D0568428

Growing Unequal?

INCOME DISTRIBUTION AND POVERTY IN OECD COUNTRIES

WITHDRAWN
UTSA Libraries
OECD

Library
University of Texas
at San Antonio

ORGANISATION FOR ECONOMIC CO-OPERATION AND DEVELOPMENT

The OECD is a unique forum where the governments of 30 democracies work together to address the economic, social and environmental challenges of globalisation. The OECD is also at the forefront of efforts to understand and to help governments respond to new developments and concerns, such as corporate governance, the information economy and the challenges of an ageing population. The Organisation provides a setting where governments can compare policy experiences, seek answers to common problems, identify good practice and work to co-ordinate domestic and international policies.

The OECD member countries are: Australia, Austria, Belgium, Canada, the Czech Republic, Denmark, Finland, France, Germany, Greece, Hungary, Iceland, Ireland, Italy, Japan, Korea, Luxembourg, Mexico, the Netherlands, New Zealand, Norway, Poland, Portugal, the Slovak Republic, Spain, Sweden, Switzerland, Turkey, the United Kingdom and the United States. The Commission of the European Communities takes part in the work of the OECD.

OECD Publishing disseminates widely the results of the Organisation's statistics gathering and research on economic, social and environmental issues, as well as the conventions, guidelines and standards agreed by its members.

This work is published on the responsibility of the Secretary-General of the OECD. The opinions expressed and arguments employed herein do not necessarily reflect the official views of the Organisation or of the governments of its member countries.

Also available in French under the title:
Croissance et inégalités
DISTRIBUTION DES REVENUS ET PAUVRETÉ DANS LES PAYS DE L'OCDE

Cover illustration:
© Inmagine ltd.
Corrigenda to OECD publications may be found on line at: *www.oecd.org/publishing/corrigenda*.
© OECD 2008

You can copy, download or print OECD content for your own use, and you can include excerpts from OECD publications, databases and multimedia products in your own documents, presentations, blogs, websites and teaching materials, provided that suitable acknowledgment of OECD as source and copyright owner is given. All requests for public or commercial use and translation rights should be submitted to *rights@oecd.org*. Requests for permission to photocopy portions of this material for public or commercial use shall be addressed directly to the Copyright Clearance Center (CCC) at *info@copyright.com* or the Centre français d'exploitation du droit de copie (CFC) *contact@cfcopies.com*.

Foreword

Fears of rising income inequalities and poverty loom large in current discussions of how globalisation is affecting OECD economies and societies. Such fears are probably the single most important concern put forward by those who argue that we should resist the increased integration of our economies and societies, and that the larger cross-border flows of goods, services and people are putting at risk the living and working conditions of millions of people in developed and less-developed countries. I believe that these responses are wrong – but also that the anxieties from which they stem should be taken seriously. Globalisation offers opportunities to live fuller and better lives – but making the best of these requires correcting the asymmetries in the distribution of the benefits and costs of globalisation.

Achieving this goal requires building up and maintaining an adequate statistical infrastructure to monitor how income inequality and poverty are changing over time. This is a task that has involved the OECD over many years, reaching back to the mid-1970s with the pioneering efforts of Malcom Sawyer for the OECD Economic Outlook, and continuing in the mid-1990s with the report prepared for the OECD on the subject by a team of leading scholars (Tony Atkinson, Lee Rainwater and Tim Smeeding). Since those days, the OECD has regularly monitored changes in income inequality and poverty through a set of standard tabulations drawn from national datasets and based on common assumptions and definitions. These tabulations are provided to the OECD by a network of national consultants. While the responsibility for analysis and possible errors in the report belongs to the authors alone, this work would not have been possible without the enduring co-operation of this network of friends and colleagues.

While this report builds on a tradition of OECD work, it nevertheless represents a landmark for the OECD. First, because – for the first time – it presents information on this subject covering all 30 OECD countries. Second, because it provides fairly up-to-date information (referring to the mid-2000s), with a large reduction in the time-lag that characterised previous such OECD reports. Lastly, because it brings together information on both household income in cash (the standard concept used by the OECD to assess the distribution of resources) and other economic resources (in-kind public services, household assets) that contribute to the well-being of individuals and families.

This report reflects the contribution of several colleagues, in and outside the OECD. Michael Förster and Marco Mira d'Ercole, from the OECD Social Policy Division, have co-ordinated the data collection. Chapter 1 has been prepared by Michael Förster and Marco Mira d'Ercole; Chapters 2 and 3 by Marco Mira d'Ercole and Aderonke Osikonimu (currently at the University of Freiburg, Germany); Chapter 4 by Peter Whiteford, senior economist at the OECD Social Policy Division at the time of writing this chapter and currently professor at the Social Policy Research Centre at the University of New South Wales, Australia; Chapter 5 by Michael Förster and Marco Mira d'Ercole; Chapter 6 by Anna Cristina D'Addio, OECD Social Policy Division; Chapter 7 by Romina Boarini, OECD Economics Department, and Marco Mira d'Ercole; Chapter 8 by Anna Cristina D'Addio; Chapter 9 by François Marical (INSEE), Marco Mira d'Ercole (OECD), Maria Vaalavuo (European University Institute,

Florence) and Gerlinde Verbist (University of Antwerp); Chapter 10 by Markus Jantti (Åbo Akademi University), Eva Sierminska (CEPS), and Tim Smeeding (Syracuse University); and Chapter 11 by Michael Förster and Marco Mira d'Ercole. Supporting material can be found on the OECD web pages www.oecd.org/els/social/inequality. Patrick Hamm contributed to the editing of the report. Mark Pearson, Head of the OECD Social Policy Division, supervised the preparation of this report and provided useful comments on various versions.

Angel Gurria
OECD Secretary-General

Acknowledgements

Most of the data underlying the analysis presented in this report are gathered through a network of national consultants (detailed below) who have provided standard tabulations based on comparable definitions and methodological approaches. This report would not exist without their dedication over many years. The OECD wish to acknowledge their essential contribution.

National consultants who have provided data for the 2008 wave of the OECD income distribution questionnaire

Country	Consultant	Agency
Australia	Jan Gatenby	Australian Bureau of Statistics
Austria	Gudrun Biffl and Martina Agwi	Austrian Institute for Economic Research
Belgium	Karel Van den Bosch and Gerlinde Verbist	University of Antwerp
Canada	Shawna Brown and Brian Murphy	Statistics Canada
Czech Republic	Ales Kanka	Czech Statistical Office
Denmark	Peter Bach-Mortensen and Lars Pantmann	Ministry of Finance
EU countries	Marton Medgyesi	Social Research Centre (TARKI)
Finland	Heikki Viitamäki	Government Institute for Economic Research (VATT)
France	Jerôme Accardo and Jerôme Pujol	Institut national de la statistique et des études économiques (INSEE)
Germany	Markus Grabka	Deutsches Institut für Wirtschaftsforschung (DIW)
Greece	Mitrakos Theodoros	Bank of Greece
Hungary	Márton Medgyesi	Social Research Center (TARKI)
Iceland	Stefán Þór Jansen	Statistics Iceland
Ireland	Kathryn Carty	Central Statistics Office
Italy	Gaetano Proto	Istituto Nazionale di Statistitica (ISTAT)
Japan	Katsuhisa Kojima and Yoshihiro Kaneko	Institute of Population and Social Security Research (ISSP)
Korea	Shinho Kim	Korean National Statistical Office
Luxembourg	Frédéric Berger	Centre d'études de populations, de pauvreté et de politiques socio-économiques (CEPS/INSTEAD)
Mexico	Ana Laura Pineda Manriquez	Instituto Nacional de Estadística, Geografía e Informática (INEGI)
Netherlands	Wim Bos	Central Bureau of Statistics
New Zealand	Caroline Brooking	Statistics New Zealand
Norway	Jon Epland	Statistics Norway
Poland	Mikolaj Haponiuk	Central Statistical Office of Poland
Portugal	Eduarda Gois	Instituto Nacional de Estatística (INE)
Slovak Republic	Ludmila Ivancikova	Statistical Office of the Slovak Republic
Spain	Marta Adiego Estella	Instituto Nacional de Estadística (INE)
Sweden	Thomas Pettersson and Tomas Petterson	Ministry of Finance
Switzerland	Ueli Oetliker and Anne Cornali	Swiss Federal Statistical Office
Turkey	Murat Karakas	State Institute of Statistics
United Kingdom	Asghar Zaidi	Organisation for Economic Co-operation and Development (OECD)
United States	John Coder	Sentier Research LLC

Table of Contents

Part III
CHARACTERISTICS OF POVERTY

Part IV
ADDITIONAL DIMENSIONS OF INEQUALITY

GROWING UNEQUAL? – ISBN 978-92-64-044180-0 – © OECD 2008

Figures

GROWING UNEQUAL? – ISBN 978-92-64-044180-0 – © OECD 2008

This book has...

StatLinks

A service that delivers Excel® files from the printed page!

Look for the *StatLinks* at the bottom right-hand corner of the tables or graphs in this book. To download the matching Excel® spreadsheet, just type the link into your Internet browser, starting with the ***http://dx.doi.org*** prefix.
If you're reading the PDF e-book edition, and your PC is connected to the Internet, simply click on the link. You'll find *StatLinks* appearing in more OECD books.

GROWING UNEQUAL? – ISBN 978-92-64-044180-0 – © OECD 2008

Introduction

If you asked a typical person to list the major problems that the world faces today, the likelihood is that "inequality and poverty" would be one of the first things they mentioned. There is a widespread concern that economic growth is not being shared fairly. A poll by the BBC in February 2008 suggested that about two-third of the population in 34 countries thought that "the economic developments of the last few years" have not been shared fairly. In Korea, Portugal, Italy, Japan and Turkey, over 80% of respondents agreed with this statement.* There are many other polls and studies which suggest the same thing.

So are people right in thinking that "the rich got richer and the poor got poorer"? As is often the case with simple questions, providing simple answers is much harder. Certainly the richest countries have got richer and some of the poorest countries have done relatively badly. On the other hand, the rapid growth in incomes in China and India has dragged millions upon millions of people out of poverty. So whether you are optimistic or pessimistic about what is happening in the world to income inequality and poverty depends on whether you think a glass is half filled or half empty. Both are true.

Even if we could agree that the world was getting more unequal, it might not be because of globalisation alone. There are other plausible explanations – skill-biased technological change (so people who know how to exploit the internet gain, for example, and those who don't, lose) or changes in policy fashion (so unions are weaker and workers less protected than before) are other reasons why inequality might have been growing. All these theories have widely-respected academic champions. In all probability, all these factors play some role.

This report looks at the 30 developed countries of the OECD. It shows that there has been an increase in income inequality that has gone on since at least the mid-1980s and probably since the mid-1970s. The widening has affected most (but not all) countries, with big increases recently in Canada and Germany, for example, but decreases in Mexico, Greece and the United Kingdom.

But the increase in inequality – though widespread and significant – has not been as spectacular as most people probably think it has been. In fact, over the 20 years, the average increase has been around 2 Gini points (the Gini is the best measure of income inequality). This is the same as the current difference in inequality between Germany and Canada – a noticeable difference, but not one that would justify to talk about the breakdown of society. This difference between what the data shows and what people think no doubt partly reflects the so-called "*Hello* magazine effect" – we read about the super rich, who have been getting much richer and attracting enormous media attention as a result. The incomes of the super rich are not considered in this report, as they cannot be measured adequately through the usual data sources on income distribution. This does not mean

* See *www.worldpublicopinion.org/pipa/pdf/feb08/BBCEcon_Feb08_rpt.pdf*.

that the incomes of the super rich are unimportant – one of the main reasons why people care about inequality is fairness, and many people consider the incomes of some to be grotesquely unfair.

The moderate increase in inequality recorded over the past two decades hides a larger underlying trend. In developed countries, governments have been taxing more and spending more to offset the trend towards more inequality – they now spend more on social policies than at any time in history. Of course, they need to spend more because of the rapid ageing of population in developed countries – more health care and pensions expenditures are necessary. The redistributive effect of government expenditures dampened the rise in poverty in the decade from the mid-1980s to the mid-1990s, but amplified it in the decade that followed, as benefits became less targeted on the poor. If governments stop trying to offset the inequalities by either spending less on social benefits, or by making taxes and benefits less targeted to the poor, then the growth in inequality would be much more rapid.

The study shows that some groups in society have done better than others. Those around retirement age – 55-75 – have seen the biggest increases in incomes over the past 20 years, and pensioner poverty has fallen very rapidly indeed in many countries, so that it is now less than the average for the OECD population as a whole. In contrast, child poverty has increased, and is now above average for the population as a whole. This is despite mounting evidence that child wellbeing is a key determinant of how well someone will do as an adult – how much they will earn, how healthy they will be, and so on. The increase in child poverty deserves more policy attention than it is currently receiving in many countries. More attention is needed to issues of child development, to ensure that (as the recent American legislation puts it) no child is left behind.

Relying on taxing more and spending more as a response to inequality can only be a temporary measure. The only sustainable way to reduce inequality is to stop the underlying widening of wages and income from capital. In particular, we have to make sure that people are capable of being in employment *and* earning wages that keep them and their families out of poverty. This means that developed countries have to do much better in getting people into work, rather than relying on unemployment, disability and early retirement benefits, in keeping them in work and in offering good career prospects.

There are a number of objections that people might make in response to the previous paragraphs. They might, for example, point to the following considerations:

- What matters is not just income. Public services such as education and health can be powerful instruments in reducing inequality.

- Some people who have low incomes nevertheless have lots of assets, so they should not be considered poor.

- We should not care unduly about poverty at a point in time – only if people have low incomes for a long period are they likely to be seriously deprived.

- A better way of looking at inequality is seeing if people are deprived of key goods and services, such as having enough food to eat, or being able to afford a television or a washing machine.

- A society in which income was distributed perfectly equally would not be a desirable place either. People who work harder, or are more talented than others, should have more income. What matters, in fact, is *equality of opportunity*, not equality of outcomes.

GROWING UNEQUAL? – ISBN 978-92-64-044180-0 – © OECD 2008

This study addresses all these issues directly – or, to be more accurate, it considers the empirical evidence for each of the statements, not the normative issues of what is and what is not a "good" society. In short, the comparative evidence in this report reveals a number of "stylised facts" pertaining to: *i)* the general features characterising the distribution of household income and its evolution; *ii)* the factors that have contributed to changes in income inequality and poverty; and *iii)* what can be learned by looking at broader measures of household resources.

Features characterising the distribution of household income in OECD countries

- Some countries have much more unequal income distributions than others, regardless of the way in which inequality is measured. Changes in the inequality measure used generally have little effect on country rankings.

- Countries with a wider distribution of income also have higher relative income poverty, with only a few exceptions. This holds regardless of whether relative poverty is defined as having income below 40, 50 or 60% of median income.

- Both income inequality and the poverty headcount (based on a 50% median income threshold) have risen over the past two decades. The increase is fairly widespread, affecting two-thirds of all countries. The rise is moderate but significant (averaging around 2 points for the Gini coefficient and 1.5 points for the poverty headcount). It is, however, much less dramatic than is often portrayed in the media.

- Income inequality has risen significantly since 2000 in Canada, Germany, Norway, the United States, Italy, and Finland, and declined in the United Kingdom, Mexico, Greece and Australia.

- Inequality has generally risen because rich households have done particularly well in comparison with middle-class families and those at the bottom of the income distribution.

- Income poverty among the elderly has continued to fall, while poverty among young adults and families with children has increased.

- Poor people in countries with high mean income and a wide income distribution (*e.g.* the United States) can have a lower living standard than poor people in countries with lower mean income but more narrow distributions (Sweden). Conversely, rich people in countries with low mean incomes and wide distributions (Italy) can have a higher living standard than rich people in countries where mean income is higher but the income distribution is narrower (Germany).

Factors that have driven changes in income inequality and poverty over time

- Changes in the structure of the population are one of the causes of higher inequality. However, this mainly reflects the rise in the number of single-adult households rather than population ageing *per se*.

- Earnings of full-time workers have become more unequal in most OECD countries. This is due to high earners becoming even more so. Globalisation, skill-biased technical change and labour market institutions and policies have all probably contributed to this outcome.

- The effect of wider wage disparities on income inequality has been offset by higher employment. However, employment rates among less-educated people have fallen and household joblessness remains high.

- Capital income and self-employment income are very unequally distributed, and have become even more so over the past decade. These trends are a major cause of wider income inequalities.

- Work is very effective at tackling poverty. Poverty rates among jobless families are almost six times higher than those among working families.

- However, work is not sufficient to avoid poverty. More than half of all poor people belong to households with some earnings, due to a combination of low hours worked during the year and/or low wages. Reducing in-work poverty often requires in-work benefits that supplement earnings.

Lessons learned by looking at broader measures of poverty and inequality

- Public services such as education and health are distributed more equally than income, so that including these under a wider concept of economic resources lowers inequality, though with few changes in the ranking of countries.

- Taking into account consumption taxes widens inequality, though not by as much as the narrowing due to taking into account public services.

- Household wealth is distributed much more unequally than income, with some countries with lower income inequality reporting higher wealth inequality. This conclusion depends, however, on the measure used, on survey design and the exclusion of some types of assets (whose importance varies across countries) to improve comparability.

- Across individuals, income and net worth are highly correlated. Income-poor people have fewer assets than the rest of the population, with a net worth generally about under half of that of the population as a whole.

- Material deprivation is higher in countries with high relative income poverty but also in those with low mean income. This implies that income poverty underestimates hardship in the latter countries.

- Older people have higher net worth and less material deprivation than younger people. This implies that estimates of old-age poverty based on cash income alone exaggerate the extent of hardship for this group.

- The number of people who are *persistently* poor over three consecutive years is quite small in most countries, but more people have low incomes at some point in that period. Countries with high poverty rates based on annual income fare worse on the basis of the share of people who are persistently poor or poor at some point in time.

- Entries into poverty mainly reflect family- and job-related events. Family events (*e.g.* divorce, child-birth, etc.) are very important for the temporarily poor, while a reduction in transfer income (*e.g.* due to changes in the conditions determining benefit eligibility) are more important for those who are poor in two consecutive years.

- Social mobility is generally higher in countries with lower income inequality, and *vice versa* . This implies that, in practice, achieving greater equality of opportunity goes hand-in-hand with more equitable outcomes.

The report leaves many questions unanswered. It does not consider whether more inequality is inevitable in the future. It does not answer questions on the relative importance of various causes of the rise in inequality. It does not even answer in any detail the question as to what developed countries should do to tackle inequality. But it does show that some countries have had smaller rises – or even falls – in inequality than others. It shows that the reason for differences across countries are, at least in part, due to different government policies, either through more effective redistribution, or better investment in the capabilities of the population to support themselves. The key policy message from this report is that – regardless of whether it is globalisation or some other reason why inequality has been rising – there is no reason to feel helpless: good government policy can make a difference.

The volume is organised as follows:

Chapter 1, which constitutes the first part of this report, describes levels and trends in income inequality among people based on a measure of household cash income adjusted for differences in economic needs across households.

The second part of the report looks in more detail at some of the main drivers of these trends in income inequality, focusing on the role of population ageing and of changes in living arrangements (Chapter 2); earnings inequality among workers, and the distribution of employment opportunities among households (Chapter 3); and government redistribution through the taxes that they collect from households and the cash transfers that they provide to them (Chapter 4).

The third part of the report focuses on the conditions of people living in poverty, in particular on the features of the lower tail of the distribution of cash income (Chapter 5); on the extent to which spells of low income last over time (Chapter 6); and on measures of poverty based on people's access to the goods and amenities needed to enjoy an acceptable standard of living (Chapter 7).

The fourth part of the report assesses how OECD countries compare when looking at additional dimensions of economic inequality, namely, at how they are passed on from parents to their offspring (Chapter 8); at the extent to which differences in cash income are reduced by publicly-provided in-kind services (Chapter 9); and at whether households with low income also experience low levels of net worth (Chapter 10).

Chapter 11 provides an overview of some of the main conclusions drawn from the previous chapters, and discusses their implications for policies aimed at narrowing income inequality and poverty.

The OECD will pursue its work on these themes in the years ahead. It will continue to monitor trends in income inequality and poverty in member countries; it will work to improve data comparability and to extend country coverage to both "accession countries" (Chile, Estonia, Israel, Russia and Slovenia) and to countries that have started a process of "enhanced engagement" with the Organisation (Brazil, China, India, Indonesia and South Africa); it will deepen its understanding of the determinants of the observed trends in inequality; and, it will pursue its analysis to understand what policies can do to moderate inequality and promote greater equality of opportunity.

PART I

Main Features of Inequality

ISBN 978-92-64-044180-0
Growing Unequal?
© OECD 2008

PART I

Chapter 1

The Distribution of Household Income in OECD Countries: What Are its Main Features?*

> *Income inequality has increased moderately but significantly over the past two decades, although with differences in the timing, intensity and even direction of these changes across countries. The wide cross-country differences in the overall shape of the income distribution at a point in time imply similarly large differences in income levels for people at similar points of the distribution – with some of the OECD countries topping the OECD league at one end of the distribution falling further behind when considering the other end.*

* This chapter has been prepared by Michael Förster and Marco Mira d'Ercole, OECD Social Policy Division.

Introduction

Policy debates in all OECD countries are increasingly marked by concerns about widening economic disparities between those who are well placed to thrive in more open and knowledge-intensive economies and those who are not. A good perspective from which to assess such concerns is provided by information on the distribution of household income. Income disparities are of course only a partial measure of economic inequalities, and only one element for the comparison of economic well-being within and across countries. Further, income disparities may reflect differences in individual preferences, and they are based on an imperfect measure of economic resources. Despite these limitations, they can be compared more reliably across countries than other measures of economic resources and such comparisons highlight patterns that are of interest to the general public and to policy makers.

This chapter provides an overview of income distribution in OECD countries over the period from the mid-1980s until the mid-2000s based on data collected through a network of national consultants. These consultants periodically provide the OECD with detailed tabulations that are based on micro-data from nationally-representative sources and employ a common methodology and assumptions. The basic income concept used in much of this report can be characterised as follows:

- it refers to the distribution of household disposable income net of household taxes in *cash* (*i.e.* excluding items such as the imputed rents of home-owners);

- it refers to the distribution among people living in private households, where each individual is attributed the income of the household where they live; and

- household income is "adjusted" to reflect differences in household needs with a common but arbitrary parameter.

The main features of the data used in this report are described in Annex 1.A1, with further details on the data sources used for each country provided in Table 1.A1.1.

This chapter first compares OECD countries in terms of the overall shape of their income distribution at a point in time. It then describes changes in these distributions over time, and finally it looks at how people at similar points in the income distribution within a country compare across nations.

How does the distribution of household income compare across countries?

The overall shape of the distribution of household disposable income differs significantly across OECD countries. Such differences may be highlighted through summary indexes of the underlying distribution. Figure 1.1 shows levels of the best known of these indexes (the Gini coefficient) in the mid-2000s, with countries ranked in increasing order of this coefficient (with increasing values denoting a wider distributions of disposable income).[1] Cross-country differences are large, with income inequality in the country at the top of the league (Mexico) twice as large as in the country at the bottom (Denmark).

Figure 1.1. **Gini coefficients of income inequality in OECD countries, mid-2000s**

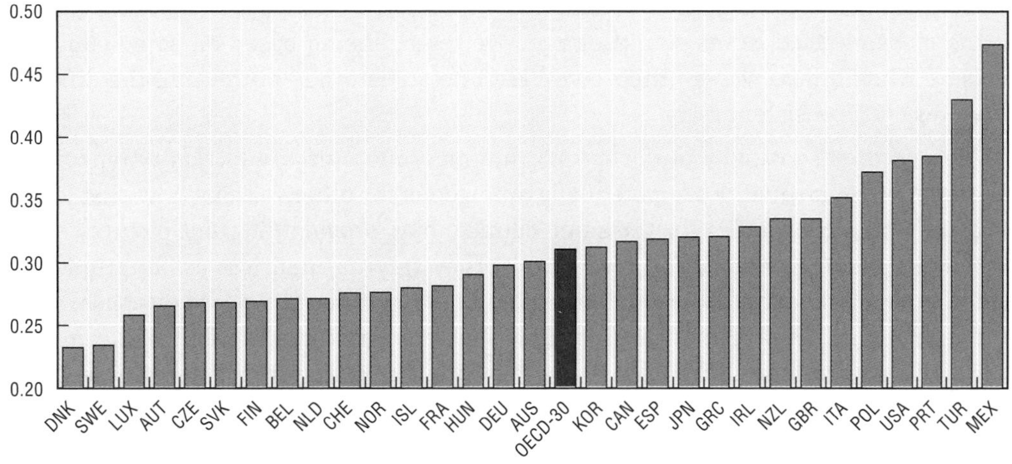

StatLink ᵐˢ᷆ http://dx.doi.org/10.1787/420515624534

Note: Countries are ranked, from left to right, in increasing order in the Gini coefficient. The income concept used is that of disposable household income in cash, adjusted for household size with an elasticity of 0.5.

Source: OECD income distribution questionnaire.

While all groupings of countries into more homogeneous clusters have a degree of arbitrariness, Figure 1.1 allows distinguishing among five groups of countries.

● At the left end of the chart are Denmark and Sweden, with Gini coefficient values of around 0.23, i.e. below the OECD average by more than 0.07 point (25%). This group of countries is characterised by "very low" income disparities.

● A second group includes countries with Gini coefficients that fall below the OECD average by a lesser extent. These are (in increasing order of the Gini coefficient) Luxembourg, Austria, the Czech and Slovak republics, Finland, the Netherlands, Belgium, Switzerland, Norway, Iceland, France, Hungary, Germany and Australia, all countries with Gini coefficients between 0.26 and around 0.30, i.e. falling below the OECD average by between 17% and 3%.

● A third group includes countries with Gini coefficients that are above the OECD average, although not much higher than those in the second group. These include Korea, Canada, Spain, Japan, Greece, Ireland, New Zealand and the United Kingdom – all countries with Gini coefficients between 0.31 and 0.34, i.e. exceeding the OECD average by up to 0.25 point (between 1% and 8%).

● A forth group includes Italy, Poland, the United States and Portugal, with Gini coefficients exceeding the OECD average by between 0.04 and 0.07 point (from 13% to 24%).

● At the upper end of the figure are Turkey and Mexico, which stand out for their very high level of income inequality (38% and 52% above the OECD average), although this is true today to a lesser extent than in the past.

The Gini coefficient is only one among many summary indexes of the underlying distribution. Because different summary indexes are especially sensitive to different parts of the Lorenz curve, the country-ranking may partly depend on the specific inequality measure used. Table 1.A2.2 shows how four other summary measures of income inequality compare to the Gini coefficient. Overall, these different measures tell a consistent story: cross-country correlations between different inequality measures and the Gini coefficient are above 0.95 for the Mean Log Deviation and the P90/P10 inter-decile ratio, and around 0.80 for the Square Coefficient of Variation and the P50/P10 inter-decile ratio.[2] Depending on the measure used, some countries improve their ranking based on some summary measure while others worsen their own based on some other, but overall the different measures tell a consistent story.

Beyond their sensitivity to the specific summary measure used, country rankings of levels of income inequality are potentially ambiguous for other reasons. The first is that different statistical sources for the same country may provide different pictures of the underlying income distribution, even when they rely on identical assumptions and computation methods; in these circumstances, it is sometimes difficult to establish, based on *a priori* arguments, which statistical source should be preferred.[3] Table 1.A2.3 compares Gini coefficients of household income in OECD countries drawn from three different data sources. Differences are relatively small in most cases but larger for some countries – although not large enough to radically modify their ranking.[4]

The second reason to suggest caution when comparing summary inequality measures across countries is that income inequality may be higher in one country than in another over one portion of the entire distribution, while the reverse occurs over a different portion.[5] In practice, this occurs only in a few cases.[6] While both factors – differences between data sources for the same country and the possibility that the assessment of inequality will vary depending on which part of the distribution is considered – suggest that cross-country comparisons of income distribution need to be taken with some caution, neither of these factors seems important enough to obscure the conclusion that the large cross-country differences in income inequalities highlighted in this section are "real" and not the product of statistical "noise".

Has the distribution of household income widened over time?

From a policy perspective, comparisons of *changes* in income distribution across countries are often more significant than comparisons of levels. In this respect the OECD data have significant advantages relative to other data sources, as they rely on series that are temporarily consistent or that (in most cases) allow correcting for discontinuities when these occur.[7] Figure 1.4, which shows point changes in the Gini coefficient for equivalised household disposable income over different time periods, highlights significant differences in income distribution across both countries and periods.

- In the decade from the mid-1980s to the mid-1990s, the dominant pattern is that of a widening of the distribution. This is especially evident in Mexico, New Zealand and Turkey but also in Italy, Portugal, the United Kingdom and the United States, as well as in the Czech Republic and Hungary (where data start in 1990). Income inequality fell in this decade in only a few countries (Canada, Denmark, France, Ireland and Spain). When averaged across the 24 OECD countries for which time-series data are available, income distribution widened by 0.018 point, *i.e.* by around 6%, and by slightly less (0.014 point, *i.e.* 5%) when excluding Mexico and Turkey.

- There is more diversity in patterns in the decade from the mid-1990s to the mid-2000s. Income distribution widened again in several countries – especially in Canada, Finland, Germany, Norway, Portugal, Sweden and the United States – but it narrowed in 10, with large declines in Mexico and Turkey and smaller ones in Australia, Greece, Ireland, the Netherlands and the United Kingdom. Statements about "average" changes of inequality in this period crucially depend on developments in Mexico and Turkey: when including them, the average increase in income inequality is only 0.002 point, while it is higher – but still below that recorded in the previous decade – when excluding them (0.07 point, i.e. 2%). Since 2000, income inequality increased strongly in Canada, Germany, Norway and the United States (and, to a lesser degree, in Italy, and Finland), while it fell in the United Kingdom, Mexico, Greece and Australia (and, to a smaller extent, in Sweden and the Netherlands).

● Overall, over the entire period from the mid-1980s to the mid-2000s, the dominant pattern is one of a fairly widespread increase in inequality (in two-thirds of all countries), with declines in France, Greece, Ireland, Spain and Turkey (but the data are limited to 2000 for Ireland and Spain). The rises are stronger in Finland, Norway and Sweden (from a low base), as well as in Germany, Italy, New Zealand and the United States (from a higher base). Across the 24 OECD countries for which data are available, the cumulative increase is of around 0.02 point, i.e. around 7%, with most of the rise experienced in the first decade, with a similar change holding when excluding Mexico and Turkey from the OECD average.[8]

Figure 1.2. **Trends in income inequality**
Point changes in the Gini coefficient over different time periods

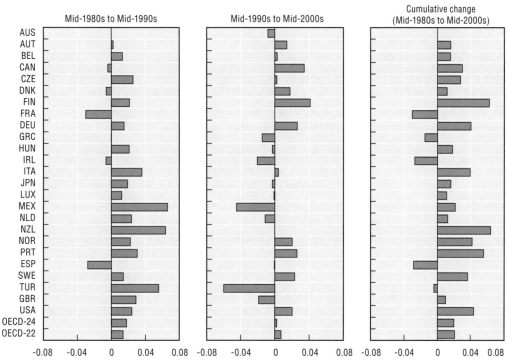

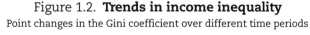
StatLink http://dx.doi.org/10.1787/420558357243

Note: In the first panel, data refer to changes from around 1990 to the mid-1990s for the Czech Republic, Hungary and Portugal and to the western Länder of Germany (no data are available for Australia, Poland and Switzerland). In the second panel, data refer to changes from the mid-1990s to around 2000 for Austria, the Czech Republic, Belgium, Ireland, Portugal and Spain (where 2005 data, based on EU-SILC, are not deemed to be comparable with those for earlier years). OECD-24 refers to the simple average of OECD countries with data spanning the entire period (all countries shown above except Australia); OECD-22 refers to the same countries except Mexico and Turkey.
Source: Computations from OECD income distribution questionnaire.

How "large" is this observed increase in income inequality? It is difficult to provide a simple answer to this (simple) question.

- First, because qualitative assessments of this type depend on the *a priori* judgments of different people: a "small" increase in the Gini coefficient for people that do not care much about inequality will appear as much larger to someone committed to a strong egalitarian agenda.

- Second, because different inequality measures have different boundaries, they will display changes of different size: for example, across the 22 OECD countries with data spanning the two decades to the mid-2000s, the inter-decile (P90/P10) ratio recorded an average increase of 0.3 point, *i.e.* 7%, while the inter-quintile share ratio (S80/S20), the MLD and the SCV increased by 10%, 9% and 30% respectively – *i.e.* larger rises than for the Gini coefficient (Table 1.A2.4).

- Third, because summary measures of income inequalities differ in their sensitivity to developments in various parts of the distribution.[9]

An intuitive metric for comparing changes in the Gini coefficient of income inequality is provided by Blackburn (1989), who argues that the difference in the Gini coefficients for two distributions is one-half the percentage value of a lump-sum transfer of average income from each individual below (above) the median to each individual above (below) the median income. On this basis, an increase in the Gini coefficient of 2 percentage points is equivalent to a (hypothetical) lump-sum transfer of 4% of average income from all those below the median to all those above it. Of course, people at the top half of the distribution have higher incomes than those at the bottom (about 2.5 times bigger, on average, in OECD countries). This means that to change the Gini coefficient by 2 points is equivalent to each person below the median transferring 7% of their own income to those above the median, whose income rises by nearly 3%. Overall, these considerations suggest that the widening of the income distribution in OECD countries recorded over the past 20 years is *moderate but significant*.

These aggregate changes in income distribution are themselves the result of differences in the pace of income growth for people at different points of the income distribution. Changes in real income by income grouping are significant for several reasons. First, if economic growth is important for the well-being of individuals in different countries, "how" the economy grows (*i.e.* which income groups benefit the most) matters for income inequalities. Second, a widening of inequalities in a country experiencing *higher* income growth throughout the distribution has different welfare implications from one occurring in a context of income declines for all. Table 1.1 shows average annual changes in real disposable income over the two decades (mid-1980s to mid-1990s and mid-1990s to mid-2000s), for people at different points in the income distribution. Patterns differ across the two time periods. In general, differences in the pace of income growth across the distribution are significant. The higher absolute pace of income growth over the past decade has generally benefitted people across the entire distribution, although with important differences across countries – *i.e.* the real income of people in the bottom quintile of the distribution fell in Belgium, Germany, Japan, Turkey and – to a lesser extent – in Mexico and the United States. On average, across all OECD countries considered, people in the top quintile recorded larger income gains than those in the bottom in both decades, but the differences were smaller in the second decade.[10]

These differences in the growth rates of equalised income across income quintiles have impacted on income distribution in various ways. The main effect is that the "middle

Table 1.1. **Trends in real household income by quintiles**

	Average annual change mid-1980s to mid-1990s					Average annual change mid-1990s to mid-2000s				
	Bottom quintile	Middle three quintiles	Top quintile	Median	Mean	Bottom quintile	Middle three quintiles	Top quintile	Median	Mean
Australia	..	..	..	..	..	2.4	2.0	1.9	2.2	2.0
Austria[1]	2.5	2.7	2.8	2.8	2.7	−2.1	−0.5	−0.4	−0.6	−0.6
Belgium[1]	1.2	0.5	1.2	0.4	0.8	1.4	1.3	1.7	1.2	1.5
Canada	0.3	−0.2	−0.1	−0.2	−0.1	0.2	1.2	2.1	1.1	1.4
Czech Republic	..	..	..	..	..	0.4	0.6	0.7	0.5	0.6
Denmark	1.3	0.9	0.8	0.9	0.9	0.6	0.9	1.5	0.9	1.1
Finland	0.9	0.9	1.0	0.8	1.2	1.6	2.5	4.6	2.5	2.9
France	1.0	0.5	−0.1	0.5	0.3	0.9	0.7	1.0	0.8	0.8
Germany	0.4	1.4	1.6	1.2	1.4	−0.3	0.5	1.3	0.6	0.7
Greece	0.3	0.1	0.1	0.3	0.1	3.6	3.0	2.7	2.9	2.9
Hungary	..	..	..	..	..	0.9	1.2	1.0	1.1	1.1
Ireland[1]	4.0	3.0	2.9	3.2	3.1	5.2	7.7	5.4	8.2	6.6
Italy	−1.3	0.5	1.5	0.6	0.8	2.2	1.0	1.6	1.0	1.3
Japan	0.8	1.8	2.1	1.8	1.9	−1.4	−1.0	−1.3	−1.0	−1.1
Luxembourg	2.3	2.5	3.0	2.4	2.7	1.5	1.5	1.7	1.5	1.6
Mexico	0.7	1.2	3.8	1.1	2.6	−0.1	−0.1	−0.6	−0.2	−0.4
Netherlands	1.1	2.7	3.9	2.8	3.0	1.8	2.0	1.4	2.0	1.8
New Zealand	−1.1	−0.5	1.6	−0.6	0.3	1.1	2.2	1.6	2.3	1.9
Norway	−0.3	0.3	1.0	0.4	0.5	4.4	3.9	5.1	3.8	4.3
Portugal[1]	5.7	6.5	8.7	6.2	7.3	5.0	4.1	4.4	4.2	4.3
Spain[1]	4.4	3.2	2.4	3.2	3.0	5.2	5.1	5.0	5.5	5.1
Sweden	0.5	0.9	1.2	0.9	0.9	1.4	2.2	2.8	2.2	2.3
Turkey	−0.6	−0.7	1.4	−0.8	0.4	−1.1	−0.5	−3.2	−0.3	−1.9
United Kingdom	0.7	2.0	4.3	1.9	2.8	2.4	2.1	1.5	2.1	1.9
United States	1.2	1.0	1.9	1.0	1.4	−0.2	0.5	1.1	0.4	0.7
OECD-22[2]	1.2	1.4	2.1	1.4	1.7	1.5	1.8	1.9	1.9	1.8
OECD-20[3]	1.3	1.5	2.1	1.5	1.7	1.7	2.0	2.2	2.1	2.1

StatLink ⧉ http://dx.doi.org/10.1787/420778364550

1. Changes over the period mid-1990s to around 2000 for Austria, the Czech Republic, Belgium, Ireland, Portugal and Spain (where 2005 data, based on EU-SILC, are not deemed to be comparable with those for earlier years).
2. OECD-22 refers to the simple average for all countries with data spanning the entire period (i.e. excluding Australia, the Czech Republic and Hungary, as well as Iceland, Korea, Poland, the Slovak Republic and Switzerland).
3. OECD-20 refers to all countries mentioned above except Mexico and Turkey.
Source: Computations from OECD income distribution questionnaire.

class" has lost ground relative to the economy-wide average in several countries. This "relative" decline may be described by looking at changes in the ratio of the "median" income (i.e. the income of the person standing exactly in the middle of the distribution) to the "mean" income of each country Figure 1.3): the more this ratio falls below 1, the more the income of the middle class falls relative to that of other people in society, in particular those in the upper tail of the distribution. The ratio of median to mean income fell since the mid-1980s (or earlier) in most countries, with the main exceptions being the Netherlands and Greece (where it increased throughout the period) and Australia, New Zealand and Turkey (where it increased since the mid-1990s). The decline in the ratio of median-to-mean income was especially sharp in New Zealand in the decade from the mid-1980s to the mid-1990s, as well as in Canada, Finland and the United States, with a decline of around 10% over the entire period.

Figure 1.3. **Changes in the ratio of median to mean household disposable income**

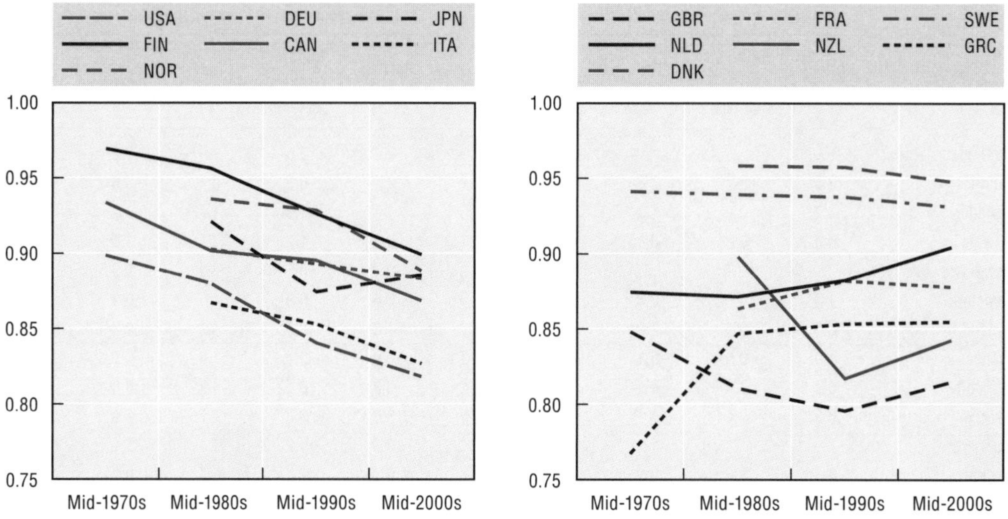

StatLink http://dx.doi.org/10.1787/420625088572

Source: Computations from OECD income distribution questionnaire.

Differences in the pace of income growth across quintiles have changed the share of total income accruing to each. Over the past decade, the income share of people in the bottom quintile was broadly constant in a majority of countries, with moderate rises in Italy and Mexico and moderate declines in Austria, Canada, Finland, Germany, Ireland, Sweden and the United States (Table 1.2). There is more diversity across countries when looking at developments in the middle and top of the income distribution. The income share of the three middle quintiles increased strongly (i.e. by more than 2 points) in Ireland, Mexico and Turkey (countries where income disparities are wide but narrowing rapidly) and, to a lesser extent (i.e. between 0.5 and 2 points), in Japan, the Netherlands and New Zealand, while it fell strongly in Norway and, to a lesser extent, Canada, Denmark, Finland, France, Germany, Italy, Sweden and the United States. Strong gains in the income share of the top quintile drove rising disparities in Canada, Finland and Norway, as well as (to a lesser extent) in Austria, Denmark, Germany, Italy, Sweden and the United States; while, conversely, strong declines in the income share of the very rich contributed to lower inequalities in Ireland, Mexico and Turkey. Income gains at the top of the distribution are likely to be under-reported in the general population surveys used in this report (Box 1.1). This is indicated by the fact that gains in the income share of the top 1% of the population, as available in the OECD income distribution questionnaire, fall short of the much larger gains (since the mid-1980s) reported in the tax records for the United States, the United Kingdom and Canada.

While the changes in income distribution described above reflect the operation of different factors (described in more detail in later chapters), a key distinction is that between inequality of *disposable income* (i.e. income after taxes and government transfers) and of *market income* (the sum of earnings, self-employment and capital income, all measured on a pre-tax basis). Changes in inequality for these two income concepts allow distinguishing (to a first approximation) between the effect of market forces and that of government policies. This distinction is important, as governments can generally counter a rise in the inequality of market income through the tax and benefit system, but not for long: there are limits to the redistribution that government can achieve, especially when

Table 1.2. **Gains and losses of income shares by income quintiles**

Point changes, mid-1990s to mid-2000s

	Bottom quintile	Middle three quintiles	Top quintile
Strong increase	..	Ireland, Mexico,Turkey	Canada, Finland, Norway
Moderate increase	Italy, Mexico	Japan, Netherlands, New Zealand, United Kingdom	Austria, Denmark, Germany, Italy, Sweden, United States
Stability	Australia, Belgium, Czech Rep., Denmark, France, Greece, Hungary, Japan, Luxembourg, Netherlands, New Zealand, Norway, Portugal, Spain, Turkey, United Kingdom	Australia, Austria, Belgium Czech Rep., Greece, Hungary Luxembourg, Portugal, Spain	Australia, Belgium, Czech Rep., France, Hungary, Japan, Luxembourg, Portugal, Spain
Moderate decline	Austria, Canada, Finland, Germany, Ireland, Sweden, United States	Canada, Denmark, France, Finland, Germany, Italy, Sweden, United States	Greece, Netherlands, New Zealand, United Kingdom
Strong decline	..	Norway	Ireland, Mexico, Turkey

Note: "Strong" increases and declines in income share are those above and below 2 percentage points, respectively; "moderate" increases and declines are those between ½ and 2 points; "stability" denotes changes in income shares between +/–½ point. For Austria, Belgium, Czech Republic, Denmark, France, Ireland, Japan, Poland, Portugal and Spain data refer to changes over the period from the mid-1990s to around 2000.
Source: OECD income distribution questionnaire.

other pressures on public spending (*e.g.* those due to population ageing) are also rising. Figure 1.4 shows changes in the Gini coefficients for these two income concepts, with both series indexed to the first observation available for each country. In the decade from the mid-1980s to the mid-1990s, greater income inequality was mainly driven by the widening distribution of market income, which affected all countries except France. In this period, governments offset this widening through household taxes and public cash benefits either in full (*e.g.* Canada and Sweden) or in part (in all others, Figure 1.4). Cross-country differences are much more significant since 1995. In this period, market income inequality fell markedly in the Netherlands and, to a lesser extent, in Australia, New Zealand, the United Kingdom and Sweden, while it stabilised in Denmark, Finland and France, and increased in other countries (rapidly in the case of Germany, Italy, Japan and Luxembourg). While the increase of disposable-income inequality was generally lower than in the previous period, a larger part of this rise reflected lower redistribution through the tax and transfers system, especially in Canada, the Netherlands, Sweden and, to a lesser extent, the United States.

Figure 1.5 plots the average trends in the dispersion of disposable and market income across the 15 OECD countries with observation spanning the entire period from the mid-1980s to the mid-2000s. The figure highlights, in a more parsimonious way than Figure 1.4, some significant differences across periods. On average, across the 15 countries here considered (the same one shown in Figure 1.4 except Australia), the widening of income inequality observed in the decade from the mid-1980s to the mid-1990s mainly reflected greater inequality in the distribution of market-income, which was partly offset by public cash transfers and households taxes. Conversely, from the mid-1990s up to around 2000, the growth of market-income inequality ebbed, and the increase in disposable income inequality mainly reflected the effect of public transfers and household taxes. The stabilisation in market-income inequality testified to the success of the welfare reforms introduced by several OECD countries in "activating" former benefit recipients, and in moving them into work (OECD, 2005). The most recent period, however, features a reversion to the older pattern of wider market-income inequality partially offset by redistribution though taxes and transfers, although at a pace lower than in the past. This

Box 1.1. **Changes at the top of the income distribution**

The survey measures of household income used in this report are not well-suited to measure income at the top of the distribution. This is due to the narrow income definition used, to confidentiality norms applied to top income and to the high non-response rates among people at the top end of the distribution. With respect to the first element, the main feature is the exclusion from the (cash) income concept used in this report of those income sources (capital and withholding gains, non-wage components of the remuneration package of managers such as stock options, and imputed rents) that disproportionately accrue to the very rich. With regard to the second element, the main feature is whether survey data cap ("top code") income or earnings beyond a given threshold. Top coding affects most analysis of income distribution in the United States, based on the "public use" data from the "Annual Social and Economic Supplement" to the *Current Population Survey,* which are affected by changes in the confidentiality limits applied by the Census Bureau on to top-income (which will dampen the recorded rise in income inequality over time); the US data presented in this report are less affected by this problem as they are based on the Census Bureau "internal" files.

An alternative to survey data for capturing changes at the top of the income distribution is provided by tax records (adjusted to take account of the income of the non-filers). Data on the share of *pre-tax income* earned by people in the top 1% of the distribution show large increases (of 70% or more) since the mid-1970s in Australia, Canada, Ireland, the United Kingdom, the United States and Canada, and smaller ones (between 10% and 25%) in Germany, Japan, New Zealand, Spain and Sweden), and declines (of around 10%) in France and the Netherlands (Leigh, 2007). With few exceptions, changes in the income share of the richest 1% of the population account for most of the increase in the income share of the top decile of the distribution. While these tax data are better at capturing what happens at the top end of the distribution – while also providing a long-term context for assessing recent trends – they are affected by changes in provisions that alter tax payers' incentives to report capital (and other) income in their tax declarations (Reynolds, 2007). In the case of the United Sates, however, the strong rise in the income share of the top 1% is confirmed by other administrative sources (*e.g.* the tabulations of the US Social Security Administration of personal earnings) and by studies that take into account payments of both personal and corporate taxes (Burtless, 2007).

Shares of pre-tax income of the richest 1% of population

StatLink ⟨⟨⟨⟨ http://dx.doi.org/10.1787/420757184562

Source: Leigh (2007), dataset downloaded from *http://econrsss.anu.edu.au/~aleigh/.*

Figure 1.4. **Inequality trends for market and disposable income**

Gini coefficients, indexed to the value in the first available year

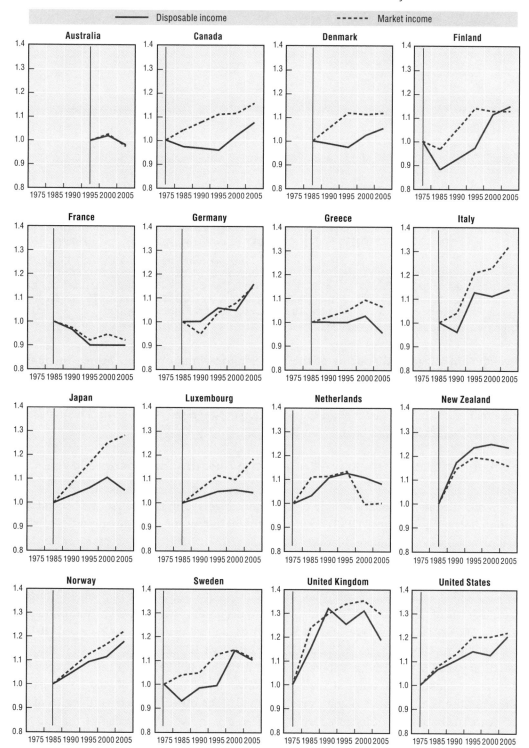

StatLink http://dx.doi.org/10.1787/420678772078

Note: Dots in each country-panel refer to the available observations. Lines are obtained as linear interpolations between these observations. Gini coefficients for market- and disposable-income are based on people ranked based on each of the two income concepts.

Source: OECD income distribution questionnaire.

Figure 1.5. **Trends in market and disposable income inequality, OECD average**

Gini coefficients, mid-1980s = 1.0

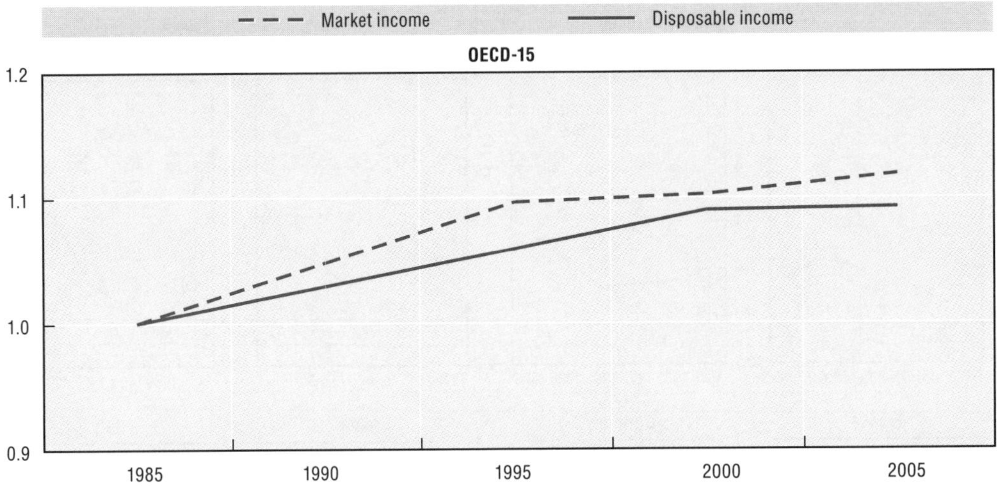

Note: OECD-15 is the average of countries for which information is available over the entire period from the mid-1980s to the mid-2000s (Canada, Denmark, Finland, France, Germany, Greece, Italy, Japan, Luxembourg, the Netherlands, New Zealand, Norway, Sweden, the United Kingdom and the United States). Gini coefficients for market and disposable income are based on people ranked based on each of the two income concepts.

Source: OECD income distribution questionnaire.

development suggests that some of the earlier narrowing in market-income inequality may have been short-lived, and that stronger reforms will be required to assure a more equal distribution of market income. While these changes in market-income inequality are often related to shifts in factor shares, the relation between the two is complex, suggesting that other factors have also been at work (Box 1.2).

Moving beyond summary measures of income distribution: income levels across deciles

While income inequality is only one element involved in comparisons of social and economic conditions across OECD countries, the data presented in this report also shed light on other aspects that are relevant to that assessment. One of these is the *absolute level* of household disposable income of people at different points of the distribution. Figure 1.6 plots the mean income (averaged across people belonging to different deciles of the distribution) of various OECD countries, as well as the average income of people belonging to each decile of the income distribution.[11] Mean disposable income per consumption unit is above USD 22 000 on average, with Luxembourg leading the league (at above USD 40 000) followed by the United States (USD 33 000) and Norway (USD 30 000). At the other extreme are Turkey and Mexico, with values of around USD 7 000. Values of mean disposable income per consumption unit are lower than conventional measures of income per capita (NNI), but the two series are highly correlated with each other.[12] The overall width of the income distribution – as measured by the difference in average income of the top and bottom income deciles, in USD at PPP rates – is also significantly different across countries, with a gap in average income between top and bottom of less than USD 20 000 in the Slovak Republic and more than USD 85 000 in the United States.

The same set of data can also be presented in a format more suited to highlight cross-country differences in the income levels of people at comparable points in the

GROWING UNEQUAL? – ISBN 978-92-64-044180-0 – © OECD 2008

Box 1.2. **Income inequality and wage shares: are they related?**

The moderate but significant rise in income inequality recorded in most OECD countries since the mid-1980s has occurred alongside significant declines in the share of wages in value added. Across 15 OECD countries with data spanning the entire period since 1976, this share has declined by around 10 points (i.e. 15%), with larger declines (of 15 points or more) in Ireland, Italy and Japan, and smaller ones (5 points or less) in Denmark, Greece, the United Kingdom and the United States (see figure below).

The share of wages in value added

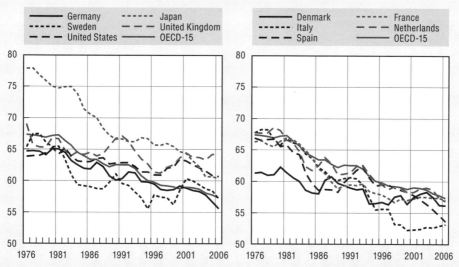

StatLink ⬛🖳 http://dx.doi.org/10.1787/420767282661

Note: Total wages are measured as total compensation of employees and the self-employed (valued at the business sector compensation rate). Total wages are expressed as a share of the Gross Domestic Product. OECD-15 is the average of the ten countries shown plus Austria, Belgium, Finland, Greece and Ireland.

Source: OECD (2007).

While there are large differences in the level of the wage share across industries, this decline has affected – to different degrees – most industrial sectors, suggesting that this downward trend reflects more than just changes in the structure of GDP (i.e. from industries with a higher wage share towards those with a lower one).[1] Empirical analysis of the determinants of the decline in the wage share at the industry level highlights the influence of higher capital-output ratios, higher real price of oil, stronger (non-labour augmenting) technological progress, as well as (in a less clear-cut way) greater adjustment costs for labour (as measured by higher employment growth) and lower bargaining power of workers (as measured by industrial conflicts, Bentolila and Saint-Paul, 2003). Other factors not explicitly included in these empirical estimates may also have contributed to the observed decline in the wage share.

As wages constitute a larger share of income for people at the bottom than at the top of the income distribution, a lower wage share is often taken to imply a decline in the share of household income going to people with lower income. In reality, there is no *necessary* connection between the share of value added paid as wages and the share of household disposable income going to low-income groups.[2] However, as described in later chapters, capital income is generally much more unequally distributed than wages: this implies that an increase in the share of capital income within households' economic resources will widen income inequality though a compositional effect.

1. De Serres *et al.* (2002) show that changes in the industrial composition of business sector output account for between 25% and 10% of the decline in the aggregate wage share from the mid-1970s to the mid-1990s in Italy, France, Belgium and the United States, with a larger influence in Germany (where a wage share adjusted for changes in the industrial composition of output rises) and a negligible one in the Netherlands.
2. Lam (1997) describes a simple model with two groups of people: low-paid workers, whose income includes only wages, and higher-income workers, who receive both wages and capital income. In this model, when assuming an elasticity of substitution between labour and capital equal to 1, an increase in the number of low-income workers will lead to an increase in their income share and to a decline in that of higher-income workers (for an unchanged share of capital income).

Figure 1.6. **Income levels across the distribution, mid-2000s**

US dollars at PPP rates

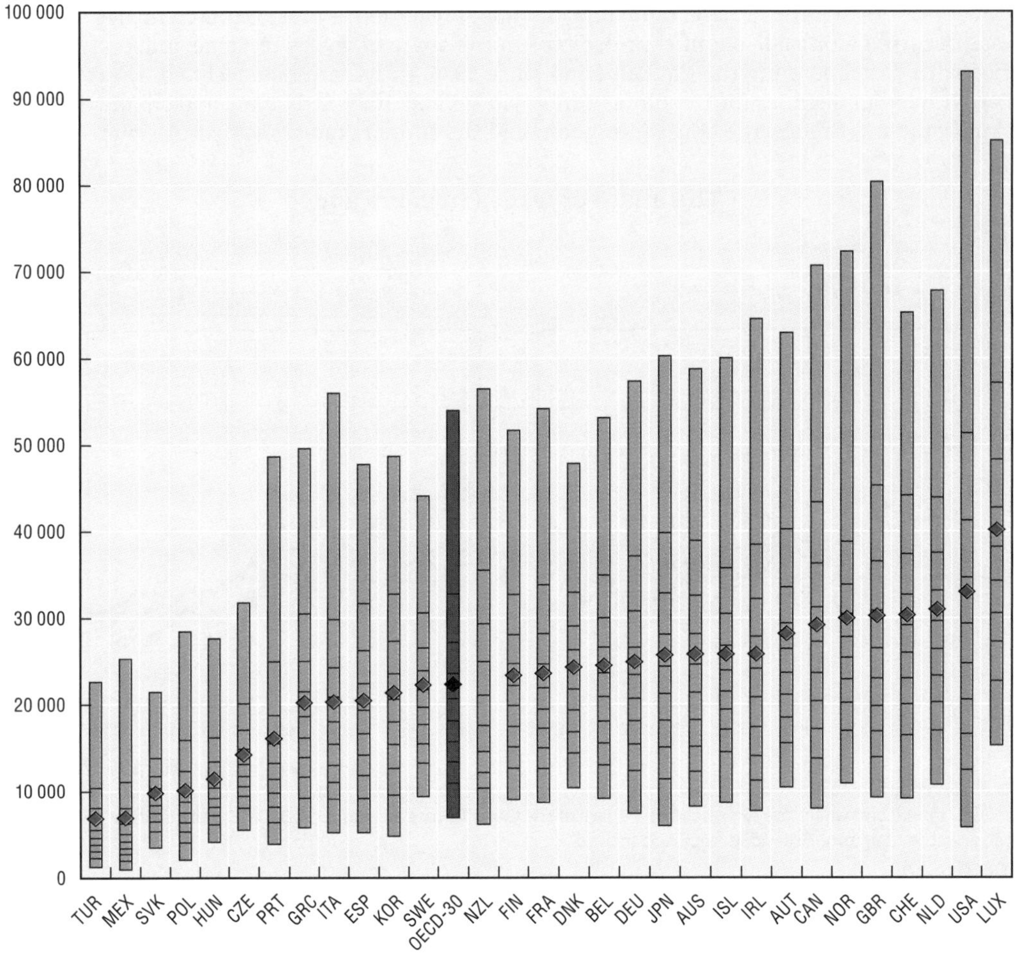

StatLink http://dx.doi.org/10.1787/420721018310

Note: The data refer to equivalised household disposable income of people at different points of the distribution. For each country, the bar starts at the average income of the first decile and ends at the average income of the 10th decile. The figure also shows the mean income over the entire population (shown as a diamond). Income data for each country are adjusted for inflation (when they refer to a year different from 2005) and then converted into US dollars based on PPP rates for actual consumption in 2005. This exchange rate expresses the costs of a standard basket of consumer goods and services purchased on the market or provided for free (or at subsidised rates) by the public sector in different countries. Countries are ranked, from left to right, in increasing order of mean equivalised income.

Source: OECD income distribution questionnaire and other OECD databases.

income distribution in different countries. Figure 1.7 presents information for middle-class people (top panel), as well for people in the bottom decile (middle panel) and top decile (bottom panel), with countries ranked in each panel in increasing order of equivalised household disposable income. Figure 1.7 highlights several patterns:

- Median income per consumption unit is marginally less than USD 20 000 on average, ranging from USD 36 000 in Luxembourg to around USD 5 000 in Mexico and Turkey. Dispersion in median income across countries is 10% higher than for mean income. Changes in country ranking (relative to that based on mean income) are small, although the Netherlands rises by two ranks (to the second-highest levels) and the United Kingdom falls by two.

 GROWING UNEQUAL? – ISBN 978-92-64-044180-0 – © OECD 2008

Figure 1.7. **Income levels for people at different points in the distribution, mid-2000s**

US dollars at PPP rates

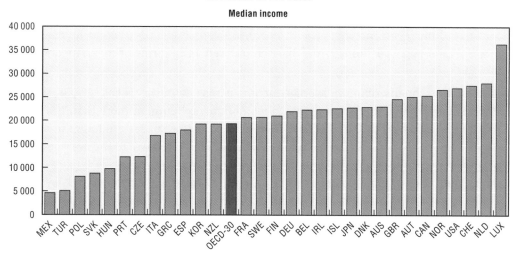

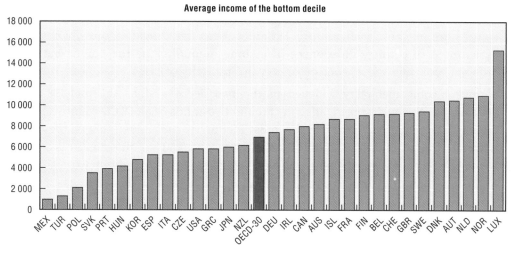

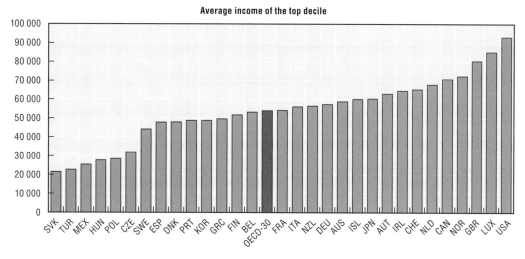

StatLink http://dx.doi.org/10.1787/420757110442

Source: OECD income distribution questionnaire and other OECD databases.

- Cross-country differences are much larger for people at the bottom of the distribution. The average income of people in the first decile is a little less than USD 7 000, ranging from 15 000 in Luxembourg to less than 1 000 in Mexico. The country-ranking for household income of those at the bottom of the distribution differs significantly from that based on mean income – *e.g.* the United States (with the second-highest mean income) falls by 11 positions while Sweden (ranked 14 in terms of mean income) rises by eight.

- At the top of the distribution, average income across countries is USD 37 000, with the United States now topping the league (ahead of Luxembourg) at more than USD 93 000 and Turkey closing it at USD 23 000. Differences across countries are larger in absolute terms than in all previous cases, but lower when assessed relative to the average income of all people at the top of income distribution. Among the countries included in the figure, Italy rises by eight positions (to the eighth-highest) while Sweden falls by four.

Conclusion

This chapter has highlighted four main patterns.

- First, the distribution of household income differs significantly across countries, and these differences persist over time – even if their exact size depends on which statistical sources are used for each country. Different measures provide a broadly consistent assessment of country differences in income inequality, as the Lorenz curves for different countries "cross" each other only in a minority of cases.

- Second, income inequality widened in the two decades since the mid-1980s. This widening is fairly widespread (affecting around two-thirds of all OECD countries), with a moderate but significant increase in most inequality measures. This widening was, however, stronger in the first decade than in the second, and has differed across countries – with several countries experiencing lower inequality in the most recent period.

- Third, the widening of the income distribution has been mainly driven by greater inequality in market income from the mid-1980s to the mid-1990s. Market-income inequality stopped rising from the mid-1990s to around 2000, followed by a renewed moderate increase in later years.

- Lastly, there are large differences across countries in terms of how people at similar points of the income distribution in different countries compare – differences that are "hidden" when countries are compared in terms of their mean income. Percentage differences in income levels across countries are larger at the bottom of the distribution than at the middle, while the top of the distribution features differences in living standards across countries that are wide in absolute terms, but smaller in percentage terms.

Notes

1. The Gini coefficient is defined as the area between the Lorenz curve (which plots cumulative shares of the population, from the poorest to the richest, against the cumulative share of income that they receive) and the 45° line, taken as a ratio of the whole triangle. The values of the Gini coefficient range between 0, in the case of "perfect equality" (i.e. each share of the population gets the same share of income), and 1, in the case of "perfect inequality" (i.e. all income goes to the individual with the highest income).

2. Relative to other indices, the Mean Log Deviation is more sensitive to changes at the bottom of the distribution, and the Squared Coefficient of Variation is more sensitive to changes at the top, while the Gini coefficient is less sensitive to changes at the two extremes of the distribution.

3. The choice of the statistical sources to use for the OECD income distribution questionnaire is made in consultation with national authorities and consultants. A key criterion for that choice is that of temporal consistency between years.

4. The OECD data show significantly higher inequality than either LIS or Eurostat in several countries (Iceland, Germany and Italy, when compared to Eurostat; Finland, Germany, Ireland, Italy, the Netherlands, Norway and Poland, when compared to LIS). Differences exist even when the three data sources rely on the same underlying survey. While these differences may partly reflect differences in the years considered (*i.e.* OECD estimates are generally more up-to-date than the LIS) and in the equivalence scale used (in the case of Eurostat), other factors also matter. In the case of Germany, Eurostat data are based on EU-SILC, which is affected by significant biases, while the OECD relies on the survey (the *German Socio-Economic Panel*) that is used by most official national reports on the subject (as well as by LIS). In the case of Italy, OECD results are based on a micro-simulation model run by the central statistical office (ISTAT), which provides estimates of household taxes for the micro-records of the Bank of Italy's *Survey of Household Income and Wealth*, which is the same household survey used by LIS. While the LIS and OECD data provide a consistent picture in terms of structural characteristics of the Italian population, the OECD data show a rise in inequality since 2000, which contrasts with the broad stability of inequality in the Bank of Italy datafiles. In the case of Japan (not covered by LIS), different sources provide significantly different estimates of inequality levels (but broadly consistent information about trends). The OECD data rely on the *Comprehensive Survey on Living Conditions* – a survey characterised by a large sample size and high response rate, which collects information based on retrospective questions and allows tracking changes in income inequality and poverty over time. The Gini coefficient from this survey is, however, significantly higher than the one computed (based on similar definitions) from the *National Survey of Family Income and Expenditure* (0.28) – the basic source of information on household spending. This second survey, which relies on diaries filled by respondents, has a larger sample but it excludes some types of households; as a result, this survey allows monitoring trends in income inequality and poverty only for a narrower population group.

5. Income inequality is unambiguously greater (lower) in one country than in another when its Lorenz curve lies strictly above (or below) that of the comparison country. Conversely, when the Lorenz curves for two countries "cross" each other, assessments of inequality based on summary measures of the entire distribution are somewhat arbitrary.

6. Table 1.A2.1 in the annex compares Lorenz curves between pairs of countries, classifying results with different colours (dark grey and dark blue in cases of "strict" dominance of the Lorenz curve of one country relative to that of another; light grey and light blue in cases where Lorenz curves of two countries cross each other at one of the two extremes; white in indeterminate cases). The table shows that, in around three quarters of all cases, binary comparisons of income distribution between countries lead to unambiguous conclusions (*i.e.* the Lorenz curve of one country lies either strictly above or strictly below than that of another). However, in 18% of all cases, Lorenz curves cross each other (cells shaded in white) and in a further 8% of all countries the crossing occurs either at the top or bottom decile (cells shaded in light blue or light grey).

7. Discontinuities, due to either changes in the statistical source used (as in the cases of Canada in 1995 and the United Kingdom in 2001) or to changes in survey design or weighting (as in the case of the Netherlands in 2000 and Sweden in 1985) are addressed by collecting data for the same year both on a "new" and "old" basis, and then "splicing" the various indicators. Statistical breaks also affect series for Belgium, Germany, Italy, Japan, Spain and Turkey (in 1995). For France, the source used for describing trends in income distribution (*Enquête Revenus Fiscaux*) differs from the one used to compare levels of the various indicators in the most recent year (EU-SILC).

8. Data spanning the period from the mid-1970s to the mid-1980s are available for seven OECD countries. These data point to a sharp increase of income inequality in the United Kingdom and, to a lesser extent, in the Netherlands and the United States, and to declines in Canada, Finland, Greece, Portugal and Sweden.

9. For example, focusing on the lower part of the distribution, it has been estimated that, for the EU15 as a whole, removing *all* means-tested benefits would increase the Gini coefficient (computed for the entire EU15 population) from 0.300 to 0.327 (Immervoll *et al.*, 2006, Table 5.3).

10. Data in Table 1.1 are shaped by the specific features of the data and definitions used. First, the income concept used in household surveys differs in important respects from that embodied in the national-accounts measures conventionally used in the analysis of living standards, and changes in the "coverage" of the survey data may distort trends over time (Siminski *et al.*, 2003). Second, changes in equivalised disposable income are affected by both the overall trends in

household income and by changes in household size across different income deciles; as average household size fell in all OECD countries over this period, the gains in equivalised income shown in Table 1.2 are lower than those for per capita income based on national accounts aggregates.

11. For the purpose of this comparison, survey-based estimate of equivalised household disposable income are first adjusted for price changes (because of differences in the years to which the data refer) to a common 2005-base, and then converted into "purchasing power" equivalents through exchange rates that express how many units of a standard basket of consumer goods residents of different countries can either purchase on the market or receive for free, or at subsidised rates, from governments (i.e. PPP rates for "actual" consumption).

12. The correlation coefficient between levels of NNI per capita and mean equivalised household disposable income in cash is around 0.95, and slightly lower when looking at rank correlations.

References

Atkinson, A.B., L. Rainwater and T.M. Smeeding (1995), *Income Distribution in OECD Countries*, OECD, Paris.

Bentolila, S. and G. Saint-Paul (2003), "Explaining Movements in the Labor Share", *Contributions to Macroeconomics*, Vol. 3, No. 1, The Berkeley Electronic Press.

Blackburn, M. (1989), "Interpreting the Magnitude of Changes in Measures of Income Inequality", *Journal of Econometrics*, No. 42.

Burniaux, J.M., T.-T. Dang, D. Fore, M.F. Förster, M. Mira d'Ercole and H. Oxley (1998), "Income Distribution and Poverty in Selected OECD Countries", OECD Economics Department Working Paper, No. 189, March, OECD, Paris.

Burtless, G. (2007), "Has US Income Inequality *Really* Increased?", mimeo, The Brookings Institution, Washington DC.

Expert Group on Household Income Statistics (2001), *Final Report and Recommendations*, The Canberra Group, Ottawa.

Förster, M. and M. Mira d'Ercole (2005), "Income Distribution and Poverty in OECD Countries in the Second Half of the 1990s", OECD Social, Employment and Migration Working Paper, No. 22, OECD, Paris.

De Serres, A., S. Scarpetta and C. Maisonneuve (2002), "Sectoral Shifts in Europe and the United States: How Do They Affect Aggregate Labour Shares and the Properties of Wage Equations", OECD Economics Department Working Papers, No. 326, OECD, Paris.

Immervoll, H., H. Levy, C. Lietz, D. Mantovani, C. O'Donoghue, H. Sutherland and G. Verbist (2006), "Household Incomes and Redistribution in the European Union: Quantifying the Equalising Properties of Taxes and Benefits", in D.B. Papadimitriou (ed.), *The Distributional Effects of Government Spending and Taxation*, Palgrave Macmillan.

Lam, D. (1997), "Demographic Variables and Income Inequality", in M.R. Rosenzweig and O. Stark (eds.), *Handbook of Population and Family Economics*, Elsevier Science.

Leigh, A. (2007), "How Closely Do Top Income Shares Track Other Measures of Inequality", *Economic Journal*, No. 117, November.

OECD (2005), *Extending Opportunities – How Active Social Policy Can Benefit Us All*, OECD, Paris.

OECD (2007), "OECD workers in the global economy: increasingly vulnerable?", *OECD Employment Outlook*, OECD, Paris.

Reynolds, A. (2007), "Has US Income Inequality *Really* Increased?", *Policy Analysis*, CATO Institute, Washington DC.

Sawyer, M. (1976), "Income Distribution in OECD Countries", *OECD Economic Outlook*, OECD, Paris.

Siminski, P., P. Saunders, S. Waseem and B. Bradbury (2003), "Reviewing the Intertemporal Consistency of ABS Household Income Data with External Aggregates", *Australian Economic Review*, Vol. 33, No. 3, September.

ANNEX 1.A1

OECD Data on Income Distribution: Key Features

Comparable data on the distribution of household income provide both a point of reference for judging the performance of any country and an opportunity to assess the role of common drivers as well as drivers that are country-specific. They also allow governments to draw on the experience of different countries in order to learn "what works best" in narrowing income disparities and poverty. But achieving comparability in this field is also difficult, as national practices differ widely in terms of concepts, measures, and statistical sources.[1] The OECD has a long association with research on the distribution of household income, which this report pursues based on a new set of data.[2] The data are collected through a network of national experts, who apply common conventions and definitions to unit record data from different national data sources and supply detailed cross-tabulations to the OECD (Table 1.A1.1 provides country details on the statistical sources used). This method of data collection allows covering a broader range of OECD countries (30, in the present volume), based on information that is both more up-to-date relative to that available through other statistical sources and better suited for assessing changes in income distribution over time. Its disadvantage is that it does not allow accessing the original micro-data, which constrains the analysis that can be performed. For this reason, data from the OECD income distribution questionnaire presented in this report are complemented, when needed, by results based on micro-records of the *Luxembourg Income Study* project (*www.lisproject.org*).

The data on income distribution presented in this volume have three key features:

- *First,* they refer to cash income – excluding imputed components such as home production and imputed rents – regularly received over the year. Data refer to disposable (*i.e.* after tax) income and its components: earnings (broken down into those of the household head, of the spouse and of other household members); self-employment income; capital income (rents, dividends and interest); public transfers; and household taxes. Information is presented for various breakdowns: by age of the individual, age of the household head (below and above 65), presence of children (persons aged below 18), presence of other adults, and work status of household members.

- *Second,* the analysis refers to the distribution among individuals, while keeping the household as the unit within which income sources are pooled and equally shared. This implies that the income of the household is attributed to each of its members, irrespectively of who in the household receives that income. The income attributed to each person is "adjusted" for household size based on a common but arbitrary equivalence elasticity (the square root of household size) that does not distinguish between adults and children and which implies that a household's economic needs increase less than proportionally with its size.[3]

● *Third,* data for most countries are drawn from household surveys, but in the case of several Nordic countries they come from comprehensive population registers integrated with survey data. The use of household surveys implies that data are affected by various sampling and non-sampling errors, whose importance can vary from country to country. It also implies that the data exclude some people at the bottom of the income distribution, such as those without a regular address (*e.g.* homeless), irregular residents and people living in institutions. Survey results may also be affected by under-reporting, which may be especially significant at the top and bottom of the distribution.

The data used in this paper, however, differ in certain aspects that escape "standardisation", and this may affect cross-country comparisons. Some of these features include the following:

● *Differences in the definition of households.* For most countries, a household refers to a group of people living in the same dwelling, but, in some others, having a common provision for essential items is an additional requirement. Countries using more restrictive definitions of households will feature lower household size and equivalised income (and higher poverty rates) relative to other countries. In Sweden until the mid-1990s, children above a given age were considered as a separate household, even if living in their parents' home, and special adjustments (described below) have been used to account for this change in the definition of households.

● *Period over which income is assessed.* Income refers to what is earned in the year preceding the interview, with most countries referring to the previous calendar year, while a few refer to the 12 months preceding the interview. In some countries, however, income or some of its components are assessed over a shorter reference period and then converted to an annual basis.[4] Countries using shorter reference periods will generally display greater income volatility and are more likely to record periods of temporary income shortfalls.

● *Availability of tax data.* All income components are reported before deduction of direct and payroll taxes (social security contributions) paid by households, but there are some exceptions.[5] Even for countries where household taxes are separately identified, there may be differences in the way these are computed, with some countries relying on self-reported data (*e.g.* Japan), others on tax records (*e.g.* Denmark and several other Nordic countries), and others on values "imputed" though microsimulation models applied to individual records (*e.g.* Italy, New Zealand, the United States). In the case of estimates based on micro-simulation models, differences in the details and assumptions used (*e.g.* with respect to tax evasion) may affect the comparability of results.

● *Temporal consistency of the data.* When statistical breaks occur – due to changes in survey methods (Japan in 1995, the Netherlands in 2000), income or household definitions (Italy in 1995, Sweden in 1985), or adoption of different surveys (Belgium, Canada and Spain in 1995; the United Kingdom in 2001) – data are collected on both the "old" and "new" bases so as to allow chain-linking various indicators. However, with the introduction of EU-SILC in 2004, several European countries (Austria, Belgium, the Czech Republic, Ireland, Portugal, Poland and Spain) discontinued the surveys used in this paper for previous years: for these countries, data for the mid-2000s are therefore not comparable with those for earlier years.

Table 1.A1.1. **National sources and data adjustments**

	Source	Income year	Period over which income is assessed	Sample size and response rate in most recent year	Definition of household and household head	Recorded income	Other data features
Australia	*Survey of income and housing*	1994/1995, 1999/2000, 2003/2004 June to June	• Current weekly income times 52.14 • Usual income in last payment period for earnings and public transfers • Payment period is previous week, fortnight or month for wages, normally fortnight for benefits)	About 11 000 households and 78% response rate	• One or more persons usually resident in the same private dwelling • Household reference chosen by applying to all household members aged 15 years and over different selection criteria • Change in definition of household head in 2003/04	• Regular and recurring cash receipts	• Changes to improve survey quality in 2003-04 may impact on the comparability with earlier data • Capital and self-employment income imputed from previous year for 1994-95 and 1999-2000, based on self-assessment of expected gross income for 2003/04
Austria	*Micro census* *EU survey of income and living conditions*	1983, 1993, 1999 2004		67% for income questions		Monthly averages Income data exclude capital and self-employment incomes (if the self-employed person is the household head)	• 2004 data not comparable with data for previous years • No data on taxes for all years (*i.e.* all data for income components recorded net of income and payroll taxes) • Data on income components refer to individuals, with imputation for non-response in 1993 and 1999
Belgium	*Tax records* *European Community household panel* *EU survey of income and living conditions*	1985, 1995 1995, 2000 2004					• 2004 data not comparable with data for previous years • Change in source in 2000 (dealt through splicing) • No data on taxes before 2004
Canada	*Survey of consumer finances* *Survey of labour and income dynamics*	1975, 1985, 1995 1995, 2000, 2005	Income over calendar year	About 30 000 households and 85% response rate	A person, or group of persons, residing in a dwelling	Market income and government benefits, net of income taxes	• Change in source in 2000 (dealt through splicing) • Income items which were coded as non-response in SLID were set to zero • Amounts received through some government transfers derived from other sources. Survey data on taxes are complete and do not require imputation
Czech Republic	*Micro census* *EU survey of income and living conditions*	1992, 1996, 2002 2004		About 38 000 dwellings and 76% response rate	Private households	Annual disposable income in each year	• Taxes exclude social security contributions • No data for 1992 • No imputation, no negative incomes
Denmark	*Danish law model system*	1983, 1994, 2000, 2005	Annual income	About 170 000 persons. For all these persons, income data are based on registers	Couples include both married and cohabitating partners. Children above 17 living at home are considered as separate households	Disposable income net of personal taxes and contributions to private pension schemes	• Data based on several tax and benefits registers • Negative incomes set to zero • Private pensions included in capital income

Table 1.A1.1. National sources and data adjustments (cont.)

	Source	Income year	Period over which income is assessed	Sample size and response rate in most recent year	Definition of household and household head	Recorded income	Other data features
Finland	Household budget survey Income distribution survey	1976 1986, 1995, 2000, 2004		Around 13 000 households and 75% response rate	Persons living in private households		
France	Enquête revenus fiscaux EU survey of income and living conditions	1984, 1989, 1994, 2000, 2005 2004	Annual income in the 12 months preceding the survey (March to March) Annual income	Around 10 000 households and 70% response rate	Persons living in the same housing unit	Values for individual income components are aggregated into total income	• Data from EU-SILC are used for cross-country comparison in mid-2000s; those from ERF for assessing trends
Germany	German Socio Economic Panel	1985, 1990, 1995 (old länder) 1995, 2000, 2004 (all länder)	Annual income in the year preceding the survey	Around 13 000 households, initial response rate over 50%, cross-sectional response rate over 95%	People living together and sharing their income	Self-employment income is included in "earnings", occupational pensions in "current transfers", private pensions in "capital income"	• Income below the social minimum of DM 5 000 per year is excluded • Taxes and social-security contributions paid by workers imputed from micro-simulation models • Only standard tax deductions considered by the micro-simulation model used to generate tax data
Greece	Household budget survey	1974, 1988, 1994, 1999, 2004		84%	Private households	All incomes in cash, net of taxes and social insurance contributions	• No data on taxes for all years • Households not providing income information excluded from the sample
Hungary	Hungarian household panel Household monitor survey	1991, 1995 2000, 2005	From April of the year in question to following March May 2000-April 2001; October 2004-September 2005	About 2 000 households and 67% response rate About 2 000 households and 49% response rate	Persons living together and sharing living expenses	Incomes in cash, net of taxes and social insurance contributions	• No data on taxes for all years • No negative incomes. Missing incomes excluded in 1991, partly replaced by imputed values in subsequent years
Iceland	EU survey of income and living conditions	2004	Annual income in the year preceding the interview	About 3 000 households	Private households	Income excluding non-monetary components	
Ireland	Living in Ireland survey	1987, 1994, 2000	Current weekly income Annual income in the year preceding the interview; continuous survey	About 3 500 households and 69% response rate	• Persons living together, sharing budget and meeting at least once per week for meals	Income excluding non-monetary components	• 2005 data not comparable with data for previous years
	EU survey of income and living conditions	2005		About 6 000 households and 72% response rate	• Persons temporarily absent and living in collective households included	Income excluding non-monetary components	
Italy	ITAXMOD95 MASTRICT (microsimulation models based on Bank of Italy survey of household income and wealth)	1984, 1991, 1993 1995, 2000, 2004	Annual income in the preceding calendar year	About 8 000 households and 36% response rate	• Persons living in the same dwelling and contributing part of their income to the household	Income excluding irregular and non-monetary components	• Income and payroll taxes estimated through microsimulation models • Break in series between 1993 and 1995 (due to change in model and income definition) dealt through splicing • Since 1995 data include income from financial assets and (imputed values of) family cash benefits (assegni famigliari)

Table 1.A1.1. **National sources and data adjustments** (cont.)

	Source	Income year	Period over which income is assessed	Sample size and response rate in most recent year	Definition of household and household head	Recorded income	Other data features
Japan	Comprehensive survey of living condition of the people on health and welfare	1985, 1995, 2000, 2003	Annual income in the year preceding the survey	About 25 000 households and 70% response rate	Persons sharing the same housing unit and livelihood Data exclude households headed by a person aged less than 17, and all individuals whose age is not recorded	All income items as reported in the survey	• Break in series in 1995 (persons with income 3 times larger than the standard deviation were excluded before that date) dealt though splicing
Korea	Household income and expenditure survey (combined with farm household economy survey)	2006	Monthly income times 12	About 14 500 households and 83% response rate	Persons sharing the same house and having a common budget Students living away from parental home counted as separate households Data on farm households (not covered by the HIES) based on Farm Household Economy Survey	Gross income All income items as reported in the survey	• Household data from the HIES and FHES integrated into a single file • All labour incomes of farm households classified as self-employment income • Data on self-employment income refer to withdrawals made by the self-employed from (net) enterprise income
Luxembourg	Panel socio-économique Liewen zu Lëtzebuerg	1986/87, 1996, 2001, 2004	Annual income	About 2 300 households and 57% response rate		All types of incomes in cash, net of taxes and social insurance contributions	Include all private households in which at least one person belongs to national social security system (around 97% of the population). Negative incomes set to zero
Mexico	Survey of household income and expenditure	1984, 1994, 2000, 2004	Income in the 3rd quarter of each year	About 20 000 households and 85% response rate	Persons normally sharing a housing unit and having common expenditure for food	Quarterly cash income net of direct taxes and soc. security contributions Income items as reported in the survey	• No data on taxes for all years (i.e. all data for income components recorded net of income and payroll taxes) • Private pensions (not separately identified) included in public transfers
Netherlands	Income panel survey	1977, 1985, 1990, 1995, 2000, 2004	Annual income in reference year	About 82 000 households and 100% response rate (register data)	• Persons living at the same dwelling and with common provisions for food and other essentials of living • Person with self-employed income, or with the higher income, or the eldest person (change in definition since 2004)	Gross annual income Taxes calculated on income in reference year	• Register data with imputation in case of incomplete information • Change in survey weighting and design in 2000 (deal through splicing)
New Zealand	Household economic survey	1986, 1991, 1996, 2001, 2004	April to March in 1986, 1991 and 1996 June to June in 2001 and 2004	About 2 800 households and 73% response rate	Persons sharing a private house and normally spending 4 or more nights a week in it	All receipts received regularly or of a recurring nature	• Income and payroll taxes imputed through microsimulation models • Missing incomes are treated as zeros
Norway	Income distribution survey	1986, 1995, 2000, 2004	Calendar year	About 13 000 households and 75% response rate	All individuals in the same dwelling having common housekeeping	Annual disposable income. All income data collected from registers	• Survey non-respondents included in sample through register data • Breakdown of earnings (into those of heads, spouse and others) not available

Table 1.A1.1. **National sources and data adjustments** (cont.)

	Source	Income year	Period over which income is assessed	Sample size and response rate in most recent year	Definition of household and household head	Recorded income	Other data features
Poland	Household budget survey / EU survey of income and living conditions	2004, 2000	Monthly income times 12	About 36 000 households and 55% response rate before substitution	Persons having a common budget for essential items	Annual disposable income	• 2004 data not comparable with earlier year • No tax data in 2000 (i.e. all income components recorded net of taxes) • Negative income values set to zero
Portugal	Household budget survey / EU survey of income and living conditions	1980, 1990, 1995, 2000 / 2004	Income in the year preceding the interview	About 10 000 households and response rate close to 100% in all years	Persons living in the same dwelling	Gross income, excluding all non-monetary components	• 2004 data not comparable with previous years • Data on taxes not available in 2004
Slovak Republic	EU survey of income and living conditions	2004	Income in previous year	6 016 households and 85.6% response rate	Persons in private dwellings who share basic household costs	Annual disposable income	• Deterministic group mean imputation for missing values • Negative income values set at zero
Spain	Continuous survey of household budgets / European community household panel / EU survey of income and living conditions	1985, 1990, 1995 / 1995, 2000 / 2004	Income in the 2nd quarter of each year	About 3 200 households and 90% response rate in 1995	Persons sharing a common budget	Quarterly disposable income	• 2004 data not comparable with those for previous years • Change in source in 2000 (dealt through splicing) No data on taxes in all years • Values of other income components recorded net of taxes
Sweden	Income distribution survey	1975, 1983, 1991, 1995, 2000, 2004	Calendar year	About 14 500 households and 75% response rate. Data from tax registers integrated with survey data	All individuals living together and sharing household resources	Annual disposable income. All income data collected from tax records	• No missing incomes, negative incomes included, households with negative disposable incomes deleted • Changes in the household definition in 1995 (dealt through splicing)
Switzerland	Income and consumption survey	2000-2001, 2004-2005	Monthly (converted into an annual basis)	About 7 000 households and 30% response rate	Persons living in the same dwelling and sharing part of their budget	Monthly gross and net income	• No negative incomes, missing incomes (about 1%) imputed • Data refer to averages of two consecutive years
Turkey	Household income and consumption survey	1984, 1994, 2004		About 8 600	People living in the same house, sharing expenditures and participating in household management and services		• No data on taxes for all years (i.e. all data for income components recorded net of income and payroll taxes) • Change in survey weighting in 1994 (dealt through splicing)
United Kingdom	Family expenditure survey / Family resources survey	1975, 1985, 1991, 1995, 2000, 2004	Income at the time of the interview for most items (over the previous 12 months for capital and self-employment income)	About 10 000 households and 60% response rate	Persons living in the same dwelling	Weekly gross income	• Data from FRS used for cross-country comparison in mid-2000s; data from FES for assessing trends • Change in source in 2000 (dealt through splicing) • Missing values excluded, negative values included
United States	Annual social and economic supplement to the current population survey	1974, 1984, 1995, 2000, 2005	Year preceding the March interview	About 50 000 households and 95% response rate	Persons occupying a housing unit	Gross annual income	• Tabulations based on Census Bureau internal files • Model-based estimates of taxes paid and in-kind public benefits added to survey data of gross annual income • Negative income allowed when below $10

Notes

1. The most important differences are the income concept and unit of analysis used: most European research has traditionally looked at the distribution of disposable income (*i.e.* after taxes and transfers) among individuals, while keeping the household (and more rarely the family) as the unit within which income is pooled and shared among its members; conversely, most analyses in the United States have focused on the distribution of pre-tax income among families (and, more rarely, households). For a detailed description of methodological features affecting income distribution statistics, see the report of the Expert Group on Household Income Statistics (2001).

2. The first milestone in OECD work on income distribution is represented by Sawyer (1976) who, in an article for *OECD Economic Outlook,* reviewed the performance of 12 OECD countries in the late 1960s and early 1970s based on the measures that were most commonly used in each country. A second milestone is represented by Atkinson, Rainwater and Smeeding (1995), who presented results referring to 12 OECD countries in the second half of the 1980s based on unit-record data from the *Luxembourg Income Study* (LIS) database, a standardised data environment that allows analysts to apply common definitions to micro records from different national surveys. A third phase began with the regular data collection undertaken by the OECD (at around five-year intervals) through a network of national consultants. The data in the present wave, covering a year as close as possible to 2005, also include revisions (for some countries) relative to the data used by Förster and Mira d'Ercole (2005).

3. The "square root elasticity" implies that the needs of a household composed of four people are twice as large as those of a single (1.4 and 1.7 times those of a single in the case of a childless couple and of a couple with one child). For further details, see *www.oecd.org/dataoecd/61/52/35411111.pdf.*

4. This is the case of Australia and the United Kingdom (where earnings data refer to the week), Austria (where data before the mid-2000s relate to monthly income) and Spain (where data until mid-1995 relate to quarterly income).

5. Data on household taxes are not available for Austria, Luxembourg and Poland (except in the mid-2000s), Greece, Hungary, Mexico, Poland, Spain and Turkey. In all these cases, data on individual components of household income are recorded on a "net" (*i.e.* post-tax) basis.

ANNEX 1.A2

Additional Tables and Figures

Table 1.A2.1. Lorenz curves' dominance across OECD countries

Mid-2000s

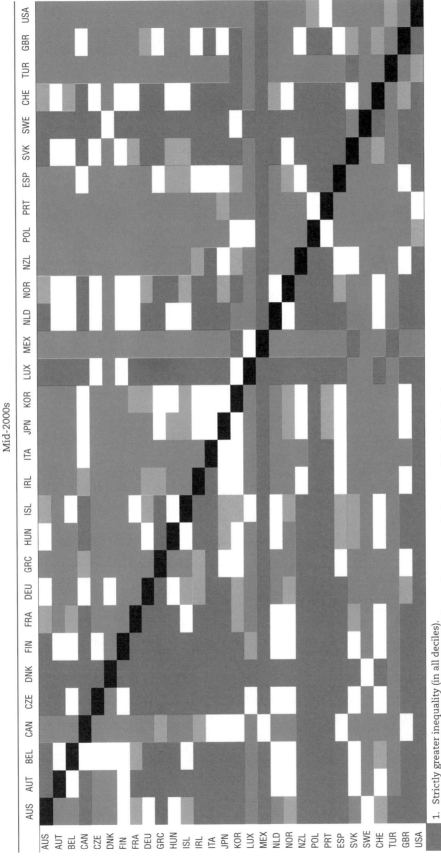

1. Strictly greater inequality (in all deciles).
2. Greater inequality (the sign is reversed either at the top or at the bottom of the distribution).
3. Multiple sign reversals (for more than 1 decile).
4. Lower inequality (the sign is reversed at either the top or the bottom of the distribution).
5. Strictly lower inequality (in all deciles).

Note: The table shows how the Lorenz curve of each OECD country (which plots the cumulative share of income received by people in each decile of the distribution) compares to that of another. It allows distinguishing among five cases: i) strictly greater inequality, when the entire curve of one country lies below that of another (denoted in dark grey); ii) greater inequality, when the curve for one country lies below that of another except at the top or bottom of the distribution denoted in light grey); iii) indeterminate situations, when the Lorenz curves of two countries intersect each other in the middle of the distribution (denoted in white); iv) lower inequality, when the curve for one country is above that of another except at the top or bottom of the distribution (denoted in light blue) ; and v) strictly lower inequality, when the entire curve of one country lies above that of another (denoted in blue). For example, the last row of the table suggests that income distribution in the United States is strictly wider than in all other OECD countries with the exceptions of Mexico (where it is strictly lower), Italy (where the two curves cross each other at the top of the distribution), Turkey (where the two curves cross each other at the bottom), as well as Poland and Portugal (where the two curves cross each other in the middle).

Source: Computations from OECD income distribution questionnaire.

GROWING UNEQUAL? – ISBN 978-92-64-044180-0 – © OECD 2008

Table 1.A2.2. **Levels of income inequality based on different summary measures in mid-2000s**

	Gini coefficient		Mean log deviation		Standard coefficient of variation		Interdecile ratio P90/P10		Interdecile ratio P50/P10	
	Level	Rank	Level	Rank	Level	Rank	Level	Rank	Level	Rank
Australia	0.30	16	0.17	15	0.39	9	3.95	15	2.09	18
Austria	0.27	4	0.13	8	0.33	3	3.27	10	1.82	7
Belgium	0.27	9	0.13	6	0.30	1	3.43	14	1.97	14
Canada	0.32	18	0.18	17	0.59	17	4.12	17	2.14	20
Czech Republic	0.27	5	0.12	4	0.38	8	3.20	5	1.74	2
Denmark	0.23	1	0.10	2	0.60	18	2.72	1	1.75	3
Finland	0.27	7	0.13	7	0.81	24	3.21	6	1.86	11
France	0.28	13	0.14	9	0.37	7	3.39	13	1.82	8
Germany	0.30	15	0.16	14	0.45	13	3.98	16	2.08	17
Greece	0.32	21	0.18	16	0.43	12	4.39	21	2.18	21
Hungary	0.29	14	0.14	10	0.48	15	3.36	12	1.78	6
Iceland	0.28	12	0.16	13	0.54	16	3.10	4	1.76	4
Ireland	0.33	22	0.19	18	0.79	22	4.41	22	2.29	22
Italy	0.35	25	0.24	23	1.10	25	4.31	20	2.11	19
Japan	0.32	20	0.20	20	0.41	11	4.77	25	2.43	26
Korea	0.31	17	0.20	22	0.35	5	4.73	24	2.50	27
Luxembourg	0.26	3	0.12	3	0.30	2	3.25	8	1.86	10
Mexico	0.47	30	0.41	28	2.70	28	8.53	30	2.86	30
Netherlands	0.27	8	..	..	..	..	3.23	7	1.86	12
New Zealand	0.34	23	..	..	..	..	4.27	19	2.06	16
Norway	0.28	11	0.16	12	0.46	14	2.83	3	1.77	5
Poland	0.37	26	0.26	24	0.71	20	5.63	26	2.42	25
Portugal	0.42	28	0.31	26	1.13	26	6.05	28	2.35	24
Slovak Republic	0.27	5	0.13	5	0.37	6	3.26	9	1.86	13
Spain	0.32	19	0.20	21	0.41	10	4.59	23	2.32	23
Sweden	0.23	2	0.10	1	0.65	19	2.79	2	1.72	1
Switzerland	0.28	10	0.15	11	0.34	4	3.29	11	1.83	9
Turkey	0.43	29	0.32	27	1.45	27	6.49	29	2.67	28
United Kingdom	0.34	23	0.20	19	0.71	21	4.21	18	1.99	15
United States	0.38	27	0.29	25	0.81	23	5.91	27	2.69	29
Average OECD	0.31	..	0.19	..	0.66	..	4.16		2.09	..
Corr. with Gini coeff.	..	..	0.99	..	0.80	..	0.96		0.88	..

StatLink ⟲ http://dx.doi.org/10.1787/420888675468

Note: The mean log deviation is the average value of the natural logarithm of the ratio of mean income to the income of each decile. The squared coefficient of variation is the variance of average income of each decile, divided by the square of the average income of the entire population. The P90/P10 inter-decile ratio is the ratio of the upper bound value of the ninth decile to that of the first. The P50/P10 inter-decile ratio is the ratio of median income to the upper bound value of the first decile. All these summary indicators have different upper and lower bounds: the mean log deviation and inter-decile ratios have a lower value of 1 and no upper bound, while the squared coefficient of variation has a lower bound of 0 and upper bound of infinity.
Source: OECD income distribution questionnaire.

Table 1.A2.3. **Gini coefficients from different sources**

Most recent year

	Reference years (incomes)			Gini coefficient			Difference in Gini coefficients rel. to OECD questionnaire	
	OECD questionnaire	Eurostat	LIS	OECD questionnaire	Eurostat	LIS	Eurostat	LIS
Australia	2004	2004	2003	0.301	..	0.312	..	−0.01
Austria	2004	2004	2000	0.265	0.260	0.257	0.01	0.01
Belgium	2004	2004	2000	0.271	0.280	0.279	−0.01	−0.01
Canada	2005	..	2000	0.317	..	0.315	..	0.00
Czech Republic	2004	2004	..	0.268	0.260	..	0.01	..
Denmark	2004	2004	2004	0.232	0.240	0.228	−0.01	0.00
Finland	2004	2004	2004	0.269	0.260	0.252	0.01	0.02
France	2004	2004	2000	0.281	0.280	0.278	0.00	0.00
Germany	2004	2004	2000	0.298	0.260	0.275	0.04	0.02
Greece	2004	2004	2000	0.321	0.330	0.333	−0.01	−0.01
Hungary	2005	2004	1999	0.291	0.280	0.295	0.01	0.00
Iceland	2004	2004	..	0.280	0.250	..	0.03	..
Ireland	2004	2004	2000	0.328	0.320	0.313	0.01	0.02
Italy	2004	2004	2000	0.352	0.330	0.333	0.02	0.02
Japan	2003	..	..	0.321	..	..	..	..
Korea	2005	..	..	0.312	..	..	..	..
Luxembourg	2004	2004	2000	0.258	0.260	0.260	0.00	0.00
Mexico	2004	..	2002	0.474	..	0.471	..	0.00
Netherlands	2004	2004	2000	0.271	0.270	0.231	0.00	0.04
New Zealand	2003	..	..	0.335	..	..	..	..
Norway	2004	2004	2000	0.276	0.280	0.251	0.00	0.03
Poland	2004	2004	1999	0.372	0.360	0.313	0.01	0.06
Portugal	2004	2004	..	0.385	0.380	..	..	..
Slovak Republic	2004	2004	..	0.268	0.260	..	0.01	..
Spain	2004	2004	2000	0.319	0.320	0.336	0.00	−0.02
Sweden	2004	2004	2000	0.234	0.230	0.252	0.00	−0.02
Switzerland	2004	..	2002	0.276	..	0.274	..	0.00
Turkey	2004	2002	..	0.430	0.450	..	−0.02	..
United Kingdom	2005	2004	1999	0.335	0.340	0.343	−0.01	−0.01
United States	2005	..	2004	0.381	..	0.372	..	0.01

StatLink http://dx.doi.org/10.1787/421057754822

Note: Both the OECD and LIS refer to household disposable income equivalised with the square root elasticity; Eurostat estimates rely on the so-called "modified OECD scale".

Source: OECD income distribution questionnaire, Eurostat (as at 6 February 2008); LIS key figures (as of 31 December 2007).

GROWING UNEQUAL? – ISBN 978-92-64-044180-0 – © OECD 2008

Table 1.A2.4. Trends in different inequality measures

	Levels in mid-2000s					Percentage point change									
	Gini coefficient	Interquintile share ratio (S80/S20)	Interdecile ratio (P90/P10)	Squared coefficient of variation (SCV)	Mean log deviation (MLD)	Gini Mid-80s to mid-90s	Gini Mid-90s to mid-2000s	S80/S20 Mid-80s to mid-90s	S80/S20 Mid-90s to mid-2000s	P90/P10 Mid-80s to mid-90s	P90/P10 Mid-90s to mid-2000s	SCV Mid-80s to mid-90s	SCV Mid-90s to mid-2000s	MLD Mid-80s to mid-90s	MLD Mid-90s to mid-2000s
Australia	0.301	4.8	4.0	0.387	0.170	..	-0.8	..	-0.2	..	-0.1	..	0.4	..	-1.9
Austria	0.265	4.0	3.3	0.325	0.129	0.2	1.4	0.1	0.4	0.1	0.3	1.4	1.2	-0.2	2.9
Belgium	0.271	4.0	3.4	0.332	0.130	1.4	0.3	0.3	0.1	0.2	0.2	0.0	-1.4	2.3	-1.6
Canada	0.317	5.2	4.1	0.588	0.185	-0.4	3.4	-0.2	0.9	-0.2	0.5	0.6	25.5	-1.0	3.9
Czech Rep.	0.268	3.8	3.2	0.375	0.122	2.6	0.2	0.4	0.1	0.3	0.1	5.3	0.2	1.9	0.2
Denmark	0.232	3.3	2.7	0.599	0.103	-0.6	1.1	-0.1	0.2	-0.2	0.1	3.0	49.4	-0.7	1.1
Finland	0.269	3.9	3.2	0.814	0.127	2.1	4.1	0.0	0.9	0.1	0.5	7.8	57.1	1.2	3.7
France	0.281	4.1	3.4	0.370	0.135	-3.1	0.0	-0.6	0.0	-0.2	0.0	-57.3	4.2	-4.2	1.0
Germany	0.298	4.8	4.0	0.452	0.155	1.5	2.6	0.5	0.6	0.5	0.5	-1.4	14.0	2.1	2.3
Greece	0.321	5.3	4.4	0.428	0.178	0.0	-1.5	-0.1	-0.5	-0.2	-0.3	1.1	-13.8	-0.4	-2.2
Hungary	0.291	4.3	3.4	0.482	0.143	2.1	-0.3	0.4	-0.1	0.3	-0.2	12.1	1.8	1.7	-0.2
Iceland	0.280	4.1	3.1	0.542	0.155	..	..	..	..	..	..	..	..	..	..
Ireland	0.328	5.4	4.4	0.789	0.194	-0.6	-2.1	-0.4	0.1	-0.1	0.3	32.0	-60.0	-3.0	-1.0
Italy	0.352	6.0	4.3	1.095	0.235	3.9	0.4	1.4	-0.3	0.9	-0.5	24.0	44.8	6.7	-0.3
Japan	0.321	5.8	4.8	0.412	0.199	1.9	-0.3	0.8	0.1	0.3	0.2	22.4	-10.5	4.1	-0.2
Korea	0.312	5.7	4.7	0.354	0.201	..	..	..	..	..	..	..	..	..	..
Luxembourg	0.258	3.7	3.3	0.302	0.116	1.2	-0.1	0.2	0.1	0.2	0.1	2.6	2.9	1.0	0.4
Mexico	0.474	12.1	8.5	2.703	0.409	6.6	-4.5	4.1	-3.4	2.1	-2.3	150.2	7.8	11.3	-8.0
Netherlands	0.271	4.0	3.2	..	..	2.4	-1.1	0.6	-0.1	0.4	-0.1	..	..	..	..
New Zealand	0.335	5.6	4.3	0.456	0.155	6.4	0.0	1.3	0.2	0.7	0.2	2.3	15.1	3.1	2.4
Norway	0.276	4.0	2.8	0.710	0.261	2.2	2.0	0.4	0.2	0.1	-0.2	..	..	..	..
Poland	0.372	7.2	5.6	0.802	0.256	..	..	..	..	..	..	..	..	..	..
Portugal	0.385	7.1	5.5	0.367	0.256	3.0	-0.3	0.8	-0.2	0.4	-0.1	14.5	-3.1	3.6	-0.9
Slovak Rep.	0.268	4.0	3.3	0.410	0.125	..	..	..	..	..	..	..	..	..	..
Spain	0.319	5.5	4.6	0.650	0.200	-2.8	0.0	-1.3	0.0	-0.9	0.2	-65.6	-3.0	-6.0	0.0
Sweden	0.234	3.3	2.8	0.337	0.007	1.4	2.3	0.2	0.4	0.1	0.3	7.9	44.7	-6.2	0.1
Switzerland	0.276	4.3	3.4	..	0.009	..	..	..	..	..	..	..	..	..	..
Turkey	0.430	9.1	6.5	1.450	0.320	5.5	-6.0	2.1	-2.2	0.3	-0.4	9.5	24.3	..	..
United Kingdom	0.335	5.4	4.2	0.714	0.195	2.9	-1.9	0.8	-0.5	0.6	-0.2	30.5	8.6	3.7	-1.3
United States	0.381	7.9	5.9	0.813	0.291	2.4	2.0	0.5	0.9	0.0	0.4	2.6	10.1	2.5	5.3
OECD-22	0.300	4.8	3.9	0.560	0.163	1.4	0.6	0.3	0.2	0.2	0.1	9.7	10.0	0.6	0.8
OECD-24	0.313	5.3	4.2	0.698	0.181	1.7	0.1	0.5	-0.1	0.2	0.0	..	..	1.1	0.4
OECD-30	0.311	5.3	4.1	0.645	0.175	..	..	..	..	..	..	..	..	..	..

StatLink http://dx.doi.org/10.1787/421061637532

Note: Data for the Czech Republic, Hungary and Portugal for the mid-1980s refer to 1990. Data for Austria, Belgium, the Czech Rep., Denmark, France, Ireland, Japan, Portugal and Spain for the mid-2000s refer to around 2000. OECD-22 excludes Australia, Iceland, Korea, Mexico, Poland, Slovak Republic, Switzerland and Turkey. OECD-24 excludes Australia, Iceland, Korea, Poland, the Slovak Republic and Switzerland.
Source: OECD income distribution questionnaire.

PART II

Main Drivers of Inequality

ISBN 978-92-64-044180-0
Growing Unequal?
© OECD 2008

PART II

Chapter 2

Changes in Demography and Living Arrangements: Are they Widening the Distribution of Household Income?*

Changes in demographic structures and lower household sizes have dampened the economic welfare of OECD populations. They have also contributed to wider income inequalities because of the increased importance of people living alone and of lone parents. These changes have been accompanied by significant shifts in the relative income of various groups, with people in their later working life gaining the most and those entering the labour market and lone parents losing ground.

* This chapter has been prepared by Marco Mira d'Ercole, OECD Social Policy Division, and Aderonke Osikominu, currently at the University of Freiburg, Germany.

Introduction

All OECD countries have experienced radical changes in their demographic profiles and the living arrangements of their populations over the last few decades. These changes have major implications not only for public budgets and other macro-economic aggregates, but also for income inequality and the distribution of economic risks between individuals. This is because these changes alter the size of different demographic groups and the ways income is shared within households. Further, these demographic shifts have occurred alongside significant changes in the relative income of various groups. Both factors – population structure and the relative income of various groups – have affected the distribution of household income, although to different extents across countries.

This chapter first describes the size of the shifts both in the demographic make-up of the population of various OECD countries and in the different income groups. It then analyses how these changes have affected trends in summary measures of income inequality in each country. It finally looks at changes in the relative income of various groups and how these are related to demographic factors.

Cross-country differences in population structure

Differences in the population structure of OECD countries have implications for the way income is shared within households and for the economic well-being of their members. While the population structure can be described for a range of dimensions, the most important are the age of individuals and the household type to which people belong.

Changes in the age profile of OECD populations are well documented. In the 20 years to 2005, all OECD countries have experienced a fall in the population share of children and youths (by around 4 and 2 points, respectively, on average, Panel A of Table 2.A1.1). Most also exhibit a roughly constant share of young adults and an increase of that of prime-age people, people in their later working life and in old age (up by around 2 points each). Population ageing has affected all OECD countries, but with different intensity. In Mexico, Turkey and Japan the population share of children fell by twice or more the average decline recorded in the OECD area. Conversely, in Portugal, Norway and Sweden the share of people aged 65 or more declined marginally, while the sharpest rise occurred for people in their later working life (41 to 50 and, especially, 51 to 65).

Even sharper changes have occurred in the population structure by household type (Panel B of Table 2.A1.1).[1] Some of these changes (the decline in the share of people living in households with children, and the increase in the share of households with a head of retirement age) simply mirror those characterising the population structure by age of individuals. Others – such as the increase in the share of people living alone and in lone-parent households – do not, and they stress the importance of additional factors bearing on living arrangements. In general, these changes have implied a gradual movement away from the "typical" family structure most prevalent in the past. Most individuals in OECD countries continue to live in households composed of couples and their children (which account for around 46% of the total population in the 24 OECD countries shown in Table 2.A1.1), but their prevalence has declined by around 9 points over the past 20 years. This fall was offset by rises in the shares of couples without children (by 3 points), of people living alone (by 2 points) and of lone parents (by 1 point).[2]

Some of these changes in living arrangements were especially pronounced in some countries. The share of single-parent households in France, Germany and the United Kingdom increased almost three times as fast as the OECD average; by 2005, they accounted for around 7% of the total population in the United Kingdom, Sweden and Norway, while remaining marginal (below 2%) in Japan, southern European countries, Turkey, Poland and the Slovak Republic. Similarly, the spread of solo living was especially pronounced in Finland, Norway and Italy. By the end of the period considered, one out of four people were living alone in Sweden and one out of five in Germany, while solo living remained marginal in Turkey. This trend can partly be explained by a rise in solo living at higher ages, due to differences in life expectancy between spouses. Yet most people living alone are persons of working age (they account for more than 10% of the total population in Germany, the Netherlands and the Nordic countries), with their rise mainly reflecting higher divorce rates and less partnership formation.

These changes in living arrangements have translated into a decline in average household size. This decline affected all OECD countries (Figure 2.1), and was especially large (above 10% in the two decades to the mid-2000s) in the United Kingdom, Mexico, Ireland, Italy, Japan and Spain. Household size matters for individual well-being, as households contribute to the standard of living of their members by allowing them to co-operate in household production and to enjoy economies of scale in consumption (Ringen, 2007). This implies that, as household size shrinks, economies of scale are lost and a higher monetary income is needed to assure the same level of well-being. Household size also matters for poverty, as highlighted by the fact that the poverty risk associated with joblessness mainly affects households comprising only one adult of working age.

Figure 2.1. **Average household size across OECD countries**

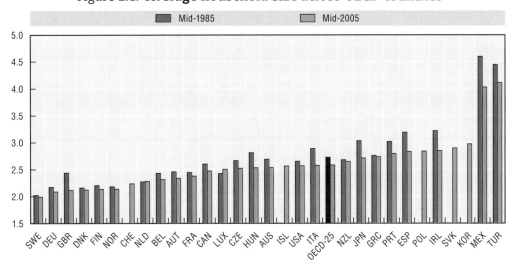

StatLink http://dx.doi.org/10.1787/421072742834

Note: Countries are ranked, from right to left, in increasing order of average household size in the mid-2000s. Average household size is computed as the total non-institutionalised population of each country divided by the number of private households in each.

Source: Computations based on the OECD income distribution questionnaire.

Demographic differences across the income distribution

Individuals with certain demographic characteristics are over-represented at certain points in the income distribution. This is especially evident when looking at age groups. Figure 2.2 plots, separately for men and women, the share of each age group in the bottom two, middle six, and top two deciles of the income distribution. It suggests large differences across countries for two main dimensions.

- First is the size of the various cohorts (as shown by the total length of the horizontal bar). For example, the demographic structure of Mexico and Turkey, characterised by a broad base (*i.e.* a large share of children) and a narrow top (*i.e.* a small share of elderly people), contrasts markedly with that of countries where the process of population ageing is more advanced (*e.g.* Japan and Italy), which translates into a more narrow base and fatter flanks.

- Second is the demographic composition of the different income quintiles. For example, children represent less than 20% of all those in the bottom income quintile in Denmark, Finland, Japan and Sweden, but up to 50% in Mexico and Turkey and more than 30% in New Zealand and the United States. Prime-age people (aged 41 to 65) account for more than half of those in the top income quintile in Denmark and Sweden, but only around one-fourth in Mexico.

Because of the assumption that people in a household share its total income equally, there are smaller differences between men and women (both are roughly equally represented at different points in the distribution). The main exception is women aged 75 and over, many of whom are living alone following the death of their spouse. They are disproportionately clustered at the bottom of the income distribution, and account for more than 10% of those in the bottom income quintile in the Nordic countries and Japan, but for only 3% in the United States and a negligible proportion in Turkey.

Changes in living arrangements have also occurred to varying extents across the income distribution. In particular, fertility rates have evolved differently across the income distribution in several countries. On the one hand, highly skilled professional women are increasingly opting to postpone childbearing and often end up having no or fewer children than desired. On the other hand, less-skilled women may have children at a very early age, and be caught in a trap where the lack of affordable child care facilities precludes them from completing their education or participating in the labour market (Dixon and Margo, 2006). Table 2.1 shows changes in fertility rates for women aged 30 to 39 who belong to households with different income levels. Taking all the countries included in Table 2.1, average fertility rates have declined more at the bottom and middle of the distribution than at the top, but these differences are small, suggesting that the impact of differential fertility on income distribution has been small. Across countries, however, fertility rates declined more strongly among low-income women than for their high-income counterparts in most countries (such as the United States, Belgium, Germany, Denmark, Spain, France, Ireland, Luxembourg and Norway), with the exceptions of Hungary, Mexico, Poland and Sweden. For low-income households, the decision to have fewer children may be part of a strategy to "spread" income over a fewer number of household members. This dampens the observed widening of the income distribution, but at the "cost" of fewer children overall.

These differences across countries in the demographic make-up of income quintiles reflect differences in both the distribution of income within each demographic group and in the average incomes of the groups. With respect to the first element, Figure 2.3 suggests that, in most OECD countries, the distribution of household income is narrower for the

Figure 2.2. **Population pyramids in mid-2000s, by gender, age and income quintiles**

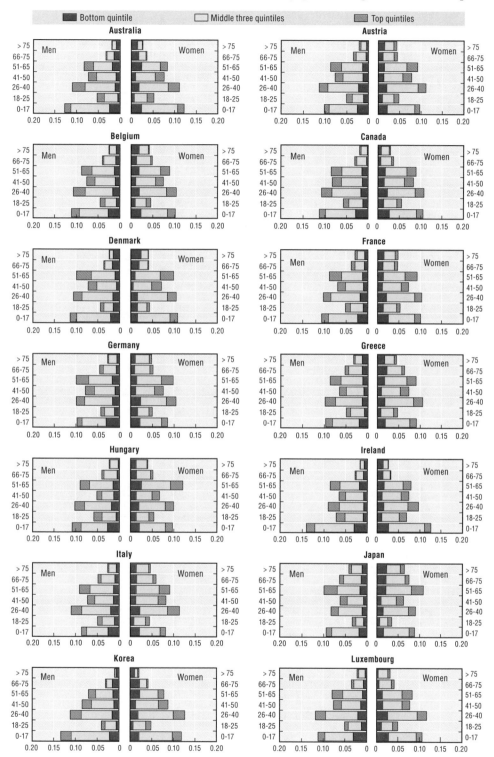

Figure 2.2. **Population pyramids in mid-2000s, by gender, age and income quintiles** (cont.)

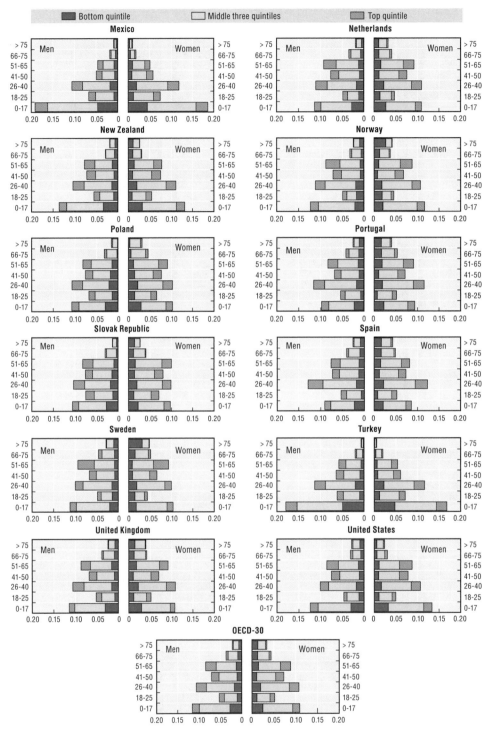

StatLink ᵐ᷈ˢᴾ http://dx.doi.org/10.1787/421136300585

Note: The figure shows, separately for men and women in each country, the share of people of a given age belonging to the bottom, top and middle-three quintiles of the distribution of equivalised household disposable income. The total length of each bar represents the share of each age group in the total population; the different colours represent the age composition of each income group. OECD-30 is the average of all OECD countries: data for countries not included in the figure are available at the StatLink below.

Source: Computations based on the OECD income distribution questionnaire.

Table 2.1. **Number of children per woman by quintile of household income**

	Period	Bottom income quintile			Middle three quintiles			Top income quintile		
		Earlier year	Later year	Point change	Earlier year	Later year	Point change	Earlier year	Later year	Point change
Australia	1985-2001	2.0	1.6	–0.4	2.0	1.7	–0.4	1.7	1.2	–0.5
Austria	1994-2000	1.1	1.0	–0.1	1.6	1.5	–0.1	1.4	1.3	–0.1
Belgium	1985-2000	1.2	0.8	–0.3	1.6	1.8	0.2	1.9	1.9	0.0
Canada	1987-2000	1.6	1.4	–0.2	1.7	1.6	–0.2	1.6	1.5	–0.1
Germany	1984-2000	1.1	0.8	–0.3	1.5	1.4	–0.2	1.3	1.2	–0.1
Denmark	1987-2000	1.0	0.9	–0.1	1.7	1.7	0.0	1.6	1.8	0.2
Spain	1990-2000	2.1	1.3	–0.8	1.9	1.3	–0.6	1.7	1.0	–0.6
Finland	1987-2000	0.7	0.7	0.0	1.7	1.7	0.0	1.9	1.9	0.0
France	1984-2000	1.4	1.1	–0.3	1.8	1.8	0.0	1.7	1.8	0.1
Greece	1995-2000	1.6	1.5	–0.1	1.6	1.6	0.0	1.4	1.6	0.2
Hungary	1991-1999	1.4	1.4	0.0	1.8	1.7	–0.1	1.8	1.5	–0.3
Ireland	1994-2000	2.1	1.7	–0.3	2.1	2.2	0.1	1.6	1.6	0.0
Italy	1986-2000	1.8	1.6	–0.2	1.7	1.3	–0.4	1.3	1.2	–0.1
Luxembourg	1985-2000	1.4	1.2	–0.2	1.6	1.5	–0.1	1.4	1.3	–0.1
Mexico	1984-2000	4.3	3.2	–1.0	3.9	2.6	–1.3	3.5	2.3	–1.2
Netherlands	1987-1999	1.2	1.1	–0.1	1.8	1.6	–0.2	1.2	1.5	0.3
Norway	1986-2000	1.1	0.9	–0.2	2.0	1.8	–0.1	2.0	1.9	–0.1
Poland	1986-1999	2.1	2.3	0.2	2.0	2.1	0.1	2.0	1.8	–0.2
Sweden	1987-2000	0.6	0.6	0.0	1.7	1.8	0.1	2.0	1.8	–0.2
United Kingdom	1986-1999	1.8	1.6	–0.2	1.9	1.7	–0.2	1.6	1.3	–0.2
United States	1986-2000	1.8	1.5	–0.2	1.7	1.6	0.0	1.5	1.6	0.0
OECD-22		1.6	1.3	–0.2	1.9	1.7	–0.2	1.7	1.6	–0.1

StatLink http://dx.doi.org/10.1787/421222675372

Note: Data refer to children aged less than 18 and to women who are classified as either head of household or as spouse and are aged 30 to 39. Quintiles based on non-equivalised household disposable income.

Source: Calculations based on the Luxembourg Income Study database.

elderly than for the non-elderly population. This mainly reflects the smaller dispersion in old-age pensions than in earnings. The exceptions are explained partly by the greater prevalence of employment among the elderly (in the United States and Japan) and partly by less mature pension systems (in Mexico and Korea).[3]

Figure 2.3. **Gini coefficients of income inequality by age of individuals, 2005**

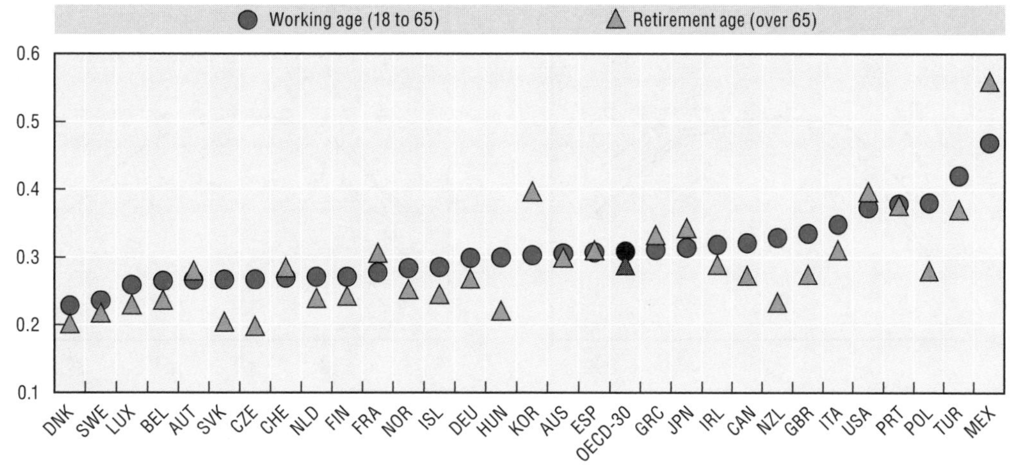

StatLink http://dx.doi.org/10.1787/421143586160

Note: Countries are ranked from left to right in increasing order of the Gini coefficient for the population of working age.

Source: OECD income distribution questionnaire.

With respect to the second element, average disposable income varies with the age of individuals and household types in similar ways across countries, with certain demographic groups overrepresented at the tails of the income distribution (Figure 2.4). In all countries, average income rises with age until the end of working life and then declines, although there are differences across countries in the age at which the highest level is reached. Similarly, when grouping people living in different household types, average income rises when moving from single-parent households to singles without children and reaches its maximum for couples with no children; average income then declines for two-adult households with children (all with a head of working age), couples with a head of

Figure 2.4. **Relative income by age of individual and household type in selected OECD countries**

Equivalised household disposable income, mid-2000s

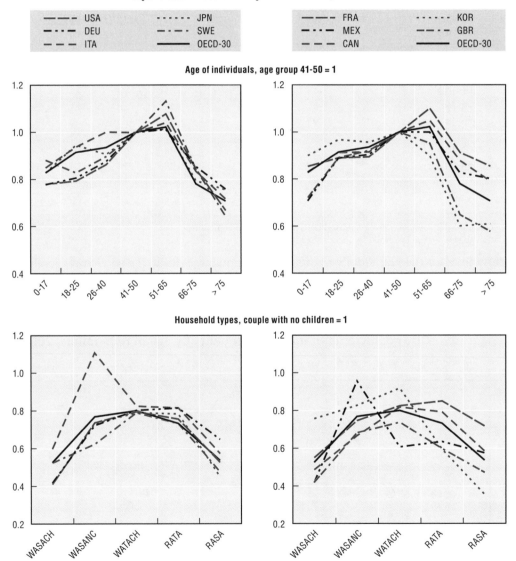

StatLink http://dx.doi.org/10.1787/421156621241

Note: WASACH = working-age head, single adult with children; WASANC = working-age head, single adult without children; WATACH = working-age head, two or more adults with children; WATANC = working-age head, two or more adults without children; RATA = retirement age head, two or more adults; RASA = retirement age head, single adult.

Source: Computations based on the OECD income distribution questionnaire.

retirement age and older people living alone (bottom panel of Figure 2.4). The income pattern by household type is generally more varied than that by age, and there is more variation across countries.

The influence of population structure on summary measures of income inequality

The previous evidence suggests that income is not uniformly distributed across individuals of different age and gender or living in different household types. Such differences matter for both levels of income inequality across countries and for the way these have changed over time. In terms of levels, most research concludes that differences in population structure do not explain much of the large differences in income inequality observed across OECD countries.[4] In Figure 2.5, the shares of different population groups are plotted against the Gini coefficient. The Gini coefficient tends to be lower in

Figure 2.5. **Shares of selected groups in the population and Gini coefficients of income inequality**

Mid-2000s

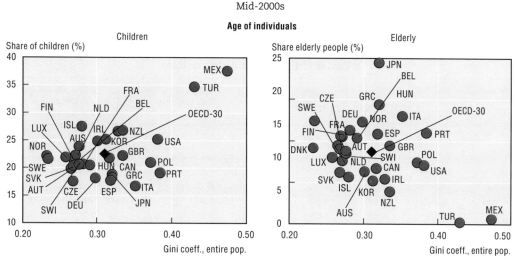

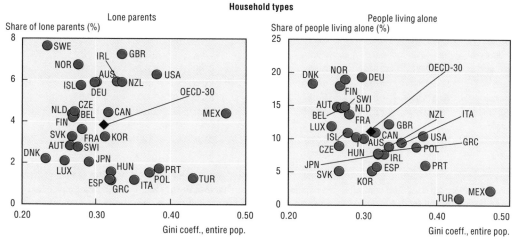

StatLink ᡦᡦᠯ http://dx.doi.org/10.1787/421188837178

Source: Computations based on the OECD income distribution questionnaire.

OECD countries with a higher share of people living alone. There is, however, no clear pattern when considering the prevalence of children, elderly people and lone parents.

In terms of changes in income inequality over time, a simple approach for assessing the overall effect of demographic trends is to compute an inequality measure while "freezing" the population structure at the level prevailing in a given reference year. Results for several OECD countries are shown in Table 2.2. Beyond the total change in the Gini coefficients of each country (shown in the first column), the table shows the change that would have prevailed with a constant population structure by age of individuals (third column), by household characteristics (fifth column) and by both age and household type (seventh column), respectively. Though age of people and household type are not independent criteria (e.g. older people are more likely to live alone), the results highlight two main patterns:

● First, changes in population structure due to the combined effect of age and household type contribute to higher income inequality in most countries, although there are some exceptions, such as Mexico, as well as (to a lesser extent) Austria, Denmark, Italy, and Sweden. The effect of changes in the demographic make-up of the population on rising inequality is large (above 20%) in Australia, Canada, France, Germany, the Netherlands and the United Kingdom.

Table 2.2. **Changes in income inequality assuming a constant population structure**

	Period	Total change in Gini coefficient	Change in Gini coefficient at constant age structure		Change in Gini coefficient at constant household structure		Change in Gini coefficient at constant age and household structure	
				Share of total change (%)		Share of total change (%)		Share of total change (%)
Australia	1995-2004	−0.008	−0.011	−31.8	−0.012	−45.0	−0.013	−57.8
Austria[1]	1987-2000	0.028	0.029	−2.0	0.031	−8.0	0.032	−10.8
Belgium[1]	1985-2000	0.053	0.049	8.8	0.045	15.4	0.044	17.1
Canada	1985-2005	0.027	0.026	4.1	0.021	22.0	0.021	21.6
Denmark[1]	1987-2004	−0.024	−0.024	2.6	−0.025	−3.7	−0.022	9.9
Finland	1986-2004	0.062	0.058	7.1	0.054	13.7	0.052	16.1
France[1]	1984-2000	−0.008	−0.008	−2.9	−0.011	−34.6	−0.011	−36.8
Germany	1985-2005	0.044	0.045	−2.5	0.005	88.2	0.026	40.8
Italy	1984-2004	0.063	0.069	−10.3	0.071	−14.0	0.073	−16.0
Luxembourg	1986-2004	0.011	0.011	2.7	0.010	12.6	0.009	14.7
Mexico	1984-2004	0.021	0.021	0.6	0.026	−20.9	0.030	−39.9
Netherlands[1]	1985-1999	−0.003	−0.002	51.4	−0.007	−129.1	−0.007	−102.1
Norway	1986-2004	0.046	0.048	−5.1	0.040	12.5	0.039	15.6
Spain[1]	1980-2000	0.018	0.020	−8.9	0.015	16.7	0.016	9.2
Sweden	1983-2004	0.019	0.018	9.4	0.020	−1.1	0.023	−18.1
United Kingdom	1985-2005	0.051	0.049	3.3	0.041	19.6	0.041	20.4
United States[1]	1986-2000	0.037	0.035	3.3	0.036	2.4	0.035	5.4
Average		0.026	0.026	0.9	0.021	17.9	0.023	11.2

StatLink ⧉ http://dx.doi.org/10.1787/421226186681

Note: The approach used first computes the population structure (across seven age groups and six household types) in the beginning and final year, and then applies re-weighting factors (defined as the ratio of the population shares in the two years) to the income records of the final year. The resulting estimate corresponds to the Gini coefficient that would have prevailed in the final year had the population structure remained unchanged. For the Netherlands, where no data on children are available in LIS, the data on household structure in the earlier year are drawn from the OECD questionnaire. Data for Germany refer to western *länder* only.
1. Based on data from the Luxembourg Income Study.
Source: Calculations based on the Luxembourg Income Study and the OECD income distribution questionnaire.

● Second, effects on income distribution are generally larger when controlling for changes by household type than for those by age of individual. This is not surprising, as changes in the latter are driven by both declines in the number of children (who have low average income in most countries) and by increases in the share of elderly (a group also characterised by low reported income). Conversely, changes in the population structure by household type tend to be dominated by the rise in the share of single adult families (both single parents with children, and elderly people living alone), *i.e.* groups with low average income.[5] Separating between age- and household type-effects is, however, difficult, as in many countries the growing importance of single households may reflect the larger share of elderly people in the total population.[6]

Changes in the relative income of different groups

Changes in population structure contribute to shaping trends in income inequality through a "compositional effect". However, trends in income inequality also reflect changes in income within and between demographic groups. Changes in average income between groups have been significant in several OECD countries. Figure 2.6 plots the

Figure 2.6. **Relative income of individuals by age**
Average household disposable income of each age group relative to that of people aged 41 to 50, mid-1980s and mid-2000s

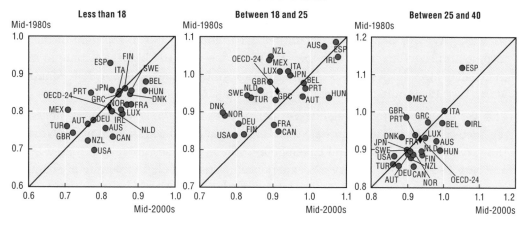

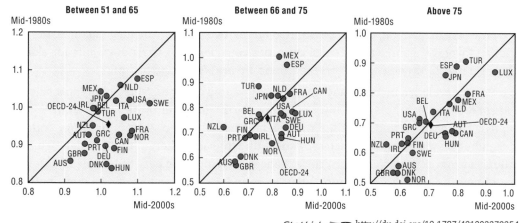

StatLink http://dx.doi.org/10.1787/421203370354

Note: The later year (on the horizontal axis) refers to the mid-2000s for all countries except Austria, Belgium, Ireland, Spain and Portugal, where it refers to around 2000. The earlier year (on the vertical axis) refers to the mid-1980s for all countries except Australia, Belgium, Poland, Portugal (1995) and Hungary (1990).

Source: OECD income distribution questionnaire.

income of various age groups of the population at two points in time (the most recent year, on the horizontal axis; and the mid-1990s, on the vertical one) relative to that of people aged 41 to 50; countries above the diagonal are those in which the relative income for the group considered has fallen. The most important changes highlighted by Figure 2.6 are the large improvements realised by people in their later working life (51 to 65) and the equally important deterioration for youths (18 to 25). However, there is also much diversity in countries' experiences.

- Children gain in most countries, especially in the United States and Canada (by 8 points or more) but also in Australia, France, New Zealand and Norway. They record large declines in Spain and Mexico, and smaller ones in Turkey and Japan.

- Youths aged 18 to 25 record a deterioration in relative income of around 4 points on average but much larger (of 10 points or more) in Denmark, Mexico, New Zealand, Norway, Sweden and Turkey. This age group improves its position only in seven countries, significantly so in Hungary, Canada and Portugal.

- There is much diversity for people aged 26 to 40, with gains in around half of the countries and losses in the other half. Changes are small in most cases, but there are large gains (of 5 points or more) in Ireland, Hungary, Australia, Canada and Finland and large losses (of the same amount) in Mexico, Denmark, Spain and Portugal.

- People in their later working life (51 to 65) experienced the largest gains (by 7 points on average, but more than twice as large in Denmark, Finland, France, Hungary, and Norway). Over this period, most countries experienced a shift to the right of the age income profile, which has made this group the one with the highest income in more than half of all countries. The position of this age group worsened in only four countries, with a large deterioration (by 5 points or more) only in Mexico.

- Changes are smaller for the elderly. For people aged 66 to 75, small improvements are recorded in all but eight countries, with large gains (of 10 points or more) in Norway, Hungary, Austria, Germany and Luxembourg, and large losses in Mexico, Turkey, Spain and New Zealand. People above 75 experienced gains in a slight majority of countries (especially in Austria, Canada and Norway) but losses in eleven countries (especially large in Japan, New Zealand, Spain and Turkey).

Changes in relative income are smaller across household types (when income is expressed relative to that of couple households with children and a working-age head). Countries are, in general, evenly distributed on the two sides of the diagonal in Figure 2.7, with an "average" gain (across the 18 countries considered) of around 4 points for elderly people living alone and a small loss (of around 1 point) for single parents.

Shifts in relative income may reflect demographic changes. This holds especially for age cohorts. For example, the entry of a large birth cohort into the labour market may depress their wages and life-time income and have indirect effects on other cohorts (depending on the extent to which they substitute for each other).[7] Similarly, demographic influences may lead to changes in social policies that alter the benefit income of different age groups, as for example when benefits are reduced or social security contributions increased in response to population ageing (von Weizsäcker, 1996). But effects may also go in the opposite direction, as larger population groups gain weight in the political process, thereby increasing their capacity to resist downward adjustments of their income and to impose policies favouring them. In practice, there is little evidence of strong links between changes in relative income and changes in population shares. First, as noted above, while

Figure 2.7. **Relative income of individuals by household type**

Household disposable income of each household type relative to couples with a working-age head without children, mid-1980s and mid-2000s

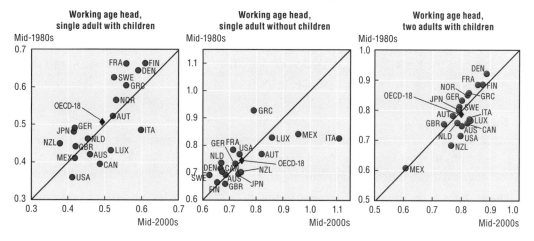

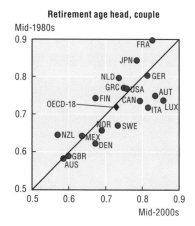

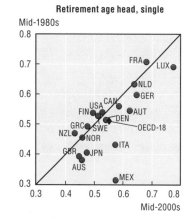

StatLink ⟨ms⟩ http://dx.doi.org/10.1787/421211338058

Note: The later year (on the horizontal axis) refers to the mid-2000s for all countries. The earlier year (on the vertical axis) refers to the mid-1980s for all countries except Australia.

Source: OECD income distribution questionnaire.

income losses of young adults have occurred alongside a rise in their population share, the gains experienced by people aged 51 to 65 occurred *despite* their larger cohort size. Second, changes in relative income for some of the groups that have experienced the most significant changes in relative income are not larger in the countries where demographic shifts are stronger. This suggests that shifts in the relative income of various groups have been driven more by changes in terms of access to jobs and support from the welfare system, rather than by demographic factors *per se*.

Conclusion

The demographic factors described in this chapter, in particular population ageing and changes in living arrangements, have shifted the distribution of economic risks among the population, with some groups losing ground relatively and others gaining. The chapter has highlighted the following patterns:

- Changes in the age structure and living arrangements of OECD populations – with more people living alone, as lone parents or as couples without children – have reduced household size and dampened the growth in equivalised income.

- These demographic shifts have widened the income distribution in most countries, more because of changes in living arrangements than in the age structure of the population. In most countries these demographic factors account for only a part of the observed change in income distribution.

- These shifts in the demographic composition of OECD countries have occurred alongside changes in the relative income of different groups. Youths and, to a lesser extent, lone parents have lost ground in most countries, while people who are closer to the end of their working life, as well as elderly people living alone, have gained the most.

These changes call for a re-orientation of social policies. Policymakers have traditionally been reluctant to implement policies with an explicit focus on demographic factors. While this situation has been changing in recent years, most of the policies introduced have aimed either at reconciling the work and family responsibilities of parents, or at increasing fertility rates. These policies, however, also affect income inequalities. Hence they need to be combined with a better understanding of what drives differences in the economic conditions of various groups, and be targeted to those families that are on the "losing end" of the redistribution of economic fortunes.

Notes

1. The OECD questionnaire on income distribution classifies individuals according to the characteristics of the households where they live, using as main criteria the age of the household head (above 65 or not), the presence of children and the number of adults (singles and couples). An additional criterion, used in later chapters, is the number of workers in the household (zero workers, one worker, two or more workers).

2. The data in the OECD questionnaire may underestimate the rise in single parenthood as they refer to people living in households with a single adult and children. A single parent living with an adult other than their partner (*e.g.* their own parent, other cohabitants) is therefore classified as a couple family.

3. With respect to changes in income inequality over time, from the mid-1990s to the mid-2000s the Gini coefficient for the retirement age population has declined in more than half of all countries; in most other countries, it has increased by *less* than that for the population of working age.

4. See, for example, Brandolini and D'Alessio (2001). These authors use LIS data to compute the mean log deviation of income that would have prevailed in 12 European countries if the demographic structure prevailing in Italy were applied to them. After controlling for differences in household size and the age and gender of the household head, they conclude that the demographic differences between Italian households and those of the other 11 European countries do not explain why inequality is higher in Italy than elsewhere (*i.e.* other European countries exhibit a lower income inequality based on the demographic profile of Italy).

5. Other approaches have aimed at disentangling the relative importance of various factors behind these changes in inequality. For inequality measures that can be decomposed additively by population subgroups (such as the MLD), the total change in inequality can be expressed as the sum of income differences "between" and "within" groups, and of a residual component representing the effect of demographic structure. While for this class of inequality measures it is possible to

derive analytically the conditions determining the overall sign of the various effects, no similar property holds for other inequality measures such as the Gini coefficient (von Weizsäcker, 1996).

6. Similar Gini-based approaches are used by Li (2005), for Australia, and Reed (2006) for the United Kingdom. The first study (which is based on a more refined methodology applied to data from the mid-1990s to the early 2000s) finds that changes in the age structure account for around one-third of the total (but insignificant) increase in income inequality, while the second study (which controls for a broader range of household characteristics over the period 1979 to 2003/04) finds that demographic change explained around 20% of the total increase in income inequality.

7. The notion of a relationship between the relative income of each cohort and its size was suggested by Easterlin (1987) who argued that, when a large cohort enters the labour market, its entry wage falls and that this fall may persist over their working career due to effects on delaying marriage and childbirth.

References

Brandolini, A. and G. D'Alessio (2001), "Household Structure and Income Inequality", Luxembourg Income Study Working Paper, No. 254, Luxembourg.

D'Addio, A. and M. Mira d'Ercole (2005), "Trends and Determinants of Fertility Rates: The Role of Policies", OECD Social, Employment and Migration Working Paper, No. 27, OECD, Paris.

Dang, T.-T., H. Immervoll, D. Mantovani, K. Orsini and H. Sutherland (2006), "An Age Perspective on Economic Well-Being and Social Protection in Nine OECD Countries", OECD Social, Employment and Migration Working Paper, No. 34, OECD, Paris.

Dixon, M. and J. Margo (2006), *Population Politics*, Institute for Public Policy Research, London.

Easterlin, R.A. (1987), "Easterlin Hypothesis", in J. Eatwell, M. Milgate and P. Newman (eds.), *The New Palgrave: A Dictionary of Economics*, The Stockton Press, NewYork, pp. 1-4.

Li, Y. (2005), "Impact of Demographic and Economic Change on Measured Income Inequality", Research Paper, Australian Bureau of Statistics, Canberra.

Reed, H. (2006), "Modelling Demographic Pressure on Poverty and Inequality", in M. Dixon and J. Margo (eds.), *Population Politics,* Institute for Public Policy Research, London.

Ringen, S. (2007), "What Do Families Do?", Chapter 5 in S. Ringen, *What Democracy Is For?*, Princeton University Press.

von Weizsäcker, R.K. (1996), "Distributive Implications of An Ageing Society", *European Economic Review*, Vol. 40.

ANNEX 2.A1

Structure of the Population in Selected OECD Countries

Table 2.A1.1. **Structure of the population in selected OECD countries**

| | | A. By age of individuals | | | | | | B. By household type | | | | | |
| | | | | | | | | Working age head | | | | Retirement age head | |
		0-17	18-25	26-40	41-50	51-65	> 65	Single adult, no children	Single adult, with children	Two adults, no children	Two adults, with children	Single adult	Two adults
Australia	1995	26	12	24	14	13	10	5	5	29	50	3	8
	2004	25	10	22	15	17	11	7	6	30	46	3	8
	Difference	*-1*	*-2*	*-2*	*1*	*3*	*1*	*1*	*1*	*1*	*-4*	*0*	*0*
Austria	1993	21	12	24	13	16	14	6	4	22	52	6	10
	2004	20	10	22	15	18	14	10	3	30	43	5	9
	Difference	*-2*	*-2*	*-2*	*3*	*2*	*1*	*4*	*-1*	*9*	*-10*	*-1*	*-1*
Belgium	1995	22	10	24	13	16	15	6	3	30	45	5	11
	2004	21	9	21	15	18	16	9	4	29	41	5	11
	Difference	*0*	*-1*	*-3*	*2*	*1*	*1*	*3*	*2*	*-1*	*-4*	*0*	*0*
Canada	1985	26	15	26	11	13	10	5	4	27	51	3	9
	2005	22	11	21	17	17	12	8	4	33	43	3	9
	Difference	*-4*	*-4*	*-4*	*5*	*4*	*2*	*2*	*1*	*6*	*-9*	*0*	*0*
Czech Rep.	1995	23	13	19	16	16	12	4	4	24	55	4	9
	2004	18	11	23	13	21	14	5	4	27	48	4	12
	Difference	*-6*	*-2*	*4*	*-3*	*5*	*2*	*1*	*1*	*3*	*-7*	*0*	*3*
Denmark	1985	23	13	23	13	16	13	9	2	28	47	6	8
	2005	22	9	21	14	20	14	12	2	28	43	6	9
	Difference	*-1*	*-4*	*-2*	*1*	*4*	*1*	*3*	*0*	*0*	*-4*	*1*	*0*
Finland	1986	24	12	25	12	15	11	9	4	26	50	5	7
	2004	21	10	19	15	19	16	12	4	29	40	6	9
	Difference	*-3*	*-3*	*-6*	*2*	*5*	*5*	*3*	*1*	*2*	*-9*	*2*	*2*
France	1985	26	11	22	11	17	13	5	5	15	62	5	9
	2005	23	10	21	14	17	16	8	8	15	52	6	11
	Difference	*-4*	*-1*	*-1*	*3*	*0*	*3*	*3*	*3*	*0*	*-9*	*1*	*3*
Germany	1985	19	13	21	15	18	14	9	3	26	46	7	10
	2004	18	9	20	15	20	17	12	6	25	36	7	13
	Difference	*-1*	*-4*	*0*	*1*	*1*	*3*	*3*	*3*	*-1*	*-9*	*1*	*3*
Greece	1988	24	12	20	12	19	14	3	2	27	53	2	13
	2004	19	10	20	14	18	19	4	1	29	43	4	19
	Difference	*-5*	*-2*	*1*	*2*	*-2*	*6*	*1*	*-1*	*2*	*-10*	*2*	*6*
Hungary	1995	24	12	21	13	15	15	3	3	28	52	4	10
	2005	20	11	20	12	21	15	5	2	37	43	5	8
	Difference	*-3*	*0*	*-1*	*-1*	*6*	*0*	*2*	*-1*	*8*	*-8*	*1*	*-2*
Iceland	2004	28	11	21	15	15	11	7	6	24	54	4	5
Ireland	1994	33	12	20	12	12	10	..	..	..	..	..	..
	2005	27	14	19	14	16	10	4	6	25	51	4	10
	Difference	*-7*	*2*	*-1*	*2*	*4*	*0*	*..*	*..*	*..*	*..*	*..*	*..*
Italy	1984	23	13	22	14	17	11	2	1	29	54	2	12
	2004	17	9	22	15	18	18	5	1	34	40	5	16
	Difference	*-6*	*-4*	*1*	*1*	*2*	*7*	*3*	*1*	*5*	*-15*	*3*	*4*
Japan	1985	27	9	23	14	17	10	3	1	26	58	1	12
	2003	18	7	17	12	21	24	4	2	28	37	4	26
	Difference	*-8*	*-2*	*-5*	*-2*	*4*	*14*	*1*	*1*	*2*	*-21*	*3*	*14*
Korea	2005	25	9	24	17	15	10	3	3	30	53	2	8
Luxembourg	1986/87	23	13	23	14	16	12	4	2	29	53	4	8
	2004	22	10	24	15	16	13	8	2	29	47	4	11
	Difference	*-1*	*-3*	*1*	*2*	*1*	*2*	*4*	*1*	*0*	*-7*	*0*	*2*

Table 2.A1.1. **Structure of the population in selected OECD countries** (cont.)

| | | A. By age of individuals | | | | | | B. By household type | | | | | |
| | | | | | | | | Working age head | | | | Retirement age head | |
		0-17	18-25	26-40	41-50	51-65	> 65	Single adult, no children	Single adult, with children	Two adults, no children	Two adults, with children	Single adult	Two adults
Mexico	1984	50	14	18	7	7	4	1	3	6	84	0	7
	2004	38	14	22	11	10	6	1	4	13	71	1	10
	Difference	−12	0	5	3	3	2	1	2	7	−13	0	3
Netherlands	1985	24	14	24	12	14	12	6	2	26	51	4	10
	2004	22	10	22	15	18	13	10	4	27	44	4	9
	Difference	−2	−4	−2	3	5	0	4	2	1	−7	0	0
New Zealand	1985	31	14	23	11	13	9	4	5	21	59	4	7
	2003	26	11	21	14	15	12	5	6	26	50	4	9
	Difference	−4	−3	−1	4	1	3	1	1	5	−9	0	1
Norway	1986	25	13	23	11	15	14	8	5	24	49	6	9
	2004	24	9	22	14	18	13	13	7	24	42	6	8
	Difference	−1	−3	−1	3	3	−1	5	2	0	−6	0	−1
Poland	2000	21	13	21	15	17	12	5	2	29	50	4	11
Portugal	1995	19	13	18	13	19	18	1	1	30	45	3	19
	2004	19	11	23	14	17	16	2	2	33	47	4	12
	Difference	0	−3	5	1	−2	−2	1	1	3	2	0	−7
Slovak Rep.	2004	20	15	20	16	18	11	3	2	32	49	5	8
Spain	1995	21	14	23	13	16	14	2	1	20	66	2	10
	2004	18	11	25	15	16	16	3	1	37	42	3	14
	Difference	−3	−3	2	2	0	2	1	0	17	−24	2	4
Sweden	1983	23	10	22	12	15	18	19	7	16	41	9	10
	2004	22	9	20	13	19	17	17	8	17	40	8	11
	Difference	−1	−1	−2	2	4	−1	−2	1	1	−1	−1	0
Switzerland	2000	21	9	23	16	18	14	10	3	31	42	5	9
Turkey	1984	42	14	20	9	11	4	0	1	13	79	0	6
	2004	35	13	23	13	11	5	1	1	18	72	0	8
	Difference	−8	−1	3	3	1	1	0	0	5	−7	0	2
United Kingdom	1985	26	11	22	11	16	13	5	4	23	53	5	10
	2005	22	10	21	14	18	14	7	7	32	39	5	10
	Difference	−4	−1	−1	3	2	2	3	3	9	−14	1	−1
United States	1984	27	12	25	11	14	11	5	6	25	50	4	10
	2005	25	10	21	15	17	12	6	7	24	49	4	10
	Difference	−2	−2	−4	4	3	1	0	1	0	−1	0	0
Average	1985	26	12	22	12	15	12	5	3	24	54	4	10
	2005	23	10	21	14	17	14	7	4	27	46	5	11
	Difference	−4	−2	−1	2	2	2	2	1	3	−9	1	2

StatLink ᴹˢᴾ http://dx.doi.org/10.1787/421247327266

Note: Average of 25 OECD countries (excluding Iceland, Korea, Poland, the Slovak Republic and Switzerland) for population structure by age of individuals; average of 24 countries (also excluding Ireland) for population structure by household type.
Source: OECD income distribution questionnaire.

ISBN 978-92-64-044180-0
Growing Unequal?
© OECD 2008

PART II

Chapter 3

Earnings and Income Inequality: Understanding the Links*

Wage disparities among full-time workers have increased over the past two decades. These disparities are much wider when looking at personal earnings of all workers, reflecting differences in the amount of work performed over the year. When looking at the distribution across the entire working-age population – whether working or not – the concentration of household earnings has remained broadly stable over the past decade, while that of capital and self-employment income has increased markedly.

* This chapter has been prepared by Marco Mira d'Ercole, OECD Social Policy Division, and Aderonke Osikonimu, currently at the University of Freiburg, Germany.

Introduction

Much of the discussion on the drivers of income inequality has focused on the distribution of earnings, and on the impact of technological development, trade with low-wage countries and institutional changes on earnings.[1] This discussion is critical to any assessment of what has happened to income inequality: earnings are the largest component of household income and, as a result, they play a key role in shaping changes in income inequality. Yet the relation between earnings and income inequality is complex: many factors are at work that can either offset the impact of earnings inequality on the distribution of household income or reinforce it.[2] Because of the variety of factors involved and differences in concepts, measures and statistical sources used to describe them, changes in the distribution of personal earnings among workers and changes in market income (the sum of earnings, self-employment and capital income) among people may sometimes move in different directions. While for most of the countries included in Figure 3.1, changes in the distribution of earnings and of market income over the past decade have moved in sympathy, there have been exceptions, and even when both distributions move consistently, there are differences in the strength of their association.[3]

This chapter focuses on the links between the distribution of personal *earnings* and the distribution of *market income* to highlight the role of labour markets in driving changes in income inequality among people of working age. Because of its focus, the chapter ignores the redistribution of income that is achieved through taxes and public transfers (these issues are considered in Chapter 4) and abstracts from the qualitatively different factors

Figure 3.1. **Changes in the distribution of personal earnings
and of household market income**

Mid-1990s to mid-2000s

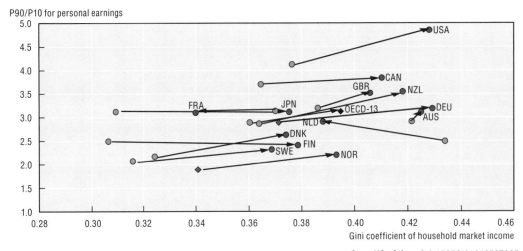

StatLink 🔗 http://dx.doi.org/10.1787/421248507235

Note: Market income inequality among persons of working age and earnings inequality among full-time workers. Data refer to the mid-1990s and mid-2000s for all countries.

Source: OECD Earnings database and income distribution questionnaire.

GROWING UNEQUAL? – ISBN 978-92-64-044180-0 – © OECD 2008

that affect income distribution among the elderly. After describing some of the main features of OECD earnings statistics (Box 3.1), this chapter reviews trends in earnings inequality among full-time workers and then discusses how the growth of non-standard jobs has shaped earnings inequality among all workers. It then describes some of the factors that come into play when moving from personal earnings to household earnings and from household earnings to market income.

Box 3.1. **Conceptual features of OECD statistics on the distribution of personal earnings**

The comparative earnings statistics collected by the OECD in its Earnings database (see Table 3.A1.1 available at *http://dx.doi.org/10.1787/424402577838*) are drawn from different sources: surveys of individuals and firms, administrative registers and tax records. The data refer to individuals of working age holding a full-time job. While full-time jobs account for the largest share of total employment in all OECD countries, the definition of full-time work used by these sources may differ from that used in labour-force surveys. These earnings data are generally reported before taxes and refer to the whole economy, although there are exceptions (*i.e.* in some countries they may exclude some sectors of employment such as general government or agriculture). The data also refer to different earnings concepts (hourly and weekly earnings in most cases, annual and monthly earnings for some countries) and include different elements of the employee remuneration packages. Because of these differences, earnings data such as those collected by the OECD are more suited for assessing *changes* in earnings distributions over time than for comparing *levels* of earnings inequality across countries (Atkinson, 2007).[*]

Beyond these methodological features, the relation between earnings and income distribution is affected by deeper conceptual differences. The most important of these relates to the unit of analysis used in each case (Saunders, 2005). Measures of earnings inequality refer to the distribution of personal earnings among *workers*. Conversely, measures of income inequality – even when using the individual as the unit of analysis – refer to the *household* as the basic unit within which income is pooled and shared by its members. This implies considering all individuals, whatever their age and employment status, and attributing to each of them the (equivalised) income of the household where they live. This difference has important implications for understanding the relationship between earnings distribution and income distribution, as the latter will be affected by how workers pool their earnings within households and by the distribution of employment opportunities among households with different characteristics.

[*] While comparability problems also affect information on the distribution of household income, they are less severe than in the case of earnings. For a description of these problems see Annex 1.A1 in Chapter 1.

Main patterns in the distribution of personal earnings among full time-workers

Changes in labour-market conditions over the past few decades have significantly affected the distribution of personal earnings in all OECD countries. The large literature that has attempted to explain these patterns has typically focused on men working full time, as they account for the largest share of total employment (Gottschalk and Danziger, 2005). Figure 3.2 highlights a sharp widening in the distribution of personal earnings – as measured by inter-decile ratios – among men working full time in most OECD countries. On average, across the 11 OECD countries for which information is available since 1985, earnings dispersion increased by around 10% since 1990, with most of this rise occurring

Figure 3.2. **Trends in earnings dispersion among men working full time**

Index 1990 = 1.0

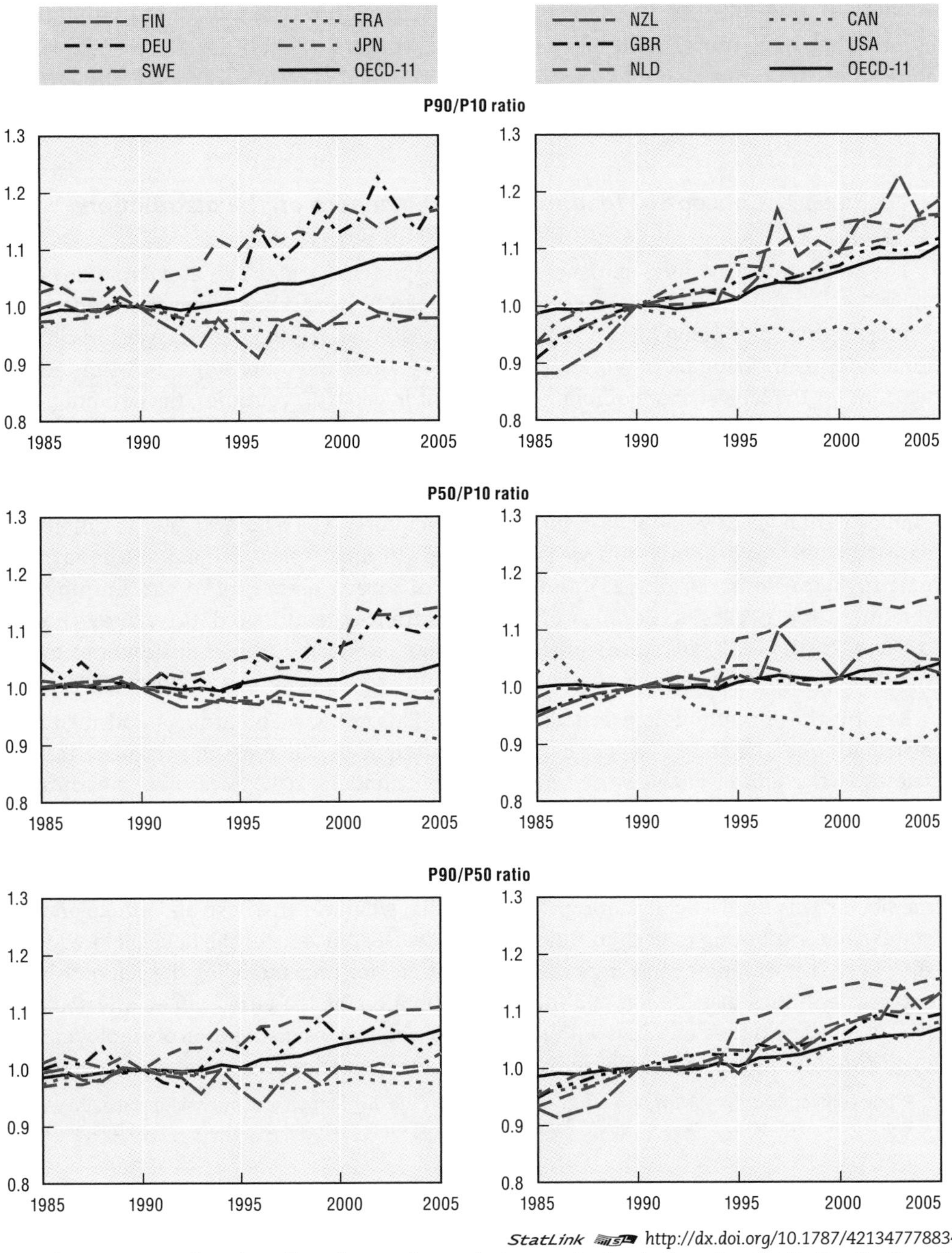

StatLink ⬛⬛🔗 http://dx.doi.org/10.1787/421347778834

Note: Three measures of earnings dispersion are shown: the top panel refers to the entire distribution (i.e. the ratio between the upper limit of the 9th decile and that of the 1st decile); the middle panel to the lower half of the distribution (the ratio of median earnings to the upper limit of the 1st decile); and the bottom panel to the upper half (the ratio of the upper limit of the 9th decile to median earnings). Wages and salaries of full-time employees are reported gross of taxes and social security contributions in all countries except France, where they exclude social security contributions paid by workers. Data for some countries have been interpolated for missing observations. OECD-11 includes Canada, Finland, France, Germany, Japan, the Netherlands, New Zealand, Sweden, the United Kingdom and the United States, as well as Korea (not shown above).

Source: OECD Earnings database.

since 1995. While this widening has affected both halves of the distribution, it is larger at the top (with an increase in P90/P50 of 7% since 1990) than at the bottom (with an increase in P50/P10 of 4% since 1990).

This average increase in earnings dispersion hides, however, significant differences across countries. In Germany, New Zealand, the Netherlands, Sweden and the United States, the increase in earnings dispersion among men working full time was large and sustained, while in Canada, France, Finland and Japan the earnings distribution was rather stable or narrowing.[4] These large cross-country differences in how the overall distribution of personal earnings changed over time mainly reflect a greater variation in the trends in the bottom half of the distribution than in the top half: the P50/P10 ratio fell in Canada, Finland, France and Japan, while it increased moderately in the United Kingdom and the United States and more sharply (exceeding 15%) in Germany. Conversely, the widening in the upper half of the distribution was common to all countries except France and Finland, and it exceeded 13% in New Zealand and the United States. Even this increase is likely to understate the widening of the earnings distribution at the very top, as OECD earnings statistics omit a large and rising share of the remuneration package of better-paid workers.[5]

Trends in earnings inequality for women working full time are generally more volatile than for men. Across the 11 OECD countries with earnings data available since 1985, the P90/P10 ratio rose by 11% since 1990, as compared to 10% for men, with most of the rise in the upper half of the distribution (an increase in P90/P50 of 8% since 1990, compared to one of 3% for P50/P10).[6] Across countries, the earnings distribution of women working full time widened in Sweden, the United States and United Kingdom, while it remained broadly stable or narrowed in France and Finland.

Additional factors come into play when looking at changes in the earnings distribution for *all full-time workers*, irrespectively of their gender. In general, these changes are significantly smaller than those experienced by men and women separately. Across the 11 OECD countries for which earnings data by gender are available since 1985, the increase in the P90/P10 ratio recorded since 1990 is 7%, *i.e.* around two-thirds that men and women separately.[7] This mainly reflected the decline in the gender wage gap (the difference in median earnings between men and women working full time), which narrowed the "distance" between the two distributions and more than offset the rise in the share of women among all full-time workers, which – had the gender wage gap stayed constant – would have "fattened" the lower tail in the total distribution.[8] As in the case of men and women separately, the widening of the earnings distribution for full-time workers was driven by a widening in the upper half.

The higher earnings dispersion is the result of differences in the pace of earnings growth for workers at various points of the distribution. However, it also matters whether these differences reflect real earnings *gains* for better-paid workers that exceed those of their lower-paid counterparts or, conversely, real earnings *losses* for workers at the bottom of the distribution. Figure 3.3 shows some significant differences in real earnings growth for full-time workers across deciles, both between men and women and across countries. In all countries, women at the lower end of the distribution have recorded stronger earnings growth than men, while differences by gender are smaller at the upper end. In the United States over the period 1980 to 2005, men working full time in the lower half of the distribution experienced real earnings losses, while workers in the middle of the distribution also experienced real declines in Canada since 1997.

Figure 3.3. **Real earnings growth for men and women working full time by decile,
1980 to 2005**

Average growth rate per year, in percentage

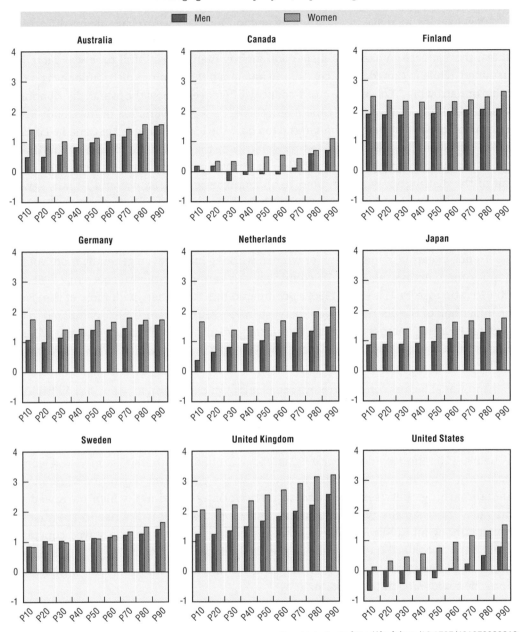

StatLink ⬛ http://dx.doi.org/10.1787/421373283813

Note: Annual growth rates over the period 1980 to 2005 for Australia, Japan and the United States; 1980 to 2004 for Finland, Germany and Sweden; 1980 to 2003 for the United Kingdom; 1985 to 2005 in the Netherlands; and 1997 to 2005 for Canada. Nominal earnings data are deflated with the CPI.

Source: OECD Earnings database.

Earnings distribution among all workers: the importance of non-standard employment

Changes in the distribution of personal earnings among *all employees* reflect the influence of a range of additional factors beyond those affecting the distribution among full-time workers. These include differences in working hours and in wage rates of other

GROWING UNEQUAL? – ISBN 978-92-64-044180-0 – © OECD 2008

groups of workers, such as those working part time and in non-standard employment, that are omitted from the OECD earnings data used above.

The importance of non-standard jobs has increased in recent years, although with different intensity across countries. For example, the incidence of part-time work in total employment since the mid-1990s has been broadly stable (at 16% in 2006) for the OECD area as a whole, but it increased sharply in Germany, Spain and Korea (OECD, 2007a). Similarly, the incidence of temporary workers (temporary help agency workers, on-call workers, seasonal workers, workers on fixed-term contracts of one year or less) has risen only marginally on average (from a little more than 10% in 1985 to around 12% in 2000) but by much more in Spain, Italy and Ireland (OECD, 2002).[9] Beyond these two categories of workers, some workers holding non-standard jobs are likely to be classified as self-employed and hence excluded from earnings statistics.

Because part-time employees work fewer hours each week and many categories of temporary employees work fewer weeks each year, the inclusion of non-standard workers significantly widens the distribution of annual earnings among all employees. This suggests that workers at the bottom of the distribution of annual earnings are typically those working a low number of hours per year, either because they work part time or because they work full time but only for part of the year (see also Burniaux, 1997).[10] This is not a cause of concern when part-time or intermittent work is "chosen": non-regular jobs often provide opportunities for people to work in flexible ways that better match their diverse lifestyles. However, surveys also suggest that many part-time workers would prefer to work more hours if suitable jobs were available, and the share of these involuntary part-timers (at 16% of part-time employment in 2005 for the OECD area as a whole) is today around three times larger than in 1985 (OECD, 2007a).[11]

Beyond differences in hours worked, workers in non-standard jobs are also typically paid less per hour. In the mid-1990s, the hourly pay of part-time workers was around 25% less than for workers in full-time jobs (OECD, 1999), and the gap between temporary workers and permanent workers was similar in a sample of European countries in the late 1990s (OECD, 2002). While part of these wage differences reflect the different characteristics of the individuals (e.g. age, tenure and qualification) and of the firms where they work (e.g. size and industrial sectors), controlling for these different characteristics does not eliminate the wage penalty associated with holding a temporary or part-time job (OECD, 1999 and 2002).[12] Further, in some countries such as Japan and Korea, earnings statistics for full-time workers exclude all those holding irregular jobs, even when their working hours are comparable to those of regular workers. In these two countries, workers holding irregular jobs are paid between 40 and 60% less per hour than regular workers, a gap that is too large to be explained by productivity differences (OECD, 2006 and 2007b). Beyond differences in pay rates, a large share of these workers are also not entitled to additional benefits and guarantees, which would imply higher gaps in actual remuneration.

One way to illustrate the importance of non-standard jobs for the distribution of personal earnings is to see how a typical measure of inequality changes when the coverage of the earnings data is broadened from full-time workers to all employees. Figure 3.4 shows estimates of the Gini coefficient for personal earnings based on micro-data for 19 OECD countries in around 2000 drawn from the *Luxembourg Income Study* project. The first panel shows how inequality in *personal earnings* changes, for each country, when moving from men working full time (on the horizontal axis) to all full-time workers, irrespective of

Figure 3.4. **Inequality in the distribution of personal earnings
when moving from full-time workers to all workers**

Gini coefficients in around 2000

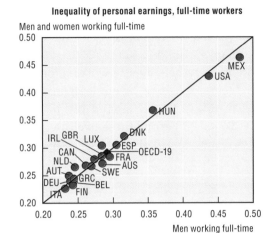

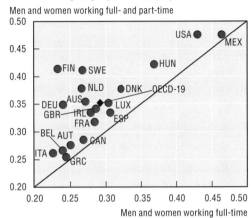

StatLink ⌗⌗⌗ http://dx.doi.org/10.1787/421380354876

Note: Gini coefficients refer to individuals belonging to households with a head aged between 18 and 65. Data refer to the year 2000, except for Australia (2001), Hungary, Netherlands and the United Kingdom (1999).

Source: Luxembourg Income Study.

their gender (on the vertical axis); the second panel shows how inequality in personal earnings changes when moving from all full-time workers (on the horizontal axis) to all employees, whether working full or part time (on the vertical axis). Two main patterns stand out from Figure 3.4:

- First, there are large cross-country differences in the width of the distribution of personal earnings among men working full time, with Gini coefficients ranging from around 0.45 in Mexico and the United States to values below 0.25 in Italy, Austria, Germany, Finland, Belgium and Greece. Conversely, including women working full time has only a small effect on the distribution of personal earnings among all full-time employees, with a small widening in most countries and a small narrowing in Mexico, Australia, Finland and the United States.[13]

- Second, the distribution of personal earnings widens significantly when including part-time workers. On average, the Gini coefficient for personal earnings among all employees exceeds that for full-timers by 0.06 point (i.e. a 20% increase), with larger rises in Finland, Sweden, Germany and the Netherlands and negligible ones in Greece and Mexico. Also, across countries, the widening of the earnings distribution when including part-time workers is larger in countries where the earnings distribution of full-time workers is narrower, which suggests that the narrower distribution may have encouraged the diffusion of part-time work in several countries.

From personal to household earnings: which factors come into play?

Moving from personal to household earnings requires broadening the analysis across individuals, considering how they pool and share their earnings with other household members, and how jobs are distributed among people. While both of these factors matter, the assessment of their role depends on how households with no earnings are included in the analysis and on how people are "ranked" (i.e. whether based on household gross earnings or on their "final" disposable income).

One summary measure of household earnings inequality is the concentration coefficient of household earnings across all people – whether working or not (as computed based on grouped data in the OECD income distribution questionnaire).[14] For most OECD countries, this measure of household earnings inequality (in Panel A of Figure 3.5) was quite stable over the decade to the mid-2000s, with significant rises in Canada, Germany, New Zealand and Norway and falls in Mexico and, to a lesser extent, Greece, Hungary, Denmark, Finland and Italy. The large differences across countries in this measure of household earnings inequality shown in Figure 3.5 partly reflect differences in the earnings measure (i.e. whether earnings are measured before or after taxes). Cross-country differences remain important, however, even when restricting the analysis to countries reporting pre-tax earnings data, ranging from values of 0.40 or more – in the United States, New Zealand, the United Kingdom and Australia – to around 0.30 – in Denmark, Sweden, Norway, Greece, Italy and Luxembourg.

Figure 3.5. **Concentration of household earnings by type of wage earner**

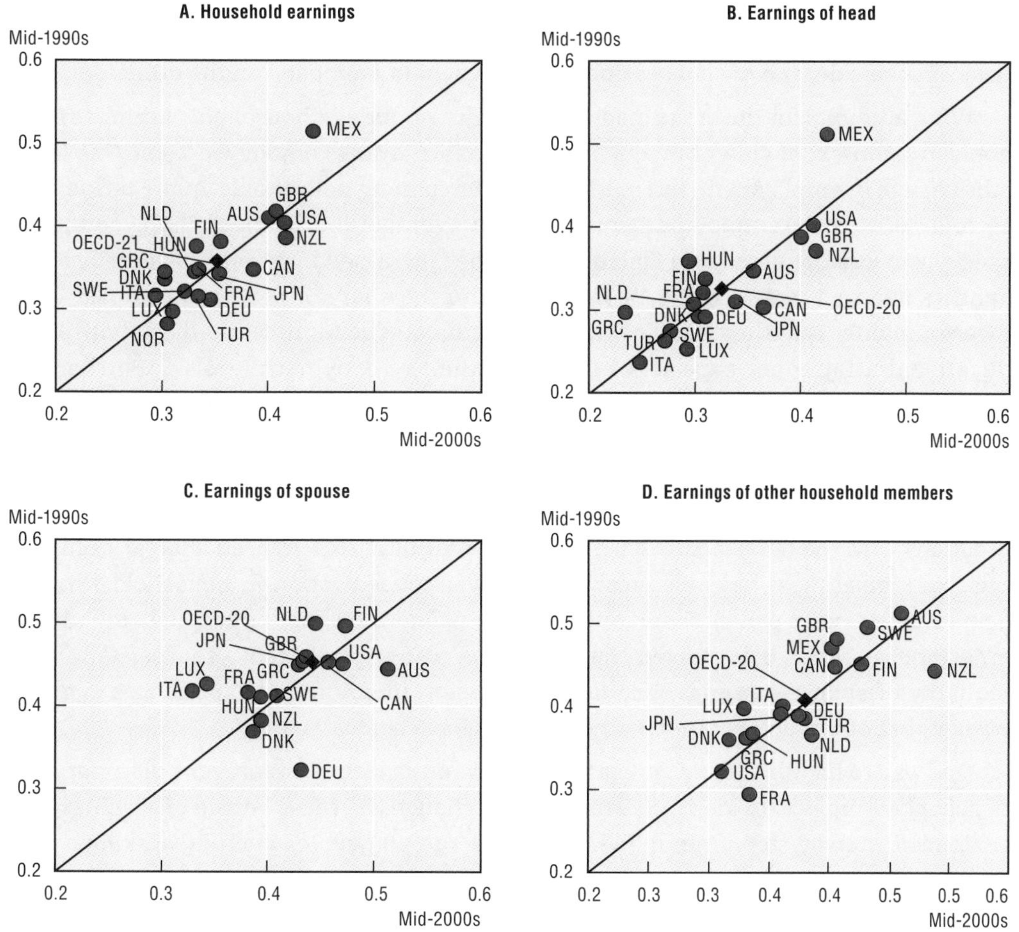

StatLink ⟨⟩ http://dx.doi.org/10.1787/421383351035

Note: The concentration coefficient is computed in the same way as the Gini coefficient, with the only difference being that individuals are not ranked by the value of the earnings they receive but rather by their equivalised disposable incomes. Concentration coefficients are computed based on grouped data for average household earnings in each income decile. Data refer to gross (i.e. pre-tax) earnings in all countries except Greece, Hungary, Mexico, Poland and Turkey, where they are measured post-tax.

Source: OECD income distribution questionnaire.

Cross-country differences in the distribution of household earnings are also evident when looking separately at the earnings of the household head, of spouses and of other household members (in Panels B, C and D of Figure 3.5). In the mid-2000s, earnings of spouses were significantly more concentrated than those of household heads (with a concentration coefficient that was, on average, one-third higher), and the same pattern applied, to a lesser extent, to the earnings of other household members (with inequality around higher). While the greater inequality of spouse earnings reflects a range of factors described in Box 3.2, cross-country differences in the size of these inequalities partly reflect how prevalent two-earner households are in each country. This is highlighted by the much larger gap between the Gini coefficient of spouse earnings and that of household heads in those countries (such as Turkey and Greece) where the share of people in two-earner households is smaller. Cross-country differences are also significant when looking at *changes* in earnings inequality among these various types of earnings: in Germany, for example, earnings of spouses became much more concentrated than those of heads, while in the United Kingdom lower inequality in the earnings of spouses and other household members was accompanied by a slight increase in that of household heads. As a result, there is only a weak correlation between changes in earnings inequality of household heads, on one side, and of spouses and other household members, on the other.

What accounts for the broad stability in the distribution of household earnings among people in a context of greater inequality in personal earnings among workers? One factor is the change in employment and in its distribution among households. In the ten years to the mid-2000s, non-employment rates fell on average and in most OECD countries, especially in Spain, Ireland and Finland, while they increased in several eastern European countries and in Turkey (Table 3.1). The decline in the share of people not in paid work, however, mainly benefited people with intermediate education, while those with lower educational attainment experienced a fall in their employment levels.[15] Further, the average decline recorded in non-employment rates has not been matched by a similar fall in the share of people living in jobless households; countries that have recorded the largest fall in non-employment rates tend to experience larger inroads into household joblessness, but the association between the two variables is not strong, and there are several exceptions.[16] In the ten years to 2005, countries that have experienced a larger decline in household joblessness have also recorded a lower concentration in household earnings (Figure 3.6, left-hand panel). Similarly, countries where the share of people living in two-earner households has increased the most have also experienced a sharper fall in the inequality of spouse-earnings. The large dispersion in countries' experiences suggests however that other factors beyond access to jobs have been at work.[17]

One way to highlight the significance of the various factors shaping the distribution of household earnings is to look at how inequality changes as the coverage of earnings data is extended, step by step, from individual workers to all people, whether working or not. Figure 3.7 shows values of the Gini coefficient for household earnings (among people living in a household with a head of working age) with people ranked by their (equivalised) household earnings (rather than income). The first panel compares the inequality in personal earnings among workers to that in household earnings among the same individuals (i.e. after allowing for partnership formation between them), with household earnings "equivalised" by the number of workers in each household. The second panel compares the inequality in household earnings as defined previously with the inequality obtained after including in the analysis non-working spouses and their children. The third

Box 3.2. **What accounts for the greater inequality of spouse earnings compared to those of household heads?**

Two factors that partly offset each other have contributed to shape the distribution of spouse earnings compared to that of household heads:

● The first reflects the characteristics of the marriage market, in particular the extent to which better-educated spouses (with a higher earnings potential) "match" with heads with similar characteristics (a phenomenon also called "assortative mating"). Much research has documented the importance of marital mating for the United States (*e.g.* Juhn and Murphy, 1997), where the growing tendency for better-educated individuals to marry each other is occurring alongside the increasing difficulty faced by less-educated women (particularly from ethnic minorities) to find suitable partners (Mare, 2000). The consequences of assortative mating are not limited to income distribution, and this phenomenon is not unique to the United States: the left-hand panel of the figure below shows a positive correlation (of 50% on average) between the educational attainment of partners within couples (with a head aged between 18 and 65), with higher values in the United States, Mexico and the southern European countries (where income inequality is above-average) and lower ones in the Nordic countries and continental Europe (with below-average income inequality).

● The second factor is the likelihood that spouses who are married to higher-earning heads (for a given level of educational attainment) will enter the labour market. For couples with an employed head, the right-hand panel of the figure below suggests that, in all countries except Denmark, spouses are more likely to enter the paid labour force when the earnings of the head are low rather than high. This result holds after controlling for the level of education of spouses as, *ceteris paribus,* labour-force participation rises with educational attainment. This suggests that many households with lower "earnings potential" offset this by having both partners participating in the paid labour market.

While these factors work in opposite directions, the evidence presented above suggests that, because of assortative mating and the higher educational levels of spouses, their earnings contribute to widening the distribution of household income.

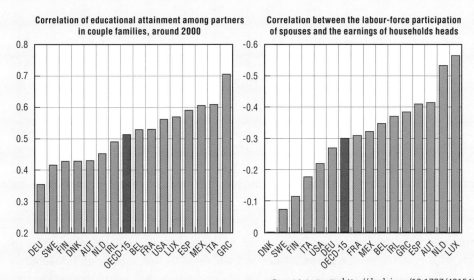

StatLink http://dx.doi.org/10.1787/421541777254

Note: Calculations based on individuals belonging to households with a head aged between 18 and 65. Data refer to the year 2000, except for Hungary and the Netherlands (1999). Values shown in the right-hand panel are partial correlation coefficients, *i.e.* computed after controlling for the educational attainment of both spouses.

Source: Luxembourg Income Study.

Table 3.1. **Non-employment rates and share of people living in jobless households**

| | Non-employment rate | | | | | | | | Share of population living in jobless households | |
| | Total | | Less educated | | Medium educated | | Highly educated | | | |
	Level, 2005	Point change since 1995	Level, 2005	Point change since 1997	Level, 2005	Point change since 1997	Level, 2005	Point change since 1997	Level, around 2005	Point change since 1995
Australia	28.4	−5.6	40.6	−3.2	21.6	−4.3	15.9	−0.9	14.2	−1.8
Austria	31.4	−0.4	52.8	1.8	26.6	1.0	15.8	0.9	11.0	−1.8
Belgium[1]	39.0	−5.2	59.6	−0.1	34.5	−2.3	17.2	−0.2	18.6	−2.2
Canada	27.5	−5.4	49.8	−3.5	25.9	−2.6	18.5	−1.0	6.2	−0.5
Czech Republic[1]	35.2	4.5	78.2	10.9	28.2	4.9	15.4	4.2	10.1	4.0
Denmark	24.5	−3.1	41.4	..	21.4	..	13.8	..	9.2	−0.5
Finland	32.0	−8.0	54.2	0.1	28.0	−6.1	15.8	−2.6	7.3	0.3
France[1]	37.7	−3.9	52.6	−3.0	31.9	−0.7	23.4	0.1	11.6	−3.1
Germany	34.5	−1.0	57.7	−2.2	30.7	−1.3	17.3	−1.1	19.4	4.2
Greece	39.7	−6.2	49.5	−0.8	39.2	−6.9	18.9	−2.3	6.5	−3.1
Hungary	43.1	−3.4	72.0	1.0	35.1	0.8	17.5	−1.1	19.1	11.2
Iceland	..	..	..	..	..	..	..	..	2.1	2.1
Ireland[1]	32.9	−15.3	50.5	−7.0	26.9	−10.9	14.5	−6.8	11.7	..
Italy	42.5	−5.9	54.1	..	33.4	..	21.5	..	9.6	−2.3
Japan	30.7	0.0	..	..	33.8	1.5	26.1	0.0	5.1	1.1
Korea	36.3	−0.9	49.9	4.8	36.2	1.7	23.6	3.2	5.5	..
Luxembourg	36.4	−3.4	49.5	..	37.0	..	17.5	..	7.1	−2.2
Mexico	40.4	−0.9	42.6	1.5	36.2	−0.4	29.2	2.4	3.8	0.4
Netherlands	28.9	−7.2	41.6	..	22.6	..	14.6	..	9.1	−1.7
New Zealand	25.4	−6.6	40.0	−5.1	23.0	−1.2	16.2	−3.4	9.3	−3.5
Norway	24.8	−3.0	42.8	3.8	19.8	−2.0	12.9	−0.1	13.1	1.8
Poland	47.0	5.3	76.9	12.4	43.1	10.0	18.7	5.2	14.0	..
Portugal[1]	32.5	−3.4	34.3	..	36.9	..	14.4	..	5.9	−1.0
Slovak Republic	42.3	2.1	86.7	12.0	33.6	5.0	16.7	5.5	10.6	..
Spain[1]	35.7	−16.9	44.4	−10.0	34.2	−23.2	19.9	−12.2	5.8	−3.6
Sweden	26.1	−2.4	47.5	4.3	21.5	−3.6	14.0	−3.4	6.2	−0.8
Switzerland	22.8	−1.6	57.8	20.3	22.8	2.3	10.3	−0.8	5.9	..
Turkey	54.1	6.5	55.4	7.9	50.1	−0.1	27.6	5.2	10.4	5.6
United Kingdom	27.4	−4.0	52.1	3.8	24.7	−1.0	12.8	−0.5	16.3	−1.1
United States	28.5	0.5	58.1	2.0	29.2	3.2	17.8	3.1	6.3	0.1
OECD	34.1	−3.3	53.3	2.3	30.6	−1.5	17.9	−0.3	9.7	0.1

StatLink ⟡ http://dx.doi.org/10.1787/421582070853

Note: Non-employment rates relative to the population of working age; share of total population living in jobless households with a head of working age.
1. Changes in the share of people in jobless households refer to the period 1995 to 2000 in the case of Austria, Belgium, the Czech Republic, Portugal and Spain; in the case of France, data on changes in household joblessness are based on a source (the *Enquête Revenus Fiscaux*) that differs from the one used to show levels of the same variable (EU-SILC).
Source: OECD Education database and income distribution questionnaire.

panel compares the dispersion of household earnings among all people living in households with positive wage income (as defined above) with that among all households (*i.e.* including those with zero earnings).[18] Inequality measures vary across countries, but to different extents:

● First, partnership formation among employees, and the economies of scale in consumption that this allows, narrows the distribution of *household earnings among all workers* relative to that for personal earnings. On average, inequality of household

Figure 3.6. **Changes in the share of the population living in households with different numbers of workers and changes in earning inequality**

Mid-1990s to mid-2000s

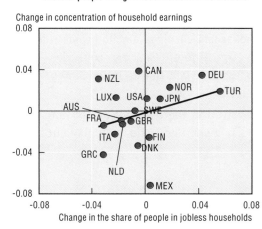
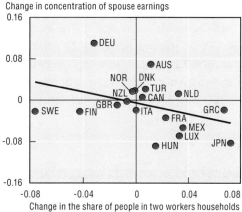

StatLink ⟶ http://dx.doi.org/10.1787/421463342772

Note: The first panel plots changes in the share of people in jobless households against changes in the Gini coefficient of household earnings; the second plots changes in the share of people living in two-earner households against changes in the Gini coefficient of spouse earnings.

Source: OECD income distribution questionnaire.

Figure 3.7. **Inequality in the distribution of household earnings when moving from households with positive earnings to all households**

Around 2000

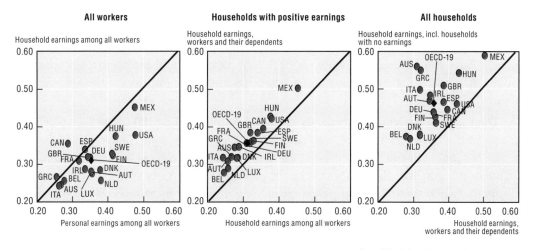

StatLink ⟶ http://dx.doi.org/10.1787/421482623283

Note: Gini coefficients calculated based on individuals belonging to households with a head aged between 18 and 65. Data refer to the year 2000, except for Australia (2001), Hungary, Netherlands and the United Kingdom (1999).

Source: Luxembourg Income Study.

earnings is around 0.04 point lower than for personal earnings (*i.e.* a 12% decline), with larger declines in the Netherlands, the United States, Denmark and Finland, with the exception of only Canada.

- Second, including dependents (children, the elderly and non-working spouses) in households of workers widens the distribution of household earnings. When each member of these households is considered as benefiting from these earnings, the distribution of *household earnings among all people in working households* widens on average, relative to the case when only workers are considered, by 0.05 point (*i.e.* a 15% increase), with only minor differences across countries.

- Third, including households with no wage income significantly widens the distribution of household earnings.[19] *The inequality in household earnings among people* rises by 0.10 point on average (*i.e.* a 30% increase) with large differences across countries – from around 0.2 point in Austria, Greece and Italy to less than 0.05 in the United States, where the share of people living in households with no earners is small.

As the importance of each of the factors involved in the distributions of household earnings may change over time, it is difficult to say *a priori* how they will play out in the aggregate.

From household earnings to market income

Moving from household earnings to market income requires broadening the analysis to include self-employment and capital income. While measurement problems for these two income sources are much larger than for earnings, both have played a significant role in shaping recent trends in the distribution of market income.

The concentration of capital and self-employment income among individuals of working age, when people are ranked by their equivalised disposable income, is in general significantly higher than that of household earnings. This reflects both greater inequality in capital and self-employment income among the households reporting them, and differences in the share of people receiving them in each decile of the income distribution. On average, the Gini coefficient for capital income exceeds that for household earnings by around one-fourth, and a similar gap is recorded for self-employment income.[20] This pattern of greater concentration holds in most countries, with the exceptions of Australia, Korea, Poland and Switzerland (where both self-employment and capital income are more equally distributed than earnings) and a few other countries (for one of the two income streams).

There have been significant changes in the concentration of capital and self-employment income in the ten years since 1995 in several OECD countries, which have contributed to greater inequality in the distribution of market income. On average, across the countries included in Figure 3.8, the concentration of capital income increased by 0.04 point, *i.e.* around 9%, while that of self-employment income increased by around 4%. Inequality in capital income has risen sharply in the Nordic countries as well as in Italy and Hungary, while it declined in Turkey, the Czech Republic and (to a lesser extent) in a few other countries. Concentration of self-employment income also increased sharply in Sweden (from a low base) as well as in Italy and Mexico. In Hungary and Norway, the increase in market-income inequality was further strengthened by the large increase in the weight of capital income within household disposable income.

There are also significant differences in the degree of concentration of the different components of capital income. While the quality of information is inevitably affected by the small number of observations for individual categories, the estimates in Table 3.2 suggest that concentration is highest for other capital income (mainly interest and returns on financial assets) and private pensions, but significantly lower for occupational pensions and private transfers.

Figure 3.8. **Concentration of capital and self-employment income, mid-2000s**

Among people of working age

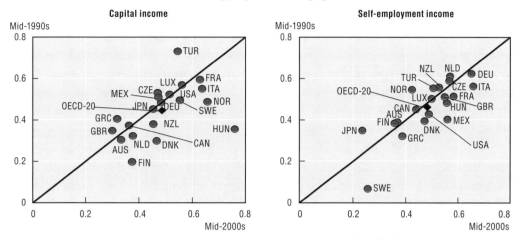

StatLink ⟨ms⟩ http://dx.doi.org/10.1787/421540540222

Note: The concentration coefficient is computed in the same way as the Gini coefficient, with the only difference being that individuals are not ranked by the value of the earnings they receive but rather by their equivalised disposable incomes. Concentration coefficients are computed based on grouped data for average income streams in each decile. Data refer to gross (*i.e.* pre-tax) income in all countries except Greece, Hungary, Mexico, Poland and Turkey, where they are measured post-tax.

Source: OECD income distribution questionnaire.

Table 3.2. **Size and concentration of different elements of capital income, mid-2000s**

Among people of working age

	Private Pensions		Occupational pensions		Private transfers		Other capital income		Total capital income	
	Concentration coefficient	Share in household disp. income (%)	Concentration coefficient	Share in household disp. income (%)	Concentration coefficient	Share in household disp. income (%)	Concentration coefficient	Share in household disp. income (%)	Concentration coefficient	Share in household disp. income (%)
Australia	..	..	0.15	2.1	0.00	1.2	0.50	4.8	0.33	8.1
Belgium	0.73	0.0	..	..	−0.12	0.7	0.54	4.1	0.44	4.8
Canada	0.32	5.5	..	..	0.31	2.9	0.48	3.6	0.36	12.0
Finland	0.49	0.6	−0.02	8.6	−0.08	1.0	0.78	9.2	0.37	19.5
Germany	0.35	0.2	0.42	0.4	−0.23	0.6	0.61	5.4	0.48	6.8
Greece	0.38	0.0	..	..	−0.20	1.7	0.55	3.8	0.32	5.5
Hungary	..	..	..	..	0.54	1.2	0.80	6.3	0.76	7.7
Italy	..	..	..	..	..	..	0.64	4.1	0.64	4.1
New Zealand	0.51	0.8	..	..	0.29	4.3	0.59	4.8	0.45	10.4
Norway	0.23	0.1	0.18	2.6	−0.25	0.3	0.81	10.7	0.66	13.8
Slovakia	0.16	0.1	..	..	−0.45	0.1	..	..	−0.05	3.0
Sweden	0.46	0.8	0.48	2.9	..	..	0.63	3.7	0.55	7.4
Turkey	0.59	0.1	..	..	0.31	2.0	0.64	5.0	0.54	7.2
United Kingdom	0.30	0.5	0.24	4.5	0.20	2.9	0.51	2.3	0.30	10.2
United States	0.51	0.1	0.16	0.7	0.45	0.5	0.65	7.8	0.61	9.2
OECD-16	0.42	0.7	0.23	3.1	0.06	1.5	0.62	5.4	0.45	8.6

StatLink ⟨ms⟩ http://dx.doi.org/10.1787/421602824576

Note: The concentration coefficient is computed in the same way as the Gini coefficient, with the only difference being that individuals are not ranked by the value of the capital income they receive but rather by their equivalised disposable incomes. Concentration coefficients are computed based on grouped data expressing the value of capital income for people in each income decile.

Source: OECD income distribution questionnaire.

Conclusion

Analyses of earnings and income distribution typically develop along parallel tracks, using different methodologies to address different questions. Research on earnings inequality typically looks at individual workers, paying little attention to household dynamics and non-wage income sources, while research on income distribution focuses on households, but may miss the importance of labour-market developments. Better integrating these two perspectives is important for understanding how labour markets affect the distribution of household income. When the two perspectives are considered jointly, the following patterns emerge:

● The distribution of personal earnings among men working full time has widened significantly in most OECD countries since 1990, mainly reflecting developments in the upper half of the distribution. The widening is smaller for all full-time workers, due to the simultaneous narrowing in the wage gap between men and women working full time. The growing incidence of non-standard employment in some OECD countries has further contributed to widening the distribution of personal earnings among all employees.

● The distribution of household earnings among all people, whether working or not, has been stable since the mid-1990s, both on average and in most countries, as the widening distribution of earnings was offset by higher employment rates. Changes in the distribution of earnings of household heads, of spouses and of other household members have evolved in different directions in various countries, due to a range of factors.

● Both capital income and self-employment income are more concentrated than household earnings, and they have become increasingly so in the last ten years, widening the distribution of market income in several OECD countries.

Overall, these patterns suggest that there are both consistencies and differences in how earnings inequality among workers and market-income inequality among people evolve over time. While both distributions have widened in most OECD countries, there are exceptions and differences in both the direction and the strength of the association between the two.[21] These differences reflect the importance of income sharing within households, the labour supply decision of spouses and the incidence of household joblessness and dual-earner households. These factors suggest that there is more than one way of countering a wider distribution of market income. As governments can only marginally affect individual decisions about household formation and living arrangements, and as the scale of redistribution is limited by the amount of tax revenues, policies to narrow income inequalities need to consider how best to improve labour-market conditions, reduce joblessness and ensure that earnings inequality does not become too large (Kenworthy, 2007).

Notes

1. Gottschalk and Smeeding (1997) and Katz and Autor (1999) discuss how trends in earnings dispersion in OECD countries are related to technological change, foreign trade and labour-market institutions. Lemieux, MacLeod and Parent (2007) discuss the importance of additional factors, such as the influence of performance pay systems; Black and Spitz-Oener (2007) relate changes in the gender wage gap to the effect of differential changes in the skill content of male and female work.

2. Atkinson and Brandolini (2005) develop a simple model to illustrate the links between different labour-market conditions, personal earnings and income inequality. Checchi and García Peñalosa

(2005) build a more complex model to explain how labour-market institutions affect the distribution of household income.

3. In Japan and Finland, for example, a widening of the distribution of market income occurred alongside stable or declining earnings dispersion among full-time workers while, conversely, the distribution of market income narrowed in the Netherlands despite a wider distribution of personal earnings.

4. The increase was also strong in Australia and Korea, where OECD earnings data are available since 1990.

5. For example, in France non-wage components of earnings (such as various incentive plans, including *intéressement, participation, abondements par les entreprises aux versements des salaries aux plan d'épargne entreprise*) account for around 3% of the wage bill, with 60% of these received by the 10% of employees with the highest earnings (CERC, 2006). Non-wage components of earnings are especially important for managers, and they account for much of the sharp rise in their remuneration. In the United States, the average remuneration of CEOs (excluding the value of "stock options") increased from 85 times average earnings in 1990 to 525 times in 2000 before declining to 410 in 2005 (*www.faireconomy.org*).

6. The P90/P10 ratio among full-time employees is generally smaller for women than for men in most OECD countries, with the exceptions of Canada and Germany.

7. From 1990 onwards consistent data on earnings inequality are available for a larger sample of 19 OECD countries (*i.e.* the same countries included in Figure 3.1, as well as Australia, the Czech Republic, Denmark, Hungary, Ireland and Poland). The cumulative increase in the interdeciles ratio since 1990 recorded by this larger set of countries is significantly higher than that recorded by the OECD-11 over the same period (a rise in the P90/P10 ratio of 18% compared to 10%), reflecting a more rapid increase in earnings inequality in the upper part of the distribution (11% rather than 7%) and, to a lesser extent, in the lower part (6% relative to 4%).

8. In 2005, the gender pay gap was highest in Japan (at 32%) and Korea (40%) and lowest in New Zealand (9%) and Poland (11%). Over the past two decades, the difference in median earnings between men and women working full time declined by between 7 and 17 points in most OECD countries, but only marginally in Australia, Germany and Sweden.

9. The two groups of workers partially overlap, as a large proportion of temporary workers hold part-time jobs (OECD, 2002).

10. Differences in the number of hours worked during the year result in the much larger disparities in annual earnings than in wage rates. In France, for example, the P90/P10 inter-decile ratio was around 3 in 2004 when looking at full-time equivalent earnings but of 13 when considering annual earnings. Employees in the first decile worked only 13 weeks during the year, as compared to 51 weeks for those in the top decile; similarly, their weekly hours of work were around 22 hours, as compared to 38 for those in the top decile (CERC, 2006).

11. Involuntary part-time employment is much higher in some countries and when using national (rather than OECD) definitions of full-time work.

12. A negative wage gap is systematically observed for women working part time even after controlling for these different characteristics, but its magnitude differs among countries and studies. In the case of men, O'Dorchai *et al.* (2007) conclude that different controls account for between 50% and 100% of the wage gap between men working full time and part time observed in the mid-1990s in European countries.

13. These earnings data, which are based on household surveys representative of the entire population, match quite closely those from the OECD Earnings database, with a correlation coefficient for P90/P10 from the two sources of over 0.9 across ten countries. The main exceptions are Denmark and the United States, where the inter-decile ratios based on the LIS are much higher than those in the OECD earnings database.

14. The concentration coefficient is computed in the same way as the Gini coefficient of household income, so that a value of zero would mean that all income groups receive an equal share of household earnings. The only difference relative to the Gini coefficient is that individuals are not ranked by the value of the earnings they receive but rather by that of their equivalised household disposable incomes.

15. Over this period, changes in employment rates have been in general more favourable for women than for men. Even in countries where total employment rates fell, those for women either increased or fell by less than for men.

16. In Germany, for example, higher employment rates have been associated with higher household joblessness; also, while employment rates increased strongly in both New Zealand and the United Kingdom, the decline in household joblessness was much stronger in the first than in the second. The correlation between changes in employment rates and changes in the share of people in jobless households as shown in Table 3.2 is less than –0.60.

17. As in the previous cases, these measures are based on data on the distribution of each earnings component among individuals ranked by their equivalised household disposable income; hence they reflect differences across deciles in both the pay workers receive and in the numbers employed.

18. Saunders (2005) conducts a similar analysis for Australia based on a somewhat different sequence of distributions. As elsewhere in this chapter, the unit of analysis used in Figure 3.7 is the individual, with household earnings equivalised by the square root elasticity to account for economies of scale in consumption.

19. Zero worker households are defined as households with zero earnings, i.e. they may include those with positive self-employment income. The inclusion of households with no earnings in measures of household earnings inequality highlights the effect of employment (and the way it is distributed) for cross-country differences in income inequality. However, this procedure effectively extends the analysis to households with no earnings while excluding their income sources other than earnings.

20. These comparisons refer to people of working age. For the population as a whole, the difference in the Gini coefficients of self-employment and capital income are slightly less.

21. Daly and Valletta (2006) and Gottschalk and Danziger (2005) show that, while the dispersion of male wages and family income evolved similarly during the last 30 years in the United States, men's earnings have not been the only driving factor in family income inequality.

References

Atkinson, A.B. (2007), "The Long Run Earnings Distribution in Five Countries: 'Remarkable Stability', U, V or W?", Second Ruggles Lecture for the International Association for Research in Income and Wealth, *Review of Income and Wealth,* Vol. 53, No. 1, March.

Atkinson, A.B. and A. Brandolini (2005), "From Earnings Dispersion to Income Inequality", in F. Farina and E. Savaglio (eds.), *Inequality and Economic Integration,* Routledge, London.

Black, S. and A. Spitz-Oener (2007), "Explaining Women's Success: Technological Change and the Skill Content of Women's Work", NBER Working Paper, No. 13116, Cambridge, Massachusetts.

Burniaux, J.-M. (1997), "Inégalités et emplois : effet de redistribution lié à la structure familiale", *Économie Internationale,* Vol. 71, No. 3.

Checchi, D. and C. García Peñalosa (2005), "Labour Market Institutions and the Personal Distribution of Income in the OECD", IZA Discussion Paper, No. 1681, Bonn.

CERC (2006), *La France en transition, 1993-2005,* Conseil de l'emploi, des revenus et de la cohésion sociale, Rapport No. 7, La Documentation Française, Paris.

Daly, M.C. and R.G. Valletta (2006), "Inequality and Poverty in the United States: The Effects of Rising Dispersion of Men's Earnings and Changing Family Behaviour", *Economica,* Vol. 73, No. 289.

Gottschalk, P. and S. Danziger (2005), "Inequality of Wage Rates and Family Income in the United States, 1975-2002", *Review of Income and Wealth,* Vol. 51, No. 2.

Gottschalk, P. and T.M. Smeeding (1997), "Cross National Comparisons of Earnings and Income Inequality", *Journal of Economic Literature,* Vol. 35, No. 2.

Juhn, C. and K.M. Murphy (1997), "Wage Inequality and Family Labor Supply", *Journal of Labor Economics,* Vol. 15, No. 1.

Katz, L. and D. Autor (1999), "Changes in the Wage Structure and Earnings Inequality", in O. Ashenfelter and D. Card (eds.), *Handbook of Labor Economics,* Vol. 3A, Amsterdam: North Holland.

Kenworthy, L. (2007), "Jobs with Equality", unpublished manuscript, University of Arizona.

Lemieux, T., W.B. Macleod and D. Parent (2007), "Performance Pay and Wage Inequality", IZA Discussion Paper, No. 2850, Bonn.

Mare, R.D. (2000), "Assortative Mating, Intergenerational Mobility and Educational Inequality", California Center for Population Research, CCPR-004-00, University of California.

O'Dorchai, S., R. Plasman and F. Rycx (2007), "The Part-time Wage Penalty in European Countries: How Large Is It for Men?", IZA Discussion Paper, No. 2591, Bonn.

OECD (1999), "Recent Labour Market Developments and Prospects – Special Focus on the Quality of Part-time Jobs", *OECD Employment Outlook*, OECD, Paris.

OECD (2002), "Taking the Measure of Temporary Employment", *OECD Employment Outlook*, OECD, Paris.

OECD (2006), *OECD Economic Survey: Japan*, OECD, Paris.

OECD (2007a), *OECD Employment Outlook*, OECD, Paris.

OECD (2007b), *OECD Economic Survey: Korea*, OECD, Paris.

Saunders, P. (2005), "Reviewing Recent Trends in Wage Income Inequality in Australia", Discussion Paper, University of New South Wales, Australia.

ISBN 978-92-64-044180-0
Growing Unequal?
© OECD 2008

PART II

Chapter 4

How Much Redistribution Do Governments Achieve? The Role of Cash Transfers and Household Taxes*

OECD countries differ significantly in how much income they redistribute through government cash transfers and household taxes – and those countries that redistribute more achieve a more narrow distribution of final income. The redistribution achieved by public cash transfers is generally larger than that of household taxes, and countries that have more targeted programmes tend to spend less than others.

* This chapter has been prepared by Peter Whiteford who, at the time of writing, was senior economist at the OECD Social Policy Division and is currently professor at the Social Policy Research Centre at the University of New South Wales, Australia. This chapter draws on a longer document, available as Whiteford (2008).

Introduction

Government policies in all OECD countries affect the distribution of household income. They do so through a range of programmes but most directly through the cash transfers paid to households and the direct taxes and social security contributions collected from them. However, different welfare states may pursue a variety of social objectives, with the balance and priority given to each of them varying across both countries and between programmes. A critical issue that all OECD governments confront – particularly when considering policy reforms – is whether the redistributive and other policy objectives of society could be more effectively or efficiently achieved through a different mix or design of policies.

This chapter provides a discussion of the varying levels of redistribution achieved by different welfare states. The chapter first outlines the framework commonly used to assess the impact of welfare state arrangements on household income and discusses briefly the definition of the targeting and progressivity of government programmes. It then compares the distributional profiles of different social programmes and tax systems before describing the combined effects of government cash transfers and household taxes in narrowing income inequality, how this effect has changed over time, and the separate contributions of taxes and public transfers to these results. The chapter then discusses how the interplay of the level of cash transfers and taxes and their targeting contribute to the economic well-being of those at the bottom of the income scale. The chapter concludes with a discussion of ways of improving the measurement of welfare state outcomes on the distribution of household income.

An accounting framework for household income

Underlying all comparisons of welfare state outcomes is a framework for analysing the process of income distribution and redistribution (Palme, 1990; Esping-Andersen, 1990). Following Ringen (1987), this will be called "the standard approach". By definition, using a common framework to analyse income distribution and redistribution across countries implies that the framework is equally applicable in all countries and gives consistent results.

Table 4.1 sets out this standard approach. In this framework, income from wages and salaries, self-employment and property sum to "factor income"; factor income plus occupational and private pensions gives "market income"; market income plus public and private transfers, as well as other types of cash income, produces "gross income"; finally, gross income minus personal income taxes and workers' social security contributions gives "cash disposable income". This last concept, when adjusted to reflect differences in household needs through an equivalence scale, gives "equivalised disposable income" – the main measure of household well-being used in this report. The approach set out in Table 4.1 is an accounting framework that allows different components of income to be related to each other and suitable aggregates to be derived but, as discussed below, the framework is both linear and static.

Table 4.1. **The income accounting framework**

Income component	Adjustment	Equivalised income component
Wages and salaries		
+		
Self-employment income		
+		
Property income		
=		
1. **Factor income**	Equivalence scales	= **Equivalent factor income**
+		
Occupational and private pensions		
=		
2. **Market income**	Equivalence scales	= **Equivalent market income**
+		
Social security cash benefits (universal, income-related, contributory)		
+		
Private transfers		
+		
Other cash income		
=		
3. **Gross income**	Equivalence scales	= **Equivalent gross income**
–		
Income tax (and employee social security contributions)		
=		
4. **Cash disposable income**	Equivalence scales	= **Equivalent cash disposable income**

Source: Adapted from O'Higgins et al. (1990), pp. 30-31.

This framework can be used to construct a number of measures of the redistributive impact of social security and taxation policies. With micro-data, this framework can be applied to each household's income to produce the four income measures identified in Table 4.1. These unit records can then be aggregated and analysed to produce measures of distribution and redistribution across the population as a whole. In particular, the degree of redistribution effected by taxes or social security transfers can be calculated by comparing income shares or other measures such as Gini coefficients at different stages in the process outlined in Table 4.1. For example, the impact of cash transfers can be evaluated by comparing the difference between measures of inequality or poverty on the basis of market income (Stage 2) and on the basis of gross income (Stage 3), while the effects of taxes can be calculated by comparing measures of gross and disposable incomes (Stage 4). As noted by Ringen (1987, p. 172), this standard approach provides a simple but ingenious and flexible model. Yet despite its widespread use, it has a number of important limitations, as discussed below.

Targeting and progressivity: how do social programmes and taxes affect income distribution?

When considering the redistributive impact of alternative systems of social protection it is important to note that their design features differ in important respects. Two of the most important features relate to the way benefits are *funded* – i.e. the different ways in which programmes are financed – and *structured* – i.e. the relationship between benefits received and the past or current income of beneficiaries. Using these criteria, the social welfare systems of OECD countries are often characterised as either "Bismarckian" or "Beveridgean" (Werding, 2003). In the first, social programmes are based on social insurance principles, with earnings-related benefits, entitlement based on contribution records and funding through employer and employee social security contributions. In the second, policies are generally characterised by universal provision, with entitlement based on residence and in some cases need, and with benefits that are flat-rate and financed through general taxation.

The differing designs of social programmes influence the distribution of household incomes in different ways. In assessing these impacts it is important to distinguish between *targeting, progressivity,* and *redistribution.*

- Targeting is a means for determining either eligibility for benefits or the level of entitlements for those eligible. In a sense, all benefit systems – apart from a universal "basic income" or "guaranteed minimum income" scheme – are targeted to specific categories of people, such as the unemployed, people with disabilities or those over retirement age. Income and asset-testing is a further form of targeting that can be applied once people satisfy categorical eligibility criteria.[1]

- Progressivity refers to the profile of benefits when compared to market or disposable incomes – how large a share of benefits is received by different income groups – *e.g.* do the poor receive more than the rich from the transfer system?

- Finally, redistribution refers to the outcomes of different tax and benefit systems – how much does the benefit system actually *change* the distribution of household income?

In this context, welfare states can have differing objectives and achieve different types of redistribution. The main objective of social transfer systems in most OECD countries is to provide income maintenance or insurance in the face of adverse risks (unemployment, disability, sickness) or to redistribute across the lifecycle, either to periods when individuals have greater needs (for example, when there are children in the household) or would otherwise have lower incomes (such as in retirement). Barr (2001) describes this as the "piggy-bank objective".[2] The second main objective of the welfare state can be described as taking from the rich to give to the poor (what Barr calls the "Robin Hood" motive). Targeting of benefits is usually justified as a means of achieving the "Robin Hood" objective. Bismarckian-type welfare states can be characterised as giving priority to the "piggy-bank" objective, while Beveridgean-type welfare states give priority to the "Robin Hood" objective.

In practice, social protection systems in all OECD countries involve a mix of redistribution between rich and poor and risk insurance or lifecycle redistribution, although the mix of elements differs between countries. However, the precise nature of the mix cannot be observed directly in annual data on incomes or social spending, since annual data cannot identify the extent to which households have already paid for their benefits, or the extent to which they will do so in the future.

As a result, various ways of modelling the lifetime distribution of benefits and taxes are required. In the United States, for example, many studies of social security evaluate the extent to which the system provides "value for money", *i.e.* the extent to which individuals with different characteristics receive back in retirement more or less than they contributed during their working lives (Leimer, 1995; Geanakoplos *et al.*, 2000). In a comparative study, Falkingham and Harding (1996) estimated that in Australia, 38% of lifetime benefits received by individuals, on average, were financed through taxes they paid at another stage in their lifecycle, and the remaining 62% of lifetime benefits involved redistribution between rich and poor; in the United Kingdom these shares were reversed, with 38% of lifetime benefits involving redistribution between individuals and 62% involving redistribution over different phases of the lifecycle of the same individual. A recent survey by Ståhlberg (2007) compares a wider range of countries and shows that the degree of redistribution across the lifecycle is negatively correlated with the level of targeting, that is, systems that target low-income households at a point in time are more redistributive between rich and poor, but achieve less lifecycle redistribution.[3]

Another measure of the balance between these two types of redistribution is shown in Figure 4.1, derived from Disney (2004). The figure shows the effective contribution rates to public pensions as a percentage of earnings (with countries ranked by the level of contributions required) as well as the part that redistributes between individuals, on one side, and across the individual's lifetime, on the other.[4] In an actuarially fair system, individual pension entitlements would exactly match individual earnings. In contrast, in a redistributive system there is little or no relationship between lifetime earnings and individual entitlements, and rates of return on contributions differ significantly between generations.

Figure 4.1. **Contribution rates to public pensions, redistributive and actuarial components, 1995**

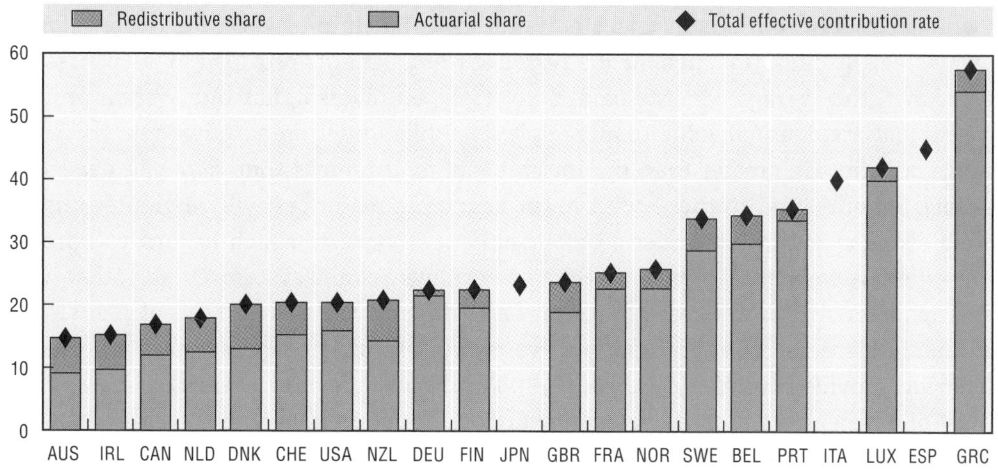

StatLink ᵃˢᵖ http://dx.doi.org/10.1787/421670886812

Source: Disney (2004).

A number of points should be emphasised. First, on this measure the share of redistribution between rich and poor varies widely across countries. Second, in all countries the larger part of pension contributions goes towards redistribution across the lifecycle. However, there is greater cross-country variability in the level of contributions going towards lifecycle redistribution than towards redistribution between rich and poor. Lastly, there tends to be an inverse relationship between the degree of redistribution between rich and poor and the level of contributions – countries that spend the most tend to concentrate more on redistribution across the lifecycle, while those that focus more on redistribution between rich and poor spend less.

Redistribution across the lifecycle cannot reduce lifetime inequality between individuals, since it is simply a way of smoothing consumption for the same person, whose total lifetime income remains unchanged; it can, however, reduce inequality at a point in time, and lower both lifetime poverty (for those whose average lifetime incomes are above the poverty line) and poverty at a point in time (Åberg, 1989).[5] Moreover, lifecycle redistribution can also occur – and in some countries may be most common – through instruments that fall outside the traditional boundaries of the welfare state. For example, home ownership is strongly redistributive across the lifecycle, as families usually face higher expenses for home purchase while they are working and then benefit from lower housing costs when in retirement. Similarly, private health insurance, personal savings, individual pension plans and endowment insurance involve either self-insurance or redistribution across an individual's or family's own lifecycle, while usually providing no redistribution between income groups. A crucial difference between private and government redistribution across the lifecycle is that private redistribution does not normally involve the pooling of risks (except in the case of insurance policies). When the risks confronting individuals (e.g. in terms of health or unemployment) are correlated with income, such pooling may also be regarded as redistributing income between individuals.

The main prerequisites for (static) redistribution to occur are that the distribution of cash transfers and that of household taxation be more progressive than the distribution of market income. Overall, the degree of redistribution achieved by the tax-benefit system[6] thus reflects both the progressivity of taxes and benefits and their size, i.e. the level of spending and of revenue collected (Barr, 1992).[7] The progressivity of benefits is determined by whether the system is means-tested (and how), flat-rate or earnings-related (and to what degree). By definition, in a means-tested system, benefits provided to the poorest are greater than the average benefits paid. Conversely, a universal, flat-rate system provides benefits that are of equal value to all recipients, while under an earnings-related system average benefits are greater than minimum benefits. It follows that, *for a given amount of spending*, benefits paid to those with fewer economic resources will be greater under a means-tested system than under a universal benefit system, which in turn will provide more generous payments to the poor than an earnings-related system. On the other hand, these characteristics of welfare systems may also impact on the overall size of spending, as the middle class may be more supportive of welfare programmes when benefits are universally provided (Korpi and Palme, 1998). The critical question, therefore, relates to the impact of different programme designs or distributional profiles when levels of spending and taxes differ across countries.

Level and characteristics of public cash transfers and household taxes

Table 4.2 shows the level of public cash transfers and of household taxes, expressed as a share of household disposable income, in various OECD countries based on the OECD income distribution questionnaire; also shown is how these shares have changed since the mid-1990s. Cash benefits are lowest in Korea and Mexico, at 4% and 6% of household disposable income, respectively, while they account for around 9% of household income in the United States. Cash benefits are between 13 and 20% of household disposable income in Australia, Canada, Finland, Iceland, Ireland, Japan, the Netherlands, New Zealand, Switzerland, Turkey and the United Kingdom; between 20 and 30% in the Czech Republic, Denmark, Germany, Greece, Italy, Norway, Portugal, Spain and the Slovak Republic; and they exceed 30% of household income in Austria, Belgium, France, Hungary, Luxembourg, Poland and Sweden. Since the mid-1990s, benefits have fallen as a share of household income in a majority of these countries, most strongly in Finland and Sweden, following the recovery from the deep recession in the early 1990s, but also in Ireland, due to strong rates of economic growth. Cash benefits have grown in significance, particularly in Turkey and Japan, as well as Germany.

Table 4.2. **Shares of cash benefits and household taxes in household disposable income**

Percentage shares in the mid-2000s and point changes in these shares since the mid-1990s

	Public cash benefits				Household taxes			
	Working age	Retirement age	Total		Working age	Retirement age	Total	
	Levels in mid-2000s			Change since mid-1990s	Levels in mid-2000s			Change since mid-1990s
Australia	10.1	48.7	14.3	−0.6	24.8	9.7	23.4	−1.4
Austria[1]	27.4	101.3	36.6	. .	35.0	27.5	33.4	. .
Belgium[1]	22.3	96.9	30.5	−2.1	42.1	19.6	38.3	. .
Canada	9.3	46.7	13.6	−4.4	27.0	15.0	25.8	−3.5
Czech Republic[2]	17.0	79.1	24.3	3.2	23.9	6.1	21.6	0.9
Denmark	19.9	81.1	25.6	−5.6	53.8	44.2	52.5	−0.7
Finland	12.4	18.1	14.4	−8.9	31.0	24.8	30.1	−3.7
France[3]	22.6	96.4	32.9	−0.1	28.8	11.1	26.0	0.5
Germany	16.4	82.2	28.2	4.9	41.1	12.5	35.5	−3.5
Greece[4]	16.7	66.4	22.7	3.3	. .	. .	. .	. .
Hungary[4]	27.5	85.6	35.1	1.1	. .	. .	. .	. .
Iceland	12.3	79.7	19.2	. .	54.1	34.2	53.1	. .
Ireland[2]	13.3	55.8	17.7	−6.7	20.7	5.4	19.4	−3.6
Italy	21.1	87.4	29.2	0.6	32.0	21.1	30.2	1.2
Japan	11.0	55.8	19.7	8.2	21.0	15.4	19.7	−0.1
Korea	3.0	15.7	3.6	. .	8.1	5.0	8.0	. .
Luxembourg[1]	22.4	91.0	30.6	. .	26.3	14.8	23.8	. .
Mexico[4]	5.4	21.3	5.8	2.2	. .	. .	. .	. .
Netherlands	12.7	53.0	17.1	−3.5	26.9	10.0	24.7	−6.0
New Zealand	13.1	76.8	13.0	−2.8	29.1	19.8	29.0	−1.5
Norway	15.4	72.7	21.7	0.4	35.0	22.7	33.2	1.3
Poland[2, 4]	30.4	92.6	35.8	. .	28.8	17.9	27.7	. .
Portugal[2, 4]	20.3	74.2	25.5	−1.5	. .	. .	. .	. .
Slovak Republic	22.0	86.0	26.0	. .	22.0	5.0	20.0	. .
Spain[2, 4]	15.0	70.4	21.3	−2.3	. .	. .	. .	. .
Sweden	21.4	96.3	32.7	−5.7	44.2	40.2	43.2	1.2
Switzerland[2]	9.7	63.6	16.0	. .	36.6	32.9	36.0	. .
Turkey[4]	18.6	46.0	16.9	10.6	. .	. .	. .	. .
United Kingdom	8.7	54.3	14.5	−0.5	26.2	10.0	24.1	0.4
United States	5.6	42.1	9.4	−1.5	27.7	16.4	25.6	−1.6
OECD-24[5]	15.8	69.7	21.9	−1.5	31.1	18.4	29.3	−1.3

StatLink ⧉ http://dx.doi.org/10.1787/421775735806

1. Data for the mid-1990s only available net of household taxes.
2. Changes refer to the period from the mid-1990s to around 2000.
3. Data on levels and changes are based on two different sources.
4. Data on public cash benefits are reported net of taxes (i.e. household taxes not separately identified).
5. Average of the 24 OECD countries with data on both gross public cash transfers and household taxes (i.e. all countries shown in the table except Greece, Hungary, Mexico, Portugal, Spain and Turkey).
Source: Computations based on OECD income distribution questionnaire.

Not surprisingly, cash benefits are most significant for the population of retirement age, amounting on average to two-thirds of their incomes, and to more than 90% in Belgium, France, Italy, Luxembourg and Sweden, and for over 100% in Austria. Cash transfers account for only around half of the household income of the elderly in Australia, Canada, Ireland, Japan, the Netherlands, Turkey, the United Kingdom and the United States, and are least significant in Korea, Mexico, and apparently Finland.[8] For households with a working-age head, benefits are much less significant, averaging around 15% of household income, but ranging from 3 to 6% in Korea, Mexico and the United States to 30% in Poland.

Measured household taxes also vary widely. They are low in Korea but account for more than 40% of household disposable income in Sweden and more than 50% in Denmark and Iceland.[9] The level of household taxes – as measured in household surveys – has decreased on average by about 1 percentage point since the middle of the 1990s, matching the decline recorded on the transfer side, with larger declines in the Netherlands, Canada, Germany, Ireland and Finland. It is clear, however, that the relationship between measured taxes and transfers differs across countries. For example, in the United States – based on the household survey data used there – household taxes (at 26% of household income) are nearly three times higher than public cash transfers. At the other extreme, in the Czech Republic, France, Luxembourg and the Slovak Republic, measured transfers account for a larger share of household disposable income than measured taxes. A major factor behind these discrepancies is the fact that employer social security contributions – which finance a large part of the welfare state in these and some other countries – are paid by employers directly to the government, and since they do not pass through the household sector they are not recorded in household income surveys.

Table 4.3 compares OECD countries in terms of how public transfers and household taxes are distributed across income groups. The measure shown is the concentration coefficient as defined in Chapter 3 (note 14); as individuals are ranked according to their disposable income, rather than by the public transfers they receive, the concentration coefficient of transfers can be negative (in the case where poorer income groups receive a higher share of transfers than their share of disposable income) – with lower and more negative values implying greater progressivity. Cash benefits are more progressively distributed than market incomes in all countries, thus reducing inequality. The distribution of cash benefits for the entire population is most progressive, by a wide margin, in Australia, followed by New Zealand, Denmark, the United Kingdom, Finland and Ireland, while it is least progressive in Mexico, Turkey, Portugal, and Poland. With the exceptions of Portugal and Turkey, transfers to people of working age are more progressively distributed than those to people of retirement age, although the differences are small in Greece, Iceland, Poland and Portugal, as well as in Italy, Luxembourg and Spain. The ranking of countries is broadly similar for transfers to people of retirement age and of working age, although Finland has the most progressive distribution of transfers to people of retirement age, rather than Australia.

The second panel of Table 4.3 shows the distribution of household taxes (income taxes and employee social security contributions). Because taxes are deducted from household incomes, higher values of the concentration coefficient imply a more progressive distribution of household taxes. Taxation is most progressively distributed in the United States, probably reflecting the greater role played there by refundable tax credits, such as the Earned Income Tax Credit and the Child Tax Credit. Overall, there is less variation in the progressivity of taxes across countries than in the case of transfers. After the United States, the distribution of taxation tends to be most progressive in the English-speaking countries – Ireland, Australia, the United Kingdom, New Zealand and Canada – together with Italy, followed by the Netherlands, the Czech Republic and Germany. Taxes tend to be least progressive in the Nordic countries, France and Switzerland. In most but not all countries taxes are more progressive for the retirement-age population than for the working-age population, reflecting the existence of various tax concessions for low-income retired people.

Table 4.3. **Progressivity of cash benefits and household taxes**

Concentration coefficients for cash benefits and household taxes, mid-2000s

	Public cash benefits			Household taxes		
	Working age	Retirement age	Total	Working age	Retirement age	Total
Australia	−0.431	−0.080	−0.400	0.492	0.816	0.533
Austria	0.130	0.256	0.157	0.365	0.464	0.381
Belgium	−0.141	0.169	−0.120	0.363	0.420	0.398
Canada	−0.173	−0.006	−0.152	0.472	0.586	0.492
Czech Republic	−0.151	0.037	−0.154	0.424	0.789	0.471
Denmark	−0.303	−0.054	−0.316	0.332	0.336	0.349
Finland	−0.258	−0.138	−0.219	0.419	0.444	0.428
France	0.098	0.285	0.136	0.354	0.474	0.374
Germany	−0.066	0.175	0.013	0.439	0.485	0.468
Greece[2]	0.176	0.202	0.115	. .	. .	. .
Hungary[2]	−0.025	0.119	−0.016	. .	. .	. .
Iceland	0.018	0.037	−0.041	0.257	0.296	0.267
Ireland	−0.205	−0.001	−0.214	0.531	0.782	0.570
Italy	0.158	0.225	0.135	0.512	0.623	0.546
Japan	0.020	0.121	0.010	0.356	0.429	0.378
Korea	0.040	0.282	−0.012	0.363	0.462	0.380
Luxembourg	0.075	0.145	0.085	0.404	0.430	0.420
Mexico[2]	0.407	0.518	0.373	. .	. .	. .
Netherlands	−0.223	−0.014	−0.198	0.436	0.705	0.471
New Zealand	−0.331	−0.011	−0.345	0.485	0.249	0.498
Norway	−0.177	0.074	−0.183	0.355	0.433	0.376
Poland[2]	0.173	0.198	0.185	0.382	0.325	0.379
Portugal[2]	0.315	0.295	0.247	. .	. .	. .
Slovak Republic	−0.030	0.104	−0.056	0.388	0.726	0.422
Spain[2]	0.102	0.175	0.063	. .	. .	. .
Sweden	−0.153	0.090	−0.145	0.330	0.312	0.337
Switzerland	−0.176	0.015	−0.170	0.211	0.202	0.223
Turkey[2]	0.320	0.288	0.347	. .	. .	. .
United Kingdom	−0.347	0.035	−0.275	0.486	0.614	0.533
United States	−0.115	0.105	−0.089	0.549	0.658	0.586
OECD-24[3]	−0.107	0.085	−0.099	0.404	0.502	0.428

StatLink ⧉ http://dx.doi.org/10.1787/421784425386

1. The concentration coefficient is computed in the same way as the Gini coefficient of household income, so that a value of zero means that all income groups receive an equal share of household transfers or pay an equal share of taxes. However, individuals are ranked by their equivalised household disposable incomes.
2. Data on public cash benefits are reported net of taxes (*i.e.* household taxes are not separately identified).
3. Average of the 24 OECD countries with data on both gross public cash transfers and household taxes (*i.e.* all countries shown in the table except Greece, Hungary, Mexico, Portugal, Spain and Turkey).

Source: Computations based on OECD income distribution questionnaire.

The progressivity of transfers varies significantly also across different types of benefits, with the highest progressivity being for housing benefits (because they tend to be income-related), "other benefits" (which include social assistance), unemployment payments and family cash benefits (Table 4.4). Housing benefits are most progressively distributed in the Nordic countries, while family benefits are most progressive in the United States and other English-speaking countries, where income-testing is more common.

However, the progressivity of the tax system also depends on the level of inequality of taxable income, and the effective progressivity of a given tax schedule will be greater in a country with a more unequal distribution of taxable income. Table 4.5 adjusts for this effect by showing the concentration coefficient of household taxes divided by the Gini coefficient for market income (in the third column), as well as the share of taxes paid by the

Table 4.4. **Progressivity of cash transfers by programme**

Concentration coefficients for cash transfers, mid-2000s

	Old age pensions	Disability benefits	Compensation for occupation injury and diseases	Survivor benefits	Family cash benefits	Unemployment benefits	Housing benefits	Other benefits
Australia	−0.47	−0.35	. .	−0.30	−0.33	−0.44	. .	−0.40
Austria	0.25	0.14	0.16	0.00	−0.09	−0.17	−0.48	−0.05
Belgium	−0.09	−0.27	−0.13	−0.14	0.03	−0.22	−0.15	−0.50
Canada	−0.11	. .	.	. .	−0.46	−0.06	. .	−0.22
Czech Republic	−0.11	−0.06	. .	0.19	−0.26	−0.28	−0.66	−0.36
Denmark	−0.49	−0.18	. .	. .	−0.04	−0.22	−0.58	−0.37
Finland	−0.44	0.07	0.12	0.02	−0.07	−0.24	−0.61	−0.39
France	0.25	0.14	. .	0.05	−0.13	0.08	−0.55	−0.23
Germany	0.10	. .	0.07	−0.04	−0.04	−0.28	0.00	−0.24
Greece	0.15	0.06	0.25	0.02	−0.02	0.04	−0.17	−0.11
Hungary	0.01	. .	. .	. .	−0.06	−0.25	. .	−0.17
Ireland	−0.32	−0.27	0.27	0.08	−0.21	−0.07	−0.46	0.02
Italy	0.22	0.90	. .	. .	−0.52	−0.04	. .	−0.05
Japan	0.02	. .	. .	. .	. .	−0.11	. .	−0.33
Luxembourg	0.17	0.00	. .	0.13	−0.02	−0.09	−0.41	−0.52
Netherlands	−0.16	−0.11	. .	−0.14	−0.36	0.03	−0.65	−0.37
New Zealand	−0.32	−0.35	−0.41	0.02	−0.43	−0.38	−0.37	−0.14
Norway	−0.27	−0.06	. .	−0.18	−0.06	−0.12	−0.65	−0.24
Poland	0.26	0.04	0.40	0.15	−0.22	0.13	−0.26	−0.13
Portugal	0.33	0.03	. .	0.03	. .	0.20	0.13	−0.77
Slovak Republic	0.00	−0.19	−0.01	0.24	−0.01	−0.07	0.84	−0.59
Spain	0.04	0.11	0.14	0.05	0.35	0.02	0.48	0.02
Sweden	−0.19	0.25	0.25	. .	−0.07	−0.10	−0.66	−0.16
Switzerland	−0.19	. .	. .	. .	−0.02	−0.15	. .	−0.29
Turkey	0.37	0.07	. .	0.25	0.17	0.08	. .	0.52
United Kingdom	−0.21	−0.20	. .	. .	. .	. .	. .	−0.37
United States	−0.04	. .	. .	. .	−0.56	0.07	. .	−0.10
OECD-27	−0.05	−0.01	0.10	0.02	−0.14	−0.10	−0.29	−0.24

StatLink ⬛⬛⬛ http://dx.doi.org/10.1787/421827523148

Note: Data refer to the mid-2000s for all countries. Data refer to "gross" public cash transfers (i.e. before taxes) for all countries except Greece, Hungary, Ireland, Mexico, Poland, Portugal, Spain and Turkey (where survey data on transfers are reported net of taxes). OECD-27 is the average across all countries with data available.
Source: Computations based on OECD income distribution questionnaire.

richest 10% of the population compared to the share of market income they receive (sixth column). Based on the concentration coefficient of household taxes, the United States has the most progressive tax system and collects the largest share of taxes from the richest 10% of the population. However, the richest decile in the United States has one of the highest shares of market income of any OECD country. After standardising for this underlying inequality, Ireland has the most progressive tax system as measured by the ratio of the concentration coefficients of household taxes and market income, while Australia and the United States collect the most tax from people in the top decile relative to the share of market income that they earn.

What is the relationship between the level of public spending on cash transfers and the progressivity of spending programmes? In other words, do OECD countries with more progressive cash programmes spend more or less than others? Figure 4.2, which plots the share of public cash transfers as a percentage of equivalised household disposable income as measured in surveys against their level of concentration in different OECD countries, provides some indication. The figure suggests the existence of a negative relationship between

Table 4.5. **Alternative measures of progressivity of taxes in OECD countries, 2005**

	A. Concentration of household taxes and market income			B. Percentage share of richest decile		
	1. Concentration coefficient for household taxes	2. Gini coefficient of market income	3. Ratio of concentration coefficients (1/2)	1. Share of taxes of richest decile	2. Share of market income of richest decile	3. Ratio of shares for richest decile (1/2)
Australia	0.53	0.46	1.16	36.8	28.6	1.29
Austria	0.38	0.43	0.88	28.5	26.1	1.10
Belgium	0.40	0.49	0.80	25.4	27.1	0.94
Canada	0.49	0.44	1.13	35.8	29.3	1.22
Czech Republic	0.47	0.47	0.99	34.3	29.4	1.17
Denmark	0.35	0.42	0.84	26.2	25.7	1.02
Finland	0.43	0.39	1.11	32.3	26.9	1.20
France	0.37	0.48	0.77	28.0	25.5	1.10
Germany	0.47	0.51	0.92	31.2	29.2	1.07
Iceland	0.27	0.37	0.72	21.6	24.0	0.90
Ireland	0.57	0.42	1.37	39.1	30.9	1.26
Italy	0.55	0.56	0.98	42.2	35.8	1.18
Japan	0.38	0.44	0.85	28.5	28.1	1.01
Korea	0.38	0.34	1.12	27.4	23.4	1.17
Luxembourg	0.42	0.45	0.92	30.3	26.4	1.15
Netherlands	0.47	0.42	1.11	35.2	27.5	1.28
New Zealand	0.50	0.47	1.05	35.9	30.3	1.19
Norway	0.38	0.43	0.87	27.4	28.9	0.95
Poland	0.38	0.57	0.67	28.3	33.9	0.84
Slovak Republic	0.42	0.46	0.92	32.0	28.0	1.14
Sweden	0.34	0.43	0.78	26.7	26.6	1.00
Switzerland	0.22	0.35	0.63	20.9	23.5	0.89
United Kingdom	0.53	0.46	1.16	38.6	32.3	1.20
United States	0.59	0.46	1.28	45.1	33.5	1.35
OECD-24	0.43	0.45	0.96	31.6	28.4	1.11

StatLink http://dx.doi.org/10.1787/422013187855

Source: Computations based on OECD income distribution questionnaire.

Figure 4.2. **Level and concentration of public cash transfers in OECD countries, mid-2000s**

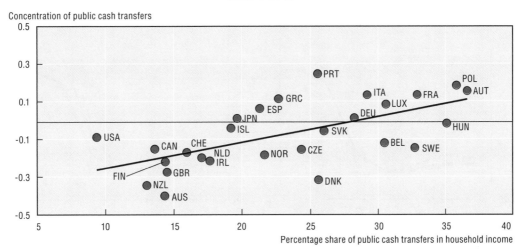

StatLink http://dx.doi.org/10.1787/421677605615

Source: Computation based on OECD income distribution questionnaire

progressivity and spending levels, with higher levels of spending associated with lower progressivity (so, for example, the countries in the bottom left of the figure tend spend less but have more progressive systems). However, lower-income OECD countries such as Mexico and Turkey (which, together with Korea, are excluded from the figure because of their less comprehensive welfare systems) combine both lower levels of spending and low progressivity.

The role of government transfers (and household taxes) also varies with individual characteristics such as age. One measure of this is provided in Figure 4.3, which shows the

Figure 4.3. **Share of net public benefits in disposable income of each age group, mid-2000s**

Percentage point differences relative to that of people aged 41-50

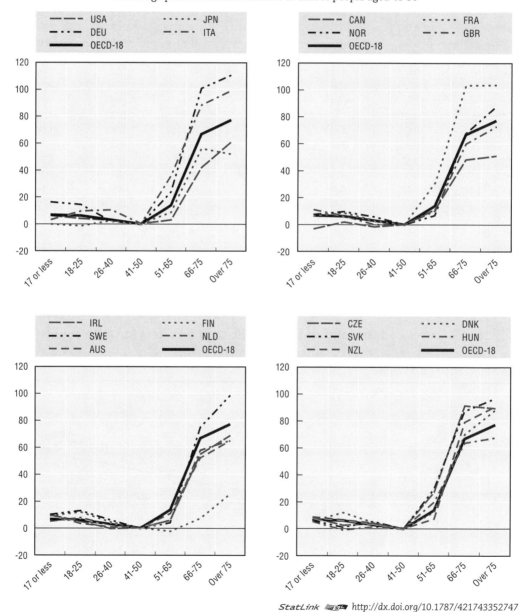

StatLink ⟜╖╜╙ http://dx.doi.org/10.1787/421743352747

Source: Computations based on the OECD Income distribution questionnaire.

GROWING UNEQUAL? – ISBN 978-92-64-044180-0 – © OECD 2008

share of net benefits (public cash benefits less household taxes) for different age groups, relative to that of people aged 41 to 50. Net benefit rates are typically positive for individuals at retirement age and negative for younger groups. When compared to those of the reference group aged 41-50 (the group that pays the highest amount of taxes relative to the benefits that they receive) children below 18 are only slightly better off. There are however large differences across countries in these profiles, which rise much more steeply in Germany, Italy and Sweden than in Australia, Canada and the United States. These age-income profiles are important not just for their influence on the current distribution of household income but also because they give an indication of how demographic changes may translate into higher public spending in the future (Dang *et al.*, 2006).

How much redistribution is achieved through government cash benefits and household taxes?

The most direct way to illustrate the effect of public cash transfers and household taxes on the distribution of household disposable income is to compare the same inequality measure computed over the various income concepts described in Table 4.1. While such comparisons will reflect differences in both size and structure of welfare programmes and tax systems across countries, they provide a convenient summary measure that is useful for comparing countries and assessing changes over time. This section presents evidence limited to those OECD countries with data covering *both* household taxes and gross public transfers (24 countries in the most recent year, excluding Greece, Hungary, Iceland, Mexico, Poland, Portugal, Spain and Turkey for analysis of levels; 19 countries, *i.e.* also excluding Austria, Belgium, Czech Republic, Korea and the Slovak Republic, for analysis of changes since 1995).

Figure 4.4 shows two measures of the "effectiveness" of the tax and benefit systems in reducing income inequality: the percentage reduction in income inequality when moving from market income to disposable income (in the top panel), and the absolute point difference between these two measures (in the bottom panel). These measures are calculated in two ways.

- In the first approach (shown as diamonds), inequality in the distribution of market income is computed by ranking people by their level of market income. On this measure, on average, across the 24 countries covered, the tax and transfer systems lower income inequality by around one-third (*i.e.* around 0.15 Gini point), with declines ranging from around 45% in Denmark, Sweden and Belgium to less than 8% in Korea.

- In the second approach (shown as bars) the Gini coefficient for market income is based on people ranked by their disposable income, *i.e.* individuals are ranked by where they end up "after" redistribution, rather than where they were placed "before" redistribution. On this second measure, the reduction of inequality achieved by taxes and transfers is a little more than one-fourth (*i.e.* 0.11 point), with declines ranging from around 40% in Sweden and Denmark to 5% in Korea.

The difference between the two measures of redistribution is a result of the re-ranking of some households as a consequence of welfare state programmes (Ankrom, 1993). This difference is of interest, as one of the limitations of the standard approach to measuring redistribution relates to the counterfactual against which redistribution is measured. Layard (1977), for example, argues that the standard approach exaggerates the redistributive impact of the welfare state because it assumes that the different levels of

Figure 4.4. **Differences in inequality before and after taxes and transfers in OECD countries**

Difference in concentration coefficients around 2005

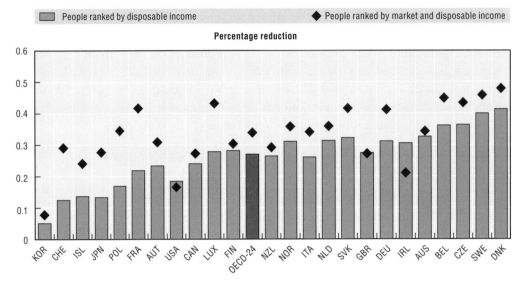

StatLink http://dx.doi.org/10.1787/421744352206

Note: Countries are ranked, from left to right, in increasing order of the percentage point reduction in the concentration coefficient achieved by household taxes and public cash transfers, based on people ranked by their household disposable income. Bars are computed based on grouped data for average market and disposable income, by deciles of people ranked by their household disposable income. Diamonds are computed based on individual data, with people ranked by market income (for the Gini coefficient of market income) and ranked by disposable income (for the Gini coefficient of disposable income).

Source: OECD income distribution questionnaire

welfare state spending and taxation have no behavioural impact on the distribution of market incomes. In particular, in countries with generous public pensions, the standard approach implies that middle-class individuals are plunged into market-income poverty on retirement simply because it is the government, rather than the market, that provides their pensions: generous earnings-related public pensions are then measured as being very effective at reducing inequality, in part because they restore middle-income retirees to their pre-retirement ranking. A comparison between the two alternative measures suggests that, in some OECD countries, a very significant part of the redistribution measured by the standard approach reflects such a re-ranking of people. In particular, the countries where the re-ranking effect is most significant are precisely those where public pensions account for more than 90% of the total disposable income of the retirement-age population – Austria, Belgium, France, Italy, Luxembourg and Sweden. In contrast, re-ranking is lower in Korea, the United States, Canada, Finland, the United Kingdom, Ireland and Australia, where public pensions are 50% or less of the disposable income of the retired.

Countries that achieve the largest redistribution through taxes and transfers generally record the lowest inequality in the distribution of household disposable income, although with considerable variation across countries (especially when looking at point changes, Figure 4.5). For example, the level of disposable-income inequality in Iceland and Switzerland is similar to that in Belgium and the Czech Republic, even though the impact of the welfare state is significantly greater in the second two countries; also, Sweden and Denmark record reductions in inequality that are nearly twice as large as that of the United States, and achieve a level of disposable-income inequality that is around half of that recorded in the United States.

Figure 4.5. **Inequality-reducing effect of public cash transfers and household taxes and relationship with income inequality, mid-2000s**

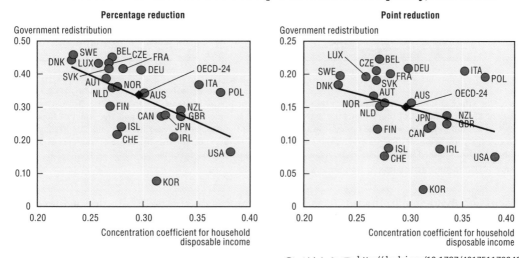

StatLink ⟨⟩ http://dx.doi.org/10.1787/421751173340

Note: Government redistribution is measured by the change in the concentration coefficient for market and disposable income, with people ranked by their disposable income. This measure is computed based on data for average (market and disposable) income by deciles of people ranked by their household disposable income.

Source: OECD income distribution questionnaire.

It is also possible to compare the size of the redistribution achieved by each of the two levers. Different approaches can be used for this purpose, but their implementation differs in terms of data requirements, and they can lead to different conclusions. One simple method, which can be applied with the available data, is to look at the difference between the concentration coefficients for market income and for gross post-transfer income as a measure of the impact of cash transfers; and at the difference between the concentration coefficients for gross post-transfer income and for disposable income as a measure of the impact of household taxes (Figure 4.6).[10] For purposes of consistency with the preferred measure used in Figure 4.4, when calculating inequality in both market and disposable income, people are ranked by their disposable incomes, so that the re-ranking effect

Figure 4.6. **Reduction in inequality due to public cash transfers and household taxes**

Point reduction in the concentration coefficient

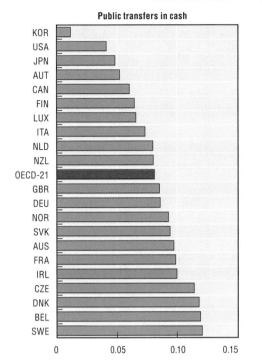
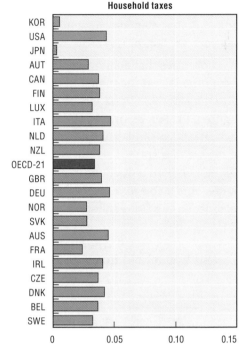

StatLink ᵐˢ☝ http://dx.doi.org/10.1787/421752256406

Note: The effect of public cash transfers in reducing income inequality is measured as the difference between the concentration coefficient of market income and that of gross income after transfers, and the effect of household taxes as the difference between the concentration coefficient of gross post-transfer income and that of disposable income. Concentration coefficients are computed based on information on the income share of transfers and taxes, with individuals ranked by their level of equivalised household disposable income.

Source: OECD income distribution questionnaire.

discussed above is eliminated. Based on this approach, the redistribution achieved by public cash transfers on average is twice as large as that achieved through household taxes, although the United States stands out for achieving greater redistribution through the tax system than through cash transfers. Korea and Japan also stand out for the very low redistribution achieved through the tax system.[11]

Based on the preferred measure of redistribution (bars in Figure 4.4), which abstracts from the effect of "re-ranking", the combined effect of transfers and taxes in reducing inequality is similar in Ireland and Australia to that achieved in Sweden and Denmark, while the redistribution in the United Kingdom and in New Zealand is similar to the levels achieved in Germany and the Netherlands, for example. It follows that the higher levels of disposable-income inequality in these four English-speaking countries do not reflect less effective welfare states but higher market-income inequality, in particular of household earnings, to start with.[12]

Has the extent of redistribution changed over time? This is shown in Figure 4.7. Countries falling above the diagonal achieve less redistribution today than in the 1990s, while those below the diagonal achieve more. Patterns are quite diverse across countries. When looking at the combined effect of public cash transfers and household taxes (top panel), a number of countries, such as Italy, Germany and the Czech Republic now achieve

GROWING UNEQUAL? – ISBN 978-92-64-044180-0 – © OECD 2008

Figure 4.7. **Changes in redistributive effects of public cash transfers and taxes over time**

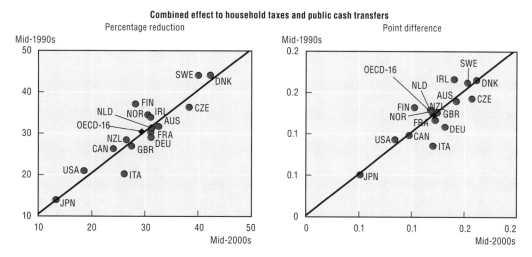

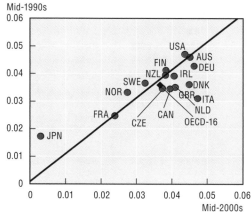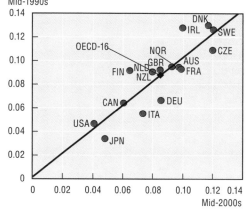

StatLink ⬛⬛ http://dx.doi.org/10.1787/421755213675

Note: Government redistribution is measured by the change in concentration coefficient for market and disposable income "without re-ranking", as computed based on data for average (market and disposable) income by deciles of people ranked by their household disposable income.

Source: OECD income distribution questionnaire.

more redistribution than in the past (although this may partly reflect greater market income inequality), while others – Finland, Norway, Sweden, Ireland, Canada and the United States – are now less redistributive, and others show very little change.[13] In some countries such as the Netherlands, an unchanged level of redistribution has gone in hand with lower inequality in the distribution of disposable income reflecting large declines in market income inequality (by close to 6 percentage points). When looking separately at changes in the two levers of government redistribution (bottom panel), the redistributive impact of household taxes appears to have declined in Japan and Norway, and increased in Italy, Denmark, the Netherlands and the United Kingdom. The redistributive impact of public cash transfers fell in Finland and Ireland, while the opposite occurred in Germany and Italy.

A further way of assessing the impact of differing welfare state arrangements is shown in Table 4.6, which provides measures of the efficiency and effectiveness of tax and

Table 4.6. **Effectiveness and efficiency of taxes and transfers in reducing inequality**

	A. Effectiveness (inequality reduction)		B. Size (share of household disp. income)		C. Efficiency index A/(B/100)		D. Concentration index	
	Household taxes	Public cash transfers	Household taxes	Public cash transfers	Household taxes	Public cash transfers	Household taxes	Public cash transfers
Australia	0.045	0.097	23.4	14.3	0.193	0.679	0.533	−0.400
Austria	0.029	0.052	33.4	36.6	0.086	0.142	0.381	0.157
Belgium	0.037	0.119	38.3	30.5	0.096	0.391	0.398	−0.120
Canada	0.037	0.060	25.8	13.6	0.145	0.444	0.492	−0.152
Czech Rep.	0.037	0.114	21.6	24.3	0.170	0.468	0.471	−0.154
Denmark	0.042	0.118	52.5	25.6	0.080	0.461	0.349	−0.316
Finland	0.038	0.065	30.1	14.4	0.127	0.449	0.428	−0.219
France	0.020	0.056	26.0	32.9	0.079	0.171	0.374	0.136
Germany	0.046	0.086	35.5	28.2	0.130	0.303	0.468	0.013
Ireland	0.041	0.100	19.4	17.7	0.210	0.565	0.570	−0.214
Italy	0.047	0.073	30.2	29.2	0.156	0.251	0.546	0.135
Japan	0.003	0.048	19.7	19.7	0.015	0.244	0.378	0.010
Korea	0.005	0.011	8.0	3.6	0.067	0.312	0.380	−0.012
Luxembourg	0.032	0.066	23.8	30.6	0.135	0.215	0.420	0.085
Netherlands	0.041	0.080	24.7	17.1	0.166	0.468	0.471	−0.198
New Zealand	0.038	0.080	29.0	13.0	0.132	0.615	0.498	−0.345
Norway	0.027	0.093	33.2	21.7	0.082	0.427	0.376	−0.183
Slovak Rep.	0.028	0.094	20.0	26.0	0.138	0.361	0.422	−0.056
Sweden	0.032	0.121	43.2	32.7	0.075	0.368	0.337	−0.145
Switzerland	−0.012	0.057	36.0	16.0	−0.034	0.355	0.223	−0.170
United Kingdom	0.039	0.085	24.1	14.5	0.164	0.586	0.533	−0.275
United States	0.044	0.041	25.6	9.4	0.170	0.434	0.586	−0.089
OECD-22	*0.032*	*0.078*	*28.3*	*21.4*	*0.117*	*0.396*	*0.438*	*−0.114*
Memorandum items								
Correlation coeff.[1]	..	0.496	0.211	0.423	0.839	0.430	0.906	−0.940

StatLink ▄▄▄ http://dx.doi.org/10.1787/422051243136

1. Correlation between effectiveness of taxes and of cash transfers in the second column; between size and effectiveness of taxes and transfers, respectively, in the third and fourth columns; between the efficiency index and effectiveness of taxes and transfers, respectively, in the fifth and sixth columns; and between the concentration index and the efficiency index of taxes and transfers, respectively, in the seventh and eighth columns.

Note: The effectiveness index is defined as the percentage point reduction in the Gini coefficient of income inequality due to household taxes (i.e. between gross and disposable income) and cash transfers (i.e. between market and gross income) in each OECD country. The efficiency index is the effectiveness index of taxes and transfers divided by the respective share of taxes and transfers in each country. The concentration index of household taxes and public cash transfer is calculated as in Table 4.2.

Source: Computations based on OECD income distribution questionnaire.

transfer systems in reducing inequality. Following Beckerman (1979), effectiveness is defined as the percentage point reduction in the concentration coefficient of income inequality associated with the household taxes and public cash transfers, respectively, in each OECD country, as shown in Figure 4.6, while efficiency is the effectiveness measure (multiplied by 100) divided by the share in household disposable income of household taxes and public cash transfers, respectively. For example, in Australia for each 1 percentage point of household taxes, the concentration coefficient for gross income is reduced by 0.193 percentage point, while for each 1 percentage point of public cash transfers, market-income inequality is reduced by 0.679 percentage point (Panel C). The table suggests that, based on the measure of "effectiveness" shown in Panel A, the tax system achieves the largest reductions of income inequality in Italy, Germany, Australia, the United States, Denmark, Ireland and the Netherlands, and the lowest ones in Japan, Korea and Switzerland (second column). When looking at public cash transfers, the largest reductions of income inequalities are recorded by Sweden, Belgium, Denmark and the Czech Republic, and the lowest ones in Korea and the United States (third column).

Overall, the efficiency measure gives a slightly different picture than some earlier measures. It remains the case that transfer systems are significantly more efficient than tax systems at reducing inequality, as well as more effective, but some countries change their ranking when the efficiency index is used rather than the concentration coefficients. For example, Australia has a slightly less progressive tax system than the United States (Panel D), but is slightly more efficient in terms of inequality reduction (Panel C).

The table also shows the correlation between various design features of OECD welfare states. Not surprisingly, the highest correlations are between the concentration and efficiency of household taxes (Panel D), and also between the concentration and efficiency of public cash transfers (in this case, the correlation is negative because the most progressive transfer systems have negative concentration coefficients, as discussed earlier). There are moderately high correlations between the other measures shown, although effectiveness and efficiency are more strongly correlated in the case of taxes than for transfers.

Redistribution towards those at the bottom of the income ladder: the interplay of size and targeting

When considering the redistributive effects of the tax and transfer systems it is important to note that the concentration coefficient gives greater weight to changes in the middle of the distribution, whereas policy-makers may be more concerned about people at the bottom of the income distribution. Beyond looking at changes in poverty rates (the subject of Chapter 5), it is possible to address this concern by considering the effect of public cash transfers and household taxes on the lowest income groups. Table 4.7 provides a measure of the redistribution towards people at the lower end of the income distribution – in the lowest income quintile – separately for gross public transfers (left-hand panel) and household taxes (right-hand panel).

The role of cash transfers in supporting the income of people in the bottom quintile is computed by first estimating the average ratio of cash transfers as a percentage of household disposable income measured in income surveys (Column A);[14] second, by calculating how much of this share goes to the poorest 20% of the population (Column B); and finally, by multiplying the size of spending by the progressivity of its distribution to calculate gross benefits accruing to people at the lower end of the distribution (divided by 100, in Column C). The same procedure is used to calculate how much tax is paid by people at the lower end of the distribution, while the difference between the two values (in Column G) represents the "net" cash transfers to the lowest income quintile.

Several patterns stand out from Table 4.7:

● First, public cash transfers are more targeted to the poorest 20% of the population in Australia, Denmark, New Zealand, Finland, the Netherlands, Ireland and the United Kingdom (where the lowest income quintile receive more than 30% of all transfers, and above 40% in Australia, Column B), and least targeted in Poland (where the poorest 20%

Table 4.7. **Redistribution through cash transfers and household taxes towards people at the bottom of the income ladder, mid-2000s**

	Gross public transfers paid to households			Direct taxes and social security contributions paid by households			G. Net transfers to lowest quintile (C-F)
	A. Average ratio of household disposable income	B. Share of public transfers paid to lowest quintile	C. Transfers to lowest quintile (A*B/100)	D. Average ratio of household disposable income	E. Share of taxes paid by lowest quintile	F. Taxes from lowest quintile (D*E/100)	
Australia	14.3	41.5	5.9	23.4	0.8	0.2	5.8
Austria	36.6	13.9	5.1	33.4	5.4	1.8	3.3
Belgium	30.5	24.1	7.3	38.3	3.9	1.5	5.8
Canada	13.6	25.7	3.5	25.8	2.3	0.6	2.9
Czech Republic	24.3	23.0	5.6	21.6	3.5	0.8	4.8
Denmark	25.6	36.0	9.2	52.5	6.1	3.2	6.0
Finland	14.4	32.9	4.7	30.1	4.0	1.2	3.5
France	32.9	16.2	5.3	26.0	5.6	1.5	3.9
Germany	28.2	17.4	4.9	35.5	2.1	0.7	4.2
Ireland	17.7	30.8	5.4	19.4	0.9	0.2	5.3
Italy	29.2	12.6	3.7	30.2	1.8	0.6	3.1
Japan	19.7	15.9	3.1	19.7	6.0	1.2	2.0
Korea	3.6	24.9	0.9	8.0	5.8	0.5	0.4
Luxembourg	30.6	13.9	4.3	23.8	5.9	1.4	2.8
Netherlands	17.1	31.5	5.4	24.7	3.4	0.8	4.5
New Zealand	13.0	34.0	4.4	29.0	1.8	0.5	3.9
Norway	21.7	27.7	6.0	33.2	4.6	1.5	4.5
Poland	35.8	9.0	3.2	27.7	6.0	1.7	1.6
Slovak Republic	26.0	19.0	4.9	20.0	5.0	1.0	3.9
Sweden	32.7	25.9	8.5	43.2	6.5	2.8	5.7
Switzerland	16.0	29.2	4.7	36.0	12.4	4.5	0.2
United Kingdom	14.5	31.4	4.6	24.1	1.7	0.4	4.1
United States	9.4	24.8	2.3	25.6	1.6	0.4	1.9
OECD-23	22.0	24.4	5.4	28.3	4.2	1.2	4.2

StatLink ⬛🖙 http://dx.doi.org/10.1787/422058728151

Note: Values in Columns A and D are the ratios of public transfers and household taxes, respectively, in the disposable income of the entire population; Columns B and E show the shares of public transfers and household taxes received and paid, respectively, by people of the bottom quintile of the population. Data refer to the mid-2000s for all countries. The table excludes countries where data on household taxes are not available (i.e. where available data on public transfers are expressed "net" of taxes).

Source: OECD income distribution questionnaire.

receive less than 10% of all transfers); on this criterion, the level of targeting is roughly similar in Canada, the United States and Sweden.

- Second, there are large differences in the overall size of the redistribution towards low income households achieved through the combined effect of public transfers and household taxes; this ranges from values (as percentages of household disposable income) above 5.5 in Australia, Belgium, Denmark and Sweden, to values of around 2 in Japan, Poland and the United States, and to less than 0.5 in Switzerland and Korea (Column G).

- Third, there are large differences in the mix of cash transfers and household taxes used to redistribute income towards people at the bottom of the income scale. For example, the value of the public transfers to people in the lowest quintile (Column C) is 30 times that of the household taxes they pay (Column F) in Australia and Ireland, and more than ten times in the United Kingdom, as compared to levels of only twice (or less) for Korea and Poland. Nordic countries transfer large amounts of gross benefits to low-income people but also levy a significant amount of household taxes on them; conversely, most English speaking countries pay less generous transfers but offset this partly by levying lower household taxes on them.

- Fourth, countries redistribute income towards people at the bottom of the income scale through different combinations of the size and progressivity of their taxes and transfers. For example, Australia and Norway pay comparable amounts of gross transfers to low-income people, with a spending effort in the former country of only two-thirds that of the latter – the difference being offset by a far greater targeting of the transfers paid (about 50% more, on the measure used here). Similarly, both Korea and the United States collect a similar amount of taxes from low-income households but achieve this through a low general tax level in the former country and through targeted tax credits in the latter.

Improving measures of welfare state outcomes

While the standard approach used in this chapter – and most of the comparative social policy literature – provides a simple but flexible model for analysing income redistribution, the framework has a number of significant limitations. These include:

- the counterfactual against which redistribution is assessed;
- the limitations in accounting for government redistributive activity; and
- the treatment of the relationship between public and private provision.

With reference to the first element, any assessment of the distributional impact of a set of policies involves comparing the observed distribution with a counterfactual – the hypothetical distribution that would exist in the absence of the policies being evaluated (Pederson, 1994). As set out in Table 4.1, the standard accounting framework is linear: it assumes that the distribution of factor and market incomes precedes the operation of the tax and transfer systems, and there are no interactions between them, apart from the direct effect of government programmes in reducing final inequality. Moreover, when applied to a range of countries, this approach implicitly assumes that the wide differences in the scope and form of different welfare states have no impact on the behaviour of people in different countries. Both assumptions – which underlie the estimates presented in this chapter – are unrealistic. Individuals make decisions about income-generating activities within existing institutional frameworks, which vary widely across countries. Layard (1977) and Reynolds and Smolensky (1977) argue that, because of these assumptions, the standard approach exaggerates both the inequality of market incomes and the amount of redistribution that is achieved by social policies. This chapter has attempted to deal with this fundamental problem by providing estimates that include and then exclude the re-ranking effects of the welfare state, showing that this effect is significant.

A second limitation of the standard approach is that the effects of government policies are only partly considered. These gaps arise in several ways. First, most income surveys only include information on cash benefits and direct taxes, while excluding in-kind benefits (discussed in Chapter 9) and consumption taxes (Warren, 2008). Second, policies can be implemented through regulations rather than direct provision, and the former are excluded from the analysis. For example, an important way in which governments affect labour-market outcomes is through the setting of minimum wages, but in the standard approach the degree of wage dispersion in each country is treated as if it has been produced by market mechanisms alone. Third, the standard framework also excludes employer social security contributions – which are insignificant in Australia, Denmark and New Zealand but account for more than 25% of total tax revenue in France and the Czech Republic (OECD, 2007b). Given that these contributions pay for a large part of social security spending in many countries, an assessment of their distributional impact would be warranted.[15] The obvious question that arises is whether a different measure of household well-being, broadened to include these factors, would change conclusions about the extent of redistribution in different countries. The answers will depend on the extent to which there is divergence between these income measures in different countries – *e.g.* on the relative weights of cash transfers and other public spending, and of direct taxes and other forms of taxation.

A final limitation of the standard approach is that public cash transfers (as well as taxes and social security contributions) can substitute for a wide range of private arrangements for individual protection, and *vice versa*.[16] A case in point arises when considering contributions to private and occupational pensions and their relation to contributions to public pensions. The standard approach (and the SNA conventions) treats contributions to government pensions as a tax that finances the retirement pensions paid out in the same year, while contributions to private pensions are effectively treated as a form of private consumption. This affects international comparisons of income distribution in several ways. For example, countries with earnings-related social security systems will look more equal because a higher proportion of the savings that well-off individuals make for retirement are made through taxes. Conversely, where flat-rate or means-tested benefits are provided, a higher proportion of savings for retirement are made through occupational and private pension contributions.[17] In summary, different social security systems produce different distributions of public and private pension rights, and the incomplete treatment of this redistributive activity may bias cross-country comparisons of income distribution. Overcoming this bias requires broadening the framework used to assess household well-being and distributive outcomes.

Conclusion

Two major objectives of the welfare state are to redistribute across the lifecycle and to redistribute between rich and poor. All OECD countries pursue both objectives, although the emphasis given to each of them varies significantly between countries. Overall, several conclusions stand out from this analysis.

- In general, countries with lower levels of transfer spending have a more progressive structure of both benefits and taxes, although there are exceptions (Mexico, with low-spending also has very low progressivity) and other cross-country differences (*e.g.* Nordic countries have higher-than-average spending and progressive benefit structures, but less progressive tax systems).

- Indicators of the redistributive activity of welfare states based on the "standard approach" show that the tax and benefit systems in all OECD countries reduce income inequality, with the impact being greatest in the Nordic countries and lowest in the United States and Korea.

- However, in a number of countries, a significant part of this redistribution results from the "re-ranking" of people, where for example, middle-income households are treated as if they fall into deep poverty upon retirement, with their income gap then ameliorated by generous, earnings-related public pensions. When accounting for re-ranking, then

Australia and Ireland prove to be nearly as effective in reducing inequality as the Nordic countries, while the United Kingdom and New Zealand are about as effective as Germany, for example

● The redistributive effect of the welfare state is generally larger for public cash benefits than for household taxes – except in the United States, which achieves more redistribution through the tax system than through the transfer system. Similarly, the degree of redistribution to the lowest income quintile varies widely across countries, and is greatest in Australia and the Nordic countries.

While useful for highlighting a number of patterns, the "standard approach" also has limits, and while some of them are addressed in later chapters, other are beyond the scope of this volume. Further efforts are therefore required to develop more comprehensive measures of the impact of redistributive policies.

Notes

1. Other forms of targeting are possible, such as benefits directed to particular geographic areas; these are more common in low-income countries.

2. Other forms of redistribution can occur as well: for example, between generations, between men and women, or across geographical regions, but these are usually a by-product of the two main objectives rather than being primary goals in their own right.

3. The actual distribution of benefits across the lifecycle for individuals is likely to differ from calculations of this sort, since both money's worth calculations and micro-simulations usually look at hypothetical lifetimes and calculate the extent of lifetime redistribution on the basis of the tax and benefit system at a specific point in time. In practice, taxation and benefit systems can be changed many times during an individual's lifetime. Some studies, therefore, attempt to estimate to what extent different generations are net beneficiaries or net contributors to social security systems (see Thomson, 1989; Williamson *et al.*, 1999).

4. The effective contribution rate is the average rate of contributions required to finance current spending on public pensions without budgetary transfers or accumulation or decumulation of pension funds.

5. While total lifetime income for an individual is unchanged by redistribution across the lifecycle, income smoothing can reduce the share of time that might otherwise be spent below the poverty line by those whose average incomes are above the poverty line. However, while people whose lifetime incomes are below the poverty line can theoretically have their incomes raised above the poverty line at different points in time, this could only be achieved at the cost of more severe poverty (i.e. a larger poverty gap) in other periods.

6. A simple example (which disregards the impact of taxes) illustrates the impact of different welfare state arrangements on the distribution of household income. Imagine two countries with the same distribution of market incomes and a concentration coefficient of 0.40. In country A transfers account for 20% of household gross income and the concentration coefficient for transfers is 0.30 (i.e. the system is earnings-related, but not as unequal as market income); in this country, market income provides 80% of gross household income and the Gini coefficient for income after transfers is 0.38 (0.40*0.8 plus 0.30*0.2). In country B transfers account for only 5% of gross income, but the concentration coefficient for transfers is zero (i.e. benefits are flat-rate) so that the Gini coefficient for income after transfers is also 0.38 (0.40*0.95 plus 0.00*0.05). In this example, the transfer systems of these two countries reduce income inequality by the same degree even though the level of spending and the distribution of benefits were very different between the two.

7. There are other influences, as well, including the incidence of unemployment by income class and differences in life expectancy and disability by income; other important factors include the take-up of benefits (low take-up reduces effective progressivity) and the coverage of the social security system – as shown below, Mexico and Turkey have the least redistributive social security systems in the OECD, with the main explanation for this being their lower level of coverage of the population.

8. The apparently low level of public cash benefits to the retirement age population in Finland reflects the fact that, in the income questionnaire used by the OECD, mandatory occupational pensions are counted as a private transfer (hence included in capital incomes) rather than as government cash transfers. More generally, level of public cash benefits from income surveys differ from those from administrative records available through the OECD Social Expenditure Database (OECD, 2007a).

9. Taxes paid by people of retirement age are by far the highest in Denmark, taking 44% of their household disposable income, followed by Sweden, Iceland and Switzerland.

10. These concentration coefficients are computed based on information on the average income by decile – with people ranked by the level of their equivalised disposable income – rather than on micro-data. In general, results based on approaches that "add in" one component after the other depend on the order in which income sources are considered. This is because the calculated contribution of each income source will depend on both its own distribution and the degree to which it is correlated to other income sources. All approaches based on the "adding in" of various income sources – such as the one used in this section – attribute the effect on inequality due to this correlation to the income source that is added last (in this case, household taxes).

11. For Korea, this partly reflects the measurement of self-employment income as withdrawals from enterprise income which is recorded net of taxes paid by the enterprise.

12. Household earnings inequality is high in these four countries in part because of wider wage dispersion, but also because a higher share of the population of working age lives in jobless households, as discussed in Chapter 3.

13. In Figure 4.7, changes in government redistribution are measured by the difference in the concentration of market and household disposable income, with individuals ranked by their disposable income. Changes in this measure of government redistribution are quite similar to those based on the differences in the Gini coefficients for market and disposable income, with individuals "re-ranked": the correlation between the two sets of measures is around 0.80 for both point and percentage changes.

14. It is possible to apply the progressivity of the formula to measures of social spending as a percentage of GDP; when this is done, very similar results are achieved. However, social spending in the national accounts includes items that do not accrue to private households (e.g. benefits received by people in hospitals and nursing homes).

15. The incidence of employer contributions is controversial, but one straightforward approach is to assume they are incident on wages. Inclusion of employer social security contributions in both market income and household taxes would change both market-income inequality and measures of the effectiveness of different tax-transfer systems (Mitchell, 1991).

16. As noted by Atkinson (1991), consideration of the effects of social insurance should take account of the possibility of the *equivalence of transactions*: "Where for instance people are already saving for old age, the introduction of a compulsory government pension scheme on the same terms may simply displace the private savings" (p. 11).

17. These biases can be addressed in several ways. For example, the United Kingdom *Households below Average Income* statistics subtract occupational pension contributions from disposable income, on the basis that these contributions do not enhance current living standards.

References

Åberg, R. (1989), "Distributive Mechanisms of the Welfare State – A Formal Analysis and an Empirical Application", *European Sociological Review*, No. 5.

Ankrom, J. (1993), "An Analysis of Horizontal and Vertical Equity in Sweden, the US and the UK", *The Scandinavian Journal of Economics*, Vol. 95, No. 1, March.

Atkinson, A.B. (1991), "Social Insurance, The Fifteenth Annual Lecture of the Geneva Association", *The GENEVA Papers on Risk and Insurance – Theory*, Vol. 16, No. 2, December.

Barr, N. (1992), "Economic Theory and the Welfare State: A Survey and Reinterpretation", *Journal of Economic Literature*, Vol. 30, June.

Barr, N. (2001), *The Welfare State as Piggy Bank: Information, Risk, Uncertainty, and the Role of the State*, Oxford University Press, Oxford.

Beckerman, W. (1979), "The Impact of Income Maintenance Payments on Poverty in Britain – 1975", *Economic Journal*, June.

Dang, T.-T., H. Immervoll, D. Mantovani, K. Orsini and H. Sutherland (2006), "An Age Perspective on Economic Well-Being and Social Protection in Nine OECD Countries", OECD Social, Employment and Migration Working Paper, No. 34, OECD, Paris.

Disney, R. (2004), "Are Contributions to Public Pension Programmes a Tax on Employment?", *Economic Policy*, July.

Esping-Andersen, G. (1990), *The Three Worlds of Welfare Capitalism*, Polity Press, Cambridge.

Falkingham, J. and A. Harding (1996), "Poverty Alleviation *versus* Social Insurance: A Comparison of Lifetime Redistribution", NATSEM Discussion Paper No. 12, NATSEM, University of Canberra.

Geanakplos, J., O.S. Mitchell and S.P. Zeldes (2000), "Social Security Money's Worth", NBER Working Paper, No. 6722, available at *http://cowles.econ.yale.edu/P/cd/d11b/d1193.pdf*.

Korpi, W. and J. Palme (1998), "The Paradox of Redistribution and the Strategy of Equality: Welfare State Institutions, Inequality and Poverty in the Western Countries", *American Sociological Review*, Vol. 63, No. 5.

Layard, R. (1977), "On Measuring the Redistribution of Lifetime Income", in M.S. Feldstein and R.P. Inman (eds), *The Economics of Public Services*, Macmillan, London.

Leimer, D.R. (1995), "A Guide to Social Security Money's Worth Issues", ORS Working Paper No. 67, Social Security Administration, Washington D.C., available at *www.ssa.gov/policy/docs/workingpapers/wp67.pdf*.

Lindert, P.H. (2004), *Growing Public: Social Spending and Economic Growth Since the Eighteenth Century*, Cambridge University Press, Cambridge.

Mitchell, D. (1991), *Income Transfers in Ten Welfare States*, Aldershot, Avebury.

OECD (2007a), *OECD Social Expenditure Database 1980-2003*, OECD, Paris.

OECD (2007b), *Revenue Statistics, 1965-2006*, OECD, Paris.

O'Higgins, M, G. Schmaus and G. Stephenson (1990), "Income Distribution and Redistribution: A Microdata Analysis for Seven Countries", in T. Smeeding, M. O'Higgins and L. Rainwater (eds.), *Poverty, Inequality, and Income Distribution in Comparative Perspective*, Harvester Wheatsheaf, Hemel Hempstead.

Pederson, A.W. (1994), "The Welfare State: Still No Answer to the Big Questions?", LIS Working Paper, CEPS/INSTEAD, Luxembourg.

Palme, J. (1990), *Pension Rights in Welfare Capitalism: The Development of Old-Age Pensions in 18 OECD Countries 1930-1985*, Swedish Institute for Social Research, Stockholm.

Reynolds, M. and Smolensky, E. (1977), *Public Expenditures, Taxes and the Redistribution of Income: The USA, 1950, 1961, 1970*, Academic Press, New York.

Ringen, S. (1987), *The Possibility of Politics*, Clarendon Press, Oxford.

Siminski, P., P. Saunders, S. Waseem and B. Bradbury (2003), "Assessing the Quality and Inter-temporal Comparability of ABS Household Income Distribution Survey Data", SPRC Discussion Paper No. 123, University of New South Wales, April.

Ståhlberg, A.-C. (2007), "Redistribution across the Life Course in Social Protection Systems", *Modernising Social Policy for the New Life Course*, OECD, Paris.

Thomson, D. (1989), "The Welfare State and Generation Conflict: Winners and Losers", in P. Johnson, C. Conrad and D. Thomson (eds.), *Workers versus Pensioners: Intergenerational Justice in an Ageing World*, Manchester University Press, Manchester, New York.

Warren, N. (2008), "A Review of Studies on the Distributional Impact of Consumption Taxes in OECD Countries", OECD Social, Employment and Migration Working Paper, forthcoming, OECD, Paris.

Werding, M. (2003), "After Another Decade of Reform: Do Pension Systems in Europe Converge?", CESifo Dice Report, Vol. 1/2003.

Whiteford, P. (2008), "Redistribution in OECD Welfare States", OECD Social, Employment and Migration Working Papers, forthcoming, OECD, Paris.

Williamson, J.B., D.M. Watts-Roy and E.R. Kingson (eds.) (1999), *The Generational Equity Debate*, New York, Columbia University Press.

PART III

Characteristics of Poverty

ISBN 978-92-64-04418-0
Growing Unequal?
© OECD 2008

PART III

Chapter 5

Poverty in OECD Countries: An Assessment Based on Static Income*

Poverty rates have increased over the past decade, especially among children and people of working age. Most of this rise reflects the lower redistribution towards people at the bottom of the income scale. As a result of these changes, the risk of poverty has shifted from the elderly towards youths. Work is very effective to avoid the risk of poverty, nevertheless most poor people belong to households with some earnings.

*   This chapter has been prepared by Michael Förster and Marco Mira d'Ercole, OECD Social Policy Division.

Introduction

Concerns about income inequality have special salience when they relate to people at the bottom of the income distribution. This reflects both the shared commitment of all OECD governments to fight poverty within their borders and the fact that, while a range of factors shape the well-being of individuals, household income is the most obvious way to assess whether individuals are at risk of falling below the minimum standard of living that is considered acceptable in each country. While minimum standards will differ across countries, and are shaped by national traditions and by the political process of each country, benchmarking countries' performance on common arbitrary thresholds allows identifying patterns that are common to all OECD countries and patterns that differentiate their experiences in the field of poverty.

This chapter presents evidence on poverty based on a measure of households' annual income at a given point in time. Poverty is assessed relative to the income of a typical middle-class family in each country but also based on measures that reflect the absolute income gains for people at the bottom of the distribution. After having described levels and trends in different poverty measures for the entire population, this chapter looks at the experience of people of working age, of children and of the elderly in order to assess how poverty risks have shifted among them and to identify the factors that most contribute to these risks. The chapter then looks at the role of public transfers and household taxes in reducing poverty in each country, and presents a simple decomposition of how different factors have affected changes in the poverty rates of households with a head of either working age or retirement age. While a number of patterns, summarised in the concluding section, emerge from the analysis, their robustness is affected by measurement problems that are especially severe at the bottom end of the income scale. These data features explain the significant differences in poverty estimates across various surveys for a few countries (see Table 5.A2.1 in the Annex); further, as large proportions of the population in each country are clustered around the thresholds used here, very small changes in their income can sometimes lead to large swings in poverty measures.[1]

Levels and trends in overall income poverty

Relative income poverty

A natural starting point for assessing patterns of income poverty in various OECD countries is represented by the level of different summary measures, based on thresholds set at different proportions of median equivalised household disposable income. Figure 5.1 displays one widely used indicator – the "headcount" ratio, i.e. the share of people in each country with an income below 40%, 50% and 60% of median income[2] – with countries ranked (in increasing order) by the level of this indicator for the 50% threshold. "Absolute" values of these thresholds (in national currencies and in USD at PPP rates) are shown in Table 5.A1.1 in the Annex.

Figure 5.1. **Relative poverty rates for different income thresholds, mid-2000s**

Relative poverty rates at 40, 50 and 60% of median income thresholds

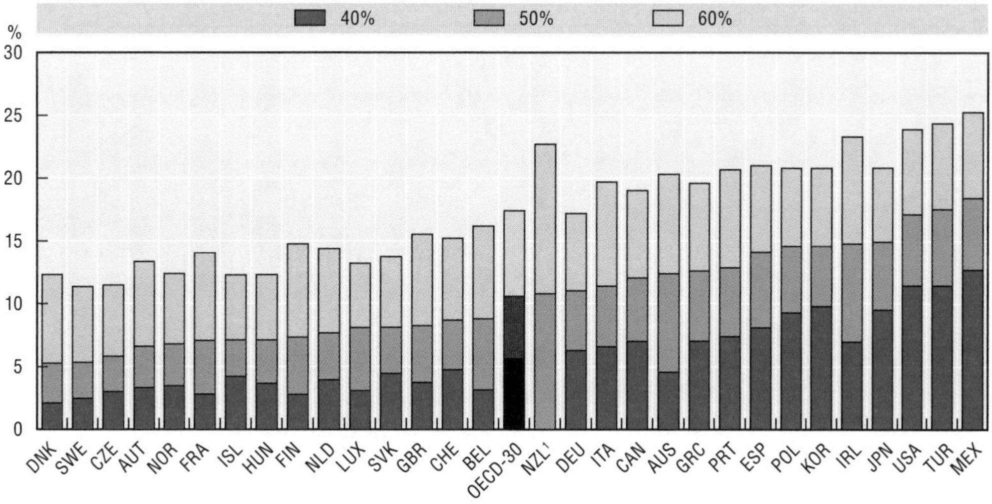

StatLink ⚙️ http://dx.doi.org/10.1787/422066332325

Note: Poverty rates are defined as the share of individuals with equivalised disposable income less than 40, 50 and 60% of the median for the entire population. Countries are ranked, from left to right, in increasing order of income poverty rates at the 50% median threshold. The income concept used is that of household disposable income adjusted for household size.

1.   Poverty rates based on a 40% threshold are not available for New Zealand.

Source: Computations from OECD income distribution questionnaire.

In the mid-2000s, around 6% of the population in the 30 OECD countries had an equivalised income of less than 40% of the median, a proportion that rises to 11% when the income threshold is set at 50% of the median and to around 17% for a threshold of 60%. There are wide disparities across countries in this measure of relative income poverty – with cross-country differences ranging between 2 and 13% for the 40% threshold, between 5 and 18% for the 50% threshold, and between 11 and 25% for the 60% threshold. These disparities remain significant even after excluding "outliers" at both ends of the distribution.[3] Cross-country dispersion (as measured by the standard deviation) rises with the threshold used.

Despite large absolute differences in headcount rates depending on the threshold used, the ranking of countries is remarkably consistent across the three measures.[4] Relative poverty rates are always lowest, whatever the threshold used, in the Czech Republic, Denmark and Sweden, while they are always highest in the United States, Turkey and Mexico. Poverty rates are below average in all Nordic and several Continental European countries, and above average in Southern European countries as well as Ireland, Japan and Korea. In Austria, Denmark, Finland, New Zealand and Sweden, the share of people with income between 50% and 60% of the median is at least as large as that below half the median, while in Japan, Korea, Mexico, Poland, Turkey and the United States this share is much smaller (less than 30%). The use of the higher income threshold would therefore increase poverty headcounts by more in the first group of countries than in the latter.

The headcount ratio is one measure of the number of poor people in each country (i.e. the frequency of poverty). Also important is the amount by which the mean income of the poor falls below the poverty line, measured as a percentage of the poverty threshold (i.e. the "poverty gap"). This gap (shown as a diamond in Figure 5.2) was – on average, across the OECD – 29%, ranging from about 20% in the Belgium, Luxembourg, Finland and the

Figure 5.2. **Poverty gap and composite measure of income poverty, mid-2000s**

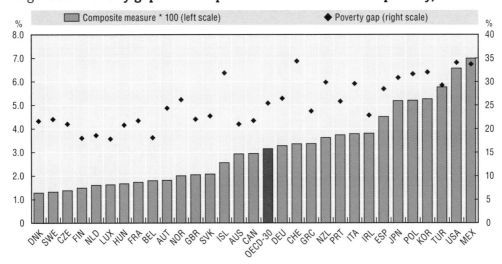

StatLink ᵃ📊 http://dx.doi.org/10.1787/422071611541

Note: The poverty gap (shown on the right-hand axis) is calculated as the distance between the poverty threshold and the mean income of the poor, expressed as a percentage of the poverty threshold. The composite measure (shown on the left-hand axis) is the product of the poverty rate and the poverty gap. Countries are ranked (from left to right) in increasing order of the composite poverty measure. Data refer to the mid-2000s for all countries except for Canada (2000). The income concept used is that of household disposable income adjusted for household size.

Source: Computations from OECD income distribution questionnaire.

Netherlands to almost 40% in Mexico, Switzerland and the United States.[5] In general, countries with a lower incidence of poverty (headcount ratios) also record lower poverty gaps, but the correlation is rather weak (0.60) and there are several exceptions: Norway, Iceland and especially Switzerland, with below-average poverty rates, have above-average poverty gaps, while Australia, Canada, Greece and Ireland, with above-average poverty rates, have below-average poverty gaps. A composite measure of poverty – which takes into account both how many poor there are in each country and the distance between their income and the poverty line (shown as bars in Figure 5.2) – was around 3%, on average, in the mid-2000s, ranging between 1.3% in Denmark and 7% in Mexico.[6]

Changes in the poverty headcount based on the 50% median income threshold since the mid-1980s highlight several patterns.

● From the mid-1980s to the mid-1990s (Figure 5.3, left-hand panel), the unweighted average of poverty rates across 24 OECD countries increased by 0.6 percentage point. Larger (2 to 4 points) rises were recorded in Germany, Italy, the Netherlands, New Zealand and the United Kingdom, while in Belgium and Spain poverty rates fell by a similar amount.[7]

● In the decade from the mid-1990s to the mid-2000s (middle panel), poverty rates increased again in a majority of countries, with the average rate across 24 OECD countries edging up by 0.6 point to almost 11% of the population. This rise extended earlier trends for Austria, Germany, Ireland, Japan, Luxembourg, the Netherlands, New Zealand and Sweden, while it reversed earlier progress for Canada, Denmark, Finland, Spain and the United States. In this decade, only Greece, Italy, Mexico and the United Kingdom experienced declines in the poverty headcount of around 1 point or more.

Figure 5.3. **Trends in poverty headcounts**

Point changes in income poverty rate at 50% median level over different time periods

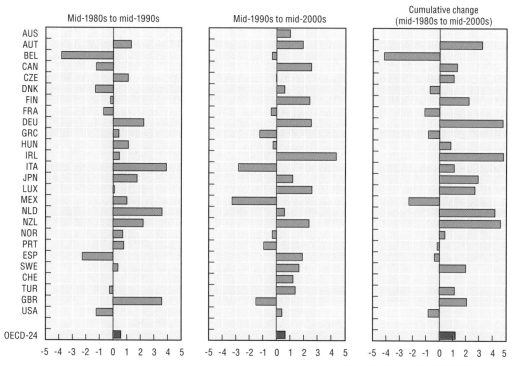

StatLink ⟨⟨⟩⟩ http://dx.doi.org/10.1787/422076001267

Note: Data in the first panel refer to changes in the poverty headcount from around 1990 to mid-1990s for Czech Republic, Hungary and Portugal; no data are available for Australia and Switzerland. Data in the second panel refer to changes from the mid-1990s to around 2000 for Austria, Belgium, Czech Republic, Ireland, Portugal and Spain (where 2005 data, based on EU-SILC, are not comparable with those for earlier years); and to changes from 2000 to 2005 for Switzerland. OECD-24 refers to the simple average of OECD countries with data spanning the entire period (all countries shown above except Australia and Switzerland).

Source: Computations from OECD income distribution questionnaire.

- Over the entire period from the mid-1980s to the mid-2000s, the poverty headcount increased in two-thirds of the OECD countries (exceptions being Belgium, Denmark, France, Greece, Mexico, Portugal, Spain and the United States). The increase was largest in Austria, Finland, Germany, Luxembourg, the Netherlands, New Zealand, Sweden and the United Kingdom (from a lower base) as well as in Ireland and Japan (from a higher base). Across the 24 OECD countries for which data are available, the cumulative increase was around 1.2 points (*i.e.* 13%) with changes of similar magnitudes in each of the two decades.[8, 9]

Changes in a broader range of poverty measures for the same countries suggest that while poverty headcounts for different thresholds typically moved in the same direction, changes in poverty rates and poverty gaps often offset each other (see Figure 5.A2.1 available at *http://dx.doi.org/10.1787/424402577838*).

Changes in "absolute" poverty

The estimates shown above refer to "relative" income poverty, *i.e.* with a threshold set as a percentage of the median income in each country in each of the years considered. Several OECD countries, however, have "official" measures of poverty that rely on "absolute" standards, typically in the form of the cost of a basket of goods and services required to assure minimum living conditions and indexed for price changes over time (*e.g.* United States). While the use of "absolute" thresholds poses difficult methodological issues for cross-country comparisons (Förster, 1994), one way to illustrate how "absolute" poverty has changed over time is to use a relative threshold in a base year which is kept unchanged in real terms in later years.[10] One such measure, based on a threshold set at half of median income in the mid-1990s, shows that – even when relative income poverty is rising – most OECD countries achieved significant reductions in absolute poverty between the mid-1990s and mid-2000s (Figure 5.4). On average, across the 15 OECD countries for which this information is available, absolute poverty rates fell by about 40% during the last decade, with larger reductions (of 60% or more) in those countries (such as Greece, Hungary) that experienced economic transformations and stronger economic growth over that period and rises since around 2000 only in Germany.[11] While there is continuing controversy about the extent to which subjective attitudes towards poverty are influenced by the actual scale of poverty in society (as measured by either absolute or relative income poverty rates), it is also clear that, in any case, these attitudes matter for the people affected and for the willingness of voters to fund programmes to alleviate poverty (Box 5.1).

Figure 5.4. **Trends in "absolute" poverty**

Threshold set at half of median income in the mid-1990s kept constant in real terms in later years, mid-1990s = 1.0

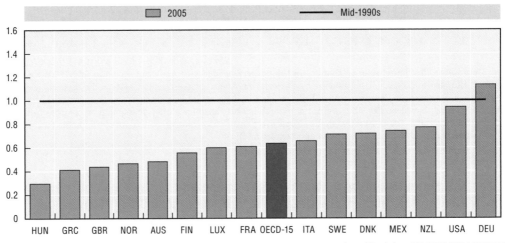

StatLink ⬛🖻⬛ http://dx.doi.org/10.1787/422162217110

Note: Countries are ranked, from left to right, in decreasing order of the reduction in "absolute poverty" from its mid-1990s level (*e.g.* in Hungary, "absolute" poverty in the mid-2000s was only 30% of the level it had reached in the mid-1990s, while in Germany it was 13% above that level).

Source: Computations from OECD income distribution questionnaire.

Poverty risks for different population groups

Poverty risks within each country vary depending on individual and household characteristics, and they have shifted significantly over time. The most significant of these shifts has been away from the elderly and towards younger people. On average – across the 23 OECD countries covered by the left-hand panel of Figure 5.5 – the poverty risk of people aged 75 and over has fallen from a level almost twice as high as that of the population average in the mid-1980s to 1.5 times by the mid-2000s. For people aged 66 to 75 this risk is now lower than for children and young adults.[12] This improvement, which appeared to have stopped in the early-2000s (Förster and Mira d'Ercole, 2005) has resumed in recent years. The reduction in the poverty risk of elderly people is even larger when looking, in a

Box 5.1. **Subjective attitudes to poverty**

The burden of poverty on individuals and families depends not just on its size but also on how others in society view its nature, in particular whether poverty is perceived as the result of individual attitudes or of the way society is organised. The chart below shows the share of respondents who believe that people are poor because of laziness or lack of will, on one side, or because society is unfair, on the other. In general, the share of respondents who believe that poverty reflects laziness is greater in the Asian and Anglo-Saxon countries than in the Nordic and Continental European countries. Beyond these cross-country differences in levels, attitudes towards poverty also change over time within individual countries. Paugman and Selz (2005) note that fewer people believe that poverty is based on laziness in times when unemployment rises, as more people are exposed to risks of job losses; they also note that "laziness" explanations of poverty have become more prevalent in most European countries in recent years.

Share of respondents attributing poverty to different factors

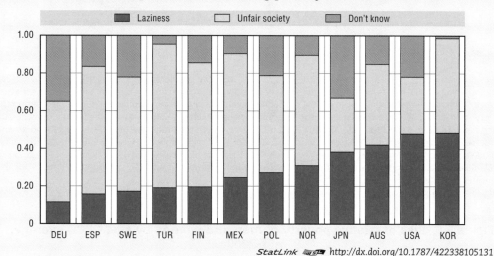

StatLink ⟶ http://dx.doi.org/10.1787/422338105131

Source: World Values Survey referring to the mid-1990s.

smaller number of OECD countries, at changes since the mid-1970s (right-hand panel). In general, poverty risks for all age groups above 50 have declined, while those for people below that age have risen. By 2005, children and young adults had poverty rates about 25% above the population average, while they were close to and below that average, respectively, 20 years ago.[13]

Poverty rates also differ by gender, despite the assumption of equal sharing of resources within households. Poverty rates of women are, on average, about 1 point higher than for men (with the only exceptions being Hungary, New Zealand and Poland, where they are less than that) but 2 points or more in Australia, Germany, Greece, Ireland, Italy, Japan, Korea and the United States. These gender differences in poverty rates are closely related to the age of individuals (Figure 5.6). Women are more likely to be living alone following the death of their spouses; and – as fewer women have gained pension rights during their working age – the risk of being poor for elderly women is one-third higher than that for men of the same age. As more women head single-parent families, the risk of poverty for prime-age women is also

Figure 5.5. **Risk of relative poverty by age of individuals, mid-1970s to mid-2000s, OECD average**

Poverty rate of the entire population in each year = 100

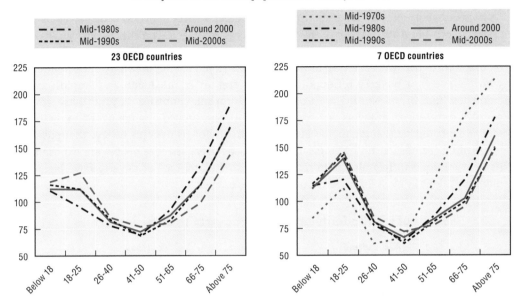

StatLink ⟶ http://dx.doi.org/10.1787/422163541278

Note: Relative poverty risk is the age-specific poverty rate divided by the poverty rate for the entire population times 100. The poverty threshold is set at 50% of median income of the entire population. OECD-23 is the average poverty rates across all OECD countries except Australia, Belgium, Iceland, Korea, Poland, the Slovak Republic and Switzerland. OECD-7 is the average for Canada, Finland, Greece, the Netherlands, Sweden, the United Kingdom and the United States. Data for mid-1980s refer to around 1990 for the Czech Republic, Hungary and Portugal; those for mid-2000s refer to 2000 for Austria, Belgium, the Czech Republic, Ireland, Portugal and Spain (where 2005 data, based on EU-SILC, are not comparable with those for earlier years). Data based on cash income (see note 12 for the implications of this).

Source: Computations from OECD income distribution questionnaire.

Figure 5.6. **Risk of relative poverty of men and women by age, OECD average, mid-2000s**

Poverty rate of the entire population = 100

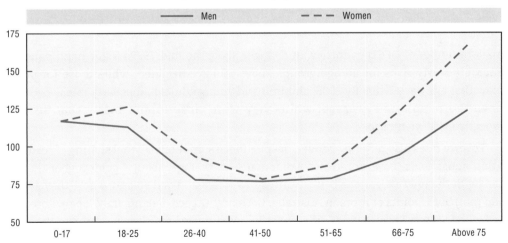

StatLink ⟶ http://dx.doi.org/10.1787/422171622463

Note: Relative poverty risk is the age-specific poverty rate of men and women divided by the poverty rate for the entire population times 100. The poverty threshold is set at 50% of the median income of the entire population.

Source: Computations from OECD income distribution questionnaire.

above that for men with the exception of the age group 41 to 50. By contrast, women below the age of 18 have no higher risk of being poor than men of the same age.

What are the differences in poverty risks across household types? In general, households with children do not face significantly higher poverty risks than those without children (10.6% in the first group, a little over 10% in the second), and in one-third of OECD countries this risk is even lower; this is especially the case in Australia, Korea and the four Nordic countries. In Poland and Turkey and, to a lesser extent, the Czech Republic, Italy and Luxembourg, however, households with children face a much higher risk of falling into poverty. Among households without children, persons living alone generally have a much higher poverty risk – twice as high on average, *i.e.* 22%. Poverty rates for persons living in single-parent families are three times higher than for the average of all households with children, and exceed 40% in one-third of OECD countries (Figure 5.7).

Figure 5.7. **Poverty rates by household type, mid-2000s**

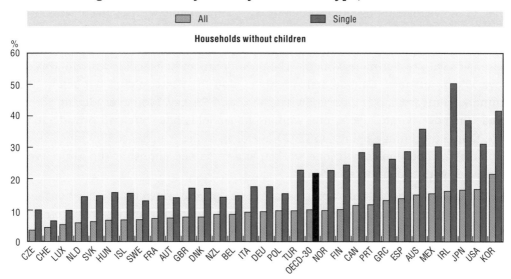

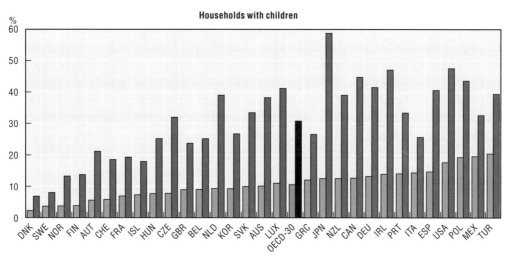

StatLink http://dx.doi.org/10.1787/422178058748

Note: Countries are ranked, from left to right, in increasing order of the poverty rate of households without children (in the top panel) and of those with children (in the bottom one). Data refer to all households, irrespectively of the age of the household head. Poverty thresholds are set at 50% of the median income of the entire population.

Source: Computations from OECD income distribution questionnaire.

Changes in poverty risks by household type over time have been small and mainly limited to single persons. On average, and in most OECD countries, the poverty risk of couples without children is around half that of the total population, while that of couples with children is slightly below average. Conversely, lone parents have a probability of falling into poverty that is around three times higher than average, with little change in the past decade. The situation for single persons without children (including both working-age and retirement-age adults) improved over the past decade.

Poverty among people of working age: the role of paid work

Across the OECD area, around 9% of people of working age had a household disposable income below the 50% threshold in the mid-2000s, a share that has increased by 0.6 point in the past decade. Poverty rates have decreased recently only in seven OECD countries, and then only slightly. While poverty rates among people belonging to this group depend on a range of factors, the most important is whether household members have a paid job. Table 5.1 shows that among all those belonging to a household with a head of working age, those living in households where no one works have a poverty rate of 36% on average, i.e. almost three times higher than in households with one worker, and 12 times higher than households with two or more workers. The poverty rate of households with no workers is above 50% in Australia, Canada, Ireland, Korea, and the United States but below 20% in Denmark, Hungary, Luxembourg, Switzerland and Turkey. Moreover, during the past decade the poverty rate among non-working households has increased considerably (by more than 3 percentage points on OECD average), while it increased by much less (by 1.6 points) for households with one worker, and remained almost at the same level for households with two or more workers.

Because households with workers have lower poverty rates than other households, countries with a higher employment rate for people of working age also tend to record a lower poverty rate among the same group (Figure 5.8, left-hand panel), although with a large variation across countries. Some countries such as Japan or the United States combine high employment rates with above-average poverty rates, while the inverse is the case in Hungary.

The effect of paid work in reducing poverty among households with a head of working age is also evident when looking at the type of job held, i.e. whether working full or part time. Among single adult households (with and without children), 46% of people in jobless households have, on average, income below the 50% threshold. This proportion declines to 28% when the single adult in these families works part time and to 8% when the person works full time. Among people living in couple families, around 33% have income below the 50% poverty line when no one in the household has a paid job. The poverty rate is thus lower for jobless couples than for singles, especially when they have children, reflecting the more generous out-of-work transfers available. The poverty rate falls to 19% when one household member is working part time and to around 4% when at least one is working full time.

Despite the importance of paid work for reducing poverty, many households with workers have income below the 50% poverty line. On average, people living in households with workers account for around 60% of the income poor, with this share ranging from around 25% in Australia and Norway to 80% or more in Japan, Greece, Luxembourg, Turkey, Iceland and Mexico (Figure 5.9). While most of these poor households have only one working member, those with two or more workers account for as much as 17% of all the income poor on average, and for more than one-third in Japan, Turkey, Iceland and

Table 5.1. **Poverty rates for people of working age and for households with a working-age head, by household characteristics**

	Poverty among people of working age		Poverty in households with a head of working age													
			Level, mid-2000s				Point changes since mid-1990s				Single			Two or more adults		
	Mid-2000s	Point changes since 1995	All	No workers	One worker	Two workers	All	No workers	One worker	Two workers	Not working	Working part-time	Working full-time	Not working	Only working part-time	At least one working full-time
Australia	10	1.2	10	55	7	1	0.4	9.0	-0.5	0.2	72	12	2	42	13	2
Austria	7	2.2	6	22	6	3	3.6	1.3	1.7	6.1	31	17	5	35	4	4
Belgium	7	0.5	8	25	8	2	0.0	6.7	0.7	-0.8	29	18	6	22	20	3
Canada	10	0.9	13	66	21	4	2.5	6.2	6.1	1.2	79	50	11	54	23	4
Czech Republic	5	0.7	6	38	7	0	0.9	2.9	-2.0	0.1	56	[.]	6	28	[.]	2
Denmark	5	1.2	5	18	8	1	1.0	4.8	1.5	0.3	22	28	1	15	6	0
Finland	7	1.7	6	34	10	1	1.8	13.4	1.2	-0.2	47	13	2	16	13	1
France	7	-0.6	7	22	10	2	0.1	7.6	0.1	-0.7	31	8	6	18	4	4
Germany	8	0.8	12	40	7	1	3.4	4.7	1.9	-0.1	49	32	5	32	25	2
Greece	9	-1.2	10	26	18	3	-0.5	4.7	3.6	-1.2	33	34	9	22	25	8
Hungary	7	1.0	7	19	6	4	0.2	-4.9	-4.6	-0.7	39	[.]	[.]	15	11	2
Iceland	7	:	7	28	19	4	:	:	:	:	23	25	10	40	13	5
Ireland	12	3.3	13	63	15	2	:	:	:	-3.1	75	36	7	55	29	3
Italy	10	-2.8	11	36	16	1	-3.1	-2.2	-1.3	-0.3	40	50	4	36	33	8
Japan	12	0.4	12	42	14	9	0.8	2.2	1.3	:	57	:	:	31	:	:
Korea	12	:	11	58	13	4	:	:	:	:	53	:	:	61	:	10
Luxembourg	8	2.8	9	19	15	3	3.3	7.3	7.3	1.6	28	35	12	14	28	:
Mexico	15	-2.2	18	37	26	10	-2.9	-3.5	-0.2	-3.5	30	:	:	41	:	:
Netherlands	7	0.7	8	34	13	2	1.4	6.5	5.9	1.0	40	:	:	27	:	6
New Zealand	11	3.3	12	46	19	4	2.5	15.2	8.5	0.1	51	41	9	42	:	:
Norway	7	1.0	6	38	4	0	0.9	1.0	0.0	0.2	47	[.]	[.]	22	[.]	:
Poland	14	:	16	33	23	5	:	:	:	:	40	:	:	31	:	:
Portugal	11	-0.4	11	37	24	3	0.0	-2.4	3.3	0.2	58	31	16	33	26	8
Slovak Republic	8	:	9	38	15	1	:	:	:	:	35	21	20	40	21	6
Spain	11	-0.4	11	49	18	4	-0.2	9.6	1.5	1.5	62	27	18	46	26	9
Sweden	5	1.0	5	23	9	1	1.4	7.6	2.6	0.2	23	16	1	21	[.]	1
Switzerland	7	0.5	6	19	4	5	0.5	4.2	3.7	-1.4	21	[.]	[.]	18	[.]	[.]
Turkey	14	0.4	17	19	17	18	1.8	-11.5	-0.1	4.2	33	[.]	3	18	22	6
United Kingdom	7	-0.3	8	33	7	1	-2.1	-2.7	-1.9	0.0	38	11	14	28	12	2
United States	15	1.0	16	71	25	5	0.0	-3.2	-0.8	-0.4	80	54	8	63	19	7
OECD	9	0.6	10	36	14	3	0.7	3.4	1.6	0.2	46	28	8	33	19	4

StatLink http://dx.doi.org/10.1787/422446454016

Note: Poverty thresholds are set at 50% of the median income of the entire population. Data for changes refer to the period from the mid-1990s to around 2000 for Austria, Belgium, the Czech Republic, Ireland, Portugal and Spain (where 2005 data, based on EU-SILC, are not comparable with those for earlier years); and to changes from 2000 to 2005 for Switzerland. [.] indicates that the sample size is too small.
Source: Computations from OECD income distribution questionnaire.

Figure 5.8. **Poverty and employment rates, around mid-2000s**

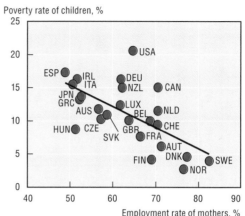

People of working age

Children and mothers

StatLink ⟨MS⟩ http://dx.doi.org/10.1787/422187281362

Note: Poverty thresholds are set at 50% of the median income of the entire population. Employment rates of persons of working age in 2003; employment rates of mothers in 2002.

Source: Computations from OECD income distribution questionnaire.

Figure 5.9. **Shares of poor people by number of workers in the household where they live, mid-2000s**

Percentage of poor people living in households with a head of working age

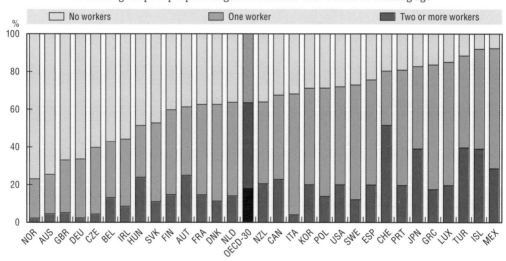

StatLink ⟨MS⟩ http://dx.doi.org/10.1787/422210017310

Note: Poverty thresholds are set at 50% of the median income of the entire population. Countries are ranked, from left to right, in increasing order of the share of poor people living in households with no workers.

Source: Computations from OECD income distribution questionnaire.

Switzerland. While such large cross-country differences may partly reflect differences in the way different sources define "workers", they also suggest that other factors beyond access to paid work – such as the number of hours worked each year and the hourly wage received – contribute to the risk of insufficient economic resources. Indeed, out of the 18 OECD countries where wages are subject to statutory minima, only in 8 (Luxembourg, the Czech Republic, Japan, New Zealand, Poland, Ireland and Australia) the net income of minimum wage earners with inactive spouses in the 2005 was high enough to keep a family with two children out of poverty (OECD, 2007).[14]

Poverty among families with children: maternal employment and number of children

In the mid-2000s, one child out of eight (12.4%) lived in households with equivalised income below the 50% median threshold, with a slightly lower share for people in households with children (*i.e.* including adult members). Both shares increased in the past decade by more than for the population as a whole. Child poverty increased by 4 points or more in Austria, Germany, Luxembourg and Turkey, while it declined slightly in Australia, Belgium, Hungary, and the United States and, more strongly, in Italy, Mexico and the United Kingdom.

Both the living arrangements and the employment status of parents shape the poverty risks of children, as can be seen in Table 5.2. Children living with a single adult have a higher probability of being in poverty than those living with two adults, and this holds for both working and non-working parents, although there are some exceptions and differences are not always large. Conversely, children whose parents are employed have much lower poverty than those in jobless households. Among single-parent families, the poverty rate of those in jobless households is 2.6 times higher than that of households with workers (Figure 5.10, top panel); among couples with children, the poverty rate of jobless households is three times higher than for one-worker households, and 12 times higher than for households with two or more workers (bottom panel). OECD countries with a larger share of mothers in paid work also record lower poverty rates among children (Figure 5.8, right-hand panel).

The risk of falling into poverty also depends on the number of children in the household. Poverty rates generally increase monotonically with the number of children present, although there are exceptions (Table 5.2, final three columns). In general, poverty rates of families with two children are only slightly above those of families with only one child. Poverty rates, however, increase more substantially when a third (or more) child is present in the family, especially in Ireland, Mexico, Poland, the United Kingdom and the United States. Conversely, in Australia, Austria and the Nordic countries, no significant increase occurs. While the general pattern of poverty rates increasing with the number of children may to some extent reflect the arbitrary nature of the elasticity of household needs to household size used here (*i.e.* a greater increase in household needs for each additional member than is actually the case), it may also reflect genuine strains on the household finances of larger families due to rising child costs.

Poverty among the elderly: the impact of earnings and living arrangements

Recent trends in poverty for elderly persons (those aged over 65) contrast with those for other age groups. On average, the poverty rate of elderly people fell slightly (by 0.5 percentage point), with a similar fall for persons living in households with a head of retirement age. Country experiences were, however, diverse. In five countries (Austria, the Czech Republic, Greece, Norway and Turkey) the decrease in income poverty was particularly pronounced (at 5 points or more), while sizeable increases were recorded in Australia, Finland, Sweden, Switzerland and particularly in Ireland.

In many OECD countries, the effective retirement age has risen recently. Nevertheless, at 27%, the share of elderly people who work (or live with persons who work) has remained remarkably stable over the past ten years. Poverty rates among elderly households with work are much lower than for those without (7% and 17%, respectively, Table 5.3), especially in Australia, France, Germany, Greece, Ireland, Italy, Norway, Portugal and the

Table 5.2. **Poverty rates for children and people in households with children by household characteristics**

Percentages

	Poverty among children		Poverty in households with children									
			All		Single		Couple			By number of children		
	Mid-2000s	Point changes since mid-1990s	Level, mid-2000s	Change from 1995	Level, mid-2000s		Level, mid-2000s					
					Not working	Working	No workers	One worker	Two and more workers	One	Two	Three and more
Australia	12	−1.2	10	−1.0	68	6	51	8	1	9	10	11
Austria	6	6.0	6	6.1	51	11	36	4	3	6	5	6
Belgium	10	−0.8	9	0.1	43	10	36	11	3	7	9	11
Canada	15	2.2	13	1.6	89	32	81	22	4	11	13	18
Czech Republic	10	1.7	8	1.4	71	10	43	9	1	8	6	[..]
Denmark	3	0.8	2	0.7	20	4	21	5	0	2	2	4
Finland	4	2.1	4	1.9	46	6	23	9	1	5	3	3
France	8	0.3	7	−0.2	46	12	48	12	2	6	7	10
Germany	16	5.1	13	4.2	56	26	47	6	1	13	13	14
Greece	13	0.9	12	0.9	84	18	39	22	4	8	13	19
Hungary	9	−1.6	8	−1.1	44	16	22	6	3	5	6	14
Iceland	8	..	7	..	23	17	51	29	4	7	6	10
Ireland	16	2.3	14	..	75	24	55	16	2	12	12	19
Italy	16	−3.4	14	−3.1	[..]	16	78	24	1	..	..	..
Japan	14	1.6	12	1.2	60	58	50	11	10	..	..	..
Korea	10	..	9	..	29	26	65	10	4	..	..	..
Luxembourg	12	4.5	11	3.8	69	38	27	16	5	7	13	14
Mexico	22	−3.8	19	−2.4	30	34	53	27	11	11	16	26
Netherlands	12	1.0	9	1.2	62	27	65	12	2	..	..	..
New Zealand	15	2.3	13	1.5	48	30	47	21	3	..	..	..
Norway	5	0.9	4	0.6	31	5	29	4	0	4	2	6
Poland	22	..	19	..	75	26	51	28	6	15	18	31
Portugal	17	0.0	14	0.4	[..]	26	53	34	5	10	17	[..]
Slovak Rep.	11	..	10	..	66	24	66	18	2	..	..	..
Spain	17	1.9	15	1.1	78	32	71	23	5	10	16	29
Sweden	4	1.5	4	1.5	18	6	36	14	1	4	3	3
Switzerland	9	1.2	6	1.3	22		8			..	..	..
Turkey	25	5.0	20	3.6	44	32	28	19	20	..	..	..
United Kingdom	10	−3.6	9	−3.7	39	7	36	9	1	4	6	20
United States	21	−1.7	18	−1.1	92	36	82	27	6	14	15	26
OECD	12	1.0	11	0.8	54	21	48	16	4	8	10	15

StatLink http://dx.doi.org/10.1787/422456583733

Note: Poverty thresholds are set at 50% of the median income of the entire population. Data for changes refer to the period from the mid-1990s to around 2000 for Austria, Belgium, the Czech Republic, Ireland, Portugal and Spain (where 2005 data, based on EU-SILC, are not comparable with those for earlier years); and to changes from 2000 to 2005 for Switzerland. [..] indicates that the sample size is too small. Data based on cash income (see note 13 for the implications of this).
Source: Computations from OECD income distribution questionnaire.

United Kingdom. Differences are much lower in Austria, Finland, the Netherlands, New Zealand and Poland, while in Turkey non-working elderly households have lower poverty rates than working ones.

Different living arrangements also affect poverty risks among the elderly. Elderly persons living alone – very often widowed women – face a much higher risk that income will fall below 50% of the median than elderly persons living with others. In the first case,

GROWING UNEQUAL – ISBN 978-92-64-04418-0 – © OECD 2008

Figure 5.10. **Poverty risk of jobless households relative to those with workers, mid-2000s**

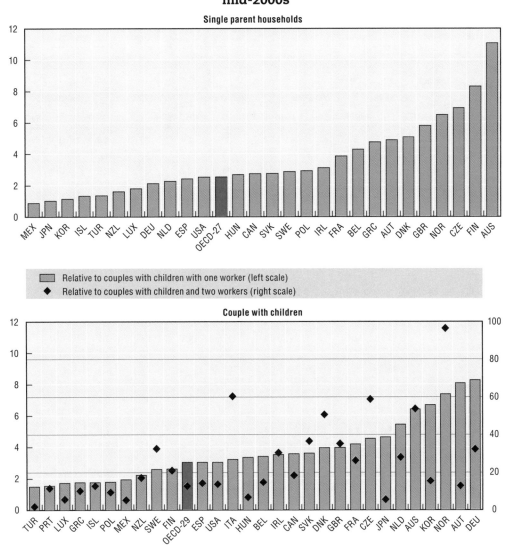

StatLink ⟨⟩ http://dx.doi.org/10.1787/422228452208

Note: The poverty risk is defined as poverty rate of non-working households divided by poverty rate of working households.

Source: Computations from OECD income distribution questionnaire.

poverty rates exceed 40% in Australia, Ireland, Japan, Korea, Mexico and the United States, countries with more limited public pension schemes. However, poverty rates have declined more significantly among the single elderly than among multiple-person households.

The role of household taxes and public cash transfers in reducing income poverty

In all OECD countries, public cash benefits and household taxes significantly reduce poverty. One measure of this is the difference between poverty rates based on disposable incomes (the income concept used so far) and those based on market income.[15] The left-hand panel of Figure 5.11 highlights differences across countries in the role of government taxes and cash benefits in reducing poverty. The point differences range from less than 10 points in Korea, Switzerland and the United States to more than 23 points in Belgium

Table 5.3. **Poverty rates among the elderly and people living in households with a retirement-age head by household characteristics**

	Poverty among people of retirement age		Poverty in households with a head of retirement age									
			All		Working		Not working		Singles		Couples	
	Mid-2000s	Point changes since mid-1990s	Mid-2000s	Point change since mid-1990s	Mid-2000s	Point change since mid-1990s	Mid-2000s	Point change since mid-1990s	Mid-2000s	Point change since mid-1990s	Mid-2000s	Point change since mid-1990s
Australia	27	4.6	27	5.6	4	3.2	32	5.4	50	−4.8	18	9.8
Austria	7	−5.7	8	−6.0	7	5.3	9	−7.6	16	−11.6	4	0.2
Belgium	13	−3.5	12	−2.3	4	−0.6	13	−3.7	17	−6.8	10	0.1
Canada	4	1.5	7	3.2	2	0.7	10	4.8	16	7.3	4	1.8
Czech Rep.	2	−6.5	3	−5.8	[..]	[..]	3	−6.2	6	−19.1	2	0.5
Denmark	10	−2.1	10	−2.2	2	0.6	12	−2.3	17	−4.4	4	0.3
Finland	13	5.3	14	5.9	11	7.7	14	5.5	28	12.5	4	2.3
France	4	−0.2	9	−2.1	1	−5.9	9	−1.4	16	0.2	4	−2.4
Germany	10	−0.6	8	−1.6	2	−4.7	9	−1.2	15	0.2	5	−1.8
Greece	23	−6.6	21	−7.0	7	−10.5	31	−3.1	34	−4.5	18	−7.1
Hungary	5	−2.5	5	−2.9	[..]	[..]	5	−5.2	11	−6.9	1	−2.7
Iceland	5	..	5	..	3	..	7	..	10	..	2	..
Ireland	31	18.8	25	..	5	..	36	..	65	..	9	..
Italy	13	−2.3	13	−2.1	3	0.4	17	−4.5	25	−7.5	9	−1.2
Japan	22	−1.0	21	−1.1	13	−1.8	30	−7.6	48	−7.9	17	−1.5
Korea	45	..	49	..	35	..	69	..	77	..	41	..
Luxembourg	3	−1.8	3	−1.6	[..]	[..]	4	−5.4	4	−5.6	3	−6.4
Mexico	28	−4.6	23	−8.6	19	−9.1	39	−7.9	45	−5.9	21	−9.2
Netherlands	2	0.9	2	0.8	2	1.1	2	0.7	3	−0.1	2	1.3
New Zealand	2	0.2	4	2.5	1	−3.8	2	1.6	3	2.1	1	−0.1
Norway	9	−6.8	9	−7.1	1	−1.1	10	−7.9	20	−13.8	1	−2.1
Poland	5	..	6	..	6	..	6	..	6	..	6	..
Portugal	17	−1.1	20	−2.2	5	−4.6	25	−1.0	35	−4.8	16	−2.0
Slovak Rep.	6	..	4	..	[..]	[..]	7	..	10	..	3	..
Spain	17	−1.1	27	16.8	12	−4.3	32	23.3	39	32.7	24	12.6
Sweden	8	4.0	6	2.7	3	1.1	7	3.2	13	5.8	1	0.5
Switzerland	18	4.3	18	−1.8	[..]	[..]	[..]	[..]	24	6.1	15	3.4
Turkey	15	−8.1	18	−4.1	20	0.6	16	−16.4	38	−6.2	17	−4.0
United Kingdom	10	−2.1	10	−0.8	1	0.1	12	−2.5	17	−0.9	7	−1.3
United States	24	2.9	24	3.2	9	1.4	34	5.0	41	3.0	17	3.2
OECD	13	−0.5	14	−0.7	7	−1.2	17	−1.4	25	−1.6	9	−0.4

StatLink ᵐˢ⁹ᵇ *http://dx.doi.org/10.1787/422457006467*

Note: Poverty thresholds are set at 50% of the median income of the entire population. Data for mid-2000s refer to around 2000 for Japan and Switzerland. Data for changes refer to the period from the mid-1990s to around 2000 for Austria, Belgium, Czech Republic, Denmark, France, Ireland, Portugal and Spain (where 2005 data, based on EU-SILC, are not comparable with those for earlier years). [..] indicates that the sample size is too small. Data based on cash income (see note 13 for the implications of this).
Source: Computations from OECD income distribution questionnaire.

and France, while the percentage difference in poverty headcounts due to the combined effect of household taxes and public cash transfers ranges from 12% in Korea to 80% in Denmark and Sweden, and is a little over 60% on average. These large cross-country differences in the poverty-reducing effects of public cash transfers and household taxes – and the significant negative correlation between disposable income poverty and the poverty-reduction effects of net public transfers – imply that countries with higher market-income poverty are not necessarily those with higher poverty based on final income.

GROWING UNEQUAL – ISBN 978-92-64-04418-0 – © OECD 2008

Figure 5.11. **Effects of taxes and transfers in reducing poverty among the entire population, mid-2000s and changes since mid-1980s**

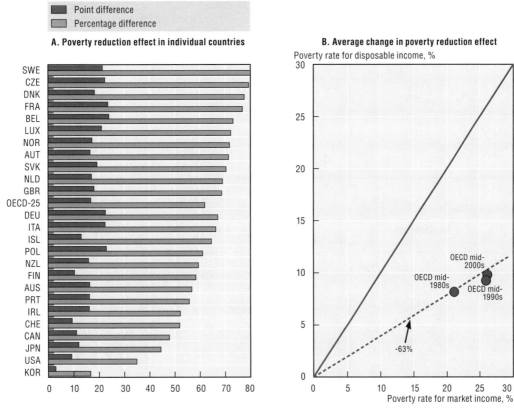

StatLink ⌐ http://dx.doi.org/10.1787/422271727828

Note: In Panel A, countries are ranked in decreasing order of poverty reduction in percentages. In Panel B, data refer to the simple average across 17 of the OECD countries shown in Figure 5.3 (except Austria, Iceland, Ireland, Korea, Luxembourg, Slovakia and Switzerland). Data for mid-2000s refer to 2000 for Belgium, Czech Republic, Denmark, France, Ireland and Portugal (where 2005 data, based on EU-SILC, are not comparable with those for earlier years). Poverty thresholds are set at 50% of the median disposable income of the entire population.

Source: Computations from OECD income distribution questionnaire.

The role of household taxes and public transfers in reducing poverty has also changed over time. Panel B of Figure 5.11 – which plots changes in the extent to which net public transfers have lowered poverty, on average, for the 17 OECD countries for which information over time is available – points to a large increase in market-income poverty from the mid-1980s to the mid-1990s (from 21% to 26%), which was only partly offset by a higher poverty-reducing effect of taxes and transfers (from 61% to 65%). Conversely, from the mid-1990s to the mid-2000s, market-income poverty stopped rising, while the effect of household taxes and public transfers in reducing poverty (at 63%) almost fell back to the level that prevailed in the mid-1980s, leading to higher poverty rates based on disposable income.

In all OECD countries, the reduction of market-income poverty achieved through taxes and transfers differs significantly across population groups and over time. This is shown in Figure 5.12 (countries situated above the diagonal recorded a decrease in poverty-reduction effects of net transfers). Because of the importance of public pensions, the effect is much greater for people of retirement age, ranging between 80% and 100% in most countries, but lower in Ireland, Finland (where occupational pensions are not classified as public

Figure 5.12. **The effect of net transfers in reducing poverty among different groups**

Percentage reductions of poverty rates, mid-1990s and mid-2000s

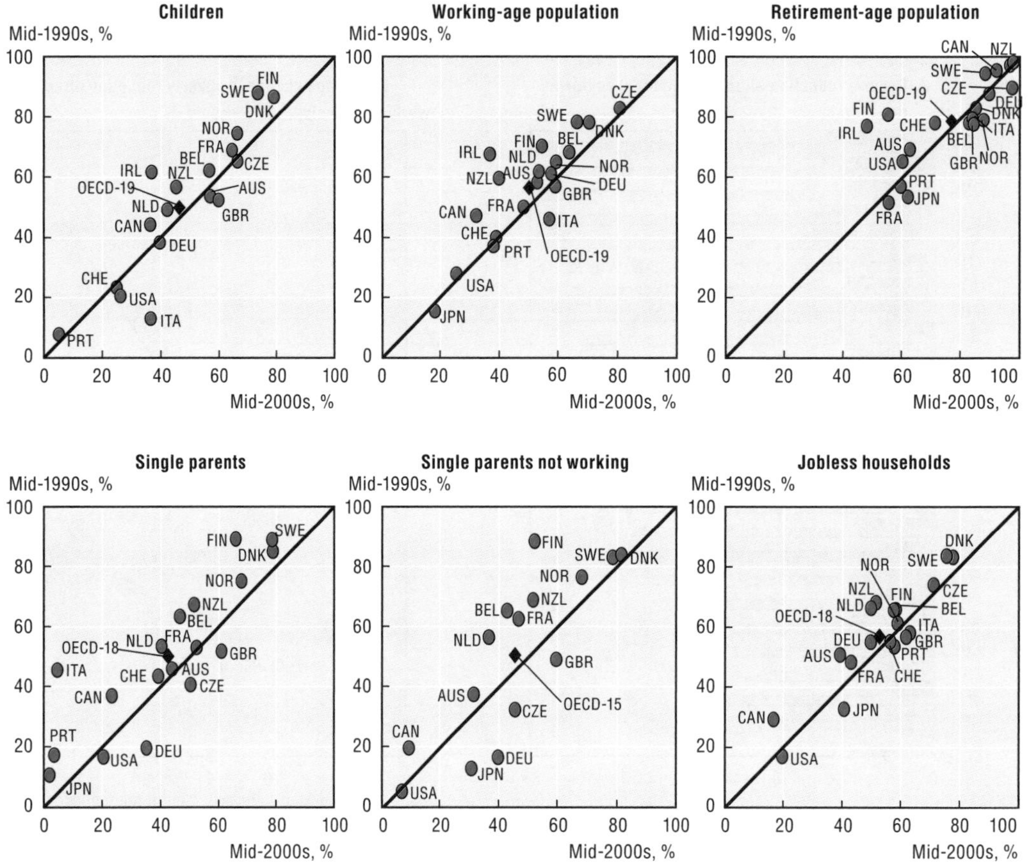

StatLink 🔗 http://dx.doi.org/10.1787/422303818851

Note: The effect of household taxes and government cash transfers in reducing poverty is measured by the percentage difference between poverty rates based on market-income and disposable income, for a threshold set at 50% of median disposable income for the entire population. Data for mid-1990s refer to 2000 for Switzerland and the United Kingdom. Data for mid-2000s refer to 2000 for Belgium, Czech Republic, Ireland and Portugal (where 2005 data, based on EU-SILC, are not comparable with those for earlier years).

Source: Computations from OECD income distribution questionnaire.

transfers), France, Portugal, Australia, Japan and the United States. Changes in the size of this effect over the past decade have been minor, with the exceptions of Ireland and Finland.

The poverty-reducing effect of taxes and transfers is much smaller for people of working age (around two-thirds, on average, of that for elderly people) and, to an even larger extent, for children (around 57% of that of the elderly). For both age groups, the impact of taxes and transfers on reducing poverty has declined over time in most OECD countries, generally with a larger reduction for people of working age than for children.[16] The decline among children was especially large in Ireland (where data are limited to 2000), as well as New Zealand, Finland and Sweden (though from very high levels in the latter two countries), while it increased in Italy and the United Kingdom and, to a lesser extent, Australia and the United States.

Differences across countries are also significant when looking at the experience of other demographic groups, although patterns may be affected by small sample sizes for some countries. For single parents, the effect of net public transfers in reducing poverty is highest in Nordic countries and lowest in Italy, Japan, Portugal and the United States – and it declined in most countries over the past decade, with the main exception of Germany. This large cross-country variation partly reflects differences in the share of lone parents who are working, rather than relying on benefits. The effect of net transfers is reducing poverty among single parents who do not work is in all countries higher than in the case of single parents as a whole, although the extent to which this is true has diminished in a majority of countries during the past decade. For persons in jobless households in general (single parents or others), the effect of net benefits in reducing poverty is lowest in Australia, Canada, France, Japan and the United States, and larger reductions (above 70%) are limited to the Czech Republic, Denmark and Sweden.[17]

These cross-country differences in the poverty-reducing effects of net public transfers partly reflect their overall size, and, as people at the bottom of the income scale typically pay few taxes, mainly the size of cash transfers to households. The poverty-reducing effect also depends on the nature of these programmes and on the characteristics of their recipients. Figure 5.13 plots cash social transfers (both public and mandatory private ones) as a share of GDP, against the (disposable income) poverty rate, based on a threshold set at half of the median, separately for people of working age and retirement age. The left-hand panel suggests a significant negative relation between the two variables, with countries spending more on social transfers towards people of working age also achieving lower poverty rates, although with large differences in poverty outcomes among countries with higher levels of social spending.[18] No similar relation exists for elderly people. While this pattern reflects the earnings-related nature of old-age pensions in most OECD countries, it

Figure 5.13. **Poverty rates and social spending for people of working age and retirement age, mid-2000s**

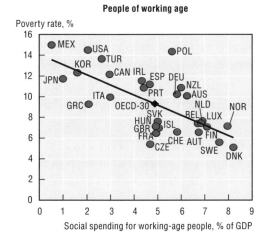

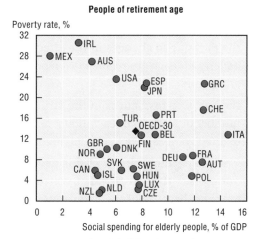

StatLink 🔗 http://dx.doi.org/10.1787/422333665216

Note: Poverty rates based on a threshold set at half of median household disposable income. Social spending includes both public and mandatory private spending in cash (i.e. excluding in-kind services). Social spending for people of working age is defined as the sum of outlays for incapacity, family, unemployment, housing and other (i.e. social assistance) programmes; social spending for people of retirement age is the sum of outlays for old-age and survivors benefits. Social spending is expressed in percentage of GDP at factor costs. Data on poverty rates refer to the mid-2000s for all countries; data for social spending refer to 2003 for all countries except Turkey (1999).

Source: Computations from OECD income distribution questionnaire and *OECD Social Expenditure database* (SOCX).

also suggests that larger inroads into reducing poverty could be achieved by redirecting spending from pension programmes towards programmes targeted to people of working age and their children at the bottom of the income scale.

Accounting for changes in poverty rates since the mid-1990s

Although both taxes and public transfers reduce poverty at a point in time, they also distort decisions of private agents in terms of employment and work efforts. Marginal effective tax rates, which are one cause of these distortions, are typically high at the lower end of the income distribution, and they may contribute both to poverty traps among people relying on benefits and to a reduced work effort by low-paid workers. Reforms implemented by several OECD countries during the second half of the 1990s (generally in the form of earnings top-up or working tax credits for low-paid workers, and of help to persons relying on benefits to move to employment) have aimed at reducing these distortions so as to improve work incentives for individuals with low income.

How have these reforms affected changes in poverty? Efforts to address this question have typically followed two tracks. The first uses individual records to assess what poverty rates would be today if the structure of wages, working hours and government benefits had remained at some base-year level; while this approach does not account for behavioural changes following reforms, it allows tracking the same individual over time.[19] A second approach, which is easier to implement when comparing a large number of countries, relies on aggregate data.[20] This approach is used here to account for changes in relative poverty rates (based on a 50% of median income threshold), separately for people living in households with a head of working age (65 or less) and of retirement age (66 or more). A simple shift-share analysis allows decomposing changes in poverty rates of each household type into three components:

- the part due to changes in market-income poverty for each of several groups within the two household types, while keeping constant both the structure of the population and the effect of taxes and transfers in reducing poverty for each group;

- the part due to changes in the effect of taxes and transfers in reducing market-income poverty for each group, for a given population structure and market-rate poverty for each group; and

- the part due to changes in the structure of the population by both household type and number of workers in each household, for a given market-income poverty rate and level of effectiveness of tax and transfers in reducing poverty in that group.[21]

While decompositions of this type do not reflect the complex links between each pair of variables,[22] they do provide a convenient summary of the role of various factors; at the same time, because of the detailed breakdown used, results may be affected by the small sample sizes of some surveys.

Table 5.4 shows results for changes in poverty rates for persons living in households with a head of working age in the period from the mid-1990s to the mid-2000s for selected OECD countries. In addition to the total change in the poverty rate of all people living in households with a working-age head (shown in the third column), the table shows the results from a decomposition based on all household categories (ten groups overall, in Panel A), and then separately when controlling only for changes in the number of workers in each household (distinguishing between no worker, one and two workers, in Panel B) and in the living arrangement of each household (single and couples, with and without

Table 5.4. **Decomposition of the change in poverty rates among people living in households with a working-age head by selected components**

Point changes

		Total change in poverty rate	Controlling for changes by:								
			A. Work attachment and household type			B. Work attachment only			C. Household type only		
			Due to changes in:								
			Market-income poverty	Taxes and public cash transfers	Change in weights	Market-income poverty	Taxes and public cash transfers	Change in weights	Market-income poverty	Taxes and public cash transfers	Change in weights
Australia	1995-2004	0.4	0.6	0.7	−0.9	0.4	0.9	−0.9	−0.6	0.2	0.7
Canada	1995-2005	2.5	0.7	2.4	−0.7	0.3	2.6	−0.4	0.0	2.1	0.3
Denmark	1995-2005	1.0	−0.2	1.1	0.1	−0.2	1.3	0.0	−0.3	1.1	0.2
Finland	1995-2004	1.8	−1.0	2.2	0.5	−0.9	2.0	0.7	−0.7	2.2	0.3
France	1996-2005	0.0	0.5	−0.3	−0.2	1.0	−0.5	−0.4	0.2	−0.4	0.2
Germany	1995-2004	3.4	0.2	0.6	2.6	0.1	1.6	1.7	1.3	0.7	1.5
Italy	1995-2004	−3.1	2.1	−3.5	−1.7	1.5	−3.7	−0.9	0.1	−3.3	0.1
Japan	1994-2003	0.8	0.2	−0.2	0.8	0.9	−0.4	0.3	0.7	−0.5	0.5
Netherlands	1995-2004	0.7	0.3	0.8	−0.4	0.6	1.0	−0.9	−0.9	1.1	0.6
New Zealand	1995-2003	2.5	1.9	2.4	−1.7	1.5	2.6	−1.6	0.0	2.9	−0.4
Norway	1995-2004	0.9	−0.6	0.6	0.8	−0.5	0.7	0.7	0.1	0.5	0.3
Sweden	1995-2004	1.4	−0.6	2.2	−0.1	−0.8	2.3	0.0	−0.9	2.2	0.1
United Kingdom	1995-2005	−1.6	−1.0	0.0	−0.6	−0.9	−0.2	−0.5	−1.6	−0.1	0.2
United States	1995-2005	0.0	−0.4	0.1	0.2	−0.7	0.0	0.6	0.1	0.0	−0.2
OECD-14		0.8	0.2	0.7	−0.1	0.2	0.7	−0.1	−0.2	0.6	0.3

StatLink 🔗 http://dx.doi.org/10.1787/422458127850

Note: Poverty rates are based on a threshold set at 50% of equivalised household disposable income. The data shown are based on a shift-share analysis applied to the population living in households with a head of working age, broken down by both work attachment and household types (ten groups, in Panel A) as well as by work attachment only (distinguishing between households with no workers, with one adult working, and with two or more adults working, in Panel B) and by household type (distinguishing between singles and couple families, with and without children, in Panel C). Within each panel, the sum of the three components (changes in market-income poverty, changes in the poverty-reducing effect of net public transfers, and changes in weights) is equal to the total change in poverty rate (shown in Column 3). The analysis is limited to countries for which the data allow distinguishing between market- and disposable-income poverty.
Source: Computations from OECD income distribution questionnaire.

children, in Panel C). In the case of Australia, for example, the poverty rate of persons living in households with a head of working age increased by 0.4 point from 1995 to 2004 (from 10% to 10.4%) as a higher market-income poverty for each group and a lower poverty-reducing effect of taxes and transfers raised poverty (by 0.6 and 0.7 point each) while changes in population structure (towards household groups with a lower poverty rate) lowered it (by 0.9 point).

On average, across the 14 countries included in Table 5.4, poverty rates of people living in a household with a head of working age increased by around 1 percentage point over the past ten years, while the rates declined in the United Kingdom and, more significantly, in Italy. The largest part of the increase in poverty rates reflected lower net public transfers to households at the bottom of the income scale (in most countries except France, Italy and Japan).[23] There are greater differences across countries in the extent to which changes in market-income poverty for each group contributed to developments in the poverty headcount, with rises in market-income poverty both on average and in most countries (especially in Italy, New Zealand, Australia and Canada) and declines in the Nordic countries as well as the United Kingdom and the United States. Changes in the structure of the population dampened the rise of the poverty headcount in most countries (shifting towards groups with lower poverty rates), with several exceptions, the most significant being Germany. Panels B and C of the table also suggest that this poverty-reducing effect of changes in population structure mainly reflected changes in work attachment (with a shift from households with no workers towards households with workers), which more than offset the poverty-increasing effect of changes by household type (from couples with children towards singles and single parents). In Germany, where changes in population structure accounted for most of the rise in the poverty rate, these structural effects mainly reflected the higher weights of people in jobless households and of singles.

A similar analysis is applied in Table 5.5 to changes in poverty rates for households with an elderly head. The previous section had shown that trends were diverse across OECD countries, with as many countries recording increases as decreases in poverty rates, a diversity that is also found across the sub-set of 13 countries in Table 5.5.[24] Where increases in poverty rates of retirement-head households occurred, this mainly reflected a smaller effect of net public transfers in reducing poverty, which more than offset the positive effect of changes in household structure (more people living in households with workers and as couples) and a small improvement in the market-income poverty rate of various groups. For those countries that recorded larger changes in poverty headcounts

Table 5.5. **Decomposition of the change in poverty rates among people living in households with a retirement-age head by selected components**

Point changes

		Total change in poverty rate	Controlling for changes by:								
			A. Work attachment and household type			B. Work attachment only			C. Household type only		
			Due to changes in:								
			Market-income poverty	Taxes and public cash transfers	Change in weights	Market-income poverty	Taxes and public cash transfers	Change in weights	Market-income poverty	Taxes and public cash transfers	Change in weights
Australia	1995-2004	5.6	−0.7	6.1	0.2	−0.3	5.3	0.6	−0.3	5.9	0.0
Canada	1995-2005	3.3	0.0	3.4	−0.1	−0.1	3.7	−0.3	−0.1	3.3	0.1
Denmark	1995-2005	−2.2	−0.3	−1.2	−0.6	−0.4	−1.4	−0.4	−0.4	−1.4	−0.4
Finland	1995-2004	5.8	−2.3	8.9	−0.8	−3.4	9.1	0.1	−2.1	8.6	−0.7
Germany	1995-2004	−1.6	−0.3	−0.8	−0.5	−0.5	−1.2	0.1	−0.2	−0.8	−0.5
Italy	1995-2004	−2.1	0.3	−3.5	1.2	0.4	−3.5	1.0	0.9	−3.5	0.5
Japan	1994-2003	−1.1	0.6	−4.8	3.1	1.2	−5.1	2.8	3.7	−5.9	1.1
Netherlands	1995-2004	0.7	0.0	0.7	0.0	0.0	0.7	0.0	0.0	0.7	0.0
New Zealand	1995-2003	2.4	−0.4	2.7	0.1	−0.5	2.7	0.2	0.0	2.4	−0.1
Norway	1995-2004	−7.1	0.0	−7.1	0.0	−0.3	−7.1	0.2	0.0	−7.1	0.0
Sweden	1995-2004	2.7	0.1	2.6	−0.1	0.0	2.7	0.0	0.1	2.6	−0.1
United Kingdom	1995-2005	−1.0	−0.3	−0.8	0.1	−0.6	−1.0	0.6	0.0	−0.8	−0.2
United States	1995-2005	3.2	0.3	3.1	−0.2	0.6	3.0	−0.3	0.1	3.1	0.1
OECD-13		0.7	−0.2	0.7	0.2	−0.3	0.6	0.3	0.1	0.6	0.0

StatLink ᴥᴥᴥ http://dx.doi.org/10.1787/422505006080

Note: Poverty rates are based on a threshold set at 50% of equivalised household disposable income. The data shown are based on a shift-share analysis applied to the population living in households with a head of retirement age, broken down by both work attachment and household types (ten groups, in Panel A) as well as by work attachment only (distinguishing between households with no workers, with one adult working, and with two or more adults working, in Panel B) and by household type (distinguishing between singles and couple families, with and without children, in Panel C). Within each panel, the sum of the three components (changes in market-income poverty, changes in the poverty-reducing effect of taxes and public cash transfers, and changes in weights) is equal to the total change in poverty rate (shown in Column 3). The analysis is limited to countries for which the data allow distinguishing between market- and disposable-income poverty.

Source: Computations from OECD income distribution questionnaire.

GROWING UNEQUAL – ISBN 978-92-64-04418-0 – © OECD 2008

(rises in Australia, Canada, Finland, New Zealand, Sweden and the United States, and declines in Denmark, Germany, Italy, Japan, Norway and the United Kingdom), changes in the poverty-reducing effect of net public transfers played the most significant role.

Conclusion

Cash income in a given year is an imperfect yardstick to assess poverty. While households with net income below a certain threshold may face a greater likelihood of falling into poverty than others, they (or the community where they live) may not perceive themselves as being "poor" in the way the term is commonly used. Further, the difficulties in measuring income are much larger for those at the bottom of the income scale than for people in the central part of the distribution. But, despite these limits, the measures of household income used in this chapter highlight several patterns that are important for assessing the conditions of the poor population and for improving the design of anti-poverty programmes.

- In the mid-2000s, the share of people at risk of poverty in OECD countries was 6%, for a threshold of 40% of median household income, 11% for a threshold of 50% and around 18% for a threshold of 60%. Differences across countries are large, with relative income poverty rates always lowest – whatever the threshold used – in Denmark, Sweden and the Czech Republic, and highest in the United States, Turkey and Mexico. The ranking of countries does not change much based on a measure that combines both the incidence and depth of poverty.

- Poverty rates (for a threshold of half of median income) increased on average by 0.6 point in the decade from the mid-1980s to the mid-1990s, and by another 0.6 point from the mid-1990s to the mid-2000s, with individual countries often experiencing contrasting developments over these two periods. In the most recent decade, poverty rates increased in a majority of OECD countries, while they declined only in Greece, Italy, Mexico and the United Kingdom, by around 1 point or more. Poverty with a threshold "anchored" in time fell, on average, by 40% since the mid-1990s, with larger declines in some countries and rises since 2000 in Germany.

- The risk of poverty varies by individual and household characteristics. The U-shaped relationship between age and poverty has shifted over the past two decades from people above 50 years of age to people below that age. Women have higher poverty risks than men, as more of them live alone in old age or head lone-parent families. The poverty risk of single persons is twice as high as that of the population as a whole, and the risk for single-parent families is three times as high.

- While both living arrangements and the employment status of household members affect the poverty rate of various population groups, work is far more important. Countries where the share of people of working age in paid employment is higher also display lower poverty rates; and the same holds for the levels of employment of mothers and child poverty.

- Work is, however, not the only factor shaping poverty. Across countries, there are large differences in the poverty rates of jobless redistribution dampened the rise in poverty in the decade from the mid-1980s to the mid-1990s, but amplified it in the following one. Countries with higher spending in social programmes targeted to people of working age record lower poverty headcounts, while no such relation is evident for programmes benefitting the elderly.

Notes

1. For example, while 4.6% of Australians have equivalised household disposable income of less than 40% of the median in 2003-04, this proportion rises to 5.3% using a 41% cutoff and to 6.9% using a 43% cutoff.

2. A threshold of 60% of median income is used as a benchmark for at-risk-of-poverty at the EU level, while the (absolute) poverty line used in the United States is closer to 40% of median income. As a mid-point between these two levels, this chapter will mainly focus on a poverty threshold of 50% of median equivalised household disposable income.

3. For example, for a threshold of half of median income, the country with the 6th highest rate – Ireland – has a poverty rate more than twice as high as the country with the 6th lowest rate – France.

4. The cross-country correlation of poverty headcounts based on different thresholds is 0.96 for thresholds set at 50% and 60% of the median as well as those set at 40% and 50% of the median, and 0.90 for thresholds of 40% and 60%.

5. Figures presented refer to the average poverty gap. Estimates for the median poverty gap generally result in lower values – some 23% on average across OECD countries. The correlation coefficient between the two measures is 0.68.

6. This measure is sometimes taken to illustrate the size of the transfer of equivalised income needed to raise all those living below the poverty line to that level. This interpretation neglects, however, behavioural changes due to, for instance, work disincentives.

7. Data for Belgium in 1983 and 1995 are based on fiscal data and are not strictly comparable with those for later years. First, the unit of analysis is that of households filling a tax declaration. Second, the method used to integrate information on households who do not fill a questionnaire differs in the two years. Alternative estimates based on household surveys from the University of Antwerp suggest broad stability of the poverty headcount in the late 1980s and a slight increase in the first half of the 1990s.

8. Changes in poverty headcounts based on a threshold set at 60% of median income (the one used by EU countries) show a cumulative rise (across 24 OECD countries) of 1.7 points (i.e. above the rise based on a 50% threshold), with a stronger rise in the first decade than in the second one.

9. Data on poverty headcounts going back to the mid-1970s are available for seven OECD countries. These data show a decline in the 50% poverty headcount from the mid-1970s to the mid-1980s in Canada, Finland and Greece, stability in the Netherlands, Sweden and the United Kingdom, and small rises in the Unites States (see Figure 5.A2.1 available at *http://dx.doi.org/10.1787/424402577838*).

10. The EU set of social inclusion indicators includes a measure of the at-risk-of-poverty rate "anchored" in year t-3 and uprated by inflation over the following three years.

11. Real income growth will cause a greater reduction of "absolute" poverty rates in countries where the level of *relative* poverty was higher at the beginning of the period (Freeman, 2001). Estimates for additional countries based on two different set of data and therefore not strictly comparable suggest that "absolute" poverty has fallen by some 32-40% in Austria, Belgium and the Czech Republic and by 60% or more in Ireland, Portugal and Spain.

12. The estimates of the elderly poverty rates shown in this report are very sensitive to methodological assumptions. First, the *cash income* definition used here exaggerates poverty rates of the elderly compared to other groups: in Denmark, for example, the inclusion of imputed rents in the income definition lowers the poverty headcount of the elderly from around 10% to around 4%, as compared to a reduction from 5.3% to 4.7% for the entire population. Second, as old-age pensions are often the main (or only) income source of the elderly, their cash income is typically clustered around the prevailing pension rates, leading to high sensitivity of poverty estimates to small changes in the income threshold used: in Australia, for example, the income-poverty rate falls from 26% for a threshold of 50% of median income, to 18% for a threshold of 47%. Third, estimates are very sensitive to the equivalence scale used: in Australia, the elderly poverty rate at 50% of median income falls from 26% based on the 0.5 equivalence scale used in this report, to 17% based on the "modified OECD equivalence scale" (where the first adult has a weight of 1.0, the second and subsequent adults a weight of 0.5, and dependent children a weight of 0.3, which is closely approximated by an equivalence scale of 0.6) conventionally used by the Australian Bureau of Statistics.

13. In some countries, however, the opposite pattern prevails. In particular, the poverty rate of children and/or young adults fell during the most recent decade in Australia, Spain and the United States while that of elderly people increased (see Table 5.A2.2 available at *http://dx.doi.org/10.1787/424402577838*).

14. These estimates are based on a threshold of 50% of median income in the early 2000s, uprated for inflation to 2005.

15. OECD measures of market-income poverty refer to the share of people with market income below a given threshold of household *disposable* income. Because of this definition, the difference between the poverty rates based on market and disposable income will reflect both the absolute size of household taxes and public cash transfers, and the extent to which these are targeted to the poor (see chapter 4).

16. Reforms implemented in this period in several OECD countries seem to have sheltered children (and their families) from the decline in the poverty-reducing effect of net benefits that affected other families. This effect was felt fully in Australia, Germany, the Czech Republic and the United States and partially in most other countries. Conversely, there has been a trend for net transfers to reduce poverty less among children than for people of working age in Italy, Japan, Norway, Denmark and Sweden, as well as Belgium and Portugal (where time series data are limited to 2000).

17. In most OECD countries, benefits of last resorts paid to people of working age in 2005 were lower than the threshold of half of median income (as defined in endnote 14), although this varied depending on whether additional housing benefits were available as well as on specific family arrangements. In the case of a married couple with two children, the net income of social assistance clients was above the threshold of half of median income only in Australia and Norway under the assumption of no housing costs and benefits; when including additional benefits conditional on rental expenditures, the list of OECD countries where the net income of social assistance clients was above that threshold also included Austria, Denmark, Finland, Germany, Ireland, Sweden and the United Kingdom (OECD, 2007).

18. For example, the Czech Republic has the same poverty rate as Sweden with a level of social spending that is 40% lower, while Poland's poverty rate is twice as high as Hungary's with the same spending level.

19. Based on this approach, Dickens and Ellwood (2001) argue that demographic conditions (*e.g.* a greater incidence of single-parent households), the earnings structure (*e.g.* wider earnings distributions) and work efforts (*i.e.* the combined effect of changes in activity rates and hours worked) account for comparable shares of the increase in relative poverty in the United Kingdom from 1979 to 1999, while greater generosity in government benefits contributed to reducing poverty rates over the same period. In the United States, the increase in relative poverty over the same period mainly reflected demographic changes and, to a lesser extent, changes in the earnings structure; greater work efforts contributed to reducing poverty, while changes in government benefits did not exert a significant influence in either direction.

20. Most often, studies using aggregate data regress poverty rates against a range of possible determinants, and use results to compare situations at two points in time. However, results from this type of analysis have typically been found to be unstable and sensitive to the specification used.

21. In this exercise, the aggregate poverty rate, at the level of disposable income, is defined as the weighted sum of group-specific poverty rates, with these rates expressed as the product of market-income poverty and of a coefficient indicating the effect of taxes and transfers in reducing market-income poverty.
$$PR_t = \Sigma \, PR^i_t * \alpha^i_t = \Sigma \, [PR(MI)^i_t * (1 - \beta)^i_t] * \alpha^i_t$$
where PR is the (disposable income) poverty rate of all people living in household with a head of working age at times t, PR^i_t is the (disposable income) poverty rate of the different groups i within all households with a head of working age; $PR(MI)^i_t$ is the poverty rate at times t at the level of market income, for each group; $(1 - \beta)^i_t$ is the poverty-reducing effect of taxes and transfers for each group; and α^i_t is the population share of each group. When analysing changes over time in the poverty headcount, changes in one variable are multiplied by the average value (between two points in time) of the other two variables (to avoid explicit consideration of the interaction between each pair of variables).

22. Changes in benefit level, for example, may encourage previously inactive individuals to take up jobs, leading to positive effects (*i.e.* a reduction in poverty) for both household structure (decline in workless households) and market-income poverty (higher earnings as former benefit recipients enter employment).

23. It should be noted that a smaller poverty-reducing effect of net public transfers may reflect a smaller increase in real benefits than in median income, and/or lower benefit take-up, rather than an absolute reduction in the real value of benefits.

24. France is excluded from the analysis because of the small number of observations in some of the household categories considered here.

References

Dickens, R. and D. Ellwood (2001), "Whither Poverty in Great Britain and the United States? The Determinants of Changing Poverty and Whether Work Will Work", NBER Working Paper, No. W8253, Cambridge, Massachusetts.

Förster, M.F. (1994), "Measurement of Low Incomes and Poverty in a Perspective of International Comparisons", OECD Labour Market and Social Policy Occasional Paper, No. 14, OECD, Paris, available at *www.oecd.org/dataoecd/45/58/1895548.pdf*.

Förster, M.F. and M. Mira d'Ercole (2005), "Income Distribution and Poverty in OECD Countries in the Second Half of the 1990s", OECD Social, Employment and Migration Working Paper, No. 22, OECD, Paris, available at *www.oecd.org/dataoecd/48/9/34483698.pdf*.

Freeman, R.B. (2001), "The Rising Tide Lifts…?", National Bureau of Economic Research Working Paper, No. 8155, March, Cambridge, Massachusetts.

OECD (2007), *Benefits and Wages – OECD Indicators*, OECD, Paris.

Paugman, S. and M. Selz (2005), "La perception de la pauvreté en Europe depuis le milieu des années 1970", *Économie et Statistique*, No. 383-385, Paris.

ANNEX 5.A1

Low-income Thresholds Used in the Analysis

Table 5.A1.1 shows the values of poverty thresholds used in this chapter. Thresholds are expressed as levels of annual income for various family types, in both national currencies (left-hand panel) and in US dollars – based on purchasing power parities for "actual" consumption (i.e. the costs of a common basket of consumer goods that are either purchased on the market or provided for free or at subsidised prices by governments), right-hand panel. For example, a couple with two children will be considered as being at risk of poverty, based on a threshold of half of median income, when their annual income is below USD 23 000 in Australia and below USD 27 000 in the United States. These estimates do not take into account the under-reporting of income at the bottom of the income scale. Also, the PPP rates used may not be fully representative of the consumption patterns of the poor across countries. The table highlights large differences between income benchmarks across countries. For a 40% threshold, a couple with two children in the United States have an income that is six times higher than a similar couple in Mexico, but 25% lower than in Luxembourg, and similar to the Netherlands, Norway and Switzerland. For a single person, the poverty threshold at 50% median income represents between 30% and 50% of the national average net wage (take-home pay) in most countries, but this share is significantly lower in Turkey and higher in the United States.

Table 5.A1.1. **Low-income thresholds used in the analysis**
2005 values in USD, at PPP rates for actual consumption

		In national currency						USD at PPP rates for actual consumption					
		50% of median				40% of median	60% of median	50% of median				40% of median	60% of median
	Currency unit	Single person (as % of take-home pay)		Childless couple	Couple with one child	Couple with two children	Couple with two children	Couple with two children	Single person	Childless couple	Couple with one child	Couple with two children	Couple with two children	Couple with two children
Australia	AUD	14 770	38	20 888	25 582	29 540	23 632	35 448	11 509	16 276	19 933	23 017	18 414	27 621
Austria	EUR	9 964	42	14 091	17 258	19 927	15 942	23 913	12 292	17 383	21 290	24 584	19 667	29 500
Belgium	EUR	9 159	43	12 953	15 864	18 318	14 654	21 981	11 163	15 786	19 334	22 325	17 860	26 790
Canada	CAD	15 049	50	21 283	26 066	30 098	24 078	36 118	12 671	17 919	21 946	25 341	20 273	30 410
Czech Rep.	CZK	76 733	46	108 516	132 905	153 465	122 772	184 158	6 176	8 734	10 696	12 351	9 881	14 821
Denmark	DKK	94 376	49	133 467	163 463	188 751	151 001	226 501	11 465	16 213	19 857	22 929	18 343	27 515
Finland	EUR	10 060	45	14 227	17 425	20 121	16 097	24 145	10 505	14 856	18 195	21 010	16 808	25 212
France	EUR	8 691	40	12 291	15 053	17 382	13 905	20 858	10 330	14 608	17 892	20 659	16 528	24 791
Germany	EUR	9 109	38	12 882	15 777	18 218	14 574	21 861	11 010	15 571	19 070	22 020	17 616	26 424
Greece	EUR	5 657	36	8 001	9 799	11 315	9 052	13 578	8 639	12 217	14 963	17 278	13 822	20 734
Hungary	HUF	544 482	45	770 014	943 071	1 088 964	871 171	1 306 757	4 887	6 912	8 465	9 775	7 820	11 730
Iceland	ISK (000s)	1 045	47	1 478	1 810	2 090	1 672	2 508	11 307	15 991	19 584	22 614	18 091	27 137
Ireland	EUR	10 775	44	15 239	18 664	21 551	17 241	25 861	11 204	15 845	19 406	22 409	17 927	26 890
Italy	EUR	7 004	42	9 905	12 131	14 008	11 206	16 809	8 394	11 871	14 539	16 788	13 430	20 146
Japan	JPN (00s)	14 975	37	21 178	25 937	29 950	23 960	35 940	11 394	16 114	19 735	22 788	18 231	27 346
Korea	KRW (000s)	7 818	30	11 056	13 541	15 636	12 509	18 763	9 707	13 728	16 813	19 414	15 531	23 297
Luxembourg	EUR	16 171	53	22 870	28 010	32 343	25 874	38 812	18 131	25 641	31 404	36 262	29 010	43 515
Mexico	MXN	15 675	..	22 167	27 149	31 349	25 079	37 619	2 307	3 263	3 996	4 615	3 692	5 538
Netherlands	EUR	11 484	44	16 241	19 891	22 968	18 374	27 562	14 017	19 823	24 278	28 034	22 427	33 640
New Zealand	NZD	13 040	41	18 442	22 587	26 081	20 865	31 297	9 633	13 623	16 684	19 265	15 412	23 118
Norway	NOK	118 294	44	167 293	204 891	236 587	189 270	283 905	13 312	18 825	23 056	26 623	21 299	31 948
Poland	PLN	6 924	36	9 793	11 994	13 849	11 079	16 619	4 056	5 736	7 025	8 111	6 489	9 734
Portugal	EUR	4 197	40	5 936	7 270	8 394	6 715	10 073	6 139	8 683	10 634	12 279	9 823	14 735
Slovak Rep.	SKK	67 213	40	95 053	116 416	134 426	107 541	161 311	4 410	6 236	7 638	8 820	7 056	10 584
Spain	EUR	6 345	39	8 973	10 989	12 690	10 152	15 227	8 990	12 713	15 571	17 979	14 384	21 575
Sweden	SEK	89 832	41	127 042	155 594	179 665	143 732	215 598	10 358	14 648	17 940	20 716	16 573	24 859
Switzerland	CHF	23 141	43	32 727	40 082	46 283	37 026	55 539	13 771	19 475	23 851	27 541	22 033	33 049
Turkey	TRY (000 000s)	2 067	19	2 924	3 581	4 135	3 308	4 962	2 532	3 581	4 386	5 065	4 052	6 078
United Kingdom	GBP	7 038	33	9 953	12 190	14 075	11 260	16 890	12 326	17 432	21 350	24 652	19 722	29 583
United States	USD	13 495	57	19 085	23 374	26 990	21 592	32 388	13 495	19 085	23 374	26 990	21 592	32 388

StatLink ⇒ http://dx.doi.org/10.1787/422525733036

Note: When the nominal income values of different countries, as available in the OECD income distribution questionnaire, refer to a year different from 2005, these values are first adjusted to a 2005 basis by the change in consumer price inflation, and then converted to USD with the PPP rate for actual consumption in 2005.
Source: Calculations based on the OECD questionnaire on distribution of household incomes.

GROWING UNEQUAL – ISBN 978-92-64-04418-0 – © OECD 2008

ANNEX 5.A2

Alternative Estimates of Main Poverty Indicators

Table 5.A2.1 shows alternative estimates of main poverty indicators from international sources (Eurostat and Luxembourg Income Study): poverty rates for the entire population at 50% and 60% of median income thresholds and child poverty rates at the 50% median income threshold, respectively. Differences in methodology are minor. The concept of disposable income is quasi-identical between the three data sources.* The equivalence scale used by Eurostat differs only slightly from that used by the OECD and LIS, giving a somewhat higher weight to additional household members and distinguishing between adults and children. For most countries, differences in poverty rates between the OECD and the alternative sources do not exceed 1 percentage point. There are, however, two exceptions (Germany and the United Kingdom), especially for estimates of child poverty.

---

* The Eurostat definition, for instance, defines inter-household transfers as transfers received minus transfers paid, while in the OECD questionnaire definition these are defined as transfers received only. Nevertheless, this will have no impact on estimates of overall poverty.

Table 5.A2.1. **Comparisons of main estimates between the OECD questionnaire and alternative data sources, latest available year**

	Reference years (incomes)			Poverty rate 50% median			Poverty rates 60% median			Child poverty rate 50% median		
	OECD question-naire	Eurostat	LIS	OECD question-naire	Eurostat	LIS	OECD question naire	Eurostat	LIS	OECD question-naire	Eurostat	LIS
Australia	2004	..	2003	12	..	12	20	..	20	12	..	14
Austria	2004	2004	2000	7	6	8	13	12	13	6	6	8
Belgium	2004	2004	2000	9	8	8	16	15	16	10	9	7
Canada	2005	..	2000	12	..	12	19	..	19	15	..	16
Czech Republic	2004	2004	..	6	5	..	11	10	..	10	9	..
Denmark	2004	2004	2004	5	6	6	12	12	13	3	5	4
Finland	2004	2004	2004	7	5	7	15	12	14	4	3	4
France	2004	2004	2000	7	6	7	14	13	14	8	6	8
Germany	2004	2004	2000	11	7	8	17	12	13	16	6	9
Greece	2004	2004	2000	13	13	14	20	20	21	13	13	13
Hungary	2005	2004	1999	7	7	6	12	13	13	9	11	8
Iceland	2004	2004	..	7	5		12	10	..	8	6	..
Ireland	2004	2004	2000	15	11	16	23	20	22	16	15	16
Italy	2004	2004	2000	11	12	13	20	19	20	16	16	17
Japan	2000	..	..	15	..	..	21	..	..	14	..	..
Korea	2005	..	..	15	..	..	21	..	..	10	..	..
Luxembourg	2004	2004	2000	8	7	6	13	13	12	12	10	9
Mexico	2004	..	2002	18	..	20	25	..	27	22	..	25
Netherlands	2004	2004	2000	8	6	5	14	11	11	12	9	6
New Zealand	2003	..	..	11	..	..	23	..	..	15	..	..
Norway	2004	2004	2000	7	7	6	12	11	12	5	5	3
Poland	2004	2004	1999	15	15	13	21	21	19	22	22	18
Portugal	2004	2004	..	13	13	..	21	19	..	17	17	..
Slovak Rep.	2004	2004	..	8	8	..	14	13	..	11	12	..
Spain	2004	2004	2000	14	13	14	21	20	21	17	16	15
Sweden	2004	2004	2000	5	5	7	11	9	12	4	5	4
Switzerland	2001	..	2002	7	..	8	12	..	14	8	..	7
Turkey	2004	2002	..	18	18	..	24	26	..	25	..	..
United Kingdom	2005	2004	1999	8	12	12	16	19	21	10	13	17
United States	2005	..	2005	17	..	17	24	..	24	21	..	21

StatLink ⧉ http://dx.doi.org/10.1787/422525733036

Note: Equivalence scale used is the square root of household size for the OECD questionnaire and LIS and the modified OECD scale for Eurostat (which gives a weight of 1 to the first person, 0.5 for each additional adult and 0.3 for each additional child). Children are defined as persons below age 18 in all three data sources.

Source: Calculations based on the OECD questionnaire on distribution of household incomes. Eurostat (as at 6 February 2008); LIS key figures (as of 31 December 2007).

ISBN 978-92-64-04418-0
Growing Unequal?
© OECD 2008

PART III

Chapter 6

Does Income Poverty Last Over Time? Evidence from Longitudinal Data*

Less than one third of people with income of less than half of median income are persistently in that condition over a three-year period, but only a small share of them move into higher strata of the distribution. Entries into poverty mainly reflect family- and job-related events, but the share of unidentified events is also important. Countries with higher poverty headcounts based on static income measures also record higher rates of persistent and recurrent poverty.

* This chapter has been prepared by Anna Cristina D'Addio, OECD Social Policy Division. The author wishes to thank Atsuhiro Yamada and Kayoko Ishii for having provided estimates for Japan based on a standard format. Also greatly appreciated was co-operation and feedback from Mary Gartley, at Statistics Canada; John Iceland and Chaowen Chan, at the University of Maryland; Dan Feenberg, at the NBER; Dean Lillard, at Cornell University; and Mark Pearson and Marco Mira d'Ercole, at the OECD Social Policy Division.

Introduction

Many people experience temporary spells of low income at some point in their lives – when they are students, when temporarily absent from work because of illness or childbirth, or when moving from job to job. But these periods of low income do not last long. As a result, a significant share of people with low income at a given point in time will move up the income distribution fairly quickly. Conversely, for a smaller group of people, the experience of poverty extends over prolonged periods, with more significant consequences for the economic well-being of the people affected and their families.

This chapter presents new cross-country evidence about the persistence of low income based on micro-data from surveys that follow the same individuals and households over time. The chapter first describes the characteristics of the surveys and the concepts used to compute the different measures of poverty dynamics. It then discusses the size of temporary and persistent poverty, and the transition into and out of it. Finally, it presents evidence about some of the reasons why people fall into poverty and about income mobility and variability.

Longitudinal data and dynamic poverty measures

Surveys that follow the *same* individual and/or household over a number of periods (*i.e.* panel data) are used in this chapter. This type of data allows examination of how individuals' income changes over time, the extent to which they experience temporary or persistent spells of poverty, and how frequently they move up and down the income distribution.

Panel data, however, also have limits. While some of these limits apply to all sample surveys (*e.g.* non-response, measurement errors), others are specific to panel data.[1] Beyond these survey features, the most important limits from the perspective of the analysis conducted here are the short number of years typically covered by these longitudinal datasets, and the small number of countries included in previous comparative analysis on the subject. As panel data extending over several years are available only for a few countries, the choice made in this chapter is to cover the largest possible number of OECD countries, although at the price of limiting the analysis to a short number of spells. This chapter relies on data spanning a period of three years – as compared to the longer periods used in OECD (2001) and Burniaux *et al.* (2006) – as this shorter period allows the analysis to cover 17 OECD countries.[2]

As in Chapter 5, estimates of poverty are based on income thresholds that capture the standard of living that is most typical in a given society at a particular time (Atkinson, 1983). While this approach is conventionally used in most comparative studies, its limits should be kept in mind – for example, poverty rates based on relative income will fall even when the incomes of the poor are declining, as long as the incomes of the non-poor are falling faster. This chapter uses different thresholds – 40%, 50% and 60% of median income – to highlight the sensitivity of results with respect to the threshold used. As in the rest of this report, the income concept used is that of annual household disposable income, *i.e.* the cash income available to the household, including public transfers and after deducting income taxes and social security contributions paid by the households.[3] To account for differences in family size, household income is "equivalised" by means of the squared root equivalence scale. This equivalised income is attributed to each household member and is used to determine the poverty status of each person in each year.

This approach allows one to distinguish between four (mutually exclusive) groups of people:

- those who are never poor over the three-year time period ("never poor");
- those with an equivalised income below the poverty threshold in only one of the three years considered ("temporary poor");
- those with an equivalised income below the poverty threshold in only two of the three years considered ("recurrent poor"); and
- those with an equivalised income below the poverty threshold over the entire period considered ("persistent poor").

These are the basic categories used in this chapter and in previous OECD reports on poverty dynamics (OECD, 1998, 2001).[4]

Distinguishing between temporary and persistent spells of poverty

Poverty measures based on annual income provide only a partial perspective on the experience of those at the bottom of the income scale, especially in a context characterised by rapid changes in the labour market and high job turnover. To highlight the limits of static income data, Figure 6.1 shows the percentage of the population falling into different categories of poverty, based on a threshold set at 50% of median income. Similar data based on thresholds of 40 and 60% can be found in the annex.[5]

Figure 6.1 highlights a number of patterns:

- First, the "average" poverty headcounts based on these longitudinal dataset were fairly similar to those based on the cross-sectional data used in Chapter 5 of this report.[6] For a threshold set at half of median income, the "average" poverty rate prevailing over the three years was around 10% for the 17 countries included in Figure 6.1, ranging between 6% or less in the Netherlands, Denmark and Germany and 14% or more in Australia, Ireland, the United States and Greece.[7]

- Second, across the 17 countries considered, around 17% had an income below the poverty threshold in at least one of the three years, implying that 83% of the population was never poor in any of the three years considered. The share of people who were poor at least once over the three years ranged from around 10% in Luxemburg and the Netherlands to 25% in Australia.

- Third, 5% of the population was, on average, poor in all three years, and a further 4% in only two of the three years considered. Rates of persistent poverty varied from 7% or more in Australia, Greece, Ireland, Portugal and the United States, to less than 2% in Denmark and the Netherlands.

Setting higher income thresholds has two results: a higher proportion of all respondents are counted as poor in each year, and a higher share of people are calculated to experience recurrent and, especially, persistent poverty among all those who are poor at least once (see Table 6.A1.1 available at *http://dx.doi.org/10.1787/424402577838*). On average,

Figure 6.1. **Share of people experiencing temporary, recurrent and persistent poverty**

Threshold set at 50% of median income, experience over three consecutive years, in percentage

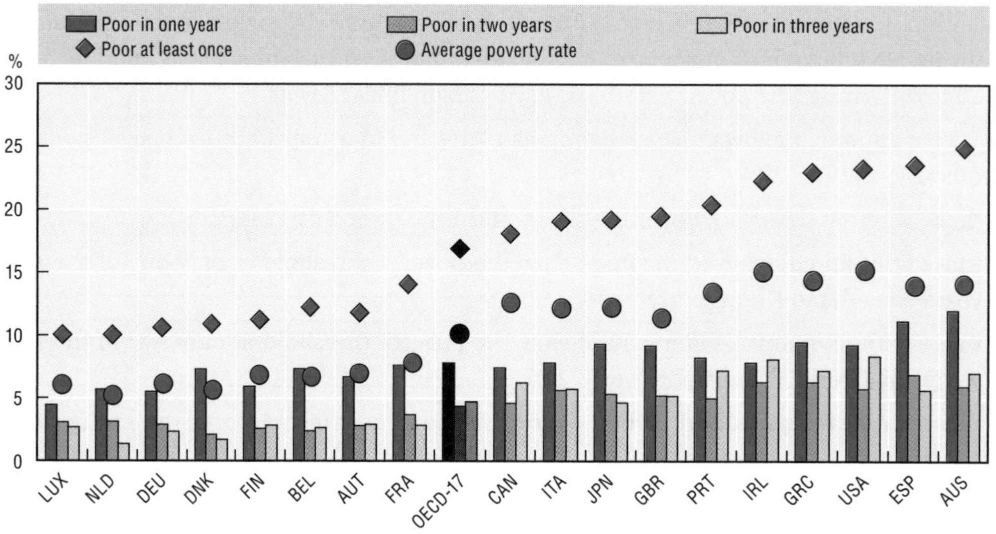

StatLink ᵐˢᵖ http://dx.doi.org/10.1787/422528522436

Note: Countries are ranked from left to right in increasing order of the share of people who have been "poor at least once" over the three years considered. OECD-17 is the simple average of the countries shown except Japan, for which estimates are based on an income definition (household income before taxes and after public transfers) that differ from that used for other countries (household disposable income, *i.e.* after taxes and public transfers).

Source: Data refer to 1999-2001 for European countries, based on the European Community Household Panel (ECHP); to 2002-2004 for Canada, based on data from the Cross National Equivalent File of the Survey of Labour and Income Dynamics (SLID); and to 2002-2004 for Australia, based on data from the Cross National Equivalent File of the survey Household Income and Labour Dynamics in Australia (HILDA). For the United States, data refer to 2001-2003 based on data from the Survey of Income and Program Participation (SIPP). For Japan, data refer to 2005-2007 and are based on the Keio Household Panel Survey.

the share of the persistent poor among all those who are poor at least once rises from 17%, for a threshold set at 40% of median income, to 28% for a threshold of 50%, and to 36% for a threshold of 60%. A similar but weaker pattern holds for the recurrent poor, whose share rises from 23% for the lower threshold to 26% for the two higher poverty lines.

Overall, cross-country differences in the prevalence of persistent and recurrent poverty are larger than those highlighted by the simple poverty headcount, although the different measures provide a consistent picture. Indeed, Figure 6.1 highlights a positive relation (statistically significant at the level of 0.01%) between the simple poverty headcount (averaged over the three years), on one side, and the rates of persistent and recurrent poverty, on the other.

The composition of persistent poverty

This section describes the composition of the poor by looking at the poverty risk, *i.e.* the ratio between the poverty rate for a specific group and that for the entire population (OECD, 2001). Groups are defined in terms of characteristics at the beginning of the period.

While the age profile of those who are poor at least once (Panel A of Figure 6.3) – averaged across the 17 countries included in the analysis – mirrors that described in Chapter 5, there are distinctive patterns for other definitions of poverty.[8]

- Individuals aged 65 and over experience not just a higher risk of being poor in each year but, especially, of persistent low income. Across the 17 countries considered, this risk

Figure 6.2. **Correlation between different indicators of poverty**

Threshold set at 50% of median income, experience over three consecutive years, in percentage

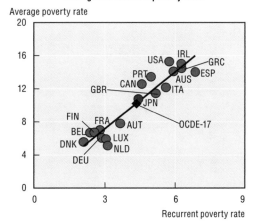

StatLink http://dx.doi.org/10.1787/422531127768

Note: OECD-17 is the simple average of the countries shown except Japan (shown as a darker dot), for which estimates are based on an income definition (household income before taxes and after public transfers) that differ from that used for other countries (equivalised household disposable income).

Source: Detailed sources are provided in Figure 6.1.

Figure 6.3. **Risks of falling into different types of poverty by age and household type, OECD average**

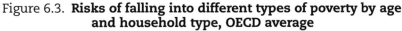

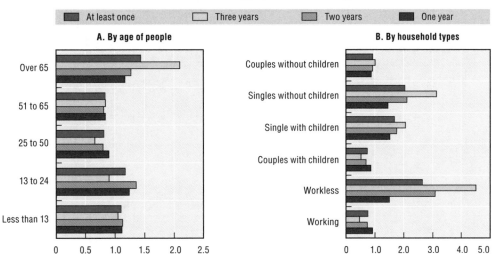

StatLink http://dx.doi.org/10.1787/422555054624

Note: OECD-17 is the simple average of the countries shown in Figure 6.1 except Japan, for which estimates are based on an income definition (household income before taxes and after public transfers) that differ from that used for other countries (household disposable income).

Source: Detailed sources are provided in Figure 6.1.

rises from 1.2 for temporary poverty (i.e. 20% above the poverty rate for the entire population) to 2.1 for persistent poverty – with much higher levels for the latter (above 3) in Australia, Austria and Denmark but a lower risk (at 1.0 or lower) in Canada, the Netherlands, Italy and Japan (Table 6.1, Panel E).

- At the other end of the age spectrum, children also experience a greater risk of poverty compared to the entire population, but this risk is evenly spread across the various poverty spells. In Denmark, virtually no child lives in persistent poverty over a three-year

Table 6.1. **Risks of falling into different types of poverty by age of the individual across OECD countries**

Poverty risk relative to the entire population, based on a threshold set at 50% of the median

	A. Less than 13 Poor in:				B. 13-24 Poor in:				C. 25-50 Poor in:				D. 51-64 Poor in:				E. 65 and over Poor in:			
	One year	Two years	Three years	At least once	One year	Two years	Three years	At least once	One year	Two years	Three years	At least once	One year	Two years	Three years	At least once	One year	Two years	Three years	At least once
Australia	1.1	1.0	0.7	1.0	1.0	1.1	0.5	0.9	0.8	0.6	0.4	0.7	0.9	1.0	1.2	1.0	1.5	2.1	3.6	2.2
Austria	1.2	0.9	0.5	1.0	0.9	1.0	0.4	0.8	0.9	0.7	0.5	0.8	1.0	0.9	0.8	0.9	1.2	2.1	3.6	2.0
Belgium	1.0	0.5	1.1	0.9	0.9	0.7	0.2	0.7	0.8	0.8	0.6	0.8	0.9	1.0	0.8	0.9	1.7	2.2	2.8	2.0
Canada	1.8	1.0	1.0	1.2	1.4	1.3	1.0	1.3	0.9	0.9	0.9	0.9	0.9	1.0	1.1	1.0	0.9	0.6	0.8	0.8
Denmark	0.5	0.1	0.0	0.3	1.4	2.9	1.2	1.6	0.7	0.5	0.3	0.6	0.6	0.5	0.7	0.6	2.5	2.5	4.2	2.8
Finland	0.7	0.3	0.1	0.5	2.1	2.5	1.1	2.0	0.9	0.8	0.6	0.8	0.7	0.6	1.2	0.8	0.9	1.2	2.6	1.4
France	1.1	1.2	1.0	1.1	1.4	1.3	1.0	1.3	0.9	0.8	0.6	0.8	0.8	0.8	0.9	0.8	1.0	1.3	2.1	1.3
Germany	0.9	1.4	0.7	1.0	1.3	1.1	1.0	1.2	0.9	1.0	0.6	0.8	1.1	1.0	1.2	1.1	1.0	0.8	1.9	1.1
Greece	1.0	1.2	0.4	0.9	1.1	1.0	0.7	0.9	0.9	0.8	0.5	0.7	1.1	1.0	1.0	1.1	1.0	1.4	2.5	1.6
Ireland	1.1	1.4	1.1	1.2	0.9	0.8	0.5	0.7	0.9	0.8	0.7	0.8	0.7	0.9	0.9	0.8	1.6	1.2	2.9	2.0
Italy	1.0	1.5	1.6	1.3	1.1	1.1	1.3	1.1	1.0	1.0	0.8	1.0	0.9	0.9	0.8	0.9	1.0	0.7	1.0	0.9
Luxembourg	1.5	1.2	1.5	1.4	1.7	1.8	1.1	1.6	1.0	0.9	1.0	1.0	0.5	0.8	0.6	0.6	0.4	0.5	0.9	0.5
Netherlands	1.0	1.8	2.0	1.4	1.4	1.9	1.8	1.6	0.9	0.9	0.9	0.9	0.9	0.3	0.2	0.6	1.1	0.1	0.1	0.6
Portugal	1.1	1.2	1.4	1.3	1.0	1.0	0.6	0.8	0.9	0.8	0.7	0.8	0.9	0.9	0.7	0.8	1.2	1.6	2.2	1.7
Spain	1.2	1.6	1.5	1.4	1.0	1.1	1.0	1.0	0.9	0.9	0.7	0.9	1.0	0.6	1.0	0.9	0.9	1.0	1.4	1.1
United Kingdom	1.4	1.4	1.8	1.5	1.4	1.3	1.0	1.3	0.8	0.7	0.7	0.8	0.6	0.6	0.5	0.6	1.0	1.3	1.3	1.2
United States	1.2	1.3	1.5	1.3	1.0	1.2	1.0	1.1	0.9	0.9	0.7	0.8	0.8	0.8	0.7	0.8	1.0	1.0	1.7	1.2
OECD-17	*1.1*	*1.1*	*1.0*	*1.1*	*1.2*	*1.4*	*0.9*	*1.2*	*0.9*	*0.8*	*0.7*	*0.8*	*0.8*	*0.8*	*0.8*	*0.8*	*1.2*	*1.3*	*2.1*	*1.4*
Memorandum items:																				
Japan	0.9	0.8	1.6	1.1	1.0	1.5	1.1	1.2	0.9	0.8	0.8	0.9	1.2	1.0	0.9	1.0	1.1	1.3	1.0	1.1
United States (PSID)	1.0	1.4	1.7	1.3	1.2	1.5	1.2	1.3	1.0	0.8	0.8	0.9	0.8	0.6	0.5	0.7	1.1	0.9	1.1	1.0

StatLink http://dx.doi.org/10.1787/422608278140

Note: The table reports poverty risk for specific age categories. The poverty risk is computed as the ratio between the poverty rate for a specific category and the poverty rate of the whole population. A value of the poverty risk higher than 1 means that the specific group has a higher risk of being in a given poverty category than that for the whole population, a value of the risk equal to one implies an equal risk, and a value less than one implies a lower risk. For example, an average value of 2.1 for people aged 65+ in the always poor group (Panel E, OECD-17 in the three years column), means that those individuals have just over twice the risk of being found in persistent poverty as the entire population. Estimates for the United States are based on SIPP (those based on PSID are shown for information only).
Source: Detailed sources are provided in Figure 6.1.

GROWING UNEQUAL – ISBN 978-92-64-04418-0 – © OECD 2008

period, while in Italy, Netherlands, the United Kingdom, the United States and Japan children face a high risk of persistent poverty (Table 6.1, Panel A).

- Youths aged 13 to 24 also have a higher probability of experiencing temporary or recurrent poverty compared to the entire population, but a lower one when looking at persistent poverty, with the exception of only Italy, the Netherlands and Japan.

- Adults aged 25 to 50 face a poverty risk below the population average for all poverty categories, and this risk falls when moving from temporary to persistent poverty.

- Older adults (aged 51 to 64) have generally lower probability of falling into poverty than the entire population, but there are exceptions – and their number rises when moving from temporary (Germany, Greece and Japan) to persistent poverty (Australia, Canada, Ireland and, especially, Finland and Germany).

The composition of the various poverty categories also varies with household characteristics (Figure 6.3, Panel B):

- Single-adult households (with and without kids) are more exposed to poverty risks than people living in couples, especially when considering the risk of having long periods with low income. On average, single adults with children face a risk of persistent poverty that is twice as high as for the whole population, particularly in Japan (where lone parents are rare), the Netherlands and Denmark (Table 6.2). The probability of persistent poverty for singles without children is even higher, being on average three times larger than for the entire population, and much more in Denmark, Finland, Ireland and Portugal.

- Couples with children face a risk of persistent poverty that is generally well below the population average with the singular exception of Italy. Patterns are more diverse for couples without children, with a higher risk than for the population average in Australia, Austria, Belgium, France, Greece, Portugal and Spain.

- A large part of these differences in the risk of chronic poverty reflects the employment status of household members. On average, people belonging to workless households have a risk of persistent poverty that is almost five times higher than that of the whole population (Figure 6.3, Panel B) and even higher in Canada, Denmark and the Netherlands (right-hand panel of Table 6.2). These cross-country differences in the risk of persistent poverty among jobless households reflect both differences in the economic conditions of these households and in the extent to which joblessness persists over time.

Finally, the risk of persistent poverty also varies by gender. Women always face a higher probability of chronic poverty than men, with a disadvantage that is especially large in Austria, Belgium, Denmark and Finland (Table 6.3). This higher risk of persistent poverty mainly reflects the situation of single women, both with and without children. Women living alone (mainly elderly women) face a risk of persistent poverty that is 2.7 times that for the entire population, and much higher in Austria, Denmark, Finland and the Netherlands. Single mothers with children have a higher probability of being poor at least once than the entire population, and this disadvantage rises when moving from transitory to recurrent and persistent poverty, especially in the Netherlands and Denmark.[9]

Poverty entries, exits and occurrences

One of the main advantages of using longitudinal data is that this allows analysis of the transitions into and out of poverty and the extent of poverty turnover. Figure 6.4 shows entry and exit rates out of income poverty (based on a threshold set at half of median

Table 6.2. **Risk of falling into different types of poverty by household type**

Poverty risk relative to the entire population, based on a threshold set at 50% of the median

	By presence of children																By employment status of household members							
	Without children								With children								Workless				Working			
	Singles				Couples				Singles				Couples											
	Poor in:				Poor in:				Poor in:				Poor in:				Poor in:				Poor in:			
	One year	Two years	Three years	At least once	One year	Two years	Three years	At least once	One year	Two years	Three years	At least once	One year	Two years	Three years	At least once	One year	Two years	Three years	At least once	One year	Two years	Three years	At least once
Australia	1.1	1.8	3.8	2.0	1.0	1.2	1.1	1.1	1.1	1.0	0.6	0.9	0.8	0.3	0.2	0.5	1.7	3.5	4.0	2.8	0.8	0.5	0.1	0.5
Austria	1.7	2.5	3.7	2.3	0.8	0.9	1.6	1.0	2.3	1.1	1.6	1.9	0.8	0.7	0.4	0.7	1.4	3.3	4.3	2.5	0.9	0.7	0.3	0.7
Belgium	1.2	2.0	3.2	1.8	1.3	1.7	1.4	1.4	1.8	1.4	1.9	1.7	0.7	0.5	0.4	0.6	2.0	3.9	4.8	3.0	0.8	0.4	0.2	0.6
Canada	1.2	1.7	2.5	1.8	0.8	0.7	0.4	0.6	1.1	1.2	1.3	1.2	0.8	0.7	0.6	0.7	1.1	3.3	7.4	3.8	1.0	0.9	0.6	0.8
Denmark	1.9	6.9	6.4	3.5	1.3	0.8	0.8	1.2	2.2	0.2	5.2	2.3	0.6	0.1	0.0	0.4	0.7	3.4	8.0	2.3	0.7	0.6	0.3	0.6
Finland	1.8	4.0	5.0	3.1	0.6	0.5	0.3	0.5	1.3	0.8	0.4	1.0	0.7	0.2	0.1	0.4	1.7	2.3	5.3	2.8	1.0	0.9	0.4	0.8
France	1.5	1.7	2.9	1.8	0.8	1.2	1.0	0.9	1.5	2.4	2.4	1.9	0.9	0.7	0.6	0.8	1.4	2.7	5.4	2.5	1.0	0.8	0.4	0.8
Germany	1.8	2.1	3.3	2.2	0.6	0.7	0.7	0.6	2.5	5.6	2.4	3.3	0.8	0.5	0.4	0.6	2.2	4.0	5.0	3.3	0.9	0.7	0.4	0.7
Greece	1.0	1.1	2.9	1.6	1.0	1.4	2.3	1.5	1.0	1.3	0.8	1.0	0.9	0.7	0.5	0.8	1.0	2.7	1.8	1.7	1.0	0.8	0.5	0.8
Ireland	1.3	1.7	5.5	2.9	1.5	1.5	0.8	1.2	1.4	1.0	0.7	1.0	0.9	1.0	0.6	0.8	1.4	2.0	5.1	2.9	0.9	0.9	0.4	0.7
Italy	1.4	1.2	1.7	1.4	0.8	0.5	0.6	0.7	0.9	1.1	1.0	1.0	1.0	1.1	1.1	1.1	1.2	1.8	2.7	1.8	1.0	1.0	0.8	0.9
Luxembourg	0.8	0.9	0.9	0.9	0.4	0.4	0.9	0.5	2.3	1.4	2.2	2.0	1.0	1.3	0.8	1.0	1.1	4.4	2.1	2.4	1.1	0.7	0.9	0.9
Netherlands	1.7	1.0	2.0	1.5	0.7	0.3	0.0	0.5	1.5	4.8	7.4	3.3	0.9	0.8	0.3	0.8	2.1	4.5	6.9	3.5	0.9	0.8	0.5	0.8
Portugal	1.4	2.1	4.3	2.6	1.1	1.5	1.9	1.5	1.2	1.4	1.3	1.3	1.0	0.9	0.7	0.9	2.5	2.9	4.2	3.2	0.9	0.8	0.6	0.8
Spain	2.0	1.9	1.1	1.8	0.9	0.9	2.1	1.2	0.8	1.0	1.6	1.1	1.1	0.9	0.9	1.0	1.3	3.2	3.5	2.4	1.0	0.8	0.7	0.8
United Kingdom	1.4	1.7	2.0	1.7	0.6	0.7	0.5	0.6	1.5	2.5	2.8	2.1	0.9	0.6	0.7	0.8	1.4	3.0	4.5	2.6	0.9	0.7	0.5	0.7
United States	1.2	1.4	2.2	1.6	0.7	0.6	0.5	0.6	1.2	1.3	1.4	1.3	0.9	0.7	0.5	0.7	1.2	1.4	1.7	1.4	0.8	0.7	0.4	0.7
OECD-17	1.4	2.1	3.1	2.0	0.9	0.9	1.0	0.9	1.5	1.7	2.1	1.7	0.9	0.7	0.5	0.7	1.5	3.1	4.5	2.6	0.9	0.7	0.5	0.8
Memorandum item:																								
Japan	1.9	1.5	2.0	1.8	0.8	0.6	0.4	0.6	1.9	3.8	8.4	4.3	0.8	0.5	0.7	0.7	1.4	1.6	2.7	1.9	0.9	1.0	0.9	0.9
United States (PSID)	1.2	1.2	1.3	1.2	0.7	0.3	0.3	0.5	1.1	1.5	1.6	1.3	0.8	0.8	0.6	0.8	1.2	2.3	5.4	2.6	1.0	1.0	0.8	0.9

Note: Estimates for the United States are based on SIPP (those based on PSID are shown for information only).
Source: Detailed sources are provided in Figure 6.1.

StatLink http://dx.doi.org/10.1787/422632758276

Table 6.3. **Risk of falling into different types of poverty for singles, by gender and presence of children**

Poverty risk relative to the entire population, based on a threshold set at 50% of median income

	Men				Women				Single women with and without children				Single women with children			
	Poor in:				Poor in:				Poor in:				Poor in:			
	One year	Two years	Three years	At least once	One year	Two years	Three years	At least once	One year	Two years	Three years	At least once	One year	Two years	Three years	At least once
Australia	0.9	0.9	0.8	0.9	1.1	1.1	1.2	1.1	1.3	1.4	1.6	1.4	1.2	1.2	0.7	1.1
Austria	0.9	0.7	0.6	0.8	1.1	1.3	1.4	1.2	2.4	2.5	3.8	2.7	3.2	1.2	1.6	2.4
Belgium	0.9	0.9	0.7	0.9	1.1	1.1	1.3	1.1	1.8	2.0	2.9	2.1	1.7	2.0	1.9	1.8
Canada	1.0	1.0	0.9	0.9	1.0	1.0	1.1	1.1	1.3	1.4	1.7	1.5	1.0	1.3	1.6	1.3
Denmark	0.9	0.6	0.7	0.8	1.1	1.4	1.3	1.2	2.7	5.7	6.1	3.8	1.8	0.5	8.6	2.6
Finland	1.0	0.9	0.7	0.9	1.0	1.1	1.3	1.1	2.0	3.0	4.5	2.9	1.1	0.7	0.5	0.9
France	1.0	0.9	0.9	0.9	1.0	1.1	1.1	1.1	1.9	2.3	2.7	2.1	1.8	2.4	2.2	2.0
Germany	0.9	0.8	1.0	0.9	1.1	1.2	1.0	1.1	2.2	2.9	2.6	2.5	3.2	5.1	3.3	3.7
Greece	1.0	1.0	0.9	1.0	1.0	1.0	1.1	1.0	1.1	1.2	2.3	1.5	1.0	1.3	1.0	1.1
Ireland	0.9	1.1	0.9	0.9	1.1	0.9	1.1	1.1	1.6	1.2	2.9	2.0	2.0	1.2	1.0	1.4
Italy	1.0	1.0	0.9	1.0	1.0	1.0	1.1	1.0	1.4	1.2	1.6	1.4	1.1	1.2	1.1	1.1
Luxembourg	1.0	1.1	0.9	1.0	1.0	0.9	1.1	1.0	1.8	1.4	1.7	1.6	2.7	0.9	2.6	2.1
Netherlands	0.9	1.1	0.9	1.0	1.1	0.9	1.1	1.0	1.9	1.9	3.3	2.1	1.8	4.2	7.9	3.4
Portugal	1.0	0.9	0.9	0.9	1.0	1.1	1.1	1.1	1.5	1.8	2.5	1.9	1.5	1.6	1.4	1.5
Spain	0.9	0.9	0.9	0.9	1.1	1.1	1.1	1.1	1.7	1.6	1.4	1.6	1.0	1.2	1.6	1.2
United Kingdom	0.9	0.9	0.8	0.9	1.1	1.1	1.1	1.1	1.8	2.2	2.4	2.1	2.1	2.8	2.6	2.4
United States	1.0	0.9	0.8	0.9	1.0	1.1	1.2	1.1	1.2	1.5	1.7	1.5	1.2	1.4	1.6	1.4
OECD-17	*0.9*	*0.9*	*0.8*	*0.9*	*1.1*	*1.1*	*1.2*	*1.1*	*1.7*	*2.1*	*2.7*	*2.0*	*1.7*	*1.8*	*2.4*	*1.8*
Memorandum items:																
Japan	1.0	0.9	0.9	1.0	1.0	1.1	1.1	1.0	1.7	3.1	4.1	2.8	2.1	4.1	9.2	4.7
United States (PSID)	1.0	0.9	0.9	0.9	1.0	1.1	1.1	1.1	1.2	1.5	1.6	1.4	1.0	1.6	1.9	1.4

StatLink ᐅᔍᕲ http://dx.doi.org/10.1787/422635017175

Note: Estimates for the United States are based on SIPP (those based on PSID are shown for information only).
Source: Detailed sources are provided in Figure 6.1.

Figure 6.4. **Entry and exit out of income poverty, early 2000s**

Poverty based on a threshold set at 50% of the median

A. Exit rates (percentage of those in poverty who exit it)

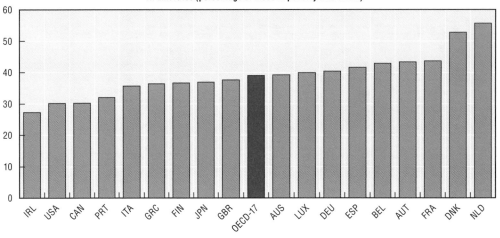

B. Entry rates (percentage of the entire population who enter poverty)

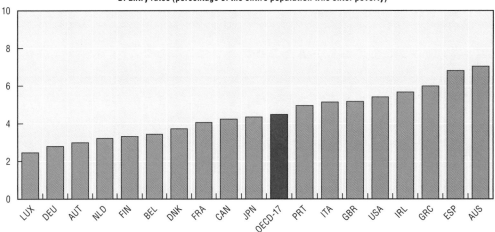

StatLink ⛬🖳 http://dx.doi.org/10.1787/422580110083

Note: Entry into poverty is measured by the share of individuals who were not poor at time *t-1* and are poor at time t. The exit rate is the share of individuals that were poor at time *t-1* and are no longer poor at time t. The two measures are averaged over the three years. Data for the United States are based on SIPP. Countries are ranked, from left to right, in increasing order of exit and entry rates. OECD-17 is the simple average of the countries shown except Japan, for which estimates are based on an income definition (household income before taxes and after public transfers) that differs from that used for other countries (household disposable income).

Source: Detailed sources are provided in Figure 6.1.

income) during the three-year period considered in this chapter, with entry rates expressed relative to the entire population and exit rates calculated over the number of people who are poor in the preceding period.[10] On average, across all OECD countries studied, about 5% of all people who were not poor in a given year have low income in the year that follows, with values ranging from above 6% in Australia, Spain and Greece to 3% or less in Luxembourg, Germany and Austria.[11] Exit rates, expressed as the share of all people who are counted as poor in any given year but who are no longer poor in the following one, are around 40% on average, ranging from more than 50% in Denmark and the Netherlands down to 30% or less in Ireland, Canada and the United States.[12] These data suggest that, overall, poverty turnover is high, but with large differences across countries (OECD, 2001).

Several empirical studies have shown that the probability of exiting poverty falls rapidly after having been poor for two or more years (Bane and Ellwood, 1986; Stevens, 1994, 1999). In theory, measures of poverty duration should allow a better understanding of the risks confronted by people at the bottom of the income distribution. In practice, such estimates are affected by biases that are especially important with the data (spanning only a few years) used in this chapter.[13] A different perspective on the characteristics of poverty is provided by looking at the extent to which poverty is recurrent. The number of poverty spells (occurrences) matters as, for a given number of years spent in poverty, an uninterrupted experience implies a more rapid reduction in accumulated savings and larger falls in living standards for people affected, as well as a greater concentration of poverty on a small number of persons for the country as a whole.[14]

Table 6.4 shows the share of the population as a whole who experience different sequences of poverty and non-poverty among those counted as income poor in either one (left-hand panel) or two (right-hand panel) of the years considered, with values of 1 or 0 denoting whether the individual is poor or not in each calendar year. For example, a sequence "101" indicates that an individual is poor in the first year, climbs out of it in the

Table 6.4. Prevalence of different sequences of poverty among the income-poor in one and two of the years considered

Poverty based on a threshold set at 50% of the median

	Poor in one year			Poor in two years		
	100	010	001	110	101	011
Australia	4.2	3.9	4.0	2.3	1.3	2.3
Austria	3.0	1.5	2.2	1.0	0.7	1.1
Belgium	2.2	2.4	2.7	0.6	0.4	1.3
Canada	2.8	1.8	2.8	1.7	0.8	2.1
Denmark	2.2	1.8	3.3	0.8	0.7	0.6
Finland	1.7	1.2	3.0	1.0	0.3	1.2
France	2.4	2.5	2.8	1.2	0.8	1.6
Germany	1.9	1.3	2.2	1.3	0.5	1.1
Greece	3.6	2.6	3.3	2.6	1.1	2.6
Ireland	2.5	2.2	3.1	1.8	1.4	3.0
Italy	2.5	2.0	3.3	2.0	1.4	2.1
Luxembourg	1.8	1.5	1.1	1.0	1.2	0.9
Netherlands	2.3	1.2	2.2	1.1	1.0	1.0
Portugal	2.9	2.0	3.3	1.6	0.8	2.5
Spain	4.5	2.6	4.1	2.8	1.4	2.7
United Kingdom	4.0	2.1	3.1	2.1	0.8	2.2
United States	3.7	1.8	3.7	2.1	1.6	2.1
OECD-17	2.8	2.0	2.9	1.6	1.0	1.8
Memorandum items:						
Japan	3.0	2.6	2.3	1.6	1.0	1.8
United States (PSID)	5.6	3.4	4.1	3.1	2.1	2.6

StatLink ᴍᴙ᷍ http://dx.doi.org/10.1787/422641132604

Note: Each column illustrates the share of individuals experiencing a specific poverty path over the three-year time period, where "0" stands for non-poor and "1" stands for poor. For example "110" means "poor in the first year, poor in the second year and non-poor in the third year". Estimates for the United States are based on SIPP (those based on PSID are shown for information only).

Source: Detailed sources are provided in Figure 6.1.

second, and re-enters it in the third year, thus experiencing two poverty occurrences over the observation period. Two main patterns stand out:

● Among those who are poor in two of the three years considered, sequences of the type "101" are generally less frequent (1% on average) than those where people remain poor for two consecutive years either at the beginning (1.6%) or at the end of the period (1.8%). Differences across countries (as measured by the standard deviation) are also larger for uninterrupted sequences (110 and 011) than for interrupted ones (101). Countries with a higher share of people experiencing uninterrupted spells of poverty over two years also record higher rates of persistent poverty over the three years, suggesting that similar factors account for the different forms of chronic poverty.

● There are also differences in the frequency of the various sequences among people who are poor in only one of the three years considered. The share of people entering poverty in the second year and exiting it in the third (010) is 2% on average, ranging from 1.2% (in Finland, Germany and the Netherlands) to above 3% (in Australia). The sequences where either entry or exit from poverty cannot be observed (100 and 001) occur more frequently (at around 3%, on average, in both cases), and people belonging to these two categories (which include people who were already poor before entering the three-year period considered here, and others whose poverty spell will continue beyond these three years) will generally experience longer poverty spells than others.

Events that trigger entry into poverty

The high turnover observed among the poor prompts questions about the nature of the events underlying the dynamics of poverty. What type of events lead households to fall into poverty? Are these events different in the case of temporary and persistent poverty? To answer these questions, this section presents evidence on the relationship between a range of events and poverty transitions. The decline in the equivalised income of each person that triggers entry into poverty will reflect changes in both household income and in household composition, and empirical studies have documented the importance of both types of event for the likelihood of entering and exiting poverty (Jenkins, 2000; OECD, 2001; Jenkins et al., 2001; Jenkins and Schluter, 2003; McKernan and Ratcliff, 2005; Valletta, 2006).

In general, this research suggests that finding a job or getting married increases the probability of moving out of poverty, while becoming unemployed or incurring separation increases the likelihood of entering it (Duncan et al., 1993; Muffels et al., 1999; Oxley et al., 2000; Finnie, 2000; Dubois and Jeandidier, 2000; Jeandidier et al., 2002; Fouarge and Layte, 2003, 2005). Other empirical studies suggest that some events, like divorce, have a stronger impact on women than on men (Bartfeld, 1998; Di Prete and McManus, 2000; Jarvis and Jenkins, 1999; Bianchi Lekha and Khan, 1999).

This section presents evidence on the events associated with entry into poverty. The approach is similar to that used in OECD (2001), but the analysis presented here distinguishes between different sequences of poverty spells during the three-year period and refers to all household members rather than being limited to the household head. As in OECD (2001), the analysis tries to account for the fact that several events concur in triggering the entry into poverty (e.g. changes in family structure may influence the supply of labour of individuals by lowering their hours worked and wages) by focusing on specific sub-samples for each event.[15]

Figure 6.5 examines the effect of a range of events on the probability of entering into poverty. The events considered are: *i*) a change in family structure (due to either the birth of a child, divorce, separation, widowhood or similar factors); *ii*) a reduction in the number of workers in the household; *iii*) the income component (among earnings, transfers, capital and other incomes) that records the largest absolute reduction when entering poverty;[16] and *iv*) other events not identified. When looking at the importance of various events for all entries into poverty combined, a number of patterns emerge:

- Changes in family structure are generally an important trigger of entry into poverty. They account on average, for around 30% of all entries, and above 40% in Austria, Denmark, Portugal and the United Kingdom.

- Falls in the number of workers in the household – unrelated to a change in family structure – account for only 5% of all entries into poverty, and for 7% or more in Canada, Germany, Greece, the Netherlands and the United States.[17]

- The combined effect of declines in income streams accounts for around 30% of all poverty entries, with similar shares for earnings and transfers, and a smaller one for capital income. Large falls in public transfers matter more for entry into poverty than those in capital income in all countries except the United States, while declines in earnings are more important than those in transfers in a slight majority of countries (but not in Austria, Belgium, Denmark, France, Germany, Luxembourg, the Netherlands and the United Kingdom).

Figure 6.5. **Events that trigger the entry into poverty**

Share of people experiencing a given event when entering poverty

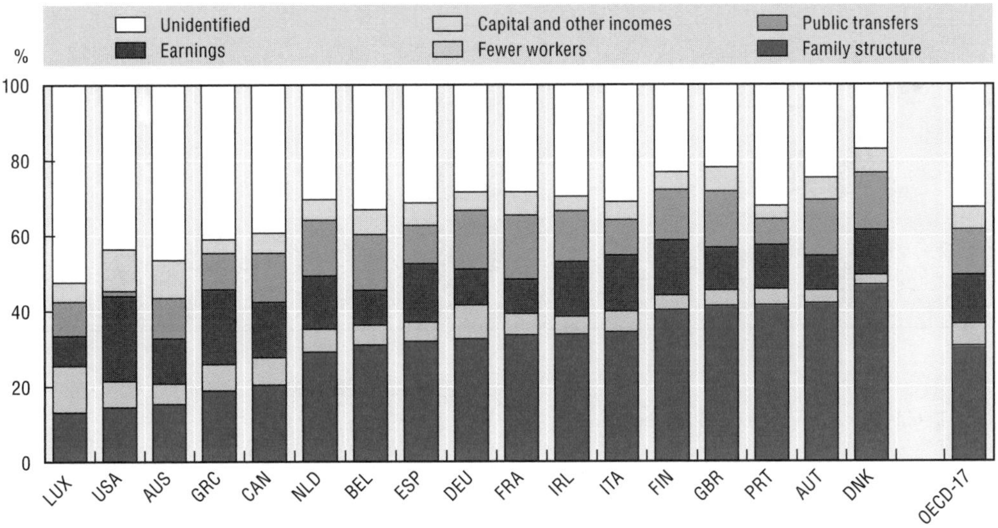

StatLink http://dx.doi.org/10.1787/422607373715

Note: Countries are ranked from left to right in increasing order of the share of people experiencing a change in family structure when entering poverty. Estimates for "fewer workers" are based on the sub-sample of people experiencing no change in family structure. Estimates referring to the income component (among earnings, public transfers and capital income) that records the largest absolute reduction when entering into poverty are based on the sub-sample of people experiencing no change in family structure and number of workers. Estimates for the United States are those based on SIPP.

Source: Detailed sources are provided in Figure 6.1.

● A large share (30% on average) of all entries into poverty is not accounted for by any of the events considered, with an even higher share in Australia, Greece, Luxembourg and the United States.

The role of various events in poverty entry differs across groups of poor people. Figure 6.6 shows – for the average of the 17 OECD countries considered – the share of entries into poverty for people who remain poor in only one year (left bar), for those who remain poor in the last two of the three years (middle), and for those who are poor in two non-consecutive years. Family events are, in general, very important for those who are temporarily poor (one year), but less so for people who are poor in two consecutive years, for whom a reduction in transfer income accounts for a larger share of poverty entries. Further, for people who are poor in two non-consecutive years (bar on the right), family and labour-market events are less important in triggering entry into poverty than among people who remain poor in only one year, while unidentified causes are more important. These patterns suggest that the duration (*i.e.* the number of years of low income) and the number of spells (interrupted and uninterrupted ones) matter for understanding the dynamics of poverty.

Figure 6.6. **Events that trigger the entry into poverty for different groups of poor people, OECD average**

Share of people experiencing a given event when entering poverty

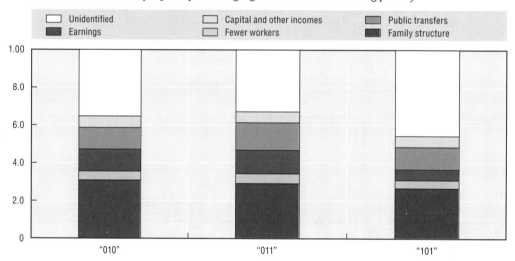

StatLink ⫘⫘ http://dx.doi.org/10.1787/422608180210

Source: Detailed sources are provided in Figure 6.1.

Income mobility and poverty persistence

The observed patterns of transition into and out of poverty and the number of poverty recurrences matter for income mobility. This is an important policy concern because the size and characteristics of poverty in society are closely linked to the extent of income mobility.[18] Higher immobility at the bottom of the income distribution implies a higher risk of chronic poverty while, conversely, persistent poverty has a bearing on lifetime income inequality and can be a "marker" of unequal opportunities. In this respect, higher income mobility may lead to a more equal distribution of lifetime incomes and also affect individual expectations about moving up the socio-economic ladder. To investigate these issues, this section looks at how people move across income quintiles between the initial and final year of the three-year period considered.

The relation between income mobility and poverty dynamics between two years – t_1 and t_2 – can be illustrated through a simple example. If incomes are unchanged in the two years, the distribution of income and the poverty rate will also be the same. However, some individuals who were poor in t_1 may have moved out of poverty in t_2, and have been replaced by an equal number of individuals who have become poor in t_2.[19] This implies that income mobility may occur even when static income measures of poverty and inequality are unchanged. Higher income mobility lowers the risk of being poor in two consecutive years and implies a more equal distribution of lifetime income and lifetime poverty. In other terms, higher income mobility gives poverty a more transitory character rather than a persistent one.

Table 6.5 illustrates the extent of mobility across the quintiles of the distribution of equivalised (household) income between the initial year and the final year of the three-year period, averaged across the 17 OECD countries considered.[20] Over this short period, the size of income mobility is fairly high, with only around 40% of the sample remaining in the same quintile during the three years. Income mobility is, however, significantly lower for people in the bottom and top quintiles; almost 70% of the people in these two quintiles remain in the same income groupings over the whole period, and most of those who move do so by one or two quintiles at most (for country specific information on transition matrices, see Table 6.A1.2 available at http://dx.doi.org/10.1787/424402577838).

Table 6.5. **Transition matrix between income quintiles, OECD average**

	Final year				
	Q1	Q2	Q3	Q4	Q5
Initial year					
Q1	0.66	0.22	0.07	0.04	0.02
Q2	0.21	0.48	0.21	0.07	0.03
Q3	0.07	0.21	0.45	0.22	0.06
Q4	0.04	0.07	0.21	0.47	0.21
Q5	0.02	0.03	0.06	0.20	0.69

StatLink ⟶ http://dx.doi.org/10.1787/422667887673

Source: Detailed sources are provided in Figure 6.1.

Table 6.6 presents additional information on mobility patterns in individual countries. The left-hand panel highlights the size of income "immobility" over the three-year period considered, i.e. the share of individuals remaining in the same income quintile in the base and final year for each country. There is evidence of "tail rigidity" in all countries, with the shares of people staying in the lowest and in the highest quintile well above those characterising other quintiles. For example, the share of people who are still in the bottom quintile after three years is above 70% in Finland and Luxembourg but below 60% in Spain, with the United States exhibiting a level of mobility around the average for other countries. The right-hand panel of Table 6.6 shows another component of mobility, i.e. mobility into adjacent quintiles as a percentage of those in each specific quintile in the initial year. On average, around 21% of those in a specific quintile move into the next one, a pattern that replicates that exhibited over longer time-periods (Yaqub, 2000).

Table 6.6 above describes the extent of income mobility for the entire sample available without looking specifically at mobility for those who are income poor in the initial year. Patterns of income mobility for the poor are illustrated in Table 6.7, which looks at people with income below the 50% threshold in the initial year who in the final year are either: i) still below the 50% threshold; ii) between 50% and 75% of median income; iii) between 75% of the median and the median itself; or iv) above the median. The table suggests that, on average, around 55% of the income poor in the initial year have incomes still below half of the median in the final year, with higher shares (at 60% or more) in Ireland, Italy, Portugal and the United States. On average, only 8% of those with income less than 50% of the median in the initial year have income above the median in the final year, but this share exceeds 10% in Austria, Belgium, the Netherlands and the United Kingdom. More than half of those who move above the 50% threshold have income between 50 and 75% of the median by the end of the period, with this share exceeding 30% in Denmark, Germany, France, Luxembourg and the Netherlands.

Table 6.6. **Measures of income mobility and immobility over a three-year period**

Shares of people in each quintile in the initial year

	Share of people staying in the same quintile					Share of people moving across adjacent quintiles			
	Q1	Q2	Q3	Q4	Q5	From Q1 to Q2	From Q2 to Q3	From Q3 to Q4	From Q4 to Q5
Australia	62.5	46.7	40.0	43.5	61.1	21.5	23.5	23.8	24.8
Austria	67.2	52.4	49.6	50.1	70.9	21.8	16.1	20.2	17.8
Belgium	65.5	43.1	46.4	43.0	60.3	21.7	23.3	21.4	23.4
Canada	69.5	52.2	47.3	50.9	71.8	20.2	21.7	22.8	19.4
Denmark	60.5	43.2	38.8	37.7	62.4	24.8	24.5	27.5	24.1
Finland	71.9	58.1	51.3	49.3	71.0	16.8	13.7	20.8	20.6
France	67.6	50.5	45.7	50.9	73.7	21.7	20.8	23.5	18.9
Germany	67.6	47.9	46.3	55.0	73.6	20.8	26.7	19.2	16.3
Greece	64.9	43.4	40.4	47.6	69.1	22.6	23.6	21.1	21.2
Ireland	66.5	41.1	39.9	36.8	62.7	24.7	20.6	25.7	30.4
Italy	66.9	52.4	45.6	49.7	70.2	17.6	15.9	20.6	18.6
Luxembourg	72.4	54.2	52.5	50.7	71.6	19.2	18.7	20.4	22.5
Netherlands	62.6	48.4	46.4	50.6	72.6	22.9	21.0	22.6	19.5
Portugal	68.2	48.6	47.8	55.2	75.8	22.9	23.7	16.3	16.2
Spain	59.6	41.7	38.4	40.3	70.0	23.9	16.8	23.7	17.1
United Kingdom	62.5	44.9	40.9	45.0	65.9	22.4	21.2	23.2	20.4
United States	66.6	43.1	41.0	44.5	66.5	23.1	24.0	24.2	23.1
OECD-17	66.0	47.8	44.6	47.1	68.8	21.7	20.9	22.2	20.8
Memorandum item:									
United States (PSID)	58.2	38.8	35.7	39.9	61.9	24.7	26.4	26.8	24.1

StatLink 🔗 *http://dx.doi.org/10.1787/422672221848*

Note: The table shows the percentage of individuals that, between the base year and the final year over a three-year time period, move from one quintile to the adjacent quintile only. Estimates for the United States are based on SIPP (those based on PSID are shown for information only).

Source: Detailed sources are provided in Figure 6.1.

Conclusion

Longitudinal income data enrich our assessment of income poverty. In particular, the evidence presented in this chapter suggests a number of patterns.

● First, for a large share of people poverty is a temporary experience, with only about 5% of people persistently poor over a three-year period. Despite this, the share of individuals for whom low income is a more chronic experience is far from being negligible, and its share rises with the poverty threshold used. Also, cross-country differences are substantial, and they increase when moving across the different categories of poverty considered.

- Second, the analysis of the socio-demographic characteristics of the persons in persistent, recurrent or temporary poverty reveals that older individuals, women, and workless households are more vulnerable to chronic poverty than other groups.

- Third, poverty turnover is high but with large differences across countries. Repeated spells (implying re-entry into poverty over the time-period considered) are also less frequent than chronic poverty. To a significant extent, entries into poverty reflect family- and job-related events, but the share of events that are not identified is also quite important. Cross-country differences are also considerable, with family-related events marginally more important in European countries, and falls in incomes more important in the United States.

- Fourth, the analysis of income mobility highlights considerable "tail rigidity" – i.e. the share of people remaining in the bottom or top quintile of the distribution is close to 70% on average, and only a small share of the income poor move into higher strata of the distribution.

The distinction between temporary and persistent spells of poverty, and the socio-demographic characteristics of those belonging to different groups of poverty, matter for

Table 6.7. **Share of income poor in the initial year at different income levels in the final year of observation**

	People with income of less than 50% of median income in the initial year who in the final year are:			
	Still below 50% of the median	Between 50% and 75% of the median	Between 75% and 100% of the median	Above the median
Australia	56.4	23.4	10.6	9.5
Austria	47.8	29.3	11.3	11.6
Belgium	51.9	28.3	7.6	12.2
Canada	61.1	24.8	7.1	7.0
Denmark	44.1	37.3	12.1	6.4
Finland	54.1	29.1	12.2	4.6
France	50.1	32.6	7.7	9.6
Germany	46.2	34.3	13.2	6.3
Greece	57.1	26.8	10.2	5.9
Ireland	68.6	13.8	11.7	5.8
Italy	61.5	22.2	7.5	8.8
Luxembourg	58.1	30.4	4.7	6.8
Netherlands	40.7	32.2	12.8	14.3
Portugal	64.0	24.2	7.6	4.2
Spain	49.6	27.7	12.6	10.1
United Kingdom	49.7	28.9	10.7	10.7
United States	63.1	23.9	7.7	5.3
OECD-17	54.4	27.8	9.8	8.2
Memorandum item:				
United States (PSID)	60.6	26.5	6.9	6.0

StatLink 🔗 http://dx.doi.org/10.1787/422672473034

Note: Estimates for the United States are based on SIPP (those based on PSID are shown for information only).
Source: Detailed sources are provided in Figure 6.1.

policy. Many recent reforms have aimed at eliminating the "poverty traps" embedded in social assistance programmes, and their success typically requires initiatives targeted towards specific groups of people. Better identifying the characteristics of these clients requires better surveys following people over time. However, and as important, the analysis in this chapter also reveals that the experience of low income affects a large part of the population.

Notes

1. The most important of these problems are attrition and censoring. Attrition occurs when some people are not present at all survey dates: as attrition is typically non-random, it implies that, without an appropriate treatment, sample estimates are biased. Censoring may occur either when the beginning of the poverty spell is not observed (left-censoring), or because the spell was still running at the end of the survey period (right-censoring). These two problems are particularly important when estimating the duration or transition models based on individual data (especially when computing the average duration of poverty spells). While the analysis in this chapter ignores the potential biases due to these selection processes, findings from national studies typically conclude that simple models provide estimates that differ little from those obtained from more complicated models (Cappellari and Jenkins, 2004).

2. Data refer to 1999-2001 for European countries, based on the European Community Household Panel (ECHP); to 2002-2004 for Canada, based on data from the Survey of Labour and Income Dynamics (SLID); and to 2002-2004 for Australia, based on data from the survey Household Income and Labour Dynamics in Australia (HILDA). For the United States, data come from two different sources: the Survey of Income and Program Participation (SIPP) for the years 2001-2003, and the Panel Survey of Income Dynamics (PSID) for 1999, 2001 and 2003; estimates based on the PSID (the source used in previous OECD analysis) are shown for information only, as the panel interviews people at two-year intervals. For Japan, data are based on the Keio Household Panel Survey for the years 2005 to 2007. Poverty estimates for Japan are based on household income *before* taxes and after public transfers; because of this difference in the income definition, estimates for Japan are shown as "memorandum items" in the figures and tables of this chapter. For Canada, Australia and the United Sates (PSID), the data for poverty estimates are those available through the Cross National Equivalent File (CNEF), see Burkhauser *et al.* (1995, 2001).

3. Household income data in the US SIPP survey are provided "before taxes and transfers". Values of income "after taxes and transfers" are obtained by applying version 8 of the internet TAXSIM model of the *National Bureau of Economic Research* to the gross income records for this survey (see *www.nber.org/~taxsim/taxsim-calc8/index.html*; and Feenberg and Coutts, 1993).

4. Several studies have analysed poverty dynamics in specific countries using econometric models. Examples of multi-state multiple spells transition models with unobserved heterogeneity are Stevens, (1999); Jenkins and Rigg (2001); Devicienti (2001a; 2001b); Hansen and Wahlberg (2004); Biewen (2006); Fertig and Tamm (2007). Studies based on a single spell of exit and re-entry include Oxley *et al.* (2000) and Fouarge and Layte (2005). See also Iceland (1997) and Jenkins (2007), as well as Duncan *et al.* (1984; 1993), Bane and Ellwood (1986), Stevens (1994; 1995; and 1999) and Burgess and Propper (1996; 1999).

5. Only individuals present in all three years of the sample are included.

6. The correlation of poverty headcounts from the two data sources is around 0.9 for thresholds set at both 60% and 50% of median income. The average poverty rates shown in Figure 6.1 are also very close to those computed on the full ("unbalanced") sample.

7. For a threshold set at 40% of the median, the OECD-average poverty rate falls to 5%, while it exceeds 16% when using a threshold of 60%. On this measure, country rankings are little affected by the specific threshold used, *i.e.* those countries that top the poverty league based on one threshold also record high values based on the others.

8. The age groups used in this chapter differ slightly from those used in Chapters 2 and 5.

9. While all data shown in this chapter are based on sample sizes of at least 50 observations, those referring to countries where the poverty headcount is low (*e.g.* Denmark) may reflect the presence of extreme values.

10. Entry into poverty is measured by the share of individuals in the population as a whole who were not poor at time t-1 and are poor at time t. The exit rate is the share of individuals who were poor at time t-1 and are no longer poor at time t.

11. The correlation between the rate of entry into poverty and the poverty headcount is positive and statistically significant (with a correlation coefficient of 0.89), i.e. the risk of entering poverty is higher in those countries where the poverty rate is also higher.

12. In this case the correlation between the rate of exit out of poverty and the poverty rate is negative and statistically significant (with a correlation coefficient equal to –0.74). Thus the probability of exiting poverty is lower where the poverty headcount is higher.

13. This is because entries into poverty are not observed for those who are classified as poor in the initial year and exits are not observed for people who are still in poverty at the end of the period. More generally, biases in the estimation of poverty duration may arise due to inadequate treatment of the right and left-censoring of the data.

14. However, as noted by Fouarge and Layte (2005), "Whether or not long spells of poverty are worse than recurrent short spells depends, to a large extent, on the degree of one's aversion towards uncertainty".

15. For example, the impact of job-related events for entry into poverty is measured by first identifying all households experiencing a change in family structure and then calculating the role of job-hrelated events only for the sub-sample of households with a stable family structure.

16. This variable was used in OECD (2001) to capture the effect of income losses due to a move to a lower-paying job or a reduction in benefits or in capital income.

17. This, however, may simply reflect the specific order in which events are considered (i.e. when a fall in the number of workers is associated with family breakdown, the approach used here attributes this effect to changes in family structure; the same will apply when a reduction in public benefits is triggered by a change in family status). As noted in OECD (2001), this procedure reduces the importance of changes in the number of workers relative to family events, and of income declines relative to changes in the number of workers.

18. Although income mobility may exist even when only small changes over two points in time are observed in the overall income distribution, stability at the macro level does not necessarily imply stability at the individual level.

19. The correlation coefficient between the incomes at the times t_1 and t_2 will be equal to one only when each individual's income has not varied over the two time periods. By contrast, when some people's incomes have increased enough to allow them to escape poverty and they are replaced by exactly the same number of individuals who see their income decline so that they enter poverty, the correlation coefficient will be lower than one. See Glewwe (2005 and 2007).

20. Mobility matrices for all the countries are in the annex.

References

Atkinson, T. (1983), *The Economics of Inequality*, 2nd edition, Clarendon Press, Oxford.

Bane, M.J. and D. Ellwood (1986), "Slipping Into and Out of Poverty: The Dynamics of Spells", *Journal of Human Resources*, Vol. 21, No. 1.

Bartfeld, J. (1998), "Child Support and the Postdivorce Economic Well-being of Mothers, Fathers, and Children", Institute for Research on Poverty Discussion Paper, No. 1182-98, University of Wisconsin.

Bianchi Lekha, S.L. and J.R. Kahn (1999), "The Gender Gap in the Economic Well-Being of Non-residential Fathers and Custodial Mothers", *Demography*, Vol. 36, No. 2.

Biewen, M. (2006), "Who Are the Chronic Poor? An Econometric Analysis of Chronic Poverty in Germany", *Research on Economic Inequality*, Vol. 13.

Burgess, S. and C. Propper (1996), "Poverty Dynamics among Young Americans", Centre for Economic Policy Research, Discussion Paper No. 1362, London.

Burgess, S. and C. Propper (1999), "An Economic Model of Household Income Dynamics, With an Application to Poverty Dynamics Among American Women", University of Bristol, Centre for Economic Policy Research, Discussion Paper No. 1830, London.

Burkhauser, R.V., B.A. Butrica and M.C. Daly (1995), "The Syracuse University PSID, GSOEP Equivalent Data File: A Product of Cross-National Research", All-University Gerontology Center, Maxwell School of Citizenship and Public Affairs, Syracuse University, United States.

Burkhauser, R.V., B.A. Butrica, M.C. Daly and D.R. Lillard (2001), "The Cross-National Equivalent File: A Product of Cross-National Research", in I. Becker, N. Ott, and G. Rolf (eds.), *Soziale Sicherung in Einer Dynamischen Gesellschaf* (Social Insurance in a Dynamic Society), Campus Verlag, Frankfurt.

Burniaux, J.M., F. Pedrini and N. Brandt (2006), "Labour Market Performance, Income Inequality and Poverty in OECD Countries", OECD Economic Department Working Paper, No. 500, OECD, Paris.

Cappellari, L and S.P. Jenkins (2004), "Modelling Low Pay Transition Probabilities: Accounting for Panel Attrition, Non-Response and Initial Conditions", Institute for Social and Economic Research, ISER Working Paper No. 2004-08, University of Essex.

Devicienti, F. (2001a), "Poverty Persistence In Britain: A Multivariate Analysis Using The BHPS, 1991-1997", in P. Moyes, C. Seidl and A.F. Shorrocks (eds.), "Inequalities: Theory, Measurement and Applications", *Journal of Economics*, Suppl. No. 9.

Devicienti, F. (2001b), "Estimating Poverty Persistence in Britain", LABORatorio R. Revelli, Working Paper Series, No. 1, Torino.

Di Prete, T.A. and A. McManus (2000), "Family Change, Employment Transitions, and the Welfare State: Household Income Dynamics in the United States and Germany", *American Sociological Review*, Vol. 65.

Dubois, C. and B. Jeandidier (2000), "Dans quelle mesure les événements d'emploi et les événements familiaux peuvent-ils expliquer les transitions individuelles de pauvreté ?", in Bertrand *et al.* (eds.), *Trajectoires d'emploi et conditions d'existence des individus*, Céreq, Séminaires, No. 148, Marseille.

Duncan, G.J., R.D. Coe and M.S. Hill (1984), "The Dynamics of Poverty", in G.J. Duncan, R.D. Coe, M.E. Corcoran, M.S. Hill, S.D. Hoffman and J.N. Morgan (eds.), *Years of Poverty, Years of Plenty: The Changing Economic Fortunes of American Workers and Families*, Institute for Social Research, University of Michigan, Ann Arbor, United States.

Duncan, G., B. Gustafsson, R. Hauser, G. Schmauss, H. Messinger, R. Muffels, B. Nolan and J.-C. Ray, (1993), "Poverty Dynamics in Eight Countries", *Journal of Population Economics*, Vol. 6.

Dynan, K.E., D.W. Elmendorf, D.E. Sichel (2007), "The Evolution of Household Income Volatility", Federal Reserve Board and Brookings Institution, Draft, June.

Feenberg, D.R. and E. Coutts (1993), "An Introduction to the TAXSIM Model", *Journal of Policy Analysis and Management*, Vol. 12, No. 1.

Fertig, M. and M. Tamm (2007), "Always Poor or Never Poor and Nothing in Between? Duration of Child Poverty in Germany", Working Paper No. 59, ECINEQ, Society for the Study of Economic Inequality, Spain.

Finnie, R. (2000), "Low Income (Poverty) Dynamics in Canada: Entry, Exit, Spell Durations, and Total Time", Applied Research Branch Strategic Policy Human Resources Development Canada Working Paper, No. W-00-7E.

Fouarge, D. and R. Layte (2003), "Duration of Poverty Spells in Europe", EPAG Working Paper, No. 2003-47, University of Essex, Colchester, United Kingdom.

Fouarge, D. and R. Layte (2005), "Welfare Regimes and Poverty Dynamics: The Duration and Recurrence of Poverty Spells in Europe", *Journal of Social Policy*, Vol. 34, No. 3.

Glewwe, P. (2005), "How Much of Observed Economic Mobility Is Measurement Error? A Method to Remove Measurement Error, with an Application to Vietnam", Unpublished paper, Department of Applied Economics, University of Minnesota, United States.

Glewwe, P. (2007), "Measurement Error Bias in Estimates of Income and Income Growth among the Poor: Analytical Results and a Correction Formula", *Economic Development and Cultural Change*, Vol. 56.

Hansen, J. and R. Wahlberg (2004), "Poverty Persistence in Sweden", IZA Discussion Paper, No. 1209, Institute for the Study of Labor (IZA), Bonn.

Iceland, J. (1997), "The Dynamics of Poverty Spells and Issues of Left-Censoring", Research Report No. 97-378, Population Studies Center, University of Michigan, Ann Arbor.

Jarvis, S. and S.P. Jenkins (1999), "Marital Splits and Income Changes: Evidence from the British Household Panel Survey", *Population Studies*, Vol. 53.

Jeandidier, B., C. Bourreau-Dubois and F. Berger (2002), "Poverty Dynamics in Europe: An Approach in Terms of Work and/or Family-Related Events", Working Paper du réseau européen COST A15 Reforming Social Protection Systems in Europe, Urbino.

Jenkins, S.P. (2000), "Modelling Household Income Dynamics", *Journal of Population Economics*, Vol. 13, No. 4, Springer.

Jenkins, S.P. (2007), "Approach to Modelling Poverty Dynamics", Paper presented at the workshop "Dynamic Analysis using Panel Data: Applications to Poverty and Social Exclusion", Torino, June 25.

Jenkins, S.P. and C. Schluter (2003), "Why Are Child Poverty Rates Higher in Britain than in Germany? A Longitudinal Perspective", *Journal of Human Resources*, Vol. 38, No. 2.

Jenkins, S.P., J. Rigg and F. Devicienti (2001), "The Dynamics of Poverty in Britain", Department for Work and Pensions, Research Report No. 157, London.

McKernan, S.-M. and C. Ratcliffe (2005), "Events that Trigger Poverty Entries and Exits", *Social Science Quarterly*, Vol. 86, No. 5.

Muffels, R., D. Fouarge and R. Dekker (1999), "Longitudinal Poverty and Income Inequality. A Comparative Panel Study for the Netherlands, Germany and the UK", EPAG-Working Paper Series, No. 1, University of Essex.

OECD (1998), "Low-income Dynamics in Four OECD Countries", *OECD Economic Outlook*, Chapter VI, OECD, Paris.

OECD (2001), "When Money is Tight: Poverty Dynamics in OECD Countries", Chapter 2 in *Employment Outlook*, OECD, Paris.

OECD (2006), *Society at a Glance – OECD Social Indicators,* OECD, Paris.

Oxley, H., P. Antolín and T.-T. Dang (2000), "Poverty Dynamics in Six OECD Countries", *OECD Economic Studies*, No. 30, OECD, Paris.

Stevens, A. Huff (1994), "The Dynamics of Poverty Spells: Updating Bane and Ellwood", *American Economic Review*, American Economic Association, Vol. 84, No. 2.

Stevens, A. Huff (1995), "Climbing Out of Poverty, Falling Back In: Measuring the Persistence of Poverty over Multiple Spells", NBER Working Paper No 5390, National Bureau of Economic Research, Inc., Cambridge, Massachusetts.

Stevens, A. Huff (1999), "Climbing out of Poverty, Falling Back In: Measuring the Persistence of Poverty over Multiple Spells", *Journal of Human Resources*, Vol. 34, No. 3.

Valletta, R.G. (2006), "The Ins and Outs of Poverty in Advanced Economics: Government Policies and Poverty Dynamics in Canada, Germany, Great Britain and the United States", *Review of Income and Wealth*, Vol. 52, No. 2.

Yaqub, S. (2000), "Intertemporal Welfare Dynamics", Background paper prepared for the Human Development Report 2001 (UNDP), Brighton.

ISBN 978-92-64-04418-0
Growing Unequal?
© OECD 2008

PART III

Chapter 7

Non-income Poverty: What Can we Learn from Indicators of Material Deprivation?*

Based on a measure that aggregates data on the prevalence of different types of deprivation, non-income poverty is higher in countries with lower per capita income and higher relative income poverty headcounts. The experience of deprivation declines monotonically with people's income and age. In a given year, a large share of the income poor are not materially deprived while, conversely, a large share of the population experience either low income or deprivation.

* This chapter has been prepared by Romina Boarini, OECD Economics Department, and Marco Mira d'Ercole, OECD Social Policy Division. The authors wish to thank Marton Medgyesi, TARKI, Hungary; Aya Abe, National Institute of Population and Social Security Research, Tokyo; Aderonke Osikominu. University of Freiburg, Germany; and Mark Pearson, OECD, for providing tabulations based on individual data for, respectively, EU countries, Japan, the United States and Australia.

Introduction

Income is only a partial measure of the economic resources of people and of the extent to which these resources allow them to meet their basic needs. Some people with low income may benefit from in-kind support from public agencies and relatives, or from accumulated savings and borrowing that allow them to enjoy a decent standard of living. Conversely, even income above conventional thresholds may leave some people with insufficient resources when they have special needs due to sickness and disability, or when they incur high work-related expenses, such as child care. Because conventional income measures cannot identify such needs, a long tradition of research on poverty has looked instead at direct measures of the extent to which individuals and households have access to the goods and amenities that are deemed to be needed for an acceptable standard of living in any given society.

This chapter takes stock of what can be learned from measures of material deprivation in a comparative perspective. After having described the conceptual foundations of material deprivation, the next section provides evidence of the size and features of material deprivation using two different approaches. The first is based on measures of the *average* prevalence of a broad range of deprivation items across OECD countries, with summary measures derived as a simple average across these items: this approach allows covering a broad range of items and countries, but relies on survey questions that are not strictly comparable across countries (and are missing for some). The second approach is based on measures of the extent to which *each* individual or household experiences a more limited number of deprivation items, with summary measures derived by considering how many people cumulate several deprivations at the same time. The final section summarises the key patterns and draws some policy implications.

Material deprivation as one approach to the measurement of poverty

Poverty is a complex phenomenon, and different measures give different perspectives as to its size and evolution.[1] While a variety of alternative measures have been developed, all approaches to the measurement of poverty rely on the specification of: *i)* a threshold separating the poor and the non-poor; and *ii)* an index that expresses how far from the threshold the poor are. Different poverty measures can however be distinguished along two main dimensions:

● First, whether the metric used is "monetary" or "non-monetary".

● Second, whether these measures refer either to "inputs" (*i.e.* indirect measures of poverty) or to "outcomes" (*i.e.* direct measures).

Most poverty measures, including those presented earlier in this report, are "monetary" and "input"-based, where the inputs are the resources required to achieve well-being; income measures fall in this category, and they can be distinguished based on whether they rely on either "absolute" or "relative" thresholds.[2] A complementary approach is that of measuring poverty "outcomes", which concentrates on the final conditions of people rather than on the means required to achieve those conditions. Outcomes are generally conceived in terms of well-being or living standards, and measured based on metrics that are either monetary – as in the case of the measures that consider whether actual household expenditures fall short of some minimum level – or non-monetary. Measures of material deprivation fall in this latter category – i.e. they are "non-monetary" and "outcome"-based measures of poverty.

Much of the interest in measuring material deprivation (or "hardship", in the US literature) stems from the work of Townsend (1979), who related the concept of deprivation to the broader notion of "inability of living a decent life". Following Townsend, other scholars have emphasised the notions of "shame" and "inability to live a decent life with dignity" (Sen, 1983). Today, most authors define material deprivation as "exclusion from the minimum acceptable way of life in one's own society because of inadequate resources" (Callan et al., 1993; Nolan and Whelan, 1996; Kangas and Ritakallio, 1998; Layte et al., 2001; Whelan et al., 2002; Perry, 2002) or as "lack of socially perceived necessities" (Bradshaw and Finch, 2003; Nolan and Whelan, 1996). In all these definitions, the line separating what is acceptable or decent and what is not differs across countries and over time. As a result, at least in theory, measures of material deprivation imply a reference to a "relative" threshold. In practice, once a set of deprivation items is identified, change in material deprivation over time will reflect changes in the absolute living conditions of people. Conversely, as in the case of income-based measures, all these definitions retain the household as the fundamental unit within which resources are shared and needs satisfied.

These definitions of material deprivation are consistent with a range of measurement approaches, and much of the later research has aimed to refine empirical measures of deprivation. This research has focused on a number of questions:

● *How to distinguish between preferences and constraints?* One objection to using material deprivation concerns the failure to distinguish between the lack of a good (or of an activity) due to voluntary choice from that due to financial constraints (Piachaud, 1981). For example, lack of a TV set might be due to not having enough money to buy one, or it might reflect disgust with the quality of programmes. Today, the wording of most survey questions on material deprivation tries to distinguish between preferences and affordability, although other aspects about the nature of deprivation (*e.g.* those related to the quality of the items owned) are not adequately addressed.

● *Which deprivation items to select?* A second issue relates to the arbitrary list of items used in the early research on material deprivation. This typically relied on experts' views of the items that allow a decent life – or, most often, of whatever information happened to be available. However, people may disagree with what is and what is not included in the list. A more structured approach pioneered by Mack and Lansley (1985) for the United Kingdom aims to reduce the arbitrariness in the choice of deprivation items by asking a representative sample of people to evaluate which specific items they perceived as "social necessities".

● *How to weight different items?* A further argument stressed the importance of accounting for the seriousness of different forms of deprivation (Gordon et al., 2000). Indeed, most empirical studies relied on simple binary scores to characterise whether a person experienced each deprivation item; this approach implicitly assigns each type of deprivation an equal weight. This might not be reasonable – we might consider not having enough food to eat as more important that access to a TV. Desai and Shah (1988) adopted a different approach by, first, replacing binary deprivation scores with a continuous score (reflecting the distance between the respondent's and the modal value in the distribution of each given item) and, second, applying weights that reflected how common was access to each item among the total population. This approach to weighting deprivation items (with a larger weight given to those items that larger proportions of the population posses) is increasingly common.

A number of consistent patterns have been identified in past studies, and these are described in Box 7.1. A fuller description of results from previous research is provided in Boarini and Mira d'Ercole (2006).

Because material deprivation takes many different forms, a framework is required to describe it. The forms deprivation takes will vary even among countries at a comparable level of economic development – depending on cultural norms, the diffusion within society of various types of consumption goods, the characteristics of the social protection system – as well as over time – as the luxuries of one generation become the conveniences of the

---

Box 7.1. **Main empirical results from previous research on material deprivation**

The empirical research on material deprivation highlights a number of consistent patterns:

- The same people typically report several forms of deprivation at the same time.

- People with lower incomes are more likely to experience material deprivation, and deprived individuals are most likely to be counted among the income poor. However, the relationship between people's income and deprivation is not very strong (i.e. only between one-third and one-half of people who are income poor are deprived, and *vice versa*), with most studies reporting correlation coefficients between 0.33 and 0.54 (Perry, 2002).

- The overlap between income poverty and material deprivation increases when a higher income threshold is used (although the evidence is mixed in the United States) and when assessing deprivation over the long term. Also, the overlap between income poverty and material deprivation generally increases when relying on measures that track individuals over time.

- Multivariate studies relying on different controls suggest that the probability of being deprived is higher for: persons who are young; unemployed or with weak ties to the labour market; poorly-educated; living alone or as a lone parent; disabled; immigrants; or receiving welfare benefits.

- Tracking people over time shows that most of those reporting material deprivation are in that condition over prolonged periods of time; this implies that material deprivation provides a useful complement to poverty measures where longitudinal income data are not available.

- Material deprivation is both more concentrated among a minority of the population and tends to last longer in countries where its prevalence is also higher.*

* On average, around 17% of the population in 14 EU countries reported having been affected by material deprivation over the four years to 1997. The number of people who have been deprived at least once in this period is, on average, 50% higher than the average number of people who report material deprivation throughout the period. Further, around 70% of those reporting material deprivation over the four-year period were persistently in that state, a share that is well above the analogous share of those who are income poor (Eurostat, 2002).

---

next and the necessities of the one that follows. A simple typology of material deprivation distinguishes between the following types.

- *Satisfaction of basic needs*, which refers to items that are essential for physical survival (*e.g.* food, clothes, ability to keep the home warm during winter, etc.).

- *Capacity to afford basic leisure and social activities*, which refers to items that, while not essential for physical survival, are critical for enjoying a decent quality of life (*e.g.* having a week of holiday away from home at least once per year, or occasionally inviting friends and relatives home for drinks or meals).

- *Availability of consumer durables*, which refers to items that are essential to perform every-day life activities (*e.g.* having a telephone) or that significantly ease housework and other domestic tasks (*e.g.* having a microwave oven).

- *Housing conditions*, which relates to both the physical characteristics of the dwelling (*e.g.* availability of electricity, water supply, or indoor flushing toilet, or whether parts of the dwelling are deteriorated or damaged) and of the areas where these are located (*e.g.* exposure to noise, indoor pollution, etc.).

- *Appreciation of own personal conditions*, in terms of their financial stress and ability to make ends meet, as well as subjective perception of whether they consider themselves as poor.

- *Characteristics of the social environment* where individuals live, which describe features of the neighbourhood (*e.g.* exposure to specific hazards, fear of crime, and availability of public services such as schools and hospitals) and of the social networks of individuals (*e.g.* ability to rely on support from others in case of need).[3]

This typology provides a grid that is used in the next section to summarise the available evidence on material derivation across OECD countries. However, not all of the items listed are equally relevant and few measures exist for some. As a result, the description below excludes indicators of the extent to which individuals feel poor and indicators of neighbourhood characteristics.

Characteristics of material deprivation in a comparative perspective

The most important problem in making international comparisons is data availability: no survey currently exists that includes a common set of questions on material deprivation and covers a significant number of OECD countries – although a common survey (the *EU Survey on Income and Living Conditions*) now exists for EU countries. It follows that any attempt to shed some light on how material deprivation compares across OECD countries will need to identify items for which comparisons are *less* arbitrary. This section uses two different approaches to make international comparisons. The first describes the prevalence of material deprivation in each country for a large number of items, and derives summary measures of deprivation for the country as a whole by *averaging* across these items. The second approach restricts attention to a more narrow set of items and countries, and reverses the order of aggregation, *i.e.* a composite measure of material deprivation is derived by looking at, first, the extent to which each person lacks various items and, second, at how many people are in these conditions.

Prevalence of material deprivation based on aggregate data

Table 7.1 presents information on the prevalence of various types of deprivation across households within each of the six main categories described above. The information

Table 7.1. **Share of households reporting different types of material deprivation, around 2000**

Based on aggregate data

Households deprived in terms of

	Basic needs			Basic leisure	Consumer durables			Housing			Financial stress		Support from others
	Inability to adequately heat home	Inability to have a healthy diet	Restricted access to health care	Having one week holiday away from home per year	Television	Telephone	Personal computer	Needing repair	Lacking indoor toilet	Exposed to pollution	Arrears in bills	Inability to make ends meet	Received regular help from others
Austria	1	6	5	21	0	1	9	4	3	4	1	14	13
Belgium	4	3	8	20	0	1	5	6	2	10	5	11	7
Canada	..	8	..	0	..	4	..	8	..	..	14	..	..
Czech Republic	8	19	3	34	..	..	18	9	5	20	7	19	14
Denmark	2	1	1	11	0	0	5	5	0	4	2	11	10
Finland	7	4	3	26	1	0	8	2	1	14	6	12	13
France	4	3	4	24	0	1	11	9	2	17	5	12	9
Germany	3	2	3	21	0	1	18	7	1	5	4	9	8
Greece	31	26	21	51	2	2	16	9	6	15	21	49	19
Hungary	11	34	8	63	..	..	23	19	9	22	18	28	20
Ireland	4	1	10	24	1	2	15	5	1	7	3	10	8
Italy	17	5	26	36	1	1	15	6	1	15	3	22	6
Japan	1	..	2	26	..	2	12	17	1	..	5	25	10
Luxembourg	6	2	5	8	0	0	2	6	..	16	3	7	6
Netherlands	3	2	3	13	0	0	4	8	0	11	1	9	10
New Zealand	4	11	8	21	0	2	..	14	0	7	10	..	14
Poland	30	17	19	68	..	..	40	25	11	22	28	53	17
Portugal	56	3	17	59	2	5	26	23	7	19	1	34	12
Slovak Republic	17	33	21	64	..	..	28	26	7	18	15	24	17
Spain	42	3	4	37	0	2	21	9	0	10	3	21	12
Sweden	1	2	3	15	0	..	4	4	1	5	4	5	0
Turkey	45	53	33	66	..	..	61	20	12	29	26	48	19
United Kingdom	2	8	3	24	0	0	10	6	1	7	11	7	11
United States	7	11	8	..	1	5	33	5	..	3	10	15	24
OECD-24	*13*	*11*	*9*	*32*	*1*	*2*	*18*	*10*	*3*	*13*	*9*	*20*	*12*

StatLink http://dx.doi.org/10.1787/42303053328

..: Data not available.

Source: OECD (2006), based on a selection of the indicators included in Tables 3 to 8 in Boarini et al. (2006).

presented is limited to a few items within each category, with information on a broader range of items (not always available for all countries) presented in Boarini et al. (2006). Some broad patterns emerge:

- **Basic needs.** In the early 2000s, across the OECD countries included in Table 7.1, around 10% of OECD households failed to satisfy basic needs such as adequately heating their home, having a healthy diet or having unrestricted access to health care. These shares are, in general, larger in most Southern and Eastern European countries (especially for heating and clothing). A high level of deprivation in one of these items generally means a high level in other indicators too.[4] The simple OECD-average of the share of households deprived in basic needs is 11% (and 10% when items that only a small share of the population lack are given a larger weight, Table 3 in Boarini et al., 2006) with values ranging from 5% or less in France, Ireland, Luxembourg, Netherlands, Sweden and the United Kingdom up to 20% or more in Greece, Hungary, Poland, Portugal, the Slovak Republic and Turkey.

- **Basic leisure.** On average, across all OECD countries, around one-third of all households could not afford to take one week of holiday away from home over the past 12 months, with this share exceeding 50% in Greece, Hungary, Poland, Portugal, the Slovak Republic and Turkey. Also, according to Table 4 in Boarini et al., 2006, 14% of all households report not having invited friends and relatives over the past month. The correlation between these two types of basic leisure activities is high (84%), and cross-country variability in the two items small. The average share of OECD households unable to afford basic leisure activities is 24% based on unweighted data, and 21% when the items that only a small share of the population lack are given a larger weight (Boarini et al., 2006). Lack of basic leisure activities appears to affect a larger share of people than does lack of basic needs.

- **Consumer durables.** On average, few OECD households lacked a television or a telephone, but close to one-fifth did not have a personal computer at home. Differences across OECD countries in the share of households possessing different consumer durables are large, with the shares lacking basic consumer durables generally higher in Australia, Canada and the United States than in most European countries (although this may reflect differences in the wording of survey questions, i.e. lack of a distinction between financial constraints and voluntary choices in most non-European surveys). Cross-country differences in the possession of consumer durables are generally higher than in the case of basic needs and leisure activities, in particular when looking at possession of cars and microwaves (Table 5 in Boarini et al., 2006). Lack of one type of durable is very much correlated with lack of another type. On average, 11% of OECD households report lacking some basic consumer durables (9% when considering the weighted average), with this share exceeding 25% in Hungary, Poland, the Slovak Republic and Turkey (Boarini et al., 2006).

- **Housing conditions.** If most households in OECD countries report having an indoor toilet, one in ten reported that their house was in need of repairs, and 13% that it was exposed to pollution. When looking at other characteristics of dwellings, very few households reported lacking an indoor shower or bath (2%) or hot running water (7%), while a significantly higher proportion (14% on average) reported overcrowding (based on an indicator referring, for most countries, to dissatisfaction with respect to housing space, Table 6 in Boarini et al., 2006). A larger share of households declared being exposed to noise and crime (21% and 19%), with little variation across countries. Overall, the items describing housing conditions are not very correlated with each other, with the average share of OECD households experiencing poor housing conditions around 12% (and 8% based on weighted data, Boarini et al., 2006).

- **Financial stress.** Less than 10% of OECD households reported having incurred payment arrears during the past year, but the share was 20% for those declaring that in the past year they could make ends meet only with great difficulty, or that occasionally they could not meet essential expenses (with much higher values in several East European countries). On average 9% of households declared having been unable to pay utility bills in the past year (a share that is much higher in East European countries, Turkey and Australia, Table 7 in Boarini et al., 2006), with a lower proportion reporting arrears in paying rents or mortgages (5%) and other types of loans (3%).[5] Different forms of financial stress are highly correlated with each other, with the main exception being the indicator referring to the inability to repay loans. The simple OECD average of households suffering from financial strain is 10%, while the weighted average is 8% (Boarini et al., 2006).

- **Support from others.** On average, around 13% of all households report that they regularly relied on help from persons living outside the household in the year preceding the survey.[6] A similar proportion of households declared that, in case of financial need, they would not have anyone on whom to rely (Table 8 in Boarini et al., 2006). Across countries, the correlation between the two indicators (at 36%) is smaller than for other deprivation dimensions. The OECD average for the two indicators is 14%, based on unweighted data (and marginally lower when using weighted data or excluding countries where only one indicator is available, Boarini et al., 2006).

Across countries, data on the prevalence of the six main components of deprivation are highly correlated with each other, particularly for deprivation in basic needs, social activities and consumer durables (with average correlations, across these dimensions, of 64%, 77% and 65%, respectively) and, to a lesser extent, for help from social networks and financial stress (with average correlations of 40% and 46% respectively). The high correlations between the different types of deprivation suggest that they measure the same underlying phenomenon and that they provide a reasonably consistent picture of the extent of poverty and hardship across OECD countries.

A summary measure of the overall prevalence of material deprivation can be computed by averaging first across the deprivation items within each of the six main categories, and then across the categories. Figure 7.1 plots the relation between this summary measure of material deprivation, on one side, and the relative income poverty headcount and per capita income, on the other. This summary measure of material deprivation is only weakly correlated with income poverty (at around 40% when using a threshold set at half of the median), while the correlation is stronger (over 80%) with respect to GDP per capita. This suggests that this simple measure of material deprivation provides information about the absolute living standard of the poor, which in turn depends on the economic development of each country. However, when limiting the comparisons to OECD countries with similar levels of income (i.e. those with a GDP per capita above USD 20 000), the correlation with relative income poverty rises (to around 0.60) while that with per capita GDP disappears. While it is not possible to interpret this relation in terms of causality, the figure suggests that monetary and non-monetary measures of poverty convey a broadly consistent picture.

Figure 7.1. **Higher material deprivation in countries with higher relative income poverty and lower GDP per capita**

Based on aggregate data

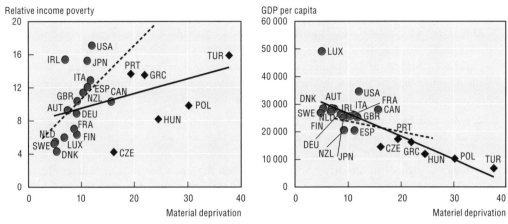

StatLink ᴍᴤᴲ http://dx.doi.org/10.1787/422677656865

Note: Material deprivation refers to the share of households reporting different forms of deprivation among the six main categories shown in Table 7.1 averaged across them. Relative income poverty is based on a threshold set at half of median disposable income. OECD countries with per capita GDP below USD 20 000 are denoted with a diamond. The grey dashed line in each panel is the trend line between the two variables obtained when limiting the analysis to countries with per capita GDP above USD 20 000.

Source: Boarini and Mira d'Ercole (2006).

Size and characteristics of material deprivation based on individual data

Despite the high correlation between the different measures of material deprivation shown above, it could be that they are not suffered by the same people. This is because the measures of material deprivation presented above do not distinguish between situations where the same person experiences different types of deprivation and those where these experiences are widely shared among the population at large. Distinguishing between these two situations requires data referring to specific individuals and households. This section presents results for 25 OECD (22 European and three non-European countries) based on household surveys referring to the mid-2000s.

The analysis refers to a small set of deprivation items that are common across surveys:

- Inadequate heating.
- Constrained food choices.
- Overcrowding.
- Poor environmental conditions.
- Arrears in utility bills.
- Arrears in rents/mortgages.
- Inability to make ends meet.

These items include both specific contingencies (such as payment arrears) and more general assessments of the respondents' own conditions (*e.g.* ability to make ends meet). It should also be noted that the wording of the survey questions differ (Box 7.2), and these differences may affect cross-country comparisons of the overall prevalence of material deprivation in each country.[7] The analysis in this section makes abstraction of these differences, trying instead to make the best possible use of the information that is currently available. The evidence below refers to the share of people affected by different

Box 7.2. **Description of deprivation items used in this section**

The analysis in this section is based on seven deprivation items that are broadly comparable across countries.

1. **Ability to adequately heat home** is assessed through questions on whether the household can "*keep the home adequately warm*" (and, if not, whether this was because it could not afford it) for European countries; is "*unable to heat home*" in Australia; "*could not afford heating and cooling devices such as air conditioners, heaters and kotatsu*" in Japan; and is "*satisfied with the warmth of home in winter*" in the United States.

2. **Constrained food choices** is assessed through questions on whether the household "*could afford to eat meat or chicken every second day if wished*" for European countries; "*went without meals because of a shortage of money*" in Australia; "*could could afford to eat a fruit each day if wished*" in Japan; and, for the United States, whether the household had "*sometimes*" or "*often*" not enough to eat, whether any member of the household has "*cut the size of the meals*", "*skipped meals*", "*eaten less than they felt they should*" or "*not eaten for a whole day*" because of shortage of money, whether they had "*enough but not always the kind of the food we want to eat*" or "*could not afford balanced meals*".

3. **Overcrowding** is assessed though questions on "*number of rooms available to the household*" for European countries; on the "*number of bedrooms*" in Australia; on whether the household "*cannot afford more than one bedroom*" or "*cannot afford to have a bedroom separate from eating room*" in Japan; and on the "*number of rooms with kitchen and without bath*" in the United States. Overcrowding is deemed to prevail when the number of household members exceeds the number of rooms (i.e. a family of four is considered as living in an overcrowded accommodation when there are only three rooms – excluding kitchen and bath but including a living room).

4. **Poor environmental conditions** are assessed through questions on whether the household's accommodation "*has noise from neighbours or outside*" or has "*any pollution, grime or other environmental problem caused by traffic or industry*" for European countries; whether there is "*vandalism in the area*", "*grime in the area*" or "*traffic noise from outside*" for Australia; whether "*noises from neighbours can be heard*" for Japan; and whether there is "*street noise or heavy street traffic*", "*trash, litter, or garbage in the street*", "*rundown or abandoned houses or buildings*" or "*odors, smoke, or gas fumes*" for the United States.

5. **Arrears in payments of utility bills** is assessed through questions on whether the household has "*been unable to pay scheduled utility bills during the past 12 months*" for European countries; whether "*over the past year could not pay gas/electricity/telephone bill because of a shortage of money*" for Australia; whether "*in the past year some services (gas, water, telephone, others) got stopped because of failure to pay bills*" for Japan; and whether "*during the past 12 months, has there been a time when household did not pay the full amount of the gas, oil or electricity bills*" in the United States.

6. **Arrears in mortgage or rent payments** is assessed through questions on whether the household "*has been unable to pay scheduled rent/mortgages for the accommodation during the past 12 months*" for European countries; whether it "*could not pay rent*" for Australia; whether "*in the past year, there has been a time when you couldn't pay the rent or the mortgage*" for Japan; and whether "*during the past 12 months, has there been a time when you did not pay the full amount of the rent or mortgage*" for the United States.

> ### Box 7.2. **Description of deprivation items used in this section** (cont.)
>
> 7. **Ability to make ends meet** is assessed through questions on whether, "*Thinking of your household's total monthly income, is your household able to make ends meet with great/some difficulty/fairly easily*" for European countries; those indicating "*very poor situation*" in response to questions about the household's "*prosperity, given current needs and financial responsibilities*" for Australia; whether "*the family runs into red every month*" for Japan; whether "*during the past 12 months, has there been a time when you did not meet all of your essential expenses*" for the United States.
>
> Data on these items are available for 22 European countries based on the Survey on Income and Living Conditions (EU-SILC) conducted in 2005; for Australia, based on the survey Household Income and Labour Dynamics in Australia (HILDA) conducted in 2005; for Japan, based on the *Shakai Seikatsu Chousa* (Survey of Living Conditions) conducted in 2003; and for the United States, based on the Survey of Income and Program Participation, SIPP, conducted in 2003. While these are large, official surveys for most countries, the survey used for Japan is an unofficial and experimental survey designed by the National Institute of Population and Social Security Research, with a (nationally representative) sample limited to around 2 000 households and around 6 000 persons aged 20 years and above, with data on household income provided through categorical answers. For the United States, where SIPP data refer to gross (*i.e.* pre-tax) income, income values "after taxes" have been obtained by applying the TAXSIM model of the National Bureau of Economic Research to the SIPP data.

types of deprivation based on responses from the household head or reference person, ignoring possible differences in assessments of their own conditions provided by various members of the same household.[8]

Prevalence of different deprivation items

The natural starting point for a comparative assessment of material deprivation is provided by prevalence rates for each of the seven items described above. Two main patterns stand out from Table 7.2:

- First, patterns differ across items. On average, across the countries considered, 20% of respondents declared being unable to make ends meet, while smaller shares of respondents report living in overcrowded housing or in areas with poor environmental conditions (18% and 16% respectively). The frequency of other deprivation items (inadequate heating and food consumption, payment arrears for utilities and rents) is, on average, below 10%.[9]

- Second, differences across countries are significant. In general, Nordic countries (except Iceland) record the lowest prevalence rates for all the items considered, Southern and Eastern European countries have some of the highest shares in almost all dimensions, while Australia, Japan and the United States are somewhere in the middle.[10]

Another perspective on the prevalence of material deprivation is provided by information on the number of items that people lacked on average. Figure 7.2 shows large differences in the share of people lacking two or more items, ranging from 10% in all Nordic countries (except Iceland), Luxembourg, Austria and the Netherlands, to 20% or more in Italy, Switzerland, the Czech Republic, Australia, the United States and Japan, and to 40% or more in Greece, Hungary, the Slovak Republic and Poland. The share of people lacking three

Table 7.2. **Prevalence of different forms of material deprivation**

Shares of total population, based on individual data

	Inadequate heating	Constrained food choices	Over-crowding	Poor environ-mental conditions	Arrears in paying utilities	Arrears in mortgage or rents	Inability to make ends meet	Average across items
European countries								
Austria	3.1	8.7	15.1	9.1	1.7	1.3	8.8	6.8
Belgium	14.0	3.8	5.1	16.8	5.7	3.0	17.1	9.4
Czech Republic	9.3	17.8	33.5	19.8	7.2	6.3	30.2	17.7
Denmark	8.9	1.9	7.7	6.7	2.8	3.1	6.8	5.4
Finland	2.6	2.9	5.9	12.8	7.4	4.4	8.5	6.3
France	5.3	6.4	6.4	17.2	7.2	6.2	16.2	9.3
Germany	4.4	10.1	6.5	21.1	2.7	2.4	11.3	8.3
Greece	15.6	5.8	33.4	33.4	18.1	26.5	6.6	19.9
Hungary	17.7	31.2	46.1	17.2	15.9	2.8	35.4	23.8
Iceland	9.4	4.2	11.9	7.7	7.7	9.9	13.3	9.1
Ireland	4.0	2.9	6.8	7.6	6.9	5.0	24.8	8.3
Italy	10.6	6.3	26.3	22.1	10.5	3.4	34.6	16.3
Luxembourg	0.9	2.4	12.0	18.6	3.2	2.2	6.3	6.5
Netherlands	3.1	2.6	3.7	14.9	3.2	3.8	16.9	6.9
Norway	1.3	3.6	5.9	7.7	7.9	5.9	8.7	5.9
Poland	33.6	35.3	52.5	13.8	24.4	2.3	51.5	30.5
Portugal	41.9	4.0	19.6	20.7	5.2	2.9	36.9	18.7
Slovak Republic	13.6	41.4	46.8	18.7	8.3	4.2	30.6	23.4
Spain	8.6	2.3	8.4	16.8	3.7	2.6	26.8	9.9
Sweden	1.4	3.2	8.4	5.0	5.0	5.1	8.5	5.2
Switzerland	2.6	9.3	41.8	20.2	12.6	2.7	27.2	16.6
United Kingdom	5.6	6.1	8.5	13.9	0.1	4.9	12.9	7.4
Non-European countries								
Australia	2.4	3.0	9.0	11.1	16.7	8.0	34.6	12.1
Japan	0.5	10.5	15.0	29.8	4.3	6.0	26.7	13.3
United States	5.1	16.4	14.1	25.4	10.0	6.3	14.2	13.0
Averages								
EU-22	9.5	9.2	17.9	14.9	7.3	4.8	19.1	11.8
OECD-25	9.0	9.7	18.0	16.3	7.9	5.2	20.6	12.4

StatLink ᵐᵖ⁴ http://dx.doi.org/10.1787/423075011583

Source: OECD Secretariat calculation based on different household surveys.

or more items is below 5% in the Nordic countries, Luxembourg, Austria, the Netherlands as well as in the United Kingdom and Germany, but above 10% in Italy, Switzerland, the Czech Republic, Portugal, Japan and the United States, and above 30% in Greece, Hungary, the Slovak Republic and Poland. The average number of items lacked varies from 0.5 or less in several European countries to around 1 in Italy, Switzerland, the Czech Republic, Australia, the United States and Japan, and to 1.5 or more in Greece, Hungary, the Slovak Republic and Poland.[11]

Characteristics of individuals experiencing multiple deprivation

People reporting multiple deprivations share a number of characteristics. The most important of these is income. Households that are experiencing material deprivation have a lower (equivalised) disposable income than those that are not, and the larger the number of items of deprivation in a household, the lower is household income. All countries shown in Figure 7.3 conform to this pattern of monotonic declines of income for increasing numbers

Figure 7.2. **Share of people lacking different numbers of deprivation items and mean number of items lacked**

Based on individual data

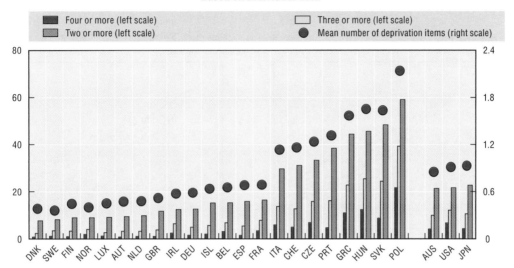

StatLink ⟨ᵣ⟩ http://dx.doi.org/10.1787/422725806623

Note: European and non-European countries are ranked separately, from left to right, in increasing order of the share of people reporting deprivation in two or more items.

Source: OECD Secretariat calculation based on different household surveys.

of deprivation items, although with differences in this profile – which is (marginally) steeper in the United Kingdom and Switzerland and flatter in Australia and Sweden.[12]

A second dimension that is important is the age of each person experiencing deprivation. Figure 7.4 shows the share of each age group reporting two or more deprivation items (top panel) and three or more items (bottom panel), relative to the corresponding share for the entire population. These profiles decline monotonically with the age of each person, a pattern that contrasts with the U-shaped profile for the income-poverty headcount described in Chapter 5. This suggests that household disposable income over-estimates the risk of inadequate consumption among the elderly. There are, however, differences in these age-deprivation profiles across countries – with high risks of deprivation for young adults in Denmark and the very elderly in Greece and Portugal, and much flatter profiles (*i.e.* small declines in the frequency of material deprivation with people's age) in Austria, Hungary, Poland, Portugal, the Slovak Republic and the United States.[13]

The risk of material deprivation also differs with the characteristics of the household where individuals live. Among households with a head of working age (Table 7.3), the experience of multiple deprivations is higher among singles than couples; among households with children than those without; and among households where no one is working than those where someone is. There are, however, exceptions and large differences in the deprivation-risk of different household types across countries. For example, couples with children have a below-average risk of deprivation (at 0.9, across the 25 OECD countries considered) when both parents work (although this is not true in eight countries) but an above-average one when only one person is working (1.8) and especially when no one works (3.1) – with a deprivation risk for jobless couples of 5 in Austria, Poland and Sweden. Among lone parents, the risk of deprivation is, on average, around 3 when the

Figure 7.3. **Relative income of individuals with different numbers of deprivation items**

Relative to people who are not materially deprived, based on individual data

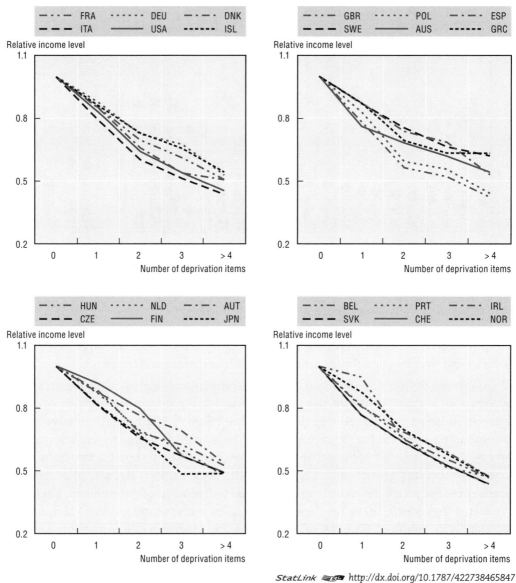

StatLink ⌨ http://dx.doi.org/10.1787/422738465847

Source: OECD Secretariat calculation based on different household surveys.

single parent is jobless (and above 5 in Luxembourg, Norway and Poland) and below 2 when he or she is working (with a deprivation risk above 2 in Denmark, Finland, France, Ireland, the Netherlands, Norway, Sweden and Japan).[14]

Overlap between material deprivation and income poverty

The pattern of income falling as the number of deprivation items experienced by people rises might be taken to imply a significant degree of consistency between income and deprivation at the individual level. In reality, the overlap between the income poor and those reporting different numbers of deprivation items is far from perfect. Figure 7.5 presents information on the number of people who are *both* deprived (in two or more

Figure 7.4. **Risk of multiple deprivation by age of individuals**

Based on individual data

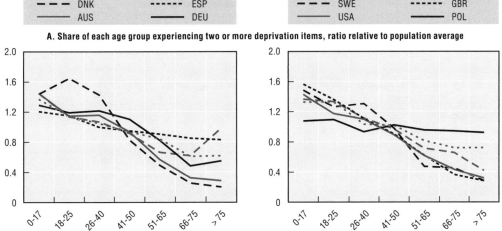

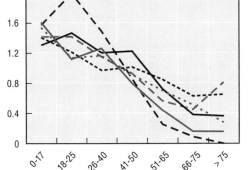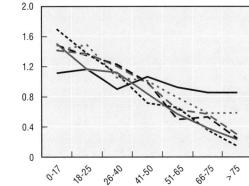

StatLink ᘎᓲᓎ *http://dx.doi.org/10.1787/422745863337*

Note: No data on deprivation by age of individuals are available for Japan.

Source: OECD Secretariat calculation based on different household surveys.

items) and income poor (based on a threshold set at half of median income) and the number in *either* of these conditions, as well as the share of all people who are materially deprived and have income of less than half of the median. Several patterns stand out:

● The overlap is in general only partial, *i.e.* only a small proportion of people reporting material deprivation are also income poor, and *vice versa*. On average, only 20% of people deprived in two or more items have income below the 50% threshold, with this share ranging from around 30% in the United States and Luxembourg, down to 10% in the Netherlands and the Slovak Republic (see Table 7.A2.1 available at *http://dx.doi.org/10.1787/424402577838*).

● Relatively few people experience *both* income poverty and material deprivation. On average, around 4% of all people have both income below the 50% threshold and experience two or more deprivations. Across countries, this share varies from less than

Table 7.3. **Risk of experiencing two or more deprivations for people living in households with a head of working age, by household characteristics**

Relative to the population average, based on individual data

	Household with a head of working age									
	Single adults				Couples					
	Without children		With children		Without children			With children		
	Working	Not working	Working	Not working	Two or more workers	One worker	No worker	Two or more workers	One worker	No worker
European countries										
Austria	0.7	2.2	1.9	4.2	0.7	0.6	0.7	1.0	1.6	5.1
Belgium	0.9	2.4	1.5	3.7	0.4	0.8	1.1	0.5	1.9	3.7
Czech Rep.	0.6	1.3	1.6	1.9	0.7	0.8	0.9	1.0	1.6	2.7
Denmark	1.4	2.9	2.5	4.7	0.4	0.5	0.5	0.8	2.8	4.7
Finland	1.2	2.5	2.7	3.9	0.5	0.7	1.3	1.0	2.2	3.1
France	1.0	2.0	2.2	3.9	0.6	0.8	0.8	0.8	1.9	3.6
Germany	1.1	2.7	1.8	3.6	0.6	0.9	0.8	0.8	1.4	3.6
Greece	0.8	0.8	1.4	0.9	1.0	0.9	1.0	0.9	1.2	1.6
Hungary	0.7	1.1	1.1	1.8	0.8	1.0	1.0	1.1	1.4	1.9
Iceland	0.9	3.0	1.8	2.0	0.6	0.7	0.8	1.1	2.6	3.0
Ireland	0.7	1.9	2.3	4.6	0.2	0.7	0.9	0.6	1.5	4.4
Italy	0.7	1.2	1.1	1.4	0.8	0.8	0.9	1.1	1.7	2.3
Luxembourg	0.5	2.4	1.8	6.0	0.4	0.6	0.6	1.4	1.6	2.2
Netherlands	1.1	2.9	2.5	5.9	0.5	0.7	1.2	0.8	1.7	4.2
Norway	1.3	2.8	2.3	5.7	0.4	0.8	1.0	0.8	2.6	6.4
Poland	0.7	1.1	1.0	1.4	0.8	0.9	1.1	0.9	1.2	1.4
Portugal	0.8	1.2	1.2	1.6	0.8	0.9	1.1	1.1	1.3	1.6
Slovak Rep.	0.6	0.9	1.0	1.7	0.9	0.9	1.0	1.1	1.2	1.5
Spain	0.9	1.9	1.5	2.0	0.8	0.9	1.1	1.1	1.2	2.2
Sweden	1.1	2.9	2.1	6.7	0.4	0.9	1.2	0.9	2.5	6.4
Switzerland	0.6	1.5	1.0	0.8	0.9	0.9	0.8	1.1	1.7	2.5
United Kingdom	0.9	2.1	1.6	3.1	0.5	0.6	1.0	0.7	1.8	2.5
Non-European countries										
Australia	1.1	1.8	1.5	3.2	0.5	0.9	0.7	0.9	1.5	2.4
Japan	2.1	1.2	3.0	2.2	0.9	1.1	0.5	1.1	1.5	2.1
United States	0.8	1.6	1.7	2.5	0.5	0.8	0.9	1.0	2.5	1.5
Averages										
EU-22	0.9	2.0	1.7	3.3	0.6	0.8	0.9	0.9	1.8	3.2
Non-EU-3	1.4	1.5	2.1	2.6	0.6	0.9	0.7	1.0	1.8	2.0
OECD-25	0.9	1.9	1.8	3.2	0.6	0.8	0.9	0.9	1.8	3.1

StatLink ᴍᴍᴤ🔗 http://dx.doi.org/10.1787/423113020872

Note: The risk of deprivation is measured as the share of people in each household type experiencing two or more deprivation items divided by the share for the entire population.
Source: OECD Secretariat calculation based on different household surveys.

2% in Sweden, Denmark, Norway, Finland and Austria, up to 6% or more in Japan, Italy, the United States, Portugal, Greece and Poland.

● While people who are *both* income poor and materially deprived may be considered as being in severe conditions, the number of those who are *either* income poor *or* deprived provides an upper bound estimate of those facing a risk of poverty. People in this group may be reducing their consumption patterns, despite having an income that is above the conventional poverty line, or they may afford typical consumption patterns, despite their low income, through additional resources. The share of people in either of these

Figure 7.5. **Share of people who are both deprived and income poor
and either deprived or income poor**

People deprived in two or more items and with income below half of median household disposable,
estimates based on individual data

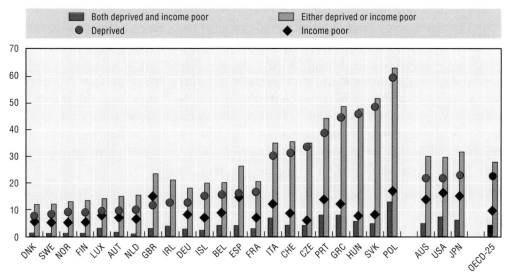

StatLink ⌐ http://dx.doi.org/10.1787/422866807520

Note: European and non-European countries are ranked separately, from left to right, in increasing order of the share
of people reporting deprivation in two or more items.

Source: OECD Secretariat calculation based on different household surveys.

two conditions is at 28% on average, ranging from 40% or more in Portugal, Hungary,
Greece, the Slovak Republic and Poland, down to 15% or less in Denmark, Sweden,
Norway, Finland, Luxembourg and Austria.[15]

Conclusion

While both of the approaches used in this chapter – *i.e.* the one based on averaging at
the country level across a large number of items, and the one based on looking at how
many people experience different types of deprivation for a more narrow range of items –
have limits, when combined they highlight a number of patterns that go beyond those
based on static income:

● There are large differences across OECD countries in the extent of material deprivation.
Based on a measure that aggregates data on the prevalence of different items,
deprivation is higher in countries with lower income and higher relative-income poverty.

● Evidence from individual data shows that the experience of deprivation declines
monotonically with income. It also declines with age, in contrast to the U-shaped
relation between relative income poverty and age described in Chapter 5, suggesting that
income-poor older people are not necessarily experiencing material hardship.

● Individual data also suggest that, while there is some overlap between low income and
deprivation, a large share of the income poor are not materially deprived; this pattern
may reflect the temporary nature of many spells of low-income, the features of the
deprivation questions considered here (*i.e.* capturing dimensions that go beyond a
minimum standard of living), and the availability of other means through which low-
income people may support their living conditions (*e.g.* in-kind transfers, the running

down of assets or the accumulation of debt). Conversely, a large share of the population as a whole experience either low income or deprivation.

This chapter is only an attempt to use the information currently available on material deprivation in a comparative setting. Better comparative measures can be achieved only through greater *ex ante* standardisation of surveys, so as to include a larger set of items that are comparable across countries. Achieving such standardisation in statistical sources is an investment worth doing in the light of the importance for social policy of measuring material deprivation accurately. Standardised measures are important not only for benchmarking countries' performance, but also in order to improve the targeting of individual programmes. This is especially important in countries where income is a poor proxy of economic needs. Indirectly, measures of material deprivation also point to the importance of looking at factors that go beyond the income and earnings capacity of people, to other constituents of an acceptable standard of living.

Notes

1. For example, Callan *et al.* (1996) shows that a much smaller minority of households in Ireland fail to satisfy their basic needs compared to those counted as income poor, and that their incidence has declined over time even when income poverty was rising.

2. Absolute thresholds define poverty on the basis of a normative judgment of, for example, what qualifies as basic needs or what is the proportion of food expenses in the household's budget. While most of these measures are not purely "absolute" – i.e. the threshold is both time- and space-specific – their common characteristic is that they build on *a priori* assumptions of what basic needs should be satisfied. Conversely, relative-income measures such as those used in Chapters 5 and 6 of this report fix an arbitrary threshold relative to the most "typical" standard of living in society (*e.g.* median income).

3. Van den Bosch (2001) provides a comprehensive discussion of the subjective dimensions of deprivation and a detailed description of methods used for the subjective assessment of poverty. Gallie and Paugam (2002) provide useful discussions of issues related to the social environment.

4. Across countries, there is in general a positive correlation between the deprivation items included in Table 3 in Boarini *et al.*, 2006 (the average of these correlation coefficients is 66%). Inability to clothe properly is the item most highly correlated with others, and inability to adequately heat the home the least (with these two items recording the highest and lowest cross-country variability).

5. Data are available, however, for only a few OECD countries. These data also raise specific problems of interpretation: first, because most households reporting material deprivation are also likely to face constraints in financial markets, hence limited indebtedness; second, because the availability of consumer loans depends on the characteristics of credit markets, which differ among OECD countries.

6. This share is higher in the United States (24%), where, however, this question is only asked to those households that experienced problems in meeting essential expenses (rather than all households). Also, the questions in the US survey refer to help received in specific contingencies (rather than in general) and to persons who did not expect to receive any help in a broader range of (non-financial) contingencies. Because of these differences in survey questions, data for the United States are not included in Table 8 in Boarini *et al.* (2006).

7. For example, overcrowding is defined more strictly in the case of Japan than for other countries while, conversely, questions about constrained food choices and poor environmental conditions encompass a larger menu of contingencies for the United States than elsewhere.

8. In the case of Australia, questions on material deprivation are answered separately by each household member. While the deprivation data for Australia used in this section are those provided by the household head, Breunig *et al.* (2005) highlight significant differences in the reporting of material deprivation among partners of the same household, especially for households with intermediate levels of income, with other household members often reporting various forms of deprivation even when the household head does not. This implies that survey which rely upon a representative individual to report about financial difficulty are missing

important information about material hardship, and suggests that, in the presence of a significant disagreement between partners on their experience of financial difficulties, many household will be misclassified.

9. The larger share of people reporting "inability to make ends meet" relative to other items partly reflects the more general and subjective nature of this type of question.

10. The share of people unable to make ends meet ranged from less than 10% in the Nordic countries (except Iceland), Luxembourg, Austria and Greece to 25% or more in the Czech Republic, Hungary, Ireland, Italy, Poland, Portugal, Switzerland and the Slovak Republic, as well as Japan and Australia. The share of people reporting inadequate heating is above 10% in Belgium, Greece, Hungary, Italy, Poland, Portugal and the Slovak Republic, and the same occurs for constrained food choices in the Czech Republic, Germany, Hungary, Poland, the Slovak Republic, as well as Japan and the United States. More than 10% of people report arrears in paying utility bills in Greece, Hungary, Italy, Poland, Switzerland, Australia and the United States, and the same share reports arrears in paying mortgages or rents in Greece and Iceland.

11. Some of the approaches that might be used to derive a measure of the prevalence of non-income poverty based on a synthetic measure of multiple deprivations are described in Annex 7.A1.

12. An alternative approach to describing the relation between income and material deprivation is used by Saunders and Adelman (2006), who plot the share of people in the various income groupings (in decreasing order of income) that are also materially deprived: their results show that this gradient is steeper and more monotonic in Australia than in the United Kingdom.

13. Across the 24 OECD countries with available data, people aged 66 to 75 and over 75 have, respectively, a risk of deprivation that is 62 and 60% lower that of the population average in the case of two or more items, but only 47 and 43% lower in the case of three or more items.

14. Among households with an elderly head, patterns mirror those by age of individuals. Households with a head of retirement age have a deprivation risk always below that of the entire population, even when the elderly person is living alone and not working. Only in Austria, Greece, Poland and Portugal is the share of elderly people living alone reporting two or more deprivations (marginally) above that for the entire population.

15. A number of other patterns stand out from Table 7.A2.1 (available at *http://dx.doi.org/10.1787/424402577838*). First, for a given number of deprivation items, the extent of overlap rises when a higher income threshold is used. For example, among people reporting deprivation in two or more items in OECD countries, 30% have income below 60% of the median, as compared to only 10% when considering those with income below 40% of the median. When considering people deprived in three of more items, the corresponding shares are 37% and 13% respectively. Second, for a given income threshold, the overlap rises when a higher number of items is considered (*e.g.*, in the case of people with income below 60% of the median, from 30% in the case of deprivation in two or more items to 37% in the case of deprivation in three or more items).

References

Boarini, R. and M. Mira d'Ercole (2006), "Measures of Material Deprivation in OECD Countries", OECD Social, Employment and Migration Working Paper No. 37, OECD, Paris.

Bradshaw, J. and N. Finch (2003), "Overlaps in Dimensions of Poverty", *Journal of Social Policy*, Vol. 32, No. 4.

Breunig, R., D. Cobb-Clark, X. Gong and D. Venn (2005), "Disagreement in Partner Reports of Financial Difficulty", IZA Discussion Paper No. 1624, Bonn, May.

Callan, T., B. Nolan and C.T. Whelan (1993), "Resources, Deprivation and the Measurement of Poverty", *Journal of Social Policy*, Vol. 22, No. 2.

Callan, T., B. Nolan, B.J. Whelan, C.J. Whelan and J. Williams (1996), *Poverty in the 1990s: Evidence from the 1994 Living in Ireland Survey*, Oak Tree Press, Dublin.

Desai, M. and A. Shah (1988), "An Econometric Approach to the Measurement of Poverty", *Oxford Economic Papers*, Vol. 40, No. 3.

Eurostat (2002), *Deuxième rapport sur le revenu, la pauvreté et l'exclusion sociale*, Statistiques sociales européennes, Luxembourg.

Gallie, D. and S. Paugam (2002), *Social Precarity and Social Integration*, Rapport pour la Direction générale de l'emploi de la Commission européenne.

Gordon, D., R. Levitas, C. Pantazis, D. Patsios, S. Payne and P. Townsend (2000), *Poverty and Social Exclusion in Britain*, Joseph Rowntree Foundation, York.

Jensen, J., M. Spittal, S. Crichton, S. Sathiyandra and V. Krishnan (2002), "Direct Measures of Living Standards: the New Zealand ELSI Scale", Ministry of Social Development, Wellington.

Kangas, O. and V.-M. Ritakallio (1998), "Different Methods – Different Results? Approaches to Multidimensional Poverty", in H.-J. Andress (ed.), *Empirical Poverty Research in a Comparative Perspective*, Aldershot, Ashgate.

Layte, R., B. Maître, B. Nolan and C. T. Whelan (2001), "Persistent and Consistent Poverty in the 1994 and 1995 waves of the European Community Household Panel", *Review of Income and Wealth*, Vol. 47, No. 4.

Mack, J. and S. Lansley (1985), *Poor Britain*, Allen and Unwin, London.

Nolan, B. and C. Whelan (1996), "Measuring Poverty using Income and Deprivation Indicators: Alternative Approaches", *Journal of European Social Policy*, Vol. 6, No. 3.

OECD (2006), *Society at a Glance – OECD Social Indicators*, OECD, Paris.

Perry, B. (2002), "The Mismatch Between Income Measures and Direct Outcome Measures of Poverty", *Social Policy Journal of New Zealand*, Vol. 19.

Piachaud, D. (1981), "Peter Townsend and the Holy Grail", *New Society*, Vol. 57.

Saunders, P. and L. Adelman (2006), "Deprivation and Exclusion: A Comparative Study of Australia and Britain", *Journal of Social Policy*, Vol. 35, No. 4.

Sen, A.K. (1983), "Poor, Relatively Speaking", *Oxford Economic Paper*, No. 35.

Townsend, P. (1979), *Poverty in the United Kingdom*, Harmondsworth, Penguin.

Van den Bosch, K. (2001), *Identifying the Poor: Using Subjective and Consensual Measures*, Ashgate, Aldershot.

Whelan, C.T., R. Layte and B. Maître (2002), "Persistent Deprivation in European Union", *Schmollers Jahrbuch: Journal of Applied Social Sciences*, Vol. 122, pp. 1-24.

ANNEX 7.A1

Prevalence of Non-income Poverty Based on a Synthetic Measure of Multiple Deprivations

While the data on individuals experiencing different forms of deprivation allow identifying a range of patterns, as described in this chapter, it is more difficult to derive a summary measure of non-income poverty based on the experience of multiple deprivations. This is for both practical and conceptual reasons. While the practical reasons mainly reflect the differences in the wording of survey questions across countries, as already noted, the conceptual reasons relate to two main issues:

- The first is the importance to be attributed to each deprivation item. The basic choice here is between measures that give equal weight to each of the seven deprivation items considered and measures that "weight" each item according to its prevalence among the entire population – i.e. giving greater weight to items that are more common in a given society.

- The second is the choice of the threshold to be used.[1] These thresholds can be based on either an absolute number of deprivation items (e.g. those lacking two or more items) or on some multiple of the typical number of items lacked by the population at large.

As there are no unambiguous answers to these two questions, Table 7.A1.1 shows different summary measures of non-income poverty, as well as income-poverty headcounts (based on different thresholds) drawn from the same surveys.[2] The first column shows a deprivation rate for unweighted items (i.e. all types of deprivation are equally important), where the number of items above which people is counted as "deprived-poor" varies across countries. This is achieved by setting the threshold at twice the average number of deprivation items that people lack.[3] This method implies, in practice, setting a deprivation threshold of two items in most countries, of three in the Czech Republic, Greece, Hungary, Italy, Portugal, Switzerland, the Slovak Republic, Australia, Japan, the United States, and of four in Poland. Based on this measure, around 14% of all people in the OECD countries considered in Table 7.A1.1 experienced multiple deprivations, a rate that is close to the income-poverty headcount based on a 60% threshold. This unweighted summary measure of multiple deprivations was above 20% in Greece, Hungary, Poland and the Slovak Republic, and below 10% in Austria, Denmark, Finland, Luxembourg, the Netherlands, Norway and Sweden. On this measure, the deprivation rate is around half of the income-poverty headcount based on a 60% threshold in Ireland, the United Kingdom, Australia, Japan and the United States, but almost double

Table 7.A1.1. **Summary measure of material deprivation and income poverty based on different thresholds**

Based on individual data

	Summary measure of material deprivation				Income-poverty rate		
	Unweighted		Weighted				
	Threshold set at:				Threshold set at:		
	Twice the mean	20%	30%	Twice the mean	60% median	50% median	40% median
European countries							
Austria	9.4	5.3	2.8	4.8	13.4	7.1	3.4
Belgium	15.2	10.8	6.6	8.5	15.6	9.0	3.7
Czech Republic	15.8	29.4	16.4	12.7	11.5	5.8	3.0
Denmark	7.6	8.2	3.3	4.4	11.1	5.5	2.7
Finland	8.9	10.4	4.1	6.5	12.3	5.7	2.3
France	16.4	16.4	8.9	11.0	14.0	7.0	2.8
Germany	12.6	11.0	5.2	7.0	14.2	8.2	3.9
Greece	22.8	32.8	20.6	13.6	19.4	12.2	7.0
Hungary	25.5	35.4	22.9	15.0	13.9	7.8	3.8
Iceland	15.2	16.2	6.9	10.5	12.1	7.0	4.2
Ireland	12.4	11.5	6.7	7.9	21.2	12.5	5.4
Italy	13.7	19.6	12.8	12.8	19.2	12.2	6.9
Luxembourg	9.2	4.8	3.4	4.4	13.1	8.0	3.0
Netherlands	9.8	8.1	4.1	6.4	10.6	6.6	4.2
Norway	8.8	9.2	4.3	5.3	10.1	5.3	3.0
Poland	21.7	43.1	25.5	17.3	22.4	16.9	11.9
Portugal	16.1	18.3	8.5	8.5	21.6	13.9	8.3
Slovak Republic	24.4	35.7	19.0	12.6	13.8	8.2	4.5
Spain	15.7	9.5	4.7	7.1	21.4	14.6	8.8
Sweden	8.1	8.6	3.8	6.0	9.4	5.0	2.8
Switzerland	12.7	16.7	7.9	8.5	13.6	8.6	4.0
Non-European countries							
Australia	9.9	12.7	6.4	10.5	20.6	13.6	6.0
Japan	10.6	10.5	4.3	6.8	20.1	15.0	8.7
United States	12.1	22.8	13.9	13.9	23.7	16.5	10.5
Averages							
EU-21	14.4	16.5	9.0	8.7	15.2	9.2	5.0
Non-EU-3	10.9	15.3	8.2	10.4	21.4	15.0	8.4
OECD-24	14.0	16.6	9.1	9.0	15.8	9.7	5.3

StatLink ⧉ http://dx.doi.org/10.1787/423114348677

Note: The deprivation rates shown in the first column are based on a threshold set at twice the mean number of items lacked by the population as a whole *i.e.* twice the difference between the number of items considered (7) and the average number of items held, as shown in Figure 7.2. In practice this threshold is equal to 2 for Austria, Belgium, Germany, Denmark, Spain, Finland, France, Ireland, Iceland, Luxembourg, the Netherlands, Norway, Sweden, the United Kingdom, as well as Japan; to 3 in the Czech Republic, Greece, Hungary, Italy, Portugal, Switzerland and the Slovak Republic, as well as Australia and the United States; and to 4 for Poland.

Source: OECD Secretariat calculation based on different household surveys.

the headcount in Hungary and the Slovak Republic (Figure 7.A1.1, left-hand panel). The correlation with the income-poverty headcount, while positive, is low.

Another way of computing a summary measure of multiple deprivations is by "weighting" each item according to its general prevalence. Weighting has the advantage of converting the discrete "1 to 7" deprivation scale into a continuous scale ranging between 0 (for people not deprived of any of the items considered) to 1 (for those deprived of all items); its disadvantage is that weights are sensitive to outliers.[4] Annex Table 7.A1.1 shows summary measures of "weighted" deprivation based on three thresholds: 20% and 30% of

Figure 7.A1.1. **The relation between a summary measure of material deprivation and income poverty headcounts**

Based on individual data

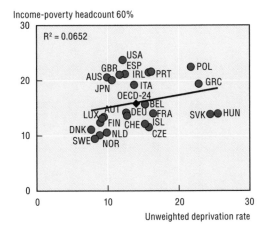
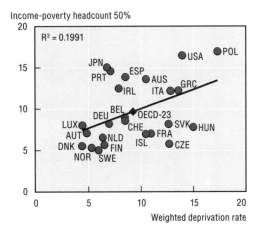

StatLink ᴴᵍ▸ http://dx.doi.org/10.1787/423021363648

Source: OECD Secretariat calculation based on different household surveys.

all items (i.e. a threshold common across countries) and a relative threshold (differing across countries) set at twice the average number of deprivation items experienced by the entire population. On average (across the 22 OECD countries included), the weighted deprivation rate based on a relative threshold is 9%, ranging between values of 12% and over in the Czech Republic, Greece, Hungary, Poland, the Slovak Republic and the United States, and below 5% in Austria, Denmark, and Luxembourg. On average, this summary measure of multiple deprivations is close to the poverty headcount based on a threshold of 50% of median income, but again with large differences across countries. This summary measure of multiple deprivations is well below the poverty headcount in Japan, Luxembourg and Spain, but well above it in the Czech and Slovak Republics, France, Iceland and Hungary (Figure 7.A1.1, left-hand panel). While the correlation between this measure of multiple deprivation and the income-poverty headcount is higher than for the "unweighted" measure, cross-country dispersion remains large.

Notes

1. Townsend (1979) considered individuals with a score equal to or greater than 5 as living in deprivation, and then derived an income threshold corresponding to the level below which "deprivation scores escalated disproportionately". Most studies of material deprivation use an absolute standard, usually defined by specifying a minimum number of items, and counting people as "poor" when they report deprivation in (at least) these items. Other approaches rely on "relative" thresholds, whereby poverty is defined by the lack of a certain number of items, the level of which is set such that the number of people lacking them is the same as the number of income poor (Layte et al., 2001). This procedure is, however, less useful if the goal is to derive an independent measure of non-income poverty that could be used alongside the income-poverty headcount.

2. The income-poverty headcounts shown in Table 7.A1.1 are very close to these based on the OECD income distribution questionnaire shown in Chapter 5, with a correlation coefficient of 0.88 for a threshold of 50% of median income, and of 91% for one at 60%.

3. This is analogous to using half of median income as the threshold for income poverty. The mean, rather than median, is used here, as the median number of items that people lack is typically zero. This approach implies that if, on average, people have six of the seven items considered (i.e. on

average they lack only one item) the threshold is set at two. The number of items "lacked" is conventionally rounded to the greater integer (*e.g.* if they lack 1.5 items, this is rounded to two).

4. When the share of people in the entire population experiencing deprivation of items is very low, the weight given to other types of deprivation becomes very small (tending to zero). For this reason, "weighted" deprivation rates for the United Kingdom are not shown in Table 7.A1.1.

PART IV

Additional Dimensions
of Inequality

ISBN 978-92-64-04418-0
Growing Unequal?
© OECD 2008

PART IV

Chapter 8

Intergenerational Mobility: Does it Offset or Reinforce Income Inequality?*

Income, education, occupation and personality traits all tend to be transmitted from parents to their offspring, especially at the top and bottom of the distribution. Countries with lower intergenerational mobility tend to feature wider income inequalities at a point in time and higher returns to education – suggesting that the education systems and the strategies used by parents for the education of their children are very important for the transmission of disadvantages from generation to generation.

* This chapter has been prepared by Anna Cristina D'Addio, OECD Social Policy Division, drawing on D'Addio (2007). Special thanks to Mark Pearson and Marco Mira d'Ercole for useful comments, and to Patrick Hamm for editorial assistance.

203

Introduction

Many OECD countries are rightly concerned about intergenerational mobility – the extent of transmission of advantages or disadvantages across generations. When children "inherit" a substantial degree of their economic status or other important social characteristics from their parents, this generates widespread perceptions of unfairness and lack of opportunity. Societies characterised by a high transmission of social and economic status from generation to generation are not only more likely to be perceived as "unfair", they may also be less productive than those where all individuals have a more equal chance to succeed, as they waste the talents and skills of youths from disadvantaged backgrounds.[1]

Drawing on a more extensive review of intergenerational mobility by D'Addio (2007), this chapter summarises the main empirical evidence about the extent to which differences in income are transmitted from one generation to the next. The first section overviews the available evidence on the transmission of income and education across generations, while also identifying the most important factors that contribute to it. The chapter then discusses some of the key policy implications of the intergenerational transmission of disadvantage, with a focus on the policies available to reduce those inequalities at birth that undermine chances of achievement and success in later life. Children's outcomes are analysed here from a lifecycle perspective; from this viewpoint, the extent to which the life chances of children are either positively or adversely affected by the circumstances and behaviours of their parents is an integral component of developing policies to give children "the best possible start to their lives".

Intergenerational transmission of disadvantages: an overview

Income, education, occupation and personality traits persist between generations in all OECD countries. However, the size of this persistence may vary across domains. It is possible, for example, to have a great deal of mobility in education, occupation or even personality traits without seeing similar mobility in income (e.g. because incomes may vary widely within the same occupation).[2] The consequences of intergenerational transmission will also vary depending on people's characteristics. For example, low-income persistence has different effects than high-income persistence, and growing up in a low-income environment may cumulate with other forms of disadvantage.

While this review mainly focuses on the transmission across generations of individuals' traits, it should be stressed that several factors shape the magnitude of this transmission. One of these factors is the macro-economic context of each country. For example, many children have enjoyed better economic and social conditions than their parents, mainly reflecting the strong economic growth recorded over the past 50 years, which has resulted in increased opportunities to move into higher-skilled, better-paid jobs. However, the overall pace of economic growth is only one factor: the more unequal a society is, the more difficult it is to move up the social ladder, simply because children have a greater gap to make up.

Intergenerational transmission of income

What do we know about the intergenerational transmission of income?

Intergenerational income mobility is commonly measured by the fraction of relative income differences between all adults at a point in time that is transmitted to their offspring: the higher this fraction (or elasticity), the lower is intergenerational income mobility. Most studies have focused on the *earnings of fathers and sons,* as family income is harder to measure and more complex to interpret. Fewer studies have considered transmission of earnings differences between fathers and daughters, despite the increasing educational attainment and participation in the labour market of recent cohorts of women.[3]

In general, the available evidence suggests that income from work – but also from assets and welfare – persists across generations. It also suggests that disadvantage tends to persist in vulnerable households. A disadvantaged family background – for example, in terms of low education, poor health, lone parenthood or non-employment – tends to boost the persistence of poverty. Similarly, growing up in areas characterised by a high concentration of poverty might also contribute to intergenerational poverty, long-term welfare dependency, crime victimisation, and family breakdowns.[4]

Intergenerational earnings mobility varies significantly across OECD countries: for example, less than 20% of the differences in parental earnings are passed on to the children in some of the Nordic countries, as well as in Australia and Canada, as compared to between 40 and 50% in some other countries, including Italy, the United Kingdom and the United States (Figure 8.1). In these latter countries, parents determine the success or failure of their offspring to a greater extent than in others, either directly (through intergenerational transfers of money, or extra investment in the success of their children) or indirectly (through living in a good neighbourhood or having a particular ethnic origin). Keeping things very simple, an elasticity value of 0.50 – as in Italy or the United Kingdom – implies that 50% of the relative difference in parental earnings is transmitted, on average, to their children. An elasticity of 0.15 (as in Denmark) implies that only 15% of the

Figure 8.1. **Estimates of the intergenerational earnings elasticity for selected OECD countries**

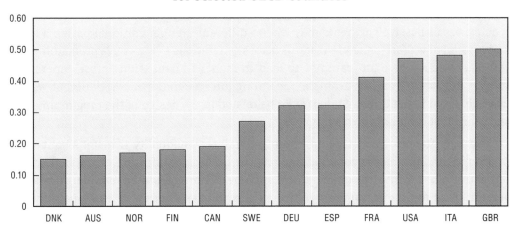

StatLink ⬛ *http://dx.doi.org/10.1787/423132685118*

Note: The height of each bar represents the best point estimate of the intergenerational earnings elasticity resulting from the meta-analysis carried out by Corak (2006), integrated with estimates from national studies for a few countries. Higher parameters indicate a higher persistence of earnings across generations (i.e. lower intergenerational mobility).

Source: D'Addio (2007) based on Corak (2006) for all countries except Italy, Spain and Australia. For these latter countries, estimates are from Leigh (2006) for Australia; Hugalde Sanchèz (2004) for Spain; and Piraino (2006) for Italy.

difference in parental earnings is transmitted to the children. The "absolute" effect of a given elasticity will, of course, be greater in more unequal societies.[5]

Evidence of lower mobility at the bottom of the earnings distribution is reported in many studies of individual countries.[6] Jäntti et al. (2006), comparing six countries (i.e. Denmark, Finland, Norway, Sweden, United Kingdom and the United States), report lower mobility in the tails of the distributions and argue that this might explain the pattern of male intergenerational mobility across countries. Table 8.1, which is drawn from this study, shows that the probability that a son is in the same earnings quintile as his father is always greater in the lowest and highest quintiles, with the probability in the United States being particularly high in the lowest earnings quintile.

Table 8.1. **Intergenerational mobility across the earnings distribution**

Probability for the son of being in the same earnings quintile as his father

	Denmark	Finland	Norway	Sweden	United Kingdom	United States
1st Quintile	0.25	0.28	0.28	0.26	0.30	0.42
2nd Quintile	0.25	0.22	0.24	0.23	0.23	0.28
3rd Quintile	0.22	0.22	0.22	0.22	0.19	0.26
4th Quintile	0.22	0.23	0.22	0.22	0.25	0.25
5th Quintile	0.36	0.35	0.35	0.37	0.35	0.36

StatLink ⟨🔗⟩ http://dx.doi.org/10.1787/423230758402

Source: Based on the diagonal of the transition matrices estimated by Jäntti et al. (2006).

A number of studies report evidence that low mobility at the bottom of the distribution increases the inheritance of poverty across generations.[7] When mobility at the bottom of the income distribution is very low, growing up in a family on welfare increases the likelihood of becoming a welfare recipient as an adult. While available research does not allow comparing the extent to which intergenerational transmission of welfare recipiency compares across countries, it does confirm that in many OECD countries welfare dependency is transmitted across generations.[8] This transmission proceeds from different mechanisms, some causal and some non-causal, which include the way that social policy is structured and delivered. For example, the structure of eligibility rules and the emphasis on active versus passive payments may lead to different intergenerational patterns in the transmission of welfare-dependent status across generations – i.e. passive programmes are more likely than active programmes to lead to higher transmission across generations (Corak et al., 2004). Thus, for example, the strong intergenerational correlation of welfare status observed in the United States might be related to the design of the programme (as it was before 1996) and how it was targeted.

The inheritance of poverty and, more generally, of inequality threatens equality of opportunity and produces economic inefficiencies. The identification of the factors that contribute most to the transmission of income differences across generations will therefore lead to a better understanding of the policies needed to make poverty less persistent. Indeed, actions directed at improving education, health, employment systems, residential mobility and urban revitalisation could contribute to break the poverty cycle through their influence on intergenerational income mobility.

What determines the extent of intergenerational income transmission?

Table 8.2 summarises the evidence, as available through several empirical studies, of how different factors contribute to the transmission of income between generations. While most of these studies suggest that the influence of schooling and household wealth is, in general, quite large, they also point to the importance of other factors.

● Wealth passed from parents to children affects the incomes of children in various ways: directly, in the form of gifts and bequests that increase the asset holdings of children from different backgrounds; and indirectly, when parental wealth contributes to the earnings of people in their adult life by improving nutrition, health, education, access to good housing and neighbourhood conditions, as well as providing start-up capital that is critical for many activities (*e.g.* Blanchflower and Oswald, 1998). Perhaps the most important intergenerational impact of wealth is that it reduces the importance of capital market failures. In an ideal world, when people seek loans on capital markets to finance investments in human capital, parental background would have no impact on whether the loan were granted. In practice, borrowing against future earnings is difficult, and liquidity constraints affect investment in human capital (Becker and Tomes, 1979). In these conditions, low-income parents will under-invest in their children's human capital, making the poverty circle harder to break. Wealth transfers may also indirectly affect intergenerational income mobility when they influence those traits that are important for economic success, such as saving and schooling propensities, the work ethic and risk-related behaviours.[9]

● Genetic factors also matter, although the mechanisms underlying their contribution to the inheritance of income are largely unexplained. Evidence suggests that inheritance of IQ makes very little contribution to the intergenerational income correlation. Other inherited traits, like personality traits (and behaviours – though not entirely genetically determined), appear to be important channels of transmission. The ethnic origin of the individual also contributes to the transmission of income across generations. This may happen because ethnicity acts as an externality in the human capital accumulation process (Borjas, 1992). This "spill-over effect" operates mainly through geographic concentrations of peers, and differs from that related to the neighbourhood in which families live: even within the same neighbourhood, children are more likely to interact with other individuals from the same ethnic group, in which case the impact of peers of the same ethnicity will outweigh that of other neighbours.

● While there is a great deal of ambiguity concerning the long-run causal effects of neighbourhoods, some studies suggest that local conditions are important in explaining intergenerational transmission of income. For example, growing up in a "good" neighbourhood, with low unemployment, is associated with higher earnings when the child reaches adulthood. The employment of parents also exerts an impact on the eventual earnings of children, independently of the income associated with work. There is evidence, in other words, that providing children with a positive role model of a working parent affects their own attitudes towards work.

● Another factor in intergenerational income transmission is the structure of the household. For example, the correlation to parental earnings is higher for first-born children than for later-born siblings. If there is "assortative mating" (*i.e.* people marry or have children with partners with similar education and earnings potential), their children are more likely to have incomes similar to their parents.

Table 8.2. **What explains the correlation of incomes across generations?**

Variable	Effect		Study	Examples
	Size	+/–		
Education				
Own schooling or parental education	Large and significant	+(*)	Blanden et al. (2006); Osborne (2005); Bowles et al. (2005); Rumberger (2006); Blanden (2005a); Piraino (2006)	Differential levels of education – measured by years of schooling – explain between 35 and 50% of intergenerational income correlation across countries (Blanden, 2005a)
Wealth	Large and significant	–	Bowles and Gintis (2002a; 2002b); Bowles et al. (2005); Boehm and Schlottmann (1999, 2002); Mazumder (2001, 2002; 2005); Askew et al. (2001)	Wealth accounts for more than 30% of the intergenerational income correlation in the United States (Bowles and Gintis, 2002a)
Social conditions				
Male unemployment rate measured at childbirth	Large and significant	–(*)	Palmer (2002);Hertz (2006); Bowles and Gintis (2002a)	Unemployment rates in the local environment at son's childbirth decrease his permanent wages (a 1% increase in the proportion of unemployed men at the local authority in 1974 leads to a 1.7% decrease in son's earnings)
Economic activity rate measured at childbirth	Large and significant			
Cognitive abilities				
IQ scores	Small and significant	–	Bowles and Gintis (2002a); Bowles et al. (2002); Blanden et al. (2006) ; Rumberger (2006); Osborne Groves (2005a)	IQ inheritance contributes very little (1-2%) to intergenerational income transmission (Bowles and Gintis, 2002a, b)
Test scores in mathematics and science; writing at age 5, mathematics at age 10	Significant and large	–	Blanden et al. (2006), Rumberger (2006)	Writing at age 5 and mathematics at age 10 concur to explain around 14% of the intergenerational earnings mobility (Blanden et al., 2006)
Other inherited traits				
Similarities measured among identical twins and fraternal twins	Significant and large	–	Bowles and Gintis (2002a, b);	Though the contribution of IQ is small, genetic factors contribute to around 22% of the intergenerational correlation of income
Genetically inherited traits other than cognitive skills (e.g. race)	Large and significant	–	Bowles and Gintis (2002a); Hertz (2005); Hertz (2006) Mazumder (2001, 2002); Harding et al. (2005)	These traits are found to matter. Mobility is lower for Blacks than for Whites: the elasticity shifts from 0.27 to 0.49 in Mazumder (2002)
Non-cognitive abilities (and personality traits)				
Locus of control and self-esteem	Significant and large	+(*)	Blanden et al. (2006), Osborne Groves (2005a); Bowles et al. (2005); Bowles et al. (2002)	Non-cognitive abilities explain around 18% of the income transmission across generations (Blanden et al. 2006)
Aggressive behaviour, anxiety at age 10		–(*)		
Health status				
Child birth-weight and height	Significant	+(*)	Blanden et al. (2006); Eriksson et al. (2005); Case and Paxson (2006); Case et al. (2004)	Conditioning on parental health status increases earnings mobility by 27% for sons (Eriksson et al., 2005)
Child's Mental illness; Parental health problems such as cancer, chronic bronchitis, asthma, allergy	Significant and large	–(*)		

GROWING UNEQUAL? – ISBN 978-92-64-04418-0 – © OECD 2008

Table 8.2. **What explains the correlation of incomes across generations?** (cont.)

Variable	Effect		Study	Examples
	Size	+/–		
Family size and structure				
Unique children	Significant	–	Grawe (2005); Lindahl (2002); Mazumder (2001); Rumberger (2006); Harding et al. (2005); Björklund et al. (2004); Anderson and Leo (2006); Björklund and Chadwick (2003)	Intergenerational elasticity is up to 14% higher than the average elasticity for first-born and up to 12% lower than the average for last-born children (Lindahl, 2002). Also, sons of divorced couples are less mobile than their peers from intact families; differences in educational attainment play an important role in explaining the variations in earnings correlations conditional on divorce (Björklund and Chadwick, 2003)
Later-born siblings	Significant	+		
Single parent	Significant	+		
Divorced parents	Significant	–		
Assortative mating				
	Large and significant	–	Lam and Schoeni (1993); Chadwick and Solon (2002); Harding et al. (2005); Hirvonen (2006); Holmlund (2006); Ermisch et al.(2006); Blanden (2005b); and Blanden, (2005c)	The higher the degree of assortative mating, the lower is mobility. Ermisch et al. (2006) show that in the United Kingdom, on average, about 40-50% of the covariance between parents' and own permanent family income can be attributed to the person to whom one is married
Labour market attachment				
Time spent not in education or in unemployment	Large and significant	– (*)	Blanden et al. (2006)	Explains a significant part of income and earnings mobility and significantly decreases sons' earnings
Migrant status				
	Significant	–	Bauer (2006); Card et al. (2005); Borjas (2004); Hertz (2005); Aydemir et al. (2006)	In Canada, differences in the extent of intergenerational income mobility of natives and immigrants are very small; in the Unites States, Sweden, Switzerland, mobility is higher among natives
Policies				
Educational (e.g. shifting the age at which the ability of students are streamed, subsidising education)	Large and significant	+	Pekkarinen et al. (2006); Holmlund (2006); Hanushek et al. (2004); Seshadri and Yuki (2004); Oreopoulous et al. (2006)	The Finnish reform of education of 1972-1977, which shifted the age at which ability was streamed (from 10 to 16) and imposed a uniform academic curriculum, has implied, approximately, a 20% decrease in intergenerational elasticity from the pre-reform average of 0.30 (Pekkarinen et al., 2006)
Reducing income labour taxes on the poor	Unclear		Hendricks (1999)	

Note: The third column reports the direction of the effect on intergenerational income mobility that is associated with the variable reported in the first column. A negative sign implies that the variable negatively affects the extent of intergenerational mobility (i.e. mobility is lower and the intergenerational income elasticity is higher); a positive sign implies that the variable positively affects the extent of intergenerational income mobility (i.e. mobility is higher and the intergenerational income elasticity lower). An asterisk (*) next to the +/– sign implies that the effect reported is on the son's earnings. Indeed, while in many situations effects on the son's earnings and on intergenerational earnings mobility are in the same direction, in other situations this association is not straightforward. For example, a negative effect of the unemployment rate on the son's earnings (at the time of his birth) does not necessarily imply that the relation between the son's and father's earnings is weakened or strengthened. Indeed, the elasticity β simply represents the extent to which income differences with respect to the average in the parent's generation are passed on to the offspring's generation.
Source: D'Addio (2007).

- Finally, educational policies may affect the extent of intergenerational income mobility. For example, public provision or funding of education may increase mobility, as it reduces the cost of education. This implicitly affects parental borrowing constraints and provides a substitute for family inputs in the education process. Of course, the relative quality of public education is also an important influence on outcomes.

Overall, the literature suggests that a large portion of the income differences transmitted from one generation to the next relates to factors that are largely beyond the control of the child (*e.g.* neighbourhood quality, family structure, and birth order) or of the parents (*e.g.* ethnic origin). Other factors, such as investment in human capital, are partly under the control of parents, but the presence of constraints (*e.g.* financial or societal), lack of information or insufficient foresight may drive parents to make sub-optimal choices. In turn, this can lead to an inefficient allocation of talents within society and to the persistence of inequalities across generations. By creating private and social benefits, education – broadly defined – is a central component of social stratification and, at the same time, a correlate of both opportunity and inequality within and across generations. The next section looks therefore at the extent to which educational inequalities are passed on from parents to their children.

Transmission of education across generations

Educational attainment and qualifications are significantly correlated across generations. The most important question that researchers have been trying to answer is to what extent this is because of genetic inheritance and to what extent it results from different behaviours (*e.g.* are more educated parents on average more effective parents?). In general, this research suggests that both inherited abilities and family background contribute to the intergenerational transmission of educational outcomes (D'Addio, 2007) but also that the way in which schooling is organised matters a lot.[10] These conclusions are highlighted by Table 8.3, which compares differences in the mathematics scores of students aged 15 in relation to various background characteristics, based on the OECD *Programme for International Students Assessment* (PISA) of 2003.

- Among the various background characteristics, *parental education* is by far the most important. Students whose fathers have low educational attainment record, on average, mathematics scores that are 62 points lower than those of students with highly educated parents, a gap in competencies that is equivalent to around 1½ years less of schooling (and more than two years of education in Hungary and the Czech and Slovak Republics).

- Students' scores are also correlated with parental occupational status. On average, children whose parents have higher *occupational status* perform better. The average gap (–77 points on a 500-point standardised scale) corresponds to around two years (grades). Gaps are highest in Luxembourg, Germany, Hungary and Belgium, where students whose parents have the highest-status jobs score, on average, about as well as the average student in Finland – the best performing country in PISA (2003) across mathematics, reading and science. In contrast, in the same countries, students whose parents have the lowest-status jobs score only a little higher than the average students in the lowest-performing countries (Greece, Italy, Mexico and Turkey).[11]

- Students from *single-parent households* also show lower performance (varying from more than one grade year in Belgium and the United States, to almost no difference in Austria, the Czech and Slovak Republics). Lower performance is also reported by *non-native*

Table 8.3. **Gaps in average achievement in mathematics scores among 15-year-olds according to various background characteristics**

Point differences in students' achievement on a 500-point standardised scale

	Father's education		Mother's education		Family type	Country of origin		Language spoken at home	Economic social and cultural index
	Low education rel. to high education	Medium education rel. to high education	Low education rel. to high education	Medium education rel. to high education	Single parents rel. to couples	First generation rel. to natives	Non-natives rel. to natives	Different language rel. to same language	Bottom quarter rel. to top quarter
Australia	−47	−35	−39	−29	−27	−5	−2	−12	−93
Austria	−46	−7	−53	−12	−3	−56	−63	−57	−94
Belgium	−62	−28	−67	−32	−42	−92	−109	−95	−133
Canada	−41	−23	−45	−21	−20	6	−7	−13	−74
Czech Republic	−111	−62	−103	−54	−5	..	..	..	−107
Denmark	−63	−41	−61	−25	−26	−70	−65	−43	−101
Finland	−34	−21	−36	−17	−9	..	..	..	−71
France	−50	−19	−55	−17	−18	−48	−72	−66	−105
Germany	−96	−30	−88	−21	−10	−93	−71	−90	−120
Greece	−48	−16	−58	−21	−19	..	−47	−48	−96
Hungary	−120	−64	−115	−58	−16	..	..	..	−127
Iceland	−38	−20	−38	−22	−8	..	..	..	−61
Ireland	−49	−24	−49	−19	−33	..	..	..	−86
Italy	−39	3	−44	−1	−15	..	..	..	−90
Japan	−66	−34	−57	−28	..	..	..	..	−88
Korea	−66	−31	−60	−20	−9	..	..	..	−90
Luxembourg	−61	−24	−53	−25	−19	−31	−45	−42	−102
Mexico	−48	11	−40	20	−10	..	..	..	−91
Netherlands	−46	−29	−40	−33	−31	−59	−79	−81	−99
New Zealand	−67	−32	−61	−13	−22	−32	−5	−16	−105
Norway	−40	−23	−53	−27	−22	..	−61	−45	−89
Poland	−86	−55	−95	−54	−13	..	..	..	−95
Portugal	−31	11	−41	−2	−10	−30	..	..	−95
Slovak Republic	−127	−62	−125	−49	−4	..	..	..	−116
Spain	−47	−27	−43	−25	−12	..	..	..	−85
Sweden	−31	−2	−48	−3	−29	−34	−92	−65	−91
Switzerland	−60	−9	−56	2	−16	−59	−89	−79	−103
Turkey	−98	−50	−108	−35	−5	..	..	..	−116
United States	−74	−35	−76	−29	−43	−22	−36	−46	−109
OECD-29	*−62*	*−27*	*−62*	*−23*	*−18*	*−45*	*−56*	*−53*	*−98*

StatLink ⬛⬛⬛ http://dx.doi.org/10.1787/423264430207

Note: Each column shows the difference in average scores in mathematics between students from disadvantaged backgrounds and those from advantaged ones. The last row shows the unweighted OECD average.

Source: OECD Secretariat computations based on data extracted from PISA (2003) as in D'Addio (2007).

students (*i.e.* students born in a different country from the one where they are attending school), by *first-generation students* (with a gap equivalent to more than one grade year, on average, relative to natives), and by *students whose parents speak a different language at home* than the language used in school classes (particularly in Belgium and Germany, while this gap is narrowest in Canada, Australia and New Zealand).

These various background characteristics are obviously correlated with one another. The PISA index of social, economic and cultural status (shown in the right-hand column of Table 8.3) summarises all elements of parental background.[12] The achievement gap of students whose parents belong to the bottom quarter of the index is 2½ grade years lower than those in the top quarter of the index (with the gap ranging from three years or more in Hungary and Belgium to less than two years in Iceland, Finland and Canada). Overall, the changes in mathematics scores associated with a one-unit change in the index of economic, social and cultural status are lowest in Iceland, Portugal and Mexico (corresponding to 0.70 of a grade), and highest in the Czech Republic, the Slovak Republic and Belgium (corresponding to around 1.25 grades).

Besides family background, policies and institutions also affect educational mobility across generations. Early streaming of children according to ability reduces educational mobility across generations, while public provision of education (which reduces the costs of human capital borne by parents) increases it. Schütz et al. (2005) report an inverted U-shaped relationship between the family background effect (FBE)[13] and pre-school enrolment – which suggests that early education may reduce the extent to which family background shapes youths life-chances. They also note that the size of the FBE increases with private expenditure and decreases with private enrolment, and argue that these features of the education system can jointly account for 40% of the cross-country variation in their estimated FBEs.

Finally, how education is rewarded in the labour market is also important. Education systems that are too egalitarian may, for example, affect the extent of educational mobility through their effects on returns to education (Checchi et al., 1999; Checchi and Flabbi, 2005; and Chevalier et al., 2005). For example, when the educational system compresses the distribution of education, the distribution of income is also likely to be narrower and returns on education to be low; and, with low returns, low-income parents may have not enough incentive to invest in their children's human capital.

In sum, the overwhelming evidence is that educational attainment persists across generations. This persistence is generated by the combined effect of education and other characteristics of the parents (such as occupation and culture) interacting with different institutions (such as the education systems and the labour market). Based on PISA, mathematics scores are least affected by family background in Iceland, Portugal and Mexico, while they are most affected by it in the Czech Republic, the Slovak Republic and Belgium – though the United States, Switzerland, Germany and Japan do not fare much better. Austria (close to France and New Zealand) occupies the median position.

Intergenerational mobility and income inequality at a point in time: what are the links?

The extent to which conventional measures of income inequality at a point in time reflect people's opportunities to move up the income ladder during their lifetime is likely to matter a lot for how income inequalities are perceived by individuals and policy makers. In fact, survey data suggest that – despite differences across countries – most people are ready to accept inequalities of income and wealth so long as these are associated with "equal opportunities" (Table 8.4). Measures of intergenerational mobility provide one yardstick against which statements about equal opportunities may be assessed.

There is, in general, no necessary association between income mobility across generation and income inequalities at a point in time. Beyond the differences in the income concept used (individual earnings, in one case, and household income, in the other), the two measures refer to different time horizons, and these differences imply that a priori the association may be either positive or negative. Because of this uncertainty, it

Table 8.4. **Share of adults agreeing with different statements about distributive justice**

Percentage share agreeing minus percentage share not agreeing

	Japan	West Germany	Great Britain	United States
It's fair if people have more money and wealth, but only if there are equal opportunities	40	72	71	74
The fairest way of distributing wealth and income would be to give everyone equal shares	−39	−37	−32	−51
It is just luck if some people are more intelligent or more skillful than others, so they don't deserve to earn more money	−37	−27	−56	−66
People who work hard deserve more money than those who do not	86	89	93	89
People are entitled to keep what they have earned even if this means some people will be wealthier than others	56	83	72	88

StatLink ᝌᝑᝍ http://dx.doi.org/10.1787/423305525101

Source: International Social Justice Project, as reported in Marshall et al. (1997).

is important to look at the empirical evidence. Figure 8.2 (left-hand panel) suggests a positive relation in a cross-section of twelve OECD countries between the extent of intergenerational earnings mobility and conventional measures of income inequality at a point in time around 2000. In general, the countries with the most equal distributions of income at a given point in time exhibit the highest income mobility across generations. The exceptions include Australia and Canada, which combine high mobility with moderately high inequality, and France which has lower mobility than would be expected from its level of inequality.[14]

Figure 8.2. **Intergenerational mobility, static income inequality and private returns on education**

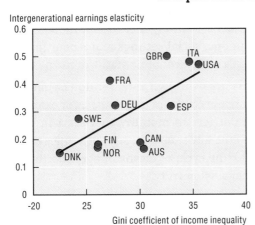
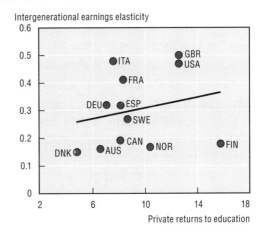

StatLink ᝌᝑᝍ http://dx.doi.org/10.1787/423218022861

Note: Intergenerational mobility is measured by the earnings elasticity between fathers and sons. Income inequality is measured by the Gini coefficient of equivalised household disposable income. The private internal rate of return on education is estimated on the basis of the addition to after-tax earnings that result from a higher level of educational attainment, net of the additional private costs (tuition and foregone earnings) that attaining this higher level of education requires; the estimates shown refer to an individual who has invested in obtaining tertiary education after having completed upper secondary education.

Source: Data on intergenerational earnings elasticity are those reported in Figure 8.1. Data on private returns on education are from OECD, Education at a Glance, various years; those on the Gini coefficient on income inequality are from previous issues of OECD, Society at Glance. See D'Addio (2007).

There are a number of possible explanations for this relation. One explanation centres on the role of private returns on education, as they affect earnings inequality. Countries with a wide distribution of earnings are also likely to be those where the private returns to education are highest – because education gives access to jobs that are even more highly paid (relative to other jobs) than is the case in countries with a narrower distribution of earnings. However, if parental income affects access to education – because of capital market constraints, or because rich parents can choose to live in neighbourhoods with good schools – then ability to take advantage of the high returns on education will be limited to children of richer households. As shown in the right-hand panel of Figure 8.2, there is indeed evidence of a (weak) positive relationship between intergenerational earnings elasticity and private returns on education. Hence, income inequality at a point in time and a strong correlation of earnings across generations can reinforce each other through the effect of the former on access to higher education.

However, there are other possible explanations of the correlation between intergenerational mobility and static income inequality. Returns on education and income inequality reflect institutional characteristics, so these relations are complex. For example, a more compressed earnings distribution, higher minimum wages and broader bargaining coverage all contribute to lower returns on education (and plausibly to lower income inequality at a point in time). A better understanding of these phenomena might provide useful insights for the study of earnings mobility across generations (Solon, 2004; Corak, 2006).

Intergenerational transmission of disadvantage: does it matter for policies?

The inequalities that arise from the transmission of low-income status have important policy implications. Educational policy, early childhood investment, access to health care and immigration policy all affect the extent to which the social and economic position of individuals in society is determined by their skills and ambitions rather than by inherited characteristics. International comparisons of intergenerational mobility are useful in helping to identify the different institutions, social settings and labour-market structures that potentially connect one generation's socio-economic status to the next.

Social policy plays an essential role in this area through interventions aimed at reducing inequality of opportunities over the entire life course of individuals. For example, family policies may help by addressing those barriers to mobility that start in early childhood, as events experienced during that age crucially shape later opportunities in life. These interventions offer an opportunity to break the cycle of disadvantage, and thus to contribute to child development and to the fight against poverty.

Social policy makers need to understand how advantages and disadvantages are passed from one generation to the next. If the degree of intergenerational transmission of disadvantage can be reduced, the aptitudes and abilities of everyone in society are more likely to be used efficiently, thus promoting both growth and equity. However, while reducing the negative effects of parental background on child outcomes is something that most policy makers would wish to promote, a society in which the circumstances and behaviours of parents had *no* effect on outcomes for their children would not be desirable either. The vast majority of parents strive to do the best that they can for their children, investing time, emotional commitment and money in them. While it is both desirable and acceptable for parents to influence the development of their children, public programmes are needed to ensure that no child is left behind because of factors for which they are not responsible.

If countries want to promote equality of opportunity, there are a number of steps they could take. The most important seems to be the reduction of different forms of inequality, including those in current income and educational results. The evidence presented earlier, while not conclusive, is suggestive of a consistent cross-country pattern of low intergenerational mobility and high income inequality. This makes intuitive sense: if the extent of mobility varies according to parental background, it is also likely that inequality linked to family characteristics and resources perpetuates over time. Unfortunately, that means that inequality in one generation is passed on to subsequent generations. This association is, however, not universal and there are some interesting anomalies. For example, when looking at the distribution of household income at a point in time, Australia and Canada are more unequal than a number of European countries, but they are among the most mobile across generations. This may be due to immigration – there is evidence that immigration increases both current inequality and income mobility – but also to public interventions in early education and care and on behalf of disadvantaged individuals as well.

The analysis of the factors shaping intergenerational mobility suggests a range of domains where policies may make a difference:

- Household wealth and parental education are two crucial determinants of children's future life-chances. Because of this, a greater public intervention in the accumulation of human capital might increase intergenerational mobility. Moreover, parents that are capital-constrained – i.e. facing tighter liquidity constraints – cannot invest as much in education as rich parents do. The effects of such liquidity constraints are also likely to vary considerably according to the ability of the child, being greater for low-income parents of high-ability children. Both factors suggest that it is important for educational and social policies to target low-income families and children with greater abilities.

- Growing up in low-income households affects children's future life-chances heavily. In fact, parental poverty is related to lower levels of good health, nutrition and housing, all of which affect child development and future incomes. High parental income is also correlated with a better quality of education (because good schools are generally in good neighbourhoods), greater transmission of verbal ability and non-cognitive skills (including self-discipline) and access to social networks that may become useful in later life (Heckman and Carneiro, 2003). Because of these effects, reducing childhood poverty may contribute to reducing intergenerational inequality.

- Family structure also matters for intergenerational mobility, perhaps for reasons that go beyond income. The home environment is where beliefs, attitudes and values are shaped, and where parents provide role models for their children. Family structure may also matter for intergenerational mobility because of the different allocation of time and money between family members. Children from lone-parent households do less well than they "should", given the income of their parents (but most evidence relates to *sons*), even if these negative effects may be related to selection rather than being a direct consequence of family structures (*e.g.* Piketty, 2003).

- Finally, there is still a good deal of ambiguity as to the long-run causal impact of the neighbourhood on child adult outcomes. The best that can be said is that they matter in the here and now for the well-being of children, and this is enough to justify policy intervention.

For policy makers, the implications of these observations reinforce the lessons of the child development literature. Childhood poverty is a route through which disadvantage is transmitted between generations, so tackling it needs to be a priority. Doing so by helping parents work can be more effective than by giving them cash transfers, as this may contribute to changing attitudes or behaviours. Targeting intensive health, nutrition and care support on particularly deprived households or areas, as well as getting good quality care in early childhood, pre-school and school years are essential tools for promoting intergenerational mobility (*e.g.* Heckman, 2006).

Conclusion

Parents transmit a broad range of resources to their children. While there is some disagreement about the mechanisms that underpin this transmission, a large part of the differences observed are related to different levels of schooling, of household wealth and of a broader set of cognitive and non-cognitive abilities. This chapter has shown the following patterns:

- While income, education, occupation and personality traits tend to be transmitted across generations in all OECD countries, there are cross-country differences: intergenerational earnings mobility, in particular, is higher in the Nordic countries, Australia and Canada, and lower in Italy, the United States and Great Britain.

- Intergenerational mobility tends to be higher in the top and bottom quintiles of the income distribution, but low-income persistence is particularly damaging, as it tends to cumulate with other forms of disadvantage.

- While many factors are involved in intergenerational income transmission – including wealth, genetics, social environment, household structure and others – parental education is by far the most important background characteristic. Educational attainment persists across generations, particularly in societies with a higher return on educational investment.

One of the main objectives of social policy is to break the cycle of disadvantage across generations and prevent the development of a self-replicating underclass. The evidence reviewed in this chapter suggests that interventions targeted at improving childhood outcomes are desirable. Such interventions have become a much more important feature of social policies in most OECD countries in recent years. Reducing the stress and anxiety of children, from whatever source, and providing them with greater educational opportunities will have a pay-off in the incomes they subsequently command and the longer-term contribution that they make to society as adults. Tapping their full potential is key to promoting both economic growth and equality.

Notes

1. The Communiqué from the 2005 meeting of OECD Social Policy Ministers stated: "Social and family policies must help give children and young people the best possible start to their lives and help them to develop and achieve through their childhood into adulthood".

2. Various types of research on intergenerational mobility face different data constraints and use different methodological tools. For example, several studies focus on intergenerational mobility in

education rather than income, as recall errors are lower in the first case than in the second. The criteria used to rank occupations may also differ across studies.

3. There are a number of specific issues to deal with when estimating intergenerational elasticity of income, such as the number of periods over which income (or earnings) is averaged and the age at which these incomes or earnings are observed. See Solon (1992), Zimmerman (1992), and Box 7 in D'Addio (2007).

4. The inheritance of poverty related to family structure might imply a widening socioeconomic gap between single-parent and two-parent families. However, Musick and Mare (2004) find very little evidence of such a divergence in the United States. This result may reflect growing income differences among single-parent families themselves. See also Blanden and Gibbons (2006) on poverty inheritance related to growing up in social housing.

5. There are no clear trends in the extent of intergenerational income mobility over time. In some countries, this is reported to have increased (e.g. Norway; see Bratberg et al., 2005), while in others it is reported to have decreased or remained stable (e.g. United Kingdom; see Blanden et al., 2005).

6. These include Hertz (2005), Atkinson et al. (1983), Dearden et al. (1997), and Blanden (2005a), for Britain; Piraino (2006), for Italy; and Bratberg et al. (2005), for Norway.

7. See D'Addio (2007) for full references to studies for individual countries.

8. For example, see Page (2004) for the United States; Corak et al. (2004) for Canada and Sweden; Maloney et al. (2003) for New Zealand; and Pech and McCoull (2000) for Australia. See D'Addio (2007) for a more extensive survey of the literature on this issue.

9. The literature suggests that personality traits, attitudes and beliefs also significantly persist across generations. The extent to which parents transmit these characteristics is important for a number of reasons. First, while evidence about how preferences or beliefs are formed is sparse, they can shape parenting styles, health and family outcomes (as in the case of the odds of experiencing divorce, Diekmann and Schmidheiny, 2006). Second, these characteristics may diverge in the long-run across different groups, leading to cleavages in societies that adversely affect social and economic outcomes. Finally, the transmission of beliefs and attitudes may matter for social policy to the extent that they lead to a "culture of dependence", which increases the likelihood of poverty for future generations (see Mulligan, 1997; Jencks, 1979; Bowles et al., 2002 and 2005).

10. For example, Belzil and Hansen (2003) suggest that household background variables (especially parents' education) account for 68% of the explained cross-sectional variations in schooling attainment, while ability correlated with background variables accounts for 17% and pure individual-specific ability accounts for 15%.

11. This result is important as occupations also persist across generations. Breen (2004) and Breen and Jonsson (2005) suggest that while absolute mobility has been substantial in all industrialised countries – as economic growth and industrialisation have fuelled the opportunities for children relative to their parents – relative mobility is rather stable and differs across countries: on this measure, the United States holds an intermediate position between the more fluid countries (Sweden, Canada, and Norway) and the most rigid nations (such as Germany, Ireland, Italy and France).

12. The index of economic, social and cultural status – ESCS – covers the highest International Socio-Economic Index of Occupational Status (ISEI) of the parents or guardians, the highest level of education of the parents (converted into years of education), an index of the educational resources in the home, and the number of books at home.

13. The family background effect (i.e. the estimated parameter) shows by how much moves from one category to the next in the number of books at home change the test scores in each country. This family background effect is interpreted by the authors as a measure of inequality of opportunity. See Schütz et al. (2005).

14. Assessing more thoroughly the relation between static income inequality and intergenerational earnings elasticity would require surveys containing data on the earnings of fathers and sons as well as on the income of the entire population. While no such surveys currently exist, Andrew and Leigh (2007) provide evidence of a significant positive relation across ten countries (excluding former communist countries) based on a variable of "predicted parental earnings" (based on information on fathers' occupation and current earnings by occupation).

References

Anderson, G.J. and T.W. Leo (2006), "Intergenerational Educational Attainment Mobility and Family Structure", Paper prepared for the 29th General Conference of the International Association for Research in Income and Wealth.

Andrews, D. and A. Leigh (2007), "More Inequality, Less Social Mobility", mimeo, Research School of Social Sciences (RSSS), Australian National University.

Askew, D., J. Brewington and A. Touhey (2001), "An Examination of Intergenerational Income Mobility Using the Panel Study of Income Dynamics", *Puget Sound eJournal of Economics*, first edition.

Atkinson, A.B., A.K. Maynard and C.G. Trinder (1983), *Parents and Children: Incomes in Two Generations*, Heinemann, London.

Aydemir, A., W.-H. Chen and M. Corak (2006), "Intergenerational Earnings Mobility among the Children of Canadian Immigrants", No. 2085, IZA Discussion Papers, Bonn.

Bauer, P. (2006), "The Intergenerational Transmission of Income in Switzerland: A Comparison between Natives and Immigrants", WWZ Discussion Paper 06/ 01, University of Basel.

Belzil, C. and J. Hansen (2003), "Structural Estimates of the Intergenerational Education Correlation", *Journal of Applied Econometrics*, Vol. 18, No. 6.

Björklund, A., T. Eriksson, M. Jäntti, O. Rauum and E. Österbacka (2004a), "Family Structure and Labour Market Success: The Influence of Siblings and Birth Order on the Earnings of Young Adults in Norway, Finland and Sweden", Chapter 9 in M. Corak (ed.), *Generational Income Mobility in North America and Europe*, Cambridge University Press.

Blanchflower, D.G. and A.J. Oswald (1998), "What Makes an Entrepreneur?", *Journal of Labor Economics*, Vol. 16.

Blanden, J. (2005a), "Essays on Intergenerational Mobility and Its Variation over Time, Place and Family Structure", PhD Thesis, University of London.

Blanden, J. (2005b), "Intergenerational Mobility and Assortative Mating in the UK", mimeo, Centre for Economic Performance, London School of Economics.

Blanden, J. (2005c), "Love and Money: Intergenerational Mobility and Marital Matching", Analytical Studies Branch Research Paper Series, Family and Labour Studies Division, Ottawa.

Blanden, J. and S. Gibbons (2006), "The Persistence of Poverty across Generations: A View from Two British Cohorts", Report, Joseph Rowntree Foundation, North Yorkshire, United Kingdom.

Blanden, J., P. Gregg and S. Machin (2005), "Intergenerational Mobility in Europe and North America. A Report supported by the Sutton Trust", Centre for Economic Performance, London School of Economics.

Blanden, J., P. Gregg and L. Macmillan (2006), "Explaining Intergenerational Income Persistence: Non-cognitive Skills, Ability and Education", Working Paper No. 06/146, Centre for Market and Public Organisation, University of Bristol.

Boehm, T. and A.M. Schlottmann (1999), "Does Home Ownership by Parents Have an Economic Impact on Their Children?", *Journal of Housing Economics*, Vol. 8.

Boehm, T. and A.M. Schlottmann (2002), "Housing and Wealth Accumulation: Intergenerational Impacts", in N.P. Retsinas and E.S. Belsky (eds.), *Low-income Homeownership: Examining the Unexamined Goal*, The Brookings Institution, Washington, DC.

Borjas, G.J. (1992), "Ethnic Capital and Intergenerational Mobility", *Quarterly Journal of Economics*, Vol. 107, No. 1.

Borjas, G.J. (2004), "Increasing the Supply of Labor Through Immigration Measuring the Impact on Native-born Workers", *Backgrounder*, Centre for Immigration Studies, Washington, DC, May.

Bowles, S. and H. Gintis (2002a), "The Inheritance of Inequality", *Journal of Economic Perspectives*, Vol. 16, No. 3.

Bowles, S. and H. Gintis (2002b), "Schooling in Capitalist America Revisited", *Sociology of Education*, Vol. 75, No. 1.

Bowles, S., H. Gintis and M. Osborne (2002), "The Determinants of Individual Earnings: Skills, Preferences, and Schooling", *Journal of Economic Literature*.

Bowles, S., H. Gintis and M. Osborne Groves (2005), "Introduction", in S. Bowles, H. Gintis, and M. Osborne Groves (eds.), *Unequal Chances: Family Background and Economic Success*, Russell Sage, New York.

Bratberg, E., Ø.A. Nilsen and K. Vaage (2005), "Intergenerational Earnings Mobility in Norway: Levels and Trends", *The Scandinavian Journal of Economics*, Vol. 107, No. 3.

Breen, R. (2004), *Social Mobility in Europe*, Oxford University Press.

Breen, R. and J.O. Jonsson (2005), "Inequality of Opportunity in Comparative Perspective: Recent Research on Educational Attainment and Social Mobility", *Annual Review of Sociology*, Vol. 31.

Card, D. (2005), "Is the New Immigration Really So Bad?", NBER Working Paper, No. 11547, National Bureau of Economic Research, Cambridge, MA.

Case, A. and C. Paxson (2006), "Children's Health and Social Mobility", *The Future of Children*, Vol. 16, No. 2.

Case, A., A. Fertig and C. Paxson (2004), "The Lasting Impact of Childhood Health and Circumstances", Centre for Health and Wellbeing Discussion Paper, Princeton.

Chadwick, L. and G. Solon (2002), "Intergenerational Income Mobility among Daughters", *American Economic Review*, Vol. 92, No. 1.

Checchi, D., A. Ichino and A. Rustichini (1999), "More equal but less mobile? Education financing and intergenerational mobility in Italy and in the US", *Journal of Public Economics*, Vol. 74.

Checchi, D. and L. Flabbi (2005), "Intergenerational mobility and schooling decisions", mimeo.

Chevalier, A., K. Denny and D. McMahon (2005), "A Multi-country Study of Inter-generational Educational Mobility", mimeo.

Corak, M. (2006), "Do Poor Children Become Poor Adults? Lessons from a Cross Country Comparison of Generational Earnings Mobility", IZA Discussion Paper, No. 1993, Bonn.

Corak, M., B. Gustafsson and T. Österberg (2004), "Intergenerational Influences on the Receipt of Unemployment Insurance in Canada and Sweden", Chapter 11 in M. Corak (ed.), *Generational Income Mobility in North America and Europe*, Cambridge University Press.

D'Addio, A.C. (2007), "Intergenerational Transmission of Disadvantage: Mobility or Immobility across Generations? A Review for OECD countries", OECD Social, Employment and Migration Working Paper, No. 52, OECD, Paris.

Dearden, L., S. Machin and H. Reed (1997), "Intergenerational Mobility in Britain", *Economic Journal*, Vol. 107.

Diekmann, A. and K. Schmidheiny (2006), "The Intergenerational Transmission of Divorce. Results from a Fifteen-Country Study with the Fertility and Family Survey", mimeo.

Eriksson, T., B. Bratsberg and O. Raaum (2005), "Earnings Persistence across Generations: Transmission through Health?", Memorandum No. 35/2005, Department of Economics, University of Oslo.

Ermisch, J., M. Francesconi and T. Siedler (2006), "Intergenerational Economic Mobility and Assortative Mating", *Economic Journal*, Vol. 116, July.

Grawe, N.D. (2004), "Intergenerational Mobility for Whom? The Experience of High- and Low-earning Sons in International Perspective", Chapter 4 in M. Corak (ed.), *Generational Income Mobility in North America and Europe*, Cambridge University Press, Cambridge.

Grawe, N.D. (2005), "Family Size and Child Achievement", Carleton College Department of Economics Working Paper, No. 2005-06, Carleton College Department of Economics, Northfield, MN.

Hanushek, E.A. and L. Woessmann (2005), Does Educational Tracking Affect Performance and Inequality? Differences-in-Differences Evidence across Countries", NBER Working Paper, No. 11124, National Bureau of Economic Research, Cambridge, MA.

Harding, D.J., C. Jencks, L.M. Lopoo and S.E. Mayer (2005), "The Changing Effect of Family Background on the Incomes of American Adults", Chapter 3 in S. Bowles, H. Gintis, and M. Osborne Groves, *Unequal Chances: Family Background and Economic Success*.

Heckman, J.J. (2006), "The Economics of Investing in Early Childhood", Presentation given at the Niftey Conference, University of New South Wales, Sydney, February.

Heckman, J. and P. Carneiro (2003), "Human Capital Policy", in J.J. Heckman and A.B. Krueger (eds.), *Inequality in America: What Role for Human Capital Policies?*, MIT Press, Cambridge, MA.

Hendricks, L. (1999), "Do Redistributive Policies Promote Intergenerational Mobility?", Working Paper No. 99/06, W.P. Carey School of Business, Arizona State University.

Hertz, T. (2006), "Understanding Mobility in America", Report, Centre for American Progress, Washington, DC.

Hirvonen, L. (2006), "Intergenerational Earnings Mobility Among Daughters and Sons: Evidence from Sweden and a Comparison with the United States", mimeo, Institute for Social Research, Stockholm University.

Holmlund, H. (2006), "Intergenerational Mobility and Assortative Mating Effects of an Educational Reform", Swedish Institute for Social Research Working Paper, No. 4/2006, Stockholm University.

Hugalde Sánchez, A. (2004), "Movilidad intergeneracional de ingresos y educativa en España (1980-90)", Working Paper No. 2004/1, Institut d'Economia de Barcelona, Centre de Recerca en Federalismo Fiscal i Economia Regional.

Jäntti, M., B. Bratsberg, K. Roed, O. Raaum, R. Naylor, E. Österbacka, A. Björklund and T. Eriksson (2006), "American Exceptionalism in a New Light: A Comparison of Intergenerational Earnings Mobility in the Nordic Countries, the United Kingdom and the United States", IZA Discussion Paper, No. 1938, IZA-Bonn.

Jencks, C. (1979), *Who Gets Ahead?*, Basic Books, New York.

Lam, D. and R.F. Schoeni (1993), "Effects of Family Background on Earnings and Returns to Schooling: Evidence from Brazil", *Journal of Political Economy*, Vol. 101, No. 4.

Leigh, A. (2006), "Intergenerational Mobility in Australia", manuscript, Social Policy Evaluation, Analysis and Research Centre, Research School of Social Sciences, Australian National University.

Lindahl, L. (2002), "Do Birth Order and Family Size Matter for Intergenerational Income Mobility? Evidence from Sweden", Working Paper No. 5/2002, Swedish Institute for Social Research, Stockholm University.

Marshall G., A. Swift and S. Roberts (1997), *Against the Odds? Social Class and Social Justice in Industrial Societies*, Oxford University Press, Oxford.

Mazumder, B. (2001), "Earnings Mobility in the US: A New Look at Intergenerational Inequality", Working Paper No. 2001-18, Federal Reserve Bank of Chicago.

Mazumder, B. (2002), "Analyzing Income Mobility over Generations", *Chicago Fed Letter*, Vol. 181, September.

Mazumder, B. (2005), "Fortunate Sons: New Estimates of Intergenerational Mobility in the US Using Social Security Earnings Data", *Review of Economics and Statistics*, Vol. 87, No. 2.

Mulligan, C.B. (1997), *Parental Priorities*, University of Chicago Press, Chicago.

Musick, K. and R.D. Mare (2004), "Family Structure, Intergenerational Mobility, and the Reproduction of Poverty: Evidence for Increasing Polarization?", *Demography*, Vol. 41, No. 4.

Osborne Groves, M.A. (2005), "Personality and the Intergenerational Transmission of Earnings from Fathers to Sons", in S. Bowles, H. Gintis and M. Osborne Groves (eds.), *Unequal Chances: Family Background and Economic Success*, Russell Sage and Princeton University Press.

Palmer, S. (2002), "Neighbourhood Effects and their Role in Intergenerational Mobility for the UK", Faculty of Social Sciences, Department of Economics, University of Southampton.

Pekkarinen, T., R. Uusitalo and S. Pekkala (2006), "Education Policy and Intergenerational Income Mobility: Evidence from the Finnish Comprehensive School Reform", IZA Discussion Paper No. 2204, Bonn.

Piketty, T. (2003), "The Impact of Divorce on School Performance: Evidence from France, 1968-2002", Centre for Economic Policy Research (CEPR), Discussion Paper No. 4146, London.

Piraino, P. (2006), "Comparable Estimates of Intergenerational Income Mobility in Italy", Working Paper No. 471, Department of Economics, University of Siena.

Rumberger, R.W. (2006), "Education and the Reproduction of Economic Inequality in the United States: An Empirical Investigation", Draft paper, University of California.

Schütz, G., H.W. Ursprung and L. Woessmann (2005), "Education Policy and Equality of Opportunity", IZA Discussion Paper, No. 1906, Bonn.

Seshadri, A. and K. Yuki (2004), "Equity and Efficiency Effects of Redistributive Policies", *Journal of Monetary Economics*, Vol. 51.

Solon, G. (1992), "Intergenerational Income Mobility in the United States", *American Economic Review* Vol. 82, No. 3.

Solon, G. (2004), "A Model of Intergenerational Mobility Variation over Time and Place", Chapter 2 in M. Corak, *Generational Income Mobility in North America and Europe*, Cambridge University Press.

Zimmerman, D. (1992), "Regression toward Mediocrity in Economic Stature", *American Economic Review*, Vol. 82, No. 3.

ISBN 978-92-64-04418-0
Growing Unequal?
© OECD 2008

PART IV

Chapter 9

Publicly-provided Services: How Do they Change the Distribution of Households' Economic Resources?*

Public services to households significantly narrow inequality, although this reduction is typically lower than that achieved by the combined effect of household taxes and public cash transfers. This inequality-reducing effect results mainly from a relatively uniform distribution of these services across the population, which implies that they account for a larger share of the resources of people at the bottom of the distribution than at the top.

* This chapter draws on a longer paper prepared by François Marical (INSEE), Marco Mira d'Ercole (OECD), Maria Vaalavuo (European University Institute, Florence) and Gerlinde Verbist (University of Antwerp). See Marical *et al.* (2006). It is also published, whith minor differences, in *OECD Economic Studies*.

Introduction

Many factors other than income contribute to individuals' well-being. By leaving these factors out of the analysis, conventional income measures bias the assessment of both the average level of well-being in each country and of how this is distributed across people. This chapter focuses on one of these factors, i.e. public services to households that confer a personal benefit to users. The case of including these services in distributive analysis is straightforward. First, households pay taxes to finance these public services: these taxes (or at least, part of them) are deducted from their gross income to arrive at a measure of households' disposable, or net, income (Table 4.1) but the public services provided in return are not considered as affecting households' consumption possibilities.[1] Secondly, the budgetary outlays for these services are, in all OECD countries, large enough to have a significant impact on households' well-being. However, important statistical and conceptual issues stand in the way of a systematic integration of these services into measures of households' resources (Box 9.1), and no consensus currently exists on the best way of addressing these problems.

This chapter looks at the impact of these public services on summary measures of income inequality, building on the results highlighted by a long tradition of research on this issue.[2] The chapter also presents quantitative estimates of the distributive effects of these services based on two different approaches. The first relies on the micro records from household surveys for 18 OECD countries and considers the distributive impact of public health care, education and social housing. The second approach is based on grouped income data by deciles from the OECD questionnaire on income distribution and provides estimates for 26 OECD countries and for all spending categories included in the OECD Social Expenditure Database. The chapter ignores other important effects of public services – such as those on labour supply and poverty – and it does not consider those public services (such as transport infrastructure, police and defence) that cannot be attributed to individual users.

Findings from previous research

Several studies have looked at the distributive implications of publicly provided services. This section summarises some of the main findings from this research in the fields of health care, education and social housing. Findings are, however, difficult to compare directly across studies, because of differences in the programmes covered and in the methodology used.

Health care

Research on the distributive effects of health care services has pursued two main approaches: the first considers the monetary value of public health care services as *adding* to household income; the second focuses on how individuals' out-of-pocket health care costs *lower* their economic resources.

Box 9.1. **Conceptual and methodological issues**

Considering the influence of government services on the distribution of economic resources available to households requires broadening the definition of resources, from the more narrow concept of disposable income – i.e. the sum of market income (earnings, rents, dividends, etc.) and cash transfers (from both public and private sources) that households receive, less the direct taxes and social security contributions they pay – to one that includes additional non-market elements, such as government-provided services, that are usually omitted from conventional statistics. Shifting from household income towards a broader concept of economic resources raises a range of questions: some are conceptual, and mainly relate to the valuation of these services and to their distribution across individual beneficiaries; others are methodological – and probably less controversial – but can crucially affect numerical results.

- *What services should be included?* The boundaries of what can be included under the heading of "public services" to households are ill defined. Major items of public expenditure such as education and health are certainly included, but a priori any public expenditure – either directly or indirectly – benefits households, from spending on military equipment to operating costs of institutions. One can, however, categorise these different types of expenditure. Some services provided by government benefit households individually, as in the case of health, education and social housing. Others, conversely, benefit the whole population more or less indivisibly, for example infrastructure or security. A few studies have sought to allocate all public expenditure to households, from agricultural subsidies to construction of motorways (*e.g.* Ruggles and O'Higgins, 1981). Others have relied on a more precise classification of public services according to their impact on households (*e.g.* Wolff and Zacharias, 2004).[1] In practice, most studies have focussed on more limited sectors of activity – notably education, health and certain other items of social expenditure – where services provided confer a personal benefit upon users.

- *How to value government services to households?* Public services are typically provided outside market settings. Because of the lack of market prices, these services are generally valued, in the national accounts system, at their production cost – which, in most cases, is further limited to labour costs, *i.e.* excluding costs for the use of capital equipment. This is a controversial choice when the objective is to value the well-being of individuals and households. An alternative to production costs would be to value these services by what an individual would have spent if similar services had been bought on the market or on the willingness of individuals to pay for them, but the information requirements of these approaches are demanding – and government services may have characteristics that differ from those purchased on the market. Despite these problems, the valuation of government output has a critical importance for all analyses of its distributive impact – underlining the importance of the ongoing discussion within the national accounts community of how best to measure government output (Atkinson, 2005). Most studies on the distributive impacts of government services value these at their production costs (*e.g.* Aaberge and Langørgen, 2006; Ruggles and O'Higgins, 1981; Smeeding *et al.*, 1993), thus neglecting differences across countries in the efficiency of service provision.[2]

- *How to distribute the aggregate value of government services among individuals?* The household surveys that are typically used to assess income distribution often provide only limited information on the actual use of different government services by each individual and household. This implies that most attempts to "individualise" these benefits rely on imputation techniques, and are therefore exposed to errors.[3] While for some services this individualisation is relatively straightforward (*e.g.* use of public education is limited to those households with a child of the relevant school age), for other types it requires more detailed information (*e.g.* on the number of medical and hospital visits in the case of public health). Most studies of the distributive impact of public health care services base the distribution of their aggregate value across individuals not on their actual use, but rather on characteristics of individuals (*e.g.* age, gender, education or income) and households (*e.g.* presence of children, work status of other adults in the family) – i.e. on the assumption that the probability that

Box 9.1. **Conceptual and methodological issues** (cont.)

a person will access these services is the same as that prevailing for other individuals with the same characteristics.[4]

● *Should the value of government services be attributed to individuals or to the household in which they live?* This methodological question is important for interpreting the results of different studies. Most studies of income distribution use the household (or, more rarely, the family) as the unit within which resources are pooled and (equally) shared by individuals (*i.e.* individuals are attributed the income of the household where they live, after an adjustment for different needs across households of different size, Canberra Group 2001). This approach raises, however, specific problems in the case of government services, *i.e.* whether their benefits accrue to the individual user (for example, those who are attending university education) or extend to other household members (*i.e.* parents who may bear the costs of their children's university studies).[5] While this second approach is the one used by most studies, its application raises specific problems in the case of students in tertiary education, many of whom may be counted as being part of an independent household with low reported income. While some studies try to overcome this problem by attaching students to their family of origin, this is not always feasible.

● *Redistribution over what period?* The benefits of government services to individual users may not be limited to the moment in which they are consumed but extend to the long term (*e.g.* education services enhance the future earnings of students). Accounting for these long-term benefits, however, requires life-cycle models whose assumptions (in terms of preferences and risk aversion) are often *ad hoc*. Because of these difficulties, most studies in this field take a more limited, but also less arbitrary, *static* view of these benefits.

Answers to many of the questions above are inevitably controversial. Some observers will question the possibility of assessing households' well-being by "adding" cash components that can be used by recipients to meet all their needs of daily living – and whose value is known with certainty – to other components that can only be used to meet some of these needs – and whose valuation is inevitably controversial. Even when accepting the usefulness of a broader concept than household income, the partial nature of this extension (*e.g.* including in-kind public services but excluding other components such as imputed rents or capital gains) can improve the ranking of some individuals (*e.g.* families with children) while an extension to all components could have the opposite effect (Verger, 2005). In other words, each additional item has the potential to affect the overall assessment of well-being and inequality.[6] These considerations have obvious implications for the interpretation of results in this report.

1. Wolff and Zacharias (2004) use a classification for the United States based on the national accounts nomenclature, which includes all services that directly benefit households but excludes general administration, national defence, justice and prisons.

2. Smeeding (1977), however, values government services based on how much households would have spent for a private service with similar characteristics, *i.e.* their cash-equivalent value. Because of differences in the characteristics of households who purchase public and private services, Smeeding relies on econometric methods (applied to households buying private services on the market) to estimate the price that households who use public services would have been ready to pay.

3. In addition, the benefits from these services may not be limited to the individual user but extend to society as a whole (*i.e.* each person may benefit from living in a community where the levels of education and heath are high). However, accounting for these externalities is difficult: as a result, they are generally ignored by most empirical analysis.

4. This assumption effectively implies that all individuals derive a benefit from knowing that, in case of need, they would have access to these services.

5. In one approach, the equivalised income of the beneficiary is increased by the non-equivalised value of government services; while in the second, the non-equivalised income of the household is first raised by the amount of government services and then equivalised.

6. Both the size and the distributive effects of various income components will depend on the valuation used. For example, Mattila-Wiro (2004) estimates that household production (*i.e.* the production by household members of goods and services for their own use that could have been delegated to individuals outside the household), when valued at the earnings of a non-skilled worker, would lower the Gini coefficient of income inequality in Finland by around 30% and the headcount poverty rate by close to 60% in 1999-2000.

Approaches based on adding public outlays to household income

Studies on the impact of public health care expenditure on overall household resources have relied on two main approaches in attributing to individuals the benefits from these services. The first is based on the notion that each individual has the same probability of benefiting from these programmes as other people with similar characteristics (*insurance value*); the second is based on the *actual use* of these services. The first approach is by far the most dominant, and is the one that will be used for the empirical analysis presented in the next section. The dominance of this approach partly reflects the high concentration of health spending on the elderly. Indeed, the profile of public health expenditure by age is remarkably similar across OECD countries: following a slight fall after an early age, use of health care services remains broadly flat until the age of 40-44 before increasing exponentially in old age, and then declining marginally after age 85 (Figure 9.1).

Figure 9.1. **Public health care expenditures per capita for each age group, as a proportion of total per capita health expenditure**

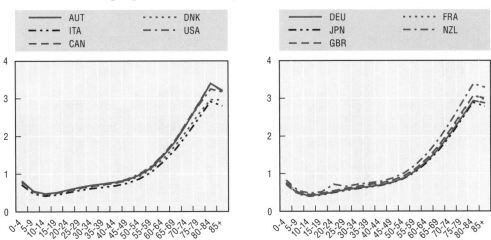

StatLink 🔗 http://dx.doi.org/10.1787/423317305521

Note: Values above 1 indicate that the per capita spending of a given age group is above the one for the population as a whole (*e.g.* health care spending going to people aged 80 and over is around three times higher than the average).
Source: Calculations based on OECD (2006).

Research that bases the imputation of public health care expenditure on people's age (extended, more rarely, to other characteristics) reports a significant effect in reducing inequality in the distribution of economic resources. This effect reflects two elements.

- The first is the heavy concentration of health spending on the elderly mentioned above, combined with the fact that most elderly, having withdrawn from the labour market, have low money income – which implies a strong redistributive effect in terms of the annual accounting period used here. Indeed, according to Gardiner *et al.* (1995), the greater concentration of health care spending in the lower quintiles mainly reflects the low income of most elderly people.

- The second is the amplification of this age-related redistributive impact by an additional equalising impact from the distribution of public health care spending within age groups.[3] This reflects both the greater importance of health care services for those at the bottom of the income distribution, even when the absolute amount provided is the same for all individuals, and – in some countries – the higher value of the health care services provided to people in the lower quintiles of the income distribution.

These patterns hold both in countries with a universal health care system (*e.g.* the United Kingdom), and, to an even greater extent, in those where access to some public health care services is limited to elderly people or to those with fewer resources (*e.g.* the United States). Estimates from national studies of the distribution of public health care expenditure across income quintiles show that the decline is both steeper and more progressive in the United States, while in both the United Kingdom and Australia those in the second quintile receive the largest share (Figure 9.2). Indeed, according to Lakin (2004), the distribution of public health care spending in the United Kingdom is relatively uniform for non-retired households, while it favours those in the lower part of the distribution when the analysis is extended to all households.

Figure 9.2. **Distribution of public health care expenditure across income quintiles, early 2000s**

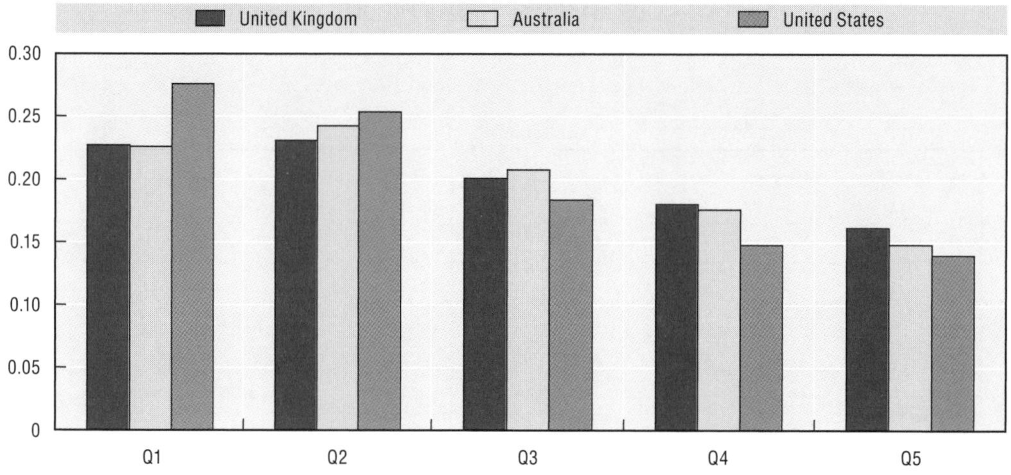

StatLink 🖳 http://dx.doi.org/10.1787/423342631545

Note: Estimates for the United States assume that outlays for public health and hospitals are available to all individuals (*i.e.* they are distributed on a per capita basis) while those for Medicare and Medicaid are only available to specific segments of the population. For each country, the five bars in the chart sum to unity.

Source: Harding *et al.* (2004) for Australia, Lakin (2004) for the United Kingdom, and Wolff and Zacharias (2004) for the United States.

Other studies have relied on *actual* consumption to assess the distributive effects of public health care. For example, both Evandrou *et al.* (1993) and Sefton (2002), who rely on detailed data on the effective use of health care services by individuals in the United Kingdom, conclude that public health care expenditure lowers inequality – with an even larger share of public health care spending accruing to people in the second quintile and a steeper fall in its distribution, relative to studies based on insurance values. Estimates based on actual health care use, however, are not immune to criticism. In effect, this approach implies that, for a given money income, sick people are better off than others simply because they receive more health-related services (Aaberge and Langørgen., 2006). In addition, many health care interventions are both very costly and concentrated over a limited period of time: as a consequence, re-ranking individuals on the basis of "final" income (*i.e.* after allowing for the effect of the public health-care benefits received) may push those people who benefit more from these services into higher income groups, thus dampening the measured effect of health care services in equalising the income distribution.

Addressing these criticisms requires considering both the greater use of health care services by people affected by health problems and their greater health needs. Research on the links between individuals income and health status suggests that poorer people have worse health conditions than others, and, as a consequence, greater needs for health care (Hernández-Quevedo et al., 2006; Humphries and van Doorslaer, 2000; Caussat et al., 2005). Studies that try to control for both needs and use of health care services (based on respondents' self-assessment of their health status and their use of various types of health care services) suggests that most OECD countries have achieved equity in terms of number of physician visits and hospital nights across different income groups, while dental health services are invariably pro-rich (Van Doorslaer et al., 2004).[4] This conclusion is further strengthened when considering that poor people may opt to forgo health care as part of the coping strategies they adopt when confronted with illness.

Approaches based on deducting out-of-pocket costs

Cross-country differences in the organisation of health care services have implications for income distribution that go beyond those implicit in the size of public expenditures. To address these, Gardiner et al. (1995) propose an alternative approach: rather than adding public health expenditures to personal income, their approach deducts from disposable income the out-of-pocket costs (including the costs of private health insurance) incurred by households.[5] The importance of out-of-pocket health care outlays for cross-country comparisons of income inequality is highlighted by the large differences across countries in both their average size and their distribution among income deciles (Gardiner et al., 1995).

Out-of-pocket health care expenditures are a special concern in countries, such as the United States, without a universal health care system.[6] Merlis (2002) observes that these payments are a major reason for income insecurity for people without health insurance in the United States (around 16% of the total population, De Navas-Walt et al., 2006), and that out-of-pocket health care payments account for more than 5% of income for 16% of all US households, and for 23% for those below the official poverty line. Also, these out-of-pocket payments are especially large for households headed by an elderly or disabled person, because of a combination of greater needs, lower income and lower coverage by employer-based health insurance. Out-of-pocket payments are also important in other countries, especially when households confront "catastrophic" events.[7] Overall, evidence suggests that out-of-pocket payments most affect the poorest families with the most serious health problems.[8]

Education

The utilisation of public education services varies from one individual to another, which a priori means significant distributive effects. An individual's age – at least up to upper secondary education – is the chief factor which determines the probability that any individual will benefit from such services (Figure 9.3). Indeed, the majority of studies of the distributive effects of public expenditure on education approach these services globally and base the imputation to individuals on the criterion of age (e.g. Garfinkel et al., 2004), although others use information on actual participation in different types of educational institutions.

However, individuals' age is not the only factor which affects the utilisation of public education services. Other factors, such as individuals' social background and income, are

Figure 9.3. **School enrolment by age in selected OECD countries, 2003**

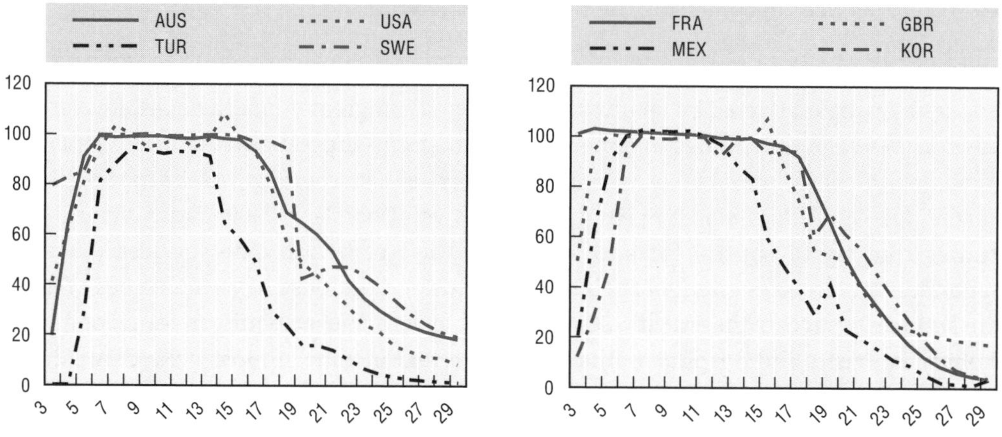

StatLink ᵐˢᵖ http://dx.doi.org/10.1787/423410322555

Note: Participation in public and private education both on a full- and part-time basis. In some countries, the rate of participation is higher than 100% because the estimates of the number of students and the number of people in each age group are based on different data sources.

Source: OECD (2005).

also important. The role of these factors depends considerably on the category of education concerned. In this regard, the fundamental distinction is between compulsory education and non-compulsory education.

Compulsory education

Compulsory education, which includes primary and lower secondary education, accounts for between 30% and 60% of public education expenditure, depending on the country. In principle, all individuals of school age benefit from this, although some households choose private education.[9] While a small minority of children (most of them from poor backgrounds) do not attend school at this age,[10] the allocation of public expenditure for compulsory education based solely on age seems *a priori* justifiable.

Studies adopting this approach to compulsory education have generally found evidence of significant reductions in inequalities in the distribution of economic resources. For example, in Greece primary and secondary education mainly benefit the three lowest quintiles of the distribution, the inclusion of each of these two categories of public spending leading to a one point reduction in the Gini coefficient (Antoninis and Tsakloglou, 2001). Greater equality generally results from the combined effect of a higher value of universal services as a proportion of income for households at the bottom of the income scale, and from the concentration of children in lower income families (in some countries). In some countries, households in the bottom deciles of the income distribution also appear to receive a higher absolute amount (*e.g.* public spending for primary and secondary education in Norway, Steckmest, 1996).

Non-compulsory education

Social background is much more significant for attendance at other levels of education. This is the case of pre-primary education, where the probability of access is higher for children from households where both parents are in paid employment and who, as a consequence, are more likely to be in the highest deciles of the distribution (CERC, 2003; Hugounenq, 1998). This phenomenon is even more apparent at post-compulsory education levels (upper secondary school and university) which, in addition, account for a much higher share of public expenditure on education.[11]

In all the OECD countries, attendance of tertiary education is associated with a more unequal distribution of resources, not least because it depends on parents' socio-economic characteristics.[12] Various factors combine to cause this.

- One factor relates to the parents' age. Parents of children aged 18 to 25 are generally at the time of their life where their salaries are highest, which helps to place them most often in the highest quintiles of the income distribution (Sefton, 2002). By contrast, older people, whose incomes are generally lower than the population average, benefit less from this expenditure because fewer of them have children of that age.[13]

- A second factor relates to family incomes. Evaluating this factor, however, raises specific problems. A large proportion of students in tertiary education live away from their family of origin and could, based on conventional definitions of household income, be considered as having low income. To take account of this factor, individuals must be grouped in their households of origin. While only a few studies appear to have used such an approach, they do highlight clear inequalities in attendance. Thus, in France, individuals aged between 18 and 24 from households in the highest quintile of the income distribution have a probability of access to university which is three times higher than that of the lowest quintile (Albouy et al., 2002). These inequalities are also evident in the United Kingdom (Evandrou et al., 1993; Sefton, 2002) and, to a lesser extent, in the United States (i.e. they are greater in those countries where the enrolment rate in higher education is lower).[14]

Both of these elements make public expenditure for tertiary education regressive, i.e. most of their benefits accrue to individuals coming from richer families.

Social housing

Housing costs are the largest item in the household budget, especially for households at the bottom of the income distribution (Ditch et al., 2001). The institutional arrangements whereby governments help the poorest to meet housing expenditure vary from one country to another (Gardiner et al., 1995). While housing aid in cash is generally included in household money income, this is not the case for social housing, even if households benefiting from this often pay a rent that is below market rates.[15] The scale of social housing varies considerably from country to country. Thus, the proportion of households in social housing ranges from 6% or less in Australia, Canada, New Zealand and Sweden, up to around 20% or more in France (18%), the United Kingdom (22%) and the Netherlands (36%, Ditch et al., 2001).

The impacts of social housing on income inequality depend on the characteristics of renters and on the size of the "implicit subsidy" provided. With respect to the first element, conditions of access to social housing vary considerably from one country to another. In Great Britain, the Netherlands, New Zealand and Sweden, access to social housing is not explicitly linked to individuals' resources, while such means-testing does exist in the other six countries considered by Ditch et al. (2001). In France, social housing primarily benefits families on low or modest incomes, even if the majority of them are not poor.[16]

While comparative evidence of the impacts of social housing on income inequality is rare, more evidence is available from national studies.[17] Both Sefton (2002) and Lakin (2004) argue that people in the two bottom quintiles of the income distribution in the United

Kingdom benefit most (receiving 36% and 34%, respectively, of the total benefits associated with social housing). Other studies, which "augment" household income for *both* the implicit subsidy provided by social housing and for the imputed rent of owner occupation, show that the effects of these two factors on income inequality offset each other. For example, Saunders and Siminski (2005) conclude that the overall effect of rental income (for all types of tenure) is a small decline of income inequality in Australia;[18] while Gardiner *et al.* (1995) report that allowing for housing subsidies and imputed rents slightly reduces income inequality and poverty in the United Kingdom and France. Overall, these studies suggest that social housing is probably the category of government services that benefits the poor most. However, its overall impact on income inequality is smaller than for health care and education because of the lower amounts of spending.

New empirical evidence

This section first describes the size of public spending on services to households, and then presents estimates of its impact on the *static* distribution of household income. These estimates are based on two different approaches, which use different methodologies to impute these expenditures to individual beneficiaries. The first approach – which is limited to a more narrow range of countries and social programmes – is based on individual records from household surveys: in this approach, household income is increased by the value of the public services received by individual beneficiaries, and inequality measures allow for possible moves of individuals in the distribution (*i.e.* for "re-ranking" of individuals). The second approach – which is applied to 26 OECD countries and covers all public expenditures for the provision of social services to households – is based on income data grouped by deciles, as available from the OECD questionnaires on income distributions. In this approach, the average income of each decile is increased by the average value of services received by people in that decile, without "re-ranking" of individuals. Both sets of estimates rely on the concept of "equivalised" household disposable income based on an arbitrary (but commonly used) assumption of how household needs change with household size (the square root elasticity).[19] The description of results presented in this section is mainly based on the inter-quintile share ratio (Q5/Q1) and refers to a single point in time, typically around 2000.

Size and composition of public services to households

Public expenditure for the provision of services that can be attributed to individual households is considerable (Figure 9.4).[20] At a minimum, these publicly provided services include health care and education, as well as spending for the provision of what are labelled as "other social services" in the OECD Social Expenditure Database.[21] On average, this expenditure represents 21% of household disposable income (according to national accounts data), with large disparities from one country to another (from less than 10% of household income in Mexico to over 40% in the Nordic countries). Health care is the biggest item (on average, 45% of total public expenditure on individualised services), closely followed by education (41%), while other social services account for 14% of the total. Within the latter category, the biggest item is services to families (34% of all "other social services") followed by services to the elderly and disabled persons (28 and 21%, respectively). Even these amounts under-estimate the size of public services to households; in particular, public spending for housing services only includes quasi-cash rental-assistance

Figure 9.4. **Public expenditure for in-kind services in OECD countries in 2000**

Percentage of household disposable income

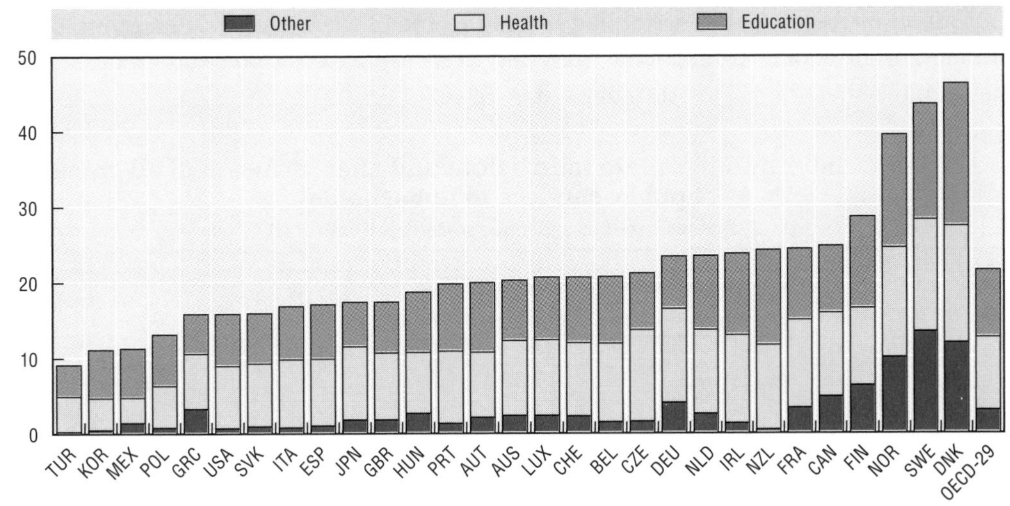

StatLink ⫘ http://dx.doi.org/10.1787/423415168781

Note: The category "other social expenditure" includes services to the elderly, survivors, disabled persons, families and unemployed, as well as those related to housing, social assistance, and active labour-market policies.

Source: Data are taken from the OECD database on social expenditure for the "health" and "other social expenditure" categories, and from the UNESCO-OECD-Eurostat database for education expenditure. For Turkey, data refer to 1999. Household disposable income is taken from the national accounts for all the countries considered except Ireland and Luxembourg (where no national accounts data for the household sector exist), where data are drawn from the OECD questionnaire on income distribution.

programmes, while excluding both the investment for the building of social housing and the "implicit subsidies" to households renting social housing at a below-market rate.[22]

On average, publicly-provided services to individual households represent an amount comparable to public cash transfers (which are included in household disposable income) and a larger amount in 11 OECD countries. In general, however, countries that spend a larger absolute amount on cash transfers also spend a larger amount on in-kind services to households (*e.g.* the Nordic countries).

Estimates based on individual records

Estimates based on individual records from household surveys cover several European countries (based on the 2001 wave of the *European Community Household Panel*, ECHP) as well as the United States, Canada and Australia (based on national surveys).[23] All these surveys provide data on the income of private households as well as information on their socio-economic characteristics that can be used to impute public services to individuals. The analysis covers health and education services, using data on public expenditures from the OECD Social Expenditure database (SOCX) and from the UNESCO-OECD-Eurostat data collection on education statistics. In addition, this section provides estimates of the distributive impact of social housing, relying on simple multivariate estimates of the implicit subsidy that is associated with the provision of social housing at below-market rents. For education and social housing, the imputation of public services to individuals is based on actual use and relies on either direct information from surveys or on "imputations" that attribute public spending to individuals based on those characteristics that most influence their use (*e.g.* age); for health care, it is based on the average costs of the services provided to individuals according to their age. For all categories of expenditures, changes in inequality relative to those based on the distribution of money disposable income depend on both the aggregate size of public expenditures and on the distribution of these services according to the income of the individuals receiving them. Estimates of the equalising impact of these services – expressed as point differences in the inter-quintile share ratio – are summarised in Table 9.1.

Table 9.1. **Inter-quintile share ratio before and after inclusion of all types of public services to households**

Estimates based on individual records, around 2000

	Money income	Income plus health		Income plus education		Income plus social housing		Income plus all public services	
	A	B	Difference (A-B)	C	Difference (A-C)	D	Difference (A-D)	E	Difference (A-E)
Denmark	3.1	2.5	0.6	2.9	0.2	3.1	0.0	2.4	0.7
Finland	3.6	3.1	0.5	3.5	0.1	3.5	0.0	2.9	0.6
Sweden	3.6	3.1	0.5	3.1	0.5	..	..	2.6	0.9
Austria	3.6	3.1	0.5	3.3	0.4	3.6	0.0	2.8	0.9
Germany	3.7	3.1	0.6	3.4	0.3	3.7	0.0	2.9	0.8
Netherlands	3.7	3.3	0.5	3.2	0.5	3.7	0.0	2.8	0.9
Luxembourg	3.8	3.2	0.5	..	..	..	..	3.2	0.5
France	4.1	3.3	0.7	3.6	0.4	4.0	0.0	3.0	1.1
Belgium	4.1	3.4	0.7	4.0	0.2	4.1	0.1	3.2	0.9
Italy	4.9	3.8	1.0	3.9	0.9	4.8	0.0	3.2	1.7
Canada	4.9	4.2	0.7	4.2	0.6	..	..	3.7	1.2
Ireland	4.9	3.9	1.0	4.4	0.5	4.7	0.2	3.4	1.4
United Kingdom	5.0	4.1	0.9	4.3	0.7	4.8	0.2	3.5	1.6
Australia	5.2	4.1	1.1	4.7	0.5			3.7	1.5
Greece	5.7	4.4	1.3	5.2	0.4	..	..	4.1	1.6
Spain	6.0	4.8	1.2	5.0	1.0	6.0	0.0	4.1	1.9
Portugal	6.5	4.8	1.7	5.1	1.3	6.4	0.1	4.0	2.5
United States	7.1	5.5	1.6	5.6	1.5	..	..	4.6	2.6
Average	*4.6*	*3.8*	*0.9*	*4.1*	*0.6*	*4.4*	*0.1*	*3.3*	*1.3*

StatLink ⬛⬛ http://dx.doi.org/10.1787/423572162200

Note: The first column presents the inter-quintile share ratio (Q5/Q1) for the conventional measure of money (disposable) income, *e.g.* in Denmark, the fifth quintile receives a money income which is 3.1 times higher than that of the first quintile; in the second column, the same measure is applied to an income concept "augmented" for the value of public services; and, the third column presents the difference between the two, *i.e.* the *change* in the income distribution which follows from the consideration of publicly-provided services. Countries are ranked, from top to bottom, in increasing order of the inter-quintile share ratio (Q5/Q1) for money income. Estimates for health care expenditure are based on insurance values; those for pre-primary education are based only on the age of the child. Data for Luxembourg exclude both education and social housing; those for Australia, Canada, the United States, Greece, Spain and Sweden exclude social housing.

Source: OECD Secretariat calculations based on ECHP for European countries and national survey data for non-European ones.

Health care

Estimates of the redistributive effects of health care are based on the insurance-value approach. This is based on the notion that what government provides is equivalent to funding an insurance policy where the value of the premium is the same for everybody sharing the same characteristics, such as age. In this section, these insurance values have been calculated on the basis of the distribution of public health care expenditures across the detailed age groups that underlie the latest set of OECD expenditure projections for health and long-term care (OECD, 2006) shown in Figure 9.1.[24] In practice, this approach implies attributing to each individual of a given age the average per capita spending amount accruing to the corresponding age group. These per capita amounts are "added" to the household disposable income of the household to which the individual belongs, and then equivalised.[25]

Based on this approach, the inter-quintile share ratio declines, on average, by 0.9 point (from 4.6 for money disposable income to 3.8 after allowing for public health services, Table 9.1, second set of columns). The reduction affects all countries and ranges between over 1 point in southern European countries, Australia and the United States to around 0.5 point in Sweden, Finland and the Netherlands.[26] In general, public health care services are distributed rather uniformly across quintiles (i.e. each quintile gets around 20% of public health care services), with marginally higher shares going to people in the lowest quintiles in Denmark, Greece and Belgium.[27] Estimates based on actual use – as available for a smaller number of countries – point to a more limited distributive impact of public health care spending (Box 9.2).

Education

Imputation of public educational expenditures to individuals based on actual use requires, first, determining whether or not an individual is participating in different levels of the education system; and second, increasing the income of the households where they live by the average public spending per student at the relevant educational level.[28] The methodology followed for determining participation applies two different approaches for individuals aged below 16 and those aged 16 and over.

- For children aged 16 and over, the survey data provide information on education participation for each individual filling out the questionnaire, although without distinguishing between public and private institutions.[29]

- For children younger than 16, the surveys provide no information on education attended. For this age group, the probability of participating in a specific education level relies on data on net enrolment rates[30] by single year of age (i.e. the probability of attending school is assumed to be the same for each individual of that age in the survey, irrespectively of their household income).

Public educational expenditure refers to total direct government expenditures for educational institutions per education level, converted to a "per student" basis through data on the number of students in each level.[31] Overall, the combined effect of public spending on all categories of education is a reduction in the inter-quintile share ratio of 0.6 point on average (Table 9.1, third set of columns). The reduction is stronger (1 point or more) in Spain, Portugal and the United States, while it is weaker (less than 0.2 point) in Finland, Denmark and Belgium.

The impact of public services in education on income inequality depends crucially on the level considered.

- *Pre-primary education* generally narrows inequalities. The effect is small because of the modest amount of expenditures for pre-primary education (in all countries below 2% of household disposable income). Different assumptions for imputing participation rates have only small effects. When the imputation is based only on the age of the child (Table 9.2, left-hand panel), the average reduction in the quintile-share ratio is 0.1 point (but twice as high in Portugal and the United States); when the imputation is based on both the age of the child and the employment status of the parents (i.e. allowing for the possibility that households where both parents work make more use of pre-primary education) the fall in inequality is marginally smaller.

- For *primary and secondary education,* public expenditures have a stronger effect in reducing inequalities, with an average decline of around 0.5 point (Table 9.3, middle panel).[32] The decline of the inter-quintile share ratio is largest in the countries with the most unequal distribution of money income (Spain, Portugal and the United States) while it is negligible in Denmark and Finland. The first outcome mainly reflects the size of public expenditures for this level of education: in most countries, primary and secondary education make up about 10% of household disposable income. On average, the distribution of this category of public expenditure is uniform across quintiles, with a marginally lower share for people in the upper part of the distribution. The share of public expenditure for primary and secondary education going to people in the bottom quintile is low in Finland and Denmark, reflecting the greater concentration of children in the middle of the income distribution in these countries.[33]

- For *tertiary education,* patterns are radically different – on average, the decline in the inter-quintile share ratio is negligible. In around un tiers of the countries included in Table 9.3

Box 9.2. **Redistributive effects of health care based on actual use**

The approach based on *actual* use of health care services can only be applied to a limited number of European countries. Several questions in ECHP relate to the use of health care services by individuals aged 15 or more (without distinguishing, however, between use of public and private facilities): questions relate to visits to a general practitioner, to a specialist and to a dentist in the year preceding the questionnaire, as well as to the number of nights spent in hospital. These data – available for eight European countries (France was excluded because of a low response rate) – have been combined with data on public health care expenditures grouped in two broad categories: hospital care, and consultations and medical examinations outside hospitals.[1]

Based on this approach, the distributive effect of health care expenditures is, on average, significantly lower than for the insurance-value approach (an average reduction of 0.2 point, as compared to one of 0.8 based on insurance value for the same countries). Results vary considerably among countries. In Denmark, inequality *rises*, and the same occurs, to a smaller extent, in Italy, Finland and the Netherlands. Conversely, public health care reduces inequality in Spain, the United Kingdom, Austria and Ireland. In those countries where inequality rises, this reflects the effect of health care services provided inside a hospital (in five of the eight countries these services widen inequalities), while health care services outside hospitals have an equalising effect in all countries.

These opposite effects reflect the large differences in how inside and outside hospital care expenditures are distributed among individuals in different income quintiles. While both inside and outside hospital expenditures tend to benefit more the lowest quintiles (based on money income), the profile is especially steep for hospital care. For example, in Denmark, 35% of hospital care expenditures go to the lowest quintile. While this may seem surprising – in the light of evidence in the table below – the result that in-hospital expenditures *increase* inequality in several countries reflects the effect of "re-ranking" individuals: as in-hospital expenditures are concentrated among a small number of individuals[2] they lead more easily to re-ranking individual beneficiaries, which dampens (or even reverses) the equalising effects of these health services. These results underline the limits (described earlier) of this approach.

Box 9.2. **Redistributive effects of health care based on actual use** (cont.)

Inter-quintile share ratio before and after inclusion of public health expenditures based on actual use

Estimates based on individual data, around 2000

		Total expenditure		In-hospital expenditures		Out-of-hospital expenditures	
	A. Money income	B. Income plus health care (consumption)	C. Difference (A-B)	B1. Income plus in-hospital health care	C1. Difference (A-B1)	B2. Income plus out-of-hospital health care	C2. Difference (A-B2)
Denmark	3.10	3.25	−0.16	3.39	−0.29	2.90	0.19
Finland	3.56	3.60	−0.04	3.77	−0.21	3.36	0.20
Austria	3.65	3.39	0.26	3.56	0.09	3.39	0.26
Netherlands	3.73	3.76	−0.02	3.99	−0.26	3.48	0.26
Italy	4.85	4.86	−0.01	5.41	−0.56	4.30	0.55
Ireland	4.88	4.69	0.20	5.01	−0.12	4.47	0.41
United Kingdom	5.02	4.37	0.66	4.97	0.06	4.35	0.67
Spain	5.99	5.24	0.75	5.90	0.09	5.23	0.76
Average	*4.35*	*4.14*	*0.20*	*4.50*	*−0.15*	*3.93*	*0.41*
Memorandum item:							
Average for the same countries based on insurance approach	*4.31*	*3.52*	*0.79*	..	..	..	..

StatLink ⬛🖝 http://dx.doi.org/10.1787/423752820478

Note: Countries are ranked, from top to bottom, in increasing order of the inter-quintile share ratio for money income.

Source: Secretariat calculations based on ECHP for European countries.

1. This breakdown of health care expenditures does not correspond exactly to the one used in ECHP (*e.g.* OECD data provide information on public health care expenditures for medical visits, without distinguishing – for most countries – between general practitioners and specialists). Imputations of in-hospital care expenditures to an individual j (DSHj) are based on the number of nights spent in hospital (nj):

$$DS^H{}_j = n_j \times \frac{DS^H}{N \times \sum_{i \in N} n_j}$$

where N indicates the population (*i.e.* those older than 15) in the sample. For expenditures outside hospital (DS^{OH}j) the criterion used is based on the number of visits to a general practitioner (vj), *i.e.*:

$$DS^{OH}{}_j = v_j \times \frac{(DS - DS^H)}{N \times \sum_{i \in N} v_j}$$

2. In the survey data used here, around 5% of the population accounted for more than 90% of the nights spent in hospital; conversely, more than 50% of the population accounted for 90% of all medical visits.

(right panel), this ratio increases slightly, a pattern suggesting that students in higher education predominantly live in better-off households. Even for countries where tertiary education lowers inequalities, such as Denmark and Sweden, this effect may predominantly reflect the large proportion of tertiary students living away from the parental home, who are classified by surveys as separate households with low reported income. Because of the earnings premium of higher education, many of these individuals will be high-income earners in the future. The share of public expenditure in tertiary education accruing to people in the top quintile of the distribution is close to 30% on average, and above 40% in Belgium, Spain and Portugal (Marical *et al.*, 2006).

Table 9.2. **Inter-quintile share ratio before and after inclusion of pre-primary education expenditures**

Estimates based on individual data, around 2000

	A. Money income	Imputation based on the age of the child		Imputation based on the age of the child and the employment status of parents	
		B1. Income plus pre-primary education	Difference (A-B1)	B2. Income plus pre-primary education	Difference (A-B2)
Denmark	3.1	3.1	0.0	3.1	0.0
Finland	3.6	3.5	0.0	3.5	0.0
Sweden	3.6	3.5	0.1	3.5	0.1
Austria	3.6	3.5	0.1	3.6	0.1
Germany	3.7	3.7	0.0	3.7	0.0
Netherlands	3.7	3.7	0.1	3.7	0.1
France	4.1	4.0	0.1	..	..
Belgium	4.1	4.1	0.1	..	..
Italy	4.9	4.7	0.2	..	..
United Kingdom	5.0	4.9	0.1	4.9	0.1
Australia	5.2	5.2	0.0	..	..
Greece	5.7	5.6	0.0	5.6	0.0
Spain	6.0	5.9	0.1	..	..
Portugal	6.5	6.2	0.2	6.1	0.3
United States	7.1	6.9	0.2	..	..
Average	*4.7*	*4.6*	*0.1*	..	..
Average across the countries included in right-hand panel	*4.3*	*4.2*	*0.1*	*4.2*	*0.1*

StatLink ⫶⫸⫶ http://dx.doi.org/10.1787/423582010573

Note: Countries are ranked, from top to bottom, in increasing order of the Q5/Q1 ratio for money income. Ireland is excluded because of the very small number of children aged 3 to 6 in pre-primary education in the survey. Estimates in the left-hand panel assume that the probability of attending pre-primary education is the same for each child, and independent of household income. Estimates on the right-hand panel assume, for countries where the participation rate of children in this age group is *below* the share of children in households where both parents work, that all children belonging to this household type have the same probability of attending and that all other children are not attending; and, for countries where the participation rate is *above* the share of children in households where both parents work, that all children in this household type are in pre-primary and that all other children have the same probability of attending. Estimates on the right-hand panel have been limited to countries where participation in pre-primary education is 80% or less in the age groups under consideration.

Source: OECD Secretariat calculations based on ECHP for European countries and national survey data for non-European ones.

Social housing

Estimating the distributive effect of social housing is more difficult than for other social services, as it requires quantifying the aggregate size of the implicit benefits provided. This section presents estimates for some European countries based on information on housing tenure (*i.e.* whether different households own or rent their residence, and whether they rent from the public or private sector)[34] and on their actual rents.

OECD countries differ not only with respect to the relative importance of various types of housing, but also in how their prevalence varies with household income. The share of individuals who are renting their main residence is close to 40% in the lowest quintile and only 13% in the top one (Marical *et al.*, 2006), with the exceptions of only Greece and Austria, where the share of renters is rather uniform across quintiles. The importance of public sector rentals also declines when moving up the income distribution.[35] Overall, the share of renters living in social housing is low in Greece and Spain (less than 10%) but more important in Ireland, the Netherlands and the United Kingdom.

Table 9.3. **Inter-quintile share ratio before and after inclusion of public expenditures on primary, secondary and tertiary education**

Estimates based on individual data, around 2000

	A. Money income	Primary and secondary education		Tertiary education	
		B1. Income plus primary and secondary education	Difference (A-B1)	B2. Income plus tertiary education	Difference (A-B2)
Denmark	3.1	3.1	0.0	2.9	0.2
Finland	3.6	3.6	−0.1	3.5	0.1
Sweden	3.6	3.4	0.2	3.4	0.2
Austria	3.6	3.4	0.3	3.7	0.0
Germany	3.7	3.5	0.2	3.7	0.0
Netherlands	3.7	3.3	0.4	3.7	0.0
France	4.1	3.8	0.3	4.0	0.1
Belgium	4.1	4.0	0.2	4.2	−0.1
Italy	4.9	4.1	0.7	4.8	0.1
Canada	4.9	4.3	0.6	4.8	0.1
Ireland	4.9	4.2	0.7	5.1	−0.2
United Kingdom	5.0	4.4	0.6	5.0	0.1
Australia	5.2	4.8	0.4	5.1	0.1
Greece	5.7	5.3	0.4	5.6	0.0
Spain	6.0	5.0	1.0	6.1	−0.1
Portugal	6.5	5.2	1.3	6.5	−0.1
United States	7.1	5.8	1.3	7.0	0.1
Average	*4.7*	*4.2*	*0.5*	*4.7*	*0.0*

StatLink ⤵ http://dx.doi.org/10.1787/423583401157

Note: Countries are ranked, from top to bottom, in increasing order of the Q5/Q1 ratio for money income.
Source: OECD Secretariat calculations based on ECHP for European countries and national survey data for non-European ones.

To evaluate the implicit subsidy associated with the provision of social housing at below-market rents, each beneficiary is attributed an amount equal to the difference between the rent effectively paid and the one they would have paid on the market for a dwelling with similar characteristics (Box 9.3). The distributive effects of social housing are in general quite limited (Table 9.1, fourth set of columns). This small equalising effect reflects the small size of the aggregate subsidy implicit in the provision of social housing (0.6% of household disposable income, on average), even though – when compared to health and education – it mainly benefits individuals in the lowest quintiles of the distribution.

Summing up

When considering the combined effect of the three categories of public services discussed above, the inter-quintile share ratio falls, on average, by around 1.3 points (i.e. from 4.6 for money disposable income to 3.3), with a reduction that is largest in the United States and Portugal (almost twice the average) and smallest in Finland and Denmark (Table 9.1, rightmost columns).[36] In general, patterns are little affected by the specific inequality measure used. Figure 9.5, which presents estimates of the effects of government services for both the inter-quintile share ratio and the Gini coefficient, suggests that:

● Both the Gini coefficient and the inter-quintile share ratio decline significantly when the income concept is broadened to include all public services considered here.

● With both measures, the ranking of countries does not change significantly when moving from money (disposable) income to a measure that includes public services (the

Box 9.3. **Estimates of the implicit subsidy provided to renters in the public sector**

Estimates are based on a simple model, which is applied separately to renters in the public and in the private sectors:

$$rent = \alpha \times rooms + \beta \times income + c.$$

where *rent* is the monthly rent paid by households, *rooms* the number of rooms in the dwelling, and *income* is the (non-equivalised) household income – a variable used to capture the neighbourhood in which households live, as individuals with the same income tend to cluster in areas with similar house prices. Coefficients (shown below) have the expected sign and are statistically significant (*i.e.* private rents are higher for households with higher income and for accommodations with a higher number of rooms), although there are exceptions and a significant fraction of the variance remains unexplained. The coefficients for private rentals are used to calculate, for households renting in the public sector, what they would have paid on the market for an accommodation with similar characteristics.

Estimates from a linear model for private rents

	Private rentals				Private rentals		
	Income	Rooms	Adjusted R7		Income	Rooms	Adjusted R7
Denmark	0.0040*	337.3*	0.21	Portugal	0.0024*	2 229.8*	0.10
	7.55	6.53			12.37	5.47	
Netherlands	0.0058*	19.3*	0.22	Austria	0.0002	671.2*	0.04
	9.54	2.08			0.28	6.12	
Belgium	0.0036*	1 136.7*	0.21	Finland	0.0041*	565.5*	0.27
	10.38	6.68			4.33	8.79	
France	0.0093*	−13.2*	0.39	Germany	0.0049*	120.8*	0.34
	31.27	−0.51			22.56	22.82	
Ireland	0.0099*	38.3*	0.32	United Kingdom	0.0048*	14.1*	0.09
	7.27	2.34			6.62	2.34	
Italy	0.0055*	66.5*	0.22				
	18.77	9.20					

StatLink ☞ http://dx.doi.org/10.1787/423763360472

Note: T statistics are reported below the estimated coefficients.* denotes significance at the 5% level.

rank correlation coefficients for both the Gini and the inter-quintile share ratio, among the 17 countries considered, is above 0.95).

- There are significant differences across countries in the size of the reduction in inequality depending on the measure used. Based on the inter-quintile share ratio, the (point) reduction is larger for countries with higher inequality in money income (United States, Portugal and Spain); conversely, declines are more uniform for the Gini coefficient, with a smaller change in the dispersion across countries.[37]

Estimates based on grouped data

The analysis of the distributive effects of government services based on individual records can be complemented by estimates based on income data for different deciles of the distribution. This grouped-data approach rests on attributing to different income deciles the monetary value of public expenditure for the provision of different types of

Figure 9.5. **Income inequality before and after inclusion of expenditures on public services in OECD countries**

Estimates based on individual data, around 2000

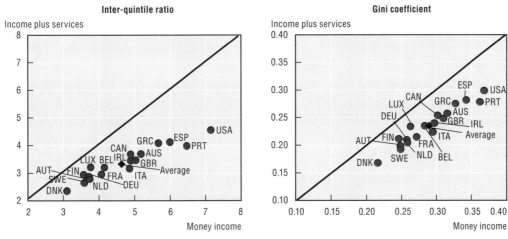

StatLink ᴍ⃝ᴎᴘ http://dx.doi.org/10.1787/423465828250

Source: OECD Secretariat calculations based on ECHP for European countries and national survey data for non-European ones.

social services, and on comparing various inequality measures before and after this imputation (*i.e.* with no re-ranking of individuals).[38] This approach is less accurate than that based on individual records, but allows the analysis to be extended to a broader range of OECD countries and public services.

The imputation of the value of the different public services to each decile of the income distribution relies on information about the average equivalised disposable income of each decile and the distribution of (nine) age groups across them.[39] The imputation of government expenditures for these services to different income deciles relies on different rules according to the type of service considered:

● *Health care.* The imputation is based on the age of individuals and on the distribution of different age groups across income deciles. Information on the latter is drawn from OECD questionnaires on income distribution. The data on the distribution of public health expenditures by age of recipients are those shown in Figure 9.1. For most countries, these age-expenditure profiles are based on national data; for countries where no national data are available,[40] the imputation relies on the "average" profile prevailing in other OECD countries.

● *Education.* The imputation of education expenditure is based on individuals' age and the distribution of different age groups across income deciles. The procedure involves three steps. The first requires determining the enrolment rates of individuals of a given age (from three to 29 years) in different levels of education and grouping them into the three age groups available in the OECD income distribution questionnaire (0-17, 18-25 and 26-40);[41] the second step involves calculating total education expenditure by age group; and the last step computes education spending in each decile based on the educational expenditure for each age group and the distribution of each age group across deciles. Expenditure data refer to the direct educational outlays of the general government, *i.e.* excluding cash transfers to private entities such as student grants and loans.[42]

- *Other social services*. This category of spending includes (in the SOCX classification) a heterogeneous set of programmes. Because of their diversity, the individualisation of public spending is based on the assumption that these services are distributed across income deciles in the same way as the corresponding cash transfers (based on information included in the OECD questionnaire on income distribution). This assumption reflects the notion that, for each type of programme, services and cash transfers typically complement each other.

While less accurate than the estimates based on individual records described above, this approach can be applied to 26 countries included in the OECD database on income distribution and to the full range of public services to households included in OECD data on social expenditure. These results can be considered as providing a "first-order" approximation of the distributive effects of public services for countries where micro records are not available.

Distributive effects, based on this approach, vary with the category of services considered:

- *Health care*. Health expenditure reduces inequalities in all the 26 OECD countries considered (by 1.1 points, on average, Table 9.4, second set of columns). Changes in country rankings are, however, small: the Nordic countries and the Czech Republic are the most egalitarian countries both before and after taking health services into account. The greatest changes in the inter-quintile ratio affect countries such as Portugal, the United States and Mexico, where the distribution of disposable income is the most unequal. Hence, overall there is a convergence of income inequalities among countries (as measured by the range of variation).[43]

- *Education*. The redistributive impact of public expenditure on education is only marginally smaller than that for health (the average inter-quintile ratio falls from 5.2, for money disposable income, to 4.2 after taking education services into account, Table 9.4, third set of columns). In general, education expenditure especially benefits the three lowest quintiles of the income distribution, even if the differences between countries are considerable. Sensitivity analysis shows that inequalities in attendance in education across income deciles have a fairly marginal impact on the results and are limited to the 18-25 age group (Marical *et al.*, 2007).[44]

- *Other social services*. While often significant, the effects of these services in narrowing income inequality (a decline of the inter-quintile share ratio of 0.3 point, on average, Table 9.4, fourth set of columns) are significantly lower than those associated with health and education, as the effect of their more targeted nature is offset by the lower amount of expenditure.

Overall, the effects of all public services on income inequalities are considerable in most countries. Thus the inter-quintile ratio falls on average from 5.2, on a cash basis, to 3.4 after taking public services into account – a fall of 1.8 points (Table 9.4, rightmost columns). The differences between countries in the size of this fall are marked, with a largest (point) fall in countries where the inequalities in the distribution of disposable income are greatest.[45] The reduction in the disparities between countries narrows without fundamentally altering their ranking, even though some countries improve their position (*e.g.* France and Australia), while that of others worsens (especially the Netherlands, Austria and Greece).

Not surprisingly, the approach based on grouped data leads, in general, to different numerical estimates of the reduction in inequality due to public services than those based on individual records. A comparison of these estimates – across the countries and programmes (education and health) that are covered by both approaches – shows the fall

Table 9.4. **Inter-quintile share ratio before and after inclusion of expenditure on all public services**

Estimates based on grouped data, around 2000

	Money income	Income plus health		Income plus education		Income plus other social services		Income plus all public services	
	A	B	Difference (A-B)	C	Difference (A-C)	D	Difference (A-D)	E	Difference (A-E)
Denmark	3.1	2.5	0.6	2.7	0.4	2.5	0.7	1.9	1.2
Sweden	3.4	2.7	0.8	2.9	0.5	2.7	0.8	2.0	1.4
Netherlands	3.6	3.1	0.5	3.1	0.5	3.4	0.2	2.6	0.9
Czech Republic	3.6	2.9	0.7	3.0	0.6	3.3	0.3	2.4	1.2
Luxembourg	3.7	3.1	0.5	3.1	0.6	3.4	0.3	2.6	1.1
Finland	3.7	3.1	0.7	3.2	0.6	3.2	0.5	2.5	1.2
Norway	3.7	2.9	0.9	3.2	0.5	3.0	0.8	2.2	1.5
Austria	3.9	3.3	0.6	3.1	0.8	3.8	0.1	2.7	1.2
Switzerland	3.9	3.2	0.7	3.4	0.6	3.7	0.2	2.8	1.1
France	4.0	3.2	0.9	3.3	0.8	3.7	0.4	2.6	1.4
Germany	4.3	3.3	1.0	3.6	0.6	3.9	0.3	2.8	1.4
Hungary	4.4	3.5	0.9	3.7	0.7	4.1	0.3	2.9	1.5
Canada	4.8	3.9	0.9	3.9	0.9	4.4	0.4	3.2	1.6
Australia	4.9	3.5	1.4	4.1	0.7	4.1	0.7	2.8	2.0
Ireland	5.0	3.7	1.3	4.3	0.7	4.7	0.4	3.2	1.8
United Kingdom	5.2	4.1	1.0	4.3	0.8	4.8	0.4	3.4	1.7
New Zealand	5.4	4.2	1.2	4.1	1.3	5.1	0.2	3.3	2.0
Spain	5.6	4.3	1.3	4.4	1.2	5.4	0.2	3.6	2.0
Japan	5.7	4.3	1.4	4.8	0.9	5.4	0.3	3.7	2.0
Greece	6.0	4.8	1.2	5.3	0.7	5.7	0.3	4.2	1.8
Poland	6.1	5.2	0.9	4.7	1.3	5.8	0.3	4.1	2.0
Italy	6.2	4.5	1.7	4.8	1.4	6.0	0.1	3.7	2.4
Portugal	6.2	4.4	1.8	4.9	1.3	6.0	0.2	3.7	2.5
United States	6.9	5.1	1.7	5.1	1.8	6.4	0.5	4.0	2.9
Turkey	9.3	7.8	1.5	7.4	1.9	9.3	0.0	6.5	2.8
Mexico	12.6	10.9	1.7	9.9	2.7	12.3	0.3	8.8	3.8
Average	*5.2*	4.1	1.1	4.2	1.0	4.8	0.3	3.4	1.8

StatLink http://dx.doi.org/10.1787/423724888582

Note: Countries are ranked, from top to bottom, in increasing order of the Q5/Q1 ratio for money income.
Source: OECD Secretariat calculation based on OECD data.

in inequality based on grouped data exceeds that based on individual records (as the first approach does not allow for individuals' re-ranking), although the difference is much lower for the Gini coefficient that for the inter-decile ratio; further the reduction in inequality based on the two approaches are highly correlated with each other (above 0.90) across countries, and this for both inequality measures.

This analysis also suggests that public services are distributed quite uniformly among the different quintiles and, in consequence, in a less inegalitarian way than money incomes. Figure 9.6 shows this result for the average of OECD countries. For all public services to households, the lowest quintile receives a share of 23% and the highest quintile 17% (left-hand panel). Similar values are recorded for health services and education, while the share of the lowest quintile is the highest for "other" public services. However, due to the different levels of cash income in the different quintiles, public services represent a much larger share of the income of those at the bottom of the distribution (around 70% of disposable income on average) than for those at the top of the distribution (11%, right-hand panel).[46] These patterns mirror closely those obtained based on individual records.

Figure 9.6. **Importance of public services in household income across the distribution, OECD average**

Estimates based on grouped data, around 2000

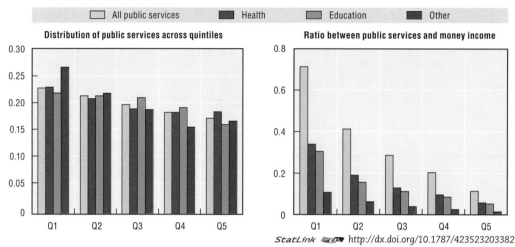

Source: OECD Secretariat computation based on different OECD databases.

A further issue is how the redistributive effect of in-kind government services compares with that of household taxes and public cash transfers. Figure 9.7 shows the point reduction of both the inter-quintile share ratio and the Gini coefficient achieved by in-kind government services (on the vertical axis) and by household taxes and public cash benefit (on the horizontal axis).[47] Three patterns stand out.

● First, the equalising impact of public in-kind services is, on average, around ¼ of that achieved by household taxes and cash transfers when looking at the inter-quintile share

Figure 9.7. **Redistributive impact of in-kind public services compared to that of household taxes and cash benefits**

Point differences in the inter-quintile ratio and Gini coefficient, estimates based on grouped data, around 2000

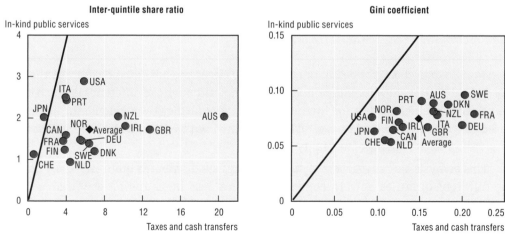

Note: The reduction in inequality due to in-kind public transfers (on the vertical axis) is measured as the absolute difference between the inequality measures (the inter-quintile share ratio, in the left-hand panel; the Gini coefficient in the right-hand panel) for disposable household income and that for income plus in-kind public services. The reduction in inequality due to household taxes and public cash transfers is the absolute difference between the inequality measures for market income and for disposable income. Points below the line denote countries where the reduction in inequality due to household taxes and public cash benefits exceeds that due to in-kind public services.

Source: OECD Secretariat computation based on different OECD databases.

GROWING UNEQUAL? – ISBN 978-92-64-04418-0 – © OECD 2008

ratio, and around ½ in the case of the Gini coefficient – although, for some countries, the reduction in inequality achieved through the two set of policies is broadly similar.[48]

- Second, the redistributive effect of household taxes and government cash transfers varies much more across countries than that of public services in-kind – around 50% more when looking at the coefficient of variation, for both inequality measures used.

- Finally, countries with a lower inequality of money disposable income also record a lower inequality after including in-kind public services (with a correlation above 95% for both inequality measures); there is conversely no correlation across countries when considering the (absolute) redistribution achieved by the two policy levers.

Conclusion

Overall, both the approach based on individual records and that based on grouped data highlight some consistent patterns that mirror, with few exceptions, those identified by previous research on the subject.

- Public expenditure for the provision of social services to households significantly narrows inequality, although for some countries – when the imputation is based on individual data – this effect is negligible for non-compulsory education. The overall effect of public services in narrowing inequalities in the distribution of households' economic resources results mainly from a relatively uniform distribution of these services across income quintiles, which translates into a larger increase in the income share at the bottom of the distribution than at the top.

- Changes in inequality measures prompted by the consideration of public services do not lead to major changes in country rankings. The dispersion of inequality across countries narrows considerably for the inter-quintile share ratio but by much less for the Gini coefficient.

- The inequality reduction due to government in-kind services is, on average, lower than that achieved by the combined effect of household taxes and public cash transfers, although this is not true in all countries.

The way various government services are distributed among the population has some important policy implications. First, because of the significant effect of the publicly-provided services considered in this chapter on the distribution of economic resources among households and individuals, it is important to take account of this redistributive impact when making policy choices about these programmes. Second, and despite economists' presumption in favour of cash transfers, provision of public services may be justified on a variety of reasons (*e.g.* when the consumption choices of parents do not take into full account the utility of their children, to improve the targeting of programmes, to increase investment is people's health and skills – and hence productivity in the long-run, Currie and Gahvari, 2007); this raises the question of how best to mix cash transfers and in-kind public services to meet any particular redistributive goal. Finally, public services may also affect the labour-supply decisions of beneficiaries, in particular for those at the bottom of the distribution; it follows that reform should consider how provision of in-kind services (*e.g.* childcare) might augment the labour supply and thus ease the trade-off between equity and efficiency goals. These considerations underscore the importance of accounting more systematically for the contribution of government services to household well-being and its distribution.

Notes

1. For example, households with children in state schools benefit from a tax-financed service that improves their well-being compared with those who have to buy the same services in the market. It should be noted, in this respect, that the OECD national accounts combine information on both the goods and services bought by households on the market, and those provided by governments free of charge or at subsidised prices within the concept of the "actual" consumption of households.

2. For example, every year the UK national statistical office publishes a report on the distribution of household income which also considers the effect of public spending in health and education (e.g. Jones, 2006); and similar reports exist for Australia (ABS, 2001). While most studies have a national focus, a few provide information extending to several countries – and their number has increased following the availability of the Luxembourg Income Study, a database providing access (within a uniform data environment) to the micro-records of household income surveys for several OECD countries (e.g. Brady, 2004; Garfinkel et al., 2004; Smeeding, 2002; Smeeding and Rainwater, 2002; Steckmest, 1996).

3. Differences in the use of health care services according to individuals' income and socio-economic status are reported even in countries with universal health care systems (e.g. Goddard et al., 2001, for the United Kingdom).

4. Exceptions include the United States, Portugal and Finland, in the case of consultations with doctors; and Mexico in the case of hospital nights.

5. Both approaches will lead to the same quantitative results when considering two countries with identical (pre-tax) money income and health care needs, and where these needs are met, in one country, through tax-financed public health care and, in the other, through private out-of-pocket health expenditures.

6. The Committee on National Statistics of the US National Academy of Sciences recommended that, for the purpose of measuring poverty, "family resources" should exclude both out-of-pocket medical care expenditures and health insurance premiums (Citro and Michael, 1995). Weinberg (2006) underscores the importance of employer-provided health insurance for a better measure of household income.

7. According to Xu et al. (2003), the share of households with out-of-pocket payments exceeding 40% of their income is almost nil in France but close to 3% in Portugal. This proportion tends to be higher in low- and middle-income countries, as well as in economies in transition.

8. Private out-of-pocket costs are only one among the different sources of health care financing. Some studies have focused on the distributive implications of all types of health care financing, i.e. taxes, contributions and out-of-pocket costs. In general, these effects will depend on the relative importance of each source, on their "progressivity" (i.e. the extent to which they weigh more heavily on higher income groups), and on various factors that shape horizontal equity (e.g. differences in contribution rates across insurance funds or in health-related tax rates across municipalities, Wagstaff et al., 1999). De Graeve and Van Ourti (2003), who examine the impact of different financing sources on income distribution in 23 European countries, find that direct taxes are progressive in all countries and indirect taxes and out-of-pocket payments regressive, while there are more differences in results for contributions to social security and private insurance. Similar results are reported by van Doorslaer et al. (1999) for 12 OECD countries including the United States. Klavus and Häkkinen (1998), who apply a similar methodology for Finland, argue that reforms to health care financing introduced following the recession of the early 1990s have moderately reduced the progressivity of the overall system without compromising its equity features, mainly because of the continuous importance of direct income taxes.

9. Private expenditure on education in OECD countries accounts on average for 18% of total expenditure at the pre-primary stage and 22% in tertiary education, but only 7% in primary and secondary education (OECD, 2005).

10. The proportion of young people aged 20 to 24 years who, in 2001, had not completed lower secondary school was less than 5% in 14 OECD countries, but highest in New Zealand (16%), Portugal (29%), Mexico (33%) and Turkey (47%).

11. Public expenditure on higher education accounts, on average, for almost half of educational spending (48%) while the share of pre-primary education is only 7%.

12. For example, the probability of access to tertiary education is three times higher for young people whose parents have a university degree than for those from less well-educated households (Machin, 2006). Differences in access to university education are also evident with regard to ethnic background. Thus, in the United States, the percentage of white students who, upon finishing high

school, enrol in university is 10 points higher than for young people of Hispanic origin and 20 points higher than for young blacks, even though these differences have declined since 1994.

13. This phenomenon is well documented by Evandrou (1993) for the United Kingdom. This study shows that the distribution of public expenditure on tertiary education is more unequal when pensioners' households are included, as compared to results obtained when limiting the analysis to households of non-pensioners.

14. Inequalities in the distribution of expenditure on tertiary education reflect not only differences in access but also differences in costs per student depending on the subject chosen. Thus, in France, students from the wealthiest families choose more expensive course (Albouy and Wanecq, 2003).

15. Governments also intervene through rent controls applied to private housing: these measures are not covered in this article.

16. Access to social housing generally means less expenditure on housing for the households concerned. In France, tenants in private accommodation pay 22% of their income on housing, compared with 18% for tenants of public housing. These differences may under-estimate the benefit, if people who live in social housing can afford a bigger or more comfortable home than if they rented in the private sector; but they may also over-estimate them, if social housing units are mainly located in disadvantaged neighbourhoods.

17. The approach used in the majority of the studies that focused on the distributive effects of social housing is to "gross up" the households' cash income by an amount equal to the difference between the market rent for a home with the same characteristic as the one occupied and the rent actually paid for it.

18. The same pattern is reported by Harding et al. (2004), who argue that social housing accounts for 13% of the disposable income of people in the first quintile of the income distribution in Australia, as compared to 3% for those in the second.

19. The "square root elasticity" implies that the needs of a household composed of four people are twice as large as those of a single (1.4 and 1.7 times those of a single in the case of a childless couple and of a couple with one child).

20. These data – as well as the estimates presented later – refer to public expenditures in 2001 (despite availability of more recent data), as the latest information on the distribution of household disposable income available at the time of writing referred to the early 2000s.

21. The category "other social expenditure" (in the SOCX nomenclature) includes services to the elderly, survivors, disabled persons, families and unemployed, as well as those related to housing, social assistance, and active labour-market policies.

22. As some of these quasi-cash housing benefits may be included in household income as measured in surveys, the estimates based on "grouped" income data in this article may imply some double counting.

23. The 2001 wave of ECHP provides information on income earned in 2000. Data for non-European countries are based on the Household Income and Labour Dynamics for Australia (HILDA); the Survey of Income and Labour Dynamics (SLID) for Canada; and the Annual Social and Economic Supplement (ASEC) to the Current Population Survey for the United States. For Canada and the United States, data are drawn from the Luxembourg Income Study database and refer to income earned in 2000. Data for Australia refer to 2004: computations were provided courtesy of Mark Pearson.

24. These projections refer to per-capita amounts of public heath care services for five-year age groups in 2003. This age profile has been applied to public expenditure data referring to 2001.

25. In most countries, public health care services make up a considerable share of disposable household income (around 13% on average), ranging between 11% (in Finland, the United Kingdom and the United States) and 16% (in Germany and Italy).

26. The larger absolute fall in the inter-quintile share ratio in countries with a wider distribution of money income implies much smaller cross-country differences in terms of percentage reduction (e.g. from 19% in Denmark to 23% in the United States).

27. In theory, the approach used here, which accounts only for differences in use by age, may underestimate the equalising effect of public health care services in countries where these are targeted to low-income households (e.g. Medicaid in the United States). In practice, estimates of the equalising impact of Medicaid and Medicare from the US Census Bureau point to a reduction of the inter-quintile share ratio and of the Gini coefficient (for non-equivalised household income)

of, respectively, 0.75 and 0.15 point (Cleveland, 2005), as compared to a decline of 1.63 and 0.37 point, respectively, reported by Marical et al. (2006).

28. The expenditures on education attributed to individual j attending education level c (DEcj) are determined on the basis of whether or not they are attending these institution (t^c_j =1 if an individual follows education in category c, otherwise it is zero) based on the following identity: formule where Nc denotes the number of students enrolled in that education category and DEc the public expenditures on education for that education level.

29. Enrolment in private schools will affect results if these students are mainly from better-off families and if public subsidies to private schools are lower than the costs of public schools; in these conditions, the approach used here will underestimate the distributive effect of public education services. As the survey data for European countries distinguish among four levels of education (tertiary, upper secondary, lower secondary, and less than lower secondary), data for other countries have been re-coded to these four levels. The survey data used for various countries differ in the information they provide on school attendance for individuals of different ages (e.g. for the United States and Canada, this information refers to all individuals aged 15 or older; for European countries, this refers to people aged 17 or older).

30. Data on net enrolment by single year of age, from OECD (2005), refer to 2003 and to individuals aged 3 to 29. For Canada; where data on enrolment by age are not available, all individuals aged between 6 and 15 are assumed to be in school (in line with the enrolment rates prevailing in other OECD countries); children aged 3 to 5 are assumed not to attend education (as no data on public expenditure on pre-primary education are available for Canada).

31. Because of lack of data, Luxembourg is not included in the analysis.

32. Primary and lower secondary education are grouped together as, for all countries considered here, they correspond to "compulsory education"; upper secondary education is also combined with these two categories as, in several countries, compulsory education, or at least part of it, extends to this level.

33. These results overestimate the equalising effect of primary and secondary education, as they do not allow for the possibility that most school drop-outs are concentrated in the lower end of the income distribution; this may affect cross-country comparisons, when drop-out rates differ across countries.

34. The definition of social housing used in the ECHP includes all accommodations provided by central and local public administrations, as well as those provided by voluntary and non-profit agencies.

35. There are, however, some exceptions. In half of the countries, the proportion of renters in the public sector is higher for the second quintile than in the first; while in Austria and the Netherlands the share of renters from the public sector is relatively uniform across quintiles.

36. The lowest reduction is recorded by Luxembourg, but for this country results only refer to health care.

37. The larger reduction in the inter-quintile share ratio (an inequality measure that is more sensitive to what happens at the two extremes of the distribution than for the Gini coefficient – a measure that is more sensitive to changes around its middle) suggests that accounting for public services is likely to have major impacts on estimates of relative income poverty.

38. The consequences of this assumption are especially important for services whose unit costs are large and actual use is concentrated over a short time-span (e.g. health care). In these circumstances, not allowing individuals to change their rank position will increase the equalizing effect of government services relative to approaches that allow for such re-ranking (Atkinson, 1980; Plotnick, 1981).

39. The values of equivalised income by deciles are converted into a non-equivalised equivalent based on estimates of the average household size for the entire population.

40. These countries are the Czech Republic, Hungary, Iceland, Japan, Korea, Mexico, New Zealand, Norway, Poland, the Slovak Republic, Switzerland and Turkey.

41. Data on school enrolment by single year of age were not available for some types of educational institutions in the case of Canada, Japan and Luxembourg. For these countries, the distribution of students aged above 17 between the aged groups 18-25 and 26-29 is based on the share of the two age groups prevailing in the United States.

42. To test the sensitivity of the results to the assumption of equal access to education, an alternative scenario (presented in Marical et al., 2006) assumes that enrolment rates for poorer people are

lower than those for better-off people, based on an arbitrary inequality coefficient that is common across countries.

43. For example, the gap in the inter-quintile share ratio between Denmark and the United States falls from 3.8, based on money income, to 2.6 after taking health services into account.

44. Marical *et al.* (2006) show estimates of the equalising impact of education based on estimates of enrolment rates by income deciles; these are based on country-specific enrolment rates by age and common coefficients for inequality in attendance (implying that disparities in attendance by household income will be higher the lower the average enrolment for educational level).

45. Thus the inter-quintile ratio falls from 6.9 to 4.0 in the United States, from 12.6 to 8.8 in Mexico and from 9.3 to 6.5 in Turkey, while it falls from 3.1 to 2.0 in Denmark.

46. A comparison of results for the inter-quintile ratio and the Gini coefficient highlights patterns that mirror quite closely those described in Figure 9.5, based on individual data, for a smaller number of OECD countries and social programmes. Both inequality measures decline after considering public spending for social services; the decline in the inter-quintile share ratio is larger for countries with a more unequal distribution of disposable income but broadly similar across countries for the Gini coefficient.

47. The comparison is made with the *combined* effect of the taxes paid by households and the cash public transfers they receive, as the information available on Gini coefficients does not allow separating the effects of the two components of disposable income.

48. The larger equalising effect of household taxes and public cash transfers, relative to that achieved by public in-kind services, reflects both differences in their distributive profile and in their size (the three items accounting for 29%, 20% and 27%, respectively, of household disposable income among the countries included in Figure 9.7).

References

Aaberge, R. and A. Langørgen (2006), "Measuring the Benefits from Public Services: The Effects of Local Government Spending on the Distribution of Income in Norway", *Review of Income and Wealth*, Vol. 52, No. 1, March.

Albouy, V., F. Bouton and N. Roth (2002), "Les effets redistributifs de l'éducation: les enseignements d'une approche monétaire statique", Communication préparée pour le séminaire organisé par le CERC, la DPD et l'INSEE, Paris.

Albouy, V. and T. Wanecq (2003), "Les inégalités sociales d'accès aux grandes écoles", *Économie et Statistique*. No. 361.

Antoninis, M. and P. Tsakloglou (2001), "Who Benefits from Public Education in Greece? Evidence and Policy Implications", *Education Economics*, Vol. 9, No. 2.

Atkinson, A.B. (1980), "Horizontal Inequity and the Distribution of the Tax Burden", in H. Aaron and M. Boskin (eds.), *The Economics of Taxation*, Studies of Government Finances, The Brookings Institutions, University of Columbia Press.

Atkinson, A.B. (2005), "Measurement of Government Output and Productivity for the National Accounts", *Atkinson Review: Final Report*, Palgrave-MacMillan.

ABS – Australian Bureau of Statistics (2001), *Government Benefits, Taxes and Household Income, Australia, 1998-99*, Catalogue No. 6537.0, Canberra.

Brady, D. (2004), "The Welfare State and Relative Poverty in Rich Western Democracies, 1967-1997", LIS Working Paper, No. 390, Luxembourg.

Canberra Group (2001), *Expert Goup on Household Income Statistics: Final Report and Recommendations*, Ottawa.

Caussat, L., S. Le Minez and D. Raynaud (2005), "L'assurance-maladie contribue-t-elle à redistribuer les revenus", Drees, Dossiers solidarité et santé, Études sur les dépenses de santé, La Documentation Francaise, Paris.

Citro, C.F. and R.T. Michael (eds.) (1995), *Measuring Poverty – A New Approach*, National Accademy Press, Washington DC.

Cleveland, R.W. (2005), "Alternative Income Estimates in the United States: 2003", *Current Population Reports*, US Census Bureau, June.

CERC – Conseil de l'Emploi, des Revenus et de la Cohésion sociale (2003), "Éducation et Redistribution", *Rapport No. 3*, Paris.

Currie, J. and F. Gahvari (2007), "Transfers in Cash and In Kind: Theory Meets the data", NBER Working Paper, No. 13557, National Bureau of Economic Analysis.

De Navas-Walt, C., B.D. Proctor and C. Hill Lee (2006), "Income Poverty, and Health Insurance Coverage in the United States: 2005", *Consumer Population Report*, US Census Bureau, August.

Ditch, J., A. Lewis and S. Wilcox (2001), "Social Housing, Tenure and Housing Allowance: An International Review", In-house Report No. 83, Department for Work and Pensions, University of York.

Evandrou, M., J. Falkingham, J. Hills and J. Le Grand (1993), "Welfare Benefits in Kind and Income Distribution", *Fiscal Studies*, Vol. 14, No. 1.

Gardiner, K., J. Hills, V. Lechene and H. Sutherland (1995), "The Effects of Differences in Housing and Health Care Systems on International Comparisons of Income Distribution", No. WSP/110, STICERD/CASE Publications.

Garfinkel, I., L. Rainwater and T. Smeeding (2004), "Welfare State Expenditures and the Redistribution of Well-being: Children, Elders, and Others in Comparative Perspective", Paper prepared for the APPAM (Association for Public Policy Analysis and Management) conference, 29 October, Atlanta.

Goddard, M. and P. Smith (2001), "Equity of Access to Health Care Services: Theory and Evidence from the UK", *Social Science and Medicine*, Vol. 53, No. 9, November.

De Graeve, D. and T. Van Ourti (2003), "The Distributional Impact of Health Financing in Europe: A Review", *The World Economy*, Vol. 26, No. 10, November.

Harding, A., R. Lloyd and N. Warren (2004), "The Distribution of Taxes and Government Benefits in Australia", Paper presented at the conference on the distributional effects of government spending and taxation, The Levy Economics Institute, October.

Hernández-Quevado, C., A.M. Jones, A. López-Nicolás and N. Rice (2006), "Socio-economic Inequalities in Health: A Comparative Longitudinal Analysis Using the European Community Household Panel", *Social Science and Medecine*, Vol. 63, No. 5, September.

Hugounenq, R. (1998), "Les consommations publiques et la redistribution : le cas de l'éducation", Document de travail, Conseil de l'emploi, des revenus et de la cohésion sociale (CERC), Paris.

Humphries, K.H. and E. van Doorslaer (2000), "Income-related Health Inequality in Canada", *Social Science and Medicine*, Vol. 50, No. 5, March.

Jones, F. (2006), "The effect of taxes and benefits on household income, 2004-2005", Office of National Statistics, London.

Klavus, J. and U. Häkkinen (1998), "Micro-level Analysis of Distributional Changes in Health Care Financing in Finland", *Journal of Health Services Research and Policy*, Vol. 3, No. 1, January.

Lakin, C. (2004), "The Effects of Taxes and Benefits on Household Income, 2002-2003", *Economic Trends*, Vol. 607, June.

Machin, S. (2006), "Social Disadvanatage and Educational Experiences", OECD Social, Employment and Migration Working Paper, No. 32, OECD, Paris.

Marical, F., M. Mira d'Ercole, M. Vaalavuo and G. Verbist (2006), "Publicly-provided Services and the Distribution of Resources", OECD Social, Employment and Migration Working Paper, DELSA/ELSA/WD/SEM(2006)14, OECD, Paris.

Mattila-Wiro, P. (2004), "Changes in the Inequality of Income and the Value of Housework Time in Finland in 1979-2000", Paper prepared for the 28th conference of the IARIW (International Association for Research in Income and Wealth), August 2004, Cork.

Merlis, M. (2002), *Family Out-of-pocket Spending for Health Services: A Continuing Source of Financial Insecurity*, CMWF (The Commonwealth Fund), New York.

OECD (2005), *Education at a Glance – OECD Indicators*, OECD, Paris.

OECD (2006), "Projecting OECD Health and Long-term Care Expenditures: What are the Main Drivers?", OECD Economic Department Working Paper, No. 477, OECD, Paris.

Plotnick, R. (1981), "A Measure of Horizontal Inequity", *Review of Economics and Statistics*, Vol. 63.

Ruggles, P. and M. O'Higgins (1981), "The Distribution of Public Expenditures and Taxes among Households in the United States", *Review of Income and Wealth*, Vol. 27, No. 3, September.

Saunders, P. and P. Siminski (2005), "Home Ownership and Inequality: Imputed Rent and Income Distribution in Australia", SPRC Discussion Paper, No. 144, September, University of New South Wales.

Sefton, T. (2002), "Recent Changes in the Distribution of the Social Wage", CASE Paper No. 62, London School of Economics, London.

Smeeding, T. (1977), "The Antipoverty Effectiveness of In-kind Transfers", *The Journal of Human Resources*, Vol. 12, No. 3, Summer.

Smeeding, T. (2002), "Real Standards of Leaving and Public Support for Children: A Cross National Comparison", LIS Working Paper, No. 345, Luxembourg.

Smeeding, T. and L. Rainwater (2002), "Comparing Living Standards across Nations: Real Incomes at the Top, the Bottom, and the Middle", SPRC Discussion Paper, No. 120, December.

Smeeding, T., S. Saunders, J. Coder, S. Jenkins, J. Fritzell, A. Hagenaars, R. Hauser and M. Wolfson (1993), "Poverty, Inequality, and Family Living Standards Impact across Seven Nations: The Effect of Noncash Subsidies for Health, Education and Housing", *Review of Income and Wealth*, Vol. 39, No. 3, September.

Steckmest, E. (1996), "Noncash Benefits and Income Distribution", LIS Working Paper, No. 100, Luxembourg.

Van Doorslaer, E., A. Wagstaff, H. Van Der Burgh, T. Christiansen, G. Citoni, R. Di Biase, U. Gerdtham, M. Gerfin, L. Gross, U. Häkkinen, J. John, P. Johnson, J. Klavus, C. Lachaud, J. Lauritsen, R. Leu, B. Nolan, J. Pereira, C. Propper, F. Puffer, L. Rochaix, M. Schellhorn, G. Sundberg and O. Winkelhake (1999), "The Distributive Effect of Health Care Finance in Twelve OECD Countries", *Journal of Health Economics*, Vol. 18.

Van Doorslaer, E. and C. Masseria (2004), "Income-related Inequality in the Use of Medical Care in 21 OECD Countries", *Towards High Performing Health Systems: Policy Studies*, OECD, Paris.

Verger, D. (2005), "Bas revenus, consommation restreinte ou faible bien-être : les approches statistiques de la pauvreté à l'épreuve des comparaisons internationales", *Économie et Statistiques*, Paris.

Wagstaff, A., E. Van Doorslaer, H. Van Der Burgh, S. Calonge, T. Christiansen, G. Citoni, U. Gerdtham, M. Gerfin., L. Gross, U. Häkkinen, P. Johnson, J. John, J. Klavus, C. Lachaud, J. Lauritsen, R. Leu, B. Nolan, E. Perán, J. Pereira, C. Propper, F. Puffer, L. Rochaix, M. Rodríguez, M. Schellhorn, G. Sundberg and O. Winkelhake (1999), "Equity in the Finance of Health Care: Some Further International Comparisons", *Journal of Health Economics*, Vol. 18, No. 3, June.

Weinberg, D.H. (2006), "Measuring Poverty in the United States", Paper prepared for the Statistics Canada-University of Toronto workshop on "Low Income, Poverty and Deprivation", Ottawa, 5-6 June.

Wolff, E. and A. Zacharias (2004), "An Overall Assessment of the Distributional Consequences of Government Spending and Taxation in the US, 1989 and 2000", Preliminary version.

Xu, K., D.B. Evans, K. Kawabata, R. Zeramdini, J. Klavus and C.J.L. Murray (2003), "Understanding Household Catastrophic Health Expenditures: A Multi-country Analysis", in C.J.L. Murray and D.B. Evans (eds.), *Health Systems Performance Assessment*, World Health Organisation, Geneva.

ISBN 978-92-64-04418-0
Growing Unequal?
© OECD 2008

PART IV

Chapter 10

How is Household Wealth Distributed? Evidence from the Luxembourg Wealth Study*

There are significant cross-country differences in both levels and distribution of household wealth compared that of income, which partly depend on the definition of wealth and on the measures used to summarise its distribution. Many of those who are classified as income poor do have some assets, although the "median" poor has negligible financial assets in all countries covered. Disposable income and net worth are positively correlated across individuals, and this association holds even after controlling for personal characteristics such as age and education.

---

* This chapter is a shorter, edited version of a longer paper prepared for the OECD by Markus Jantti (Åbo Akademi University), Eva Sierminska (CEPS), and Tim Smeeding (Syracuse University). See Jantti *et al.* (2008).

Introduction

Wealth is a key dimension of household economic resources, and the study of the size and distribution and household wealth is today a flourishing research field. Empirical analysis must, however, cope with considerable weaknesses in available data. Household surveys of assets and debts typically suffer from large sampling errors due to the high skewness of the wealth distribution as well as from serious non-sampling errors. In comparative analysis these problems are compounded by differences in the methods and definitions used in various countries.[1] Because of these methodological features – and in contrast with the quality information now available on household income – knowledge about the country-ordering in terms of wealth inequality is far more uncertain than in the case of cash income. Analyses of the joint distribution of income and assets (i.e. whether people at the bottom of the income scale also report low levels of household wealth) confront similar challenges.[2]

These and similar questions have led researchers and institutions from a number of countries to join forces to launch the Luxembourg Wealth Study (LWS) – an international project to assemble existing micro-data on household wealth into a coherent database. Building on the experience with the Luxembourg Income Study (LIS), the hope is that the availability of such a database could spur comparative research on household net worth, portfolio composition, and wealth distributions, and stimulate a process of harmonisation of definitions and methodologies.[3]

This chapter describes asset-holdings and their distribution for the entire population, as well as the composition of household assets, in terms of both diffusions and amounts. After having outlined some of the reasons why information on household wealth matters for social policies, the chapter presents measures of asset holding and inequality based on a range of wealth definitions. It then focuses on the "joint distribution" of net worth and income, so as to provide a measure of people's economic situation that goes beyond that provided by the use of income alone. Developing a more all-sided picture like this, including of that part of the population that is income-poor but asset-rich, is important for developing policies that can more accurately target the neediest sections of society and have an impact on the actual sources of poverty and inequality.

Household wealth and social policies

The joint distribution of wealth and income is affected by a large number of public policies. Because of the multiple nature of these links, any attempt to summarise the policies that affect the wealth-holding of households is inevitably partial and idiosyncratic. After all, it does not take a great effort of either imagination or evidence to make links between the human capital in a household, its income, and its holdings of other forms of capital, and between macroeconomic variables and the rate of return on financial assets. Through these two routes, virtually *any* aspect of government economic and social policy (broadly defined) can be said to influence asset-holding. Three main areas of policy are, however, worth mentioning as examples of the importance for social policies of better information about household assets:

- **Assets and means-tests in welfare programmes.** Although means-tests referring to *both* income and assets define eligibility for several social programmes in many OECD countries, most comparative studies of welfare programmes are based on income data alone. Consideration of the joint distribution of income and assets would allow determining whether income and assets tests are "biting", whether the two measures complement one another and, if so, to what extent. In general, all household decisions to accumulate assets include elements of both precautionary saving "against a rainy day" and life-cycle redistribution. The social protection system provides an alternative means for people to cope with both objectives by providing insurance particularly against unemployment and disability and through public pension savings. When eligibility for welfare benefits or the amount granted are based on the amount of liquid assets that a family holds, households are encouraged to liquidate or hide these assets. Policies that penalise or tax such assets as a condition for receiving benefits thus discourage the accumulation of private assets for possible self-protection. The system of targeted benefits in the United States, for instance (such as SSI and Food Stamps), which conditions eligibility on having liquid assets of under USD 2 000 or the value of automobiles of under USD 4 500, discourages both precautionary savings and maintaining a vehicle that could be vital for transportation to a job. Even in cases where the liquid asset limit is rather high (*e.g.*, about AUD 60 000 for the Australian means-tested old-age flat pension), potential beneficiaries are encouraged to invest in untaxed assets (such as own homes) rather than in "taxed" financial assets. Indeed, the height of policy irony is reached where "matched savings" polices are aimed at encouraging low-income persons to accumulate assets, while at the same time means-testing punishes the income poor for holding such assets.

- **Assets and means-tests in long-term care.** Social programmes and asset distribution also interact in the financing of long-term care for the frail elderly. Approximately 10-15% of those reaching retirement, especially older women, eventually need help with activities of daily living. Much attention focuses on whether healthy life expectancy is increasing at the same rate as life expectancy itself. The jury is still out on that: the best that can currently be said is that "it is possible" (compare Cutler, 2001 with Wolf, 2001), and many studies of disability at older ages do not measure trends in various types of dementia. Clearly, when provision of long-term care is provided collectively through insurance (as it is in Germany and Japan, for example), there is less need to accumulate assets to pay for it than in countries where the individual or family is expected to pay. In many countries, public support for long-term care is provided through the welfare system and is subject to means-tests. A great deal of institutional information is available on the structure of support for long-term care, though it is hard to see what form the best explanatory indicator might take. There are few good studies of the effects of means-tested long-term care benefits on asset transfers.

- **Assets and pensions.** Another area where there is little information available is the accumulation of individual assets in employer-provided pensions. Generally, the best information available in all-purpose wealth surveys consists of the proportion of the current working population who are covered. A survey of occupational pension-scheme providers and large employers is currently being carried out by the OECD, jointly with the

European Union, and may shed more light on what sort of pension entitlements are being accumulated outside of social retirement systems.

It is not possible to examine these issues in detail here. Moreover, information on pension fund accumulation is not available in comparative form at this time. However, it is useful to bear in mind these potential policy links when looking at descriptive results.

Basic LWS measures and methodology

The surveys in the LWS differ by purpose and sampling frame (see Sierminska, 2005, for details). Certain surveys have been designed for the specific purpose of collecting wealth data (i.e. Canada, Italy, and the *Survey of Consumer Finances* in the United States, US-SCF); others cover different areas and have been supplemented with special wealth modules (i.e. Germany and the *Panel Survey on Income Dynamics* in the United States, US-PSID). Some surveys over-sample the wealthy and provide better coverage of the upper tail of the distribution (Canada, Germany and the SCF in the United States) but at the cost of higher non-response rates; further, not all over-sample evenly, as only the US-SCF uses a list sample of tax authority records and a large sample of high-wealth persons. Some surveys ask detailed questions about various types of assets, while others ask only a small number of broad wealth questions, but achieve good response rates (e.g., US-PSID).[4] Finally, Germany (alone among the countries included in the LWS) applies a special case of bottom-coding (financial assets, durables and collectibles, and non-housing debt are only recorded when their respective values exceed EUR 2 500). To improve comparability, most of the data in this chapter impose the same bottom-coding on the records of other countries.

Definitions also differ across surveys:

● In general, the *unit of analysis* is the household, but it is the individual in Germany, and the nuclear family (i.e. a single adult or a couple plus dependent children) in Canada. A household is defined as including all persons living together in the same dwelling, but sharing expenses is an additional requirement in Italy, Sweden and the United States. Demographic differences in asset-holdings hence reflect both differences in the unit of analysis and "true" differences in the population structure.

● The *household head* is the main income earner in most surveys, but is the person most knowledgeable and responsible for household finances in Germany and Italy. The United States is the only country where the head is taken to be the male in mixed-sex couples.

The number and definition of recorded wealth variables also vary considerably across surveys, ranging from seven for the United Kingdom to 30 or more for Italy and the US-SCF.[5] These differences, and the different detail of the questions asked in various surveys, make the construction of comparable wealth aggregates a daunting task. The LWS has approached this problem by defining an ideal set of variables to be included in the database. This starts with a general classification of wealth components, from which totals and subtotals are obtained by aggregation. This set is then integrated with demographic characteristics (including health status) and income and consumption aggregates, plus a group of variables particularly relevant in the study of household wealth: realised lump-sum incomes (e.g., capital gains, inheritances and *inter-vivo* transfers) and "behavioural" variables such as motives for savings, perceptions about future events (e.g., bequest motivation), attitude towards risk, and so forth.

This ideal list was then pared down so that it could be crossed with the information actually available in the LWS surveys. This gives rise to the matrix shown in Table 10.A1.2

in the annex. This matrix illustrates the difficulty of transforming the original sources into a harmonised database: the coverage and aggregation of wealth items vary widely across surveys. An acceptable degree of comparability can be obtained for only four main categories of financial assets: i) deposit accounts; ii) bonds; iii) stocks; and iv) mutual funds (with the partial exception of Germany, which does not record information on checking deposits). The remaining financial components are available only for some countries. For non-financial assets the greatest comparability is obtained for both principal residence and investment real estate, while for business equity data are available only for a subset of countries. Liabilities are present in all surveys, though with a varying degree of detail. Applying the minimum common denominator criterion to this matrix, the following four LWS aggregates are then defined:

- *Financial assets,* which include transaction and savings accounts; certificate of deposits; total bonds; stocks; mutual and investment funds; life insurance; pension assets; and other financial assets.

- *Non-financial assets,* which include the principal residence; investment in real estate; business equity; vehicles; durables and collectibles; and other non-financial assets.

- *Liabilities,* including home-secured debt – *i.e.* the sum of principal residence mortgage, other property mortgage, and other home-secured debt (including lines of credit); vehicle loans; instalment debt (including credit card balance); educational loans; other loans from financial institutions; and informal debt.

- *Net worth,* i.e. the sum of financial and non-financial assets less liabilities.

These LWS aggregates still fall far short of perfect comparability, since underlying definitions and methods vary across surveys. Moreover, these aggregates fail to capture important wealth components, such as pension assets. As the importance of these components differs across countries, cross-national comparisons are bound to reflect these omissions. Some indication of the size of these omissions is provided by comparing LWS definitions of household net worth with the national accounts definitions. The LWS database includes variables that are part of the national accounts concept but are excluded from the LWS definition. This allows users to reconcile the different definitions, as shown for five countries in Table 10.A1.3 in the Annex. The first message of Table 10.A1.3 is reassuring: once the missing items are included back in net worth, the LWS figures closely approximate those released in the national accounts. On the other hand, the weight of these omissions is significant and varies considerably across countries, ranging from about a half in the two North-American nations to less than a fourth in the three European nations. This is a salutary warning of the current high cost of cross-country comparability: until a greater standardisation of wealth surveys is achieved *ex ante*, comparability comes at the price of an incomplete picture of national wealth. The section of this chapter describing the joint distribution of assets and income will use a "broad" definition of net worth that includes business equity, but this reduces the number of countries analysed. The next section, which describes basic patterns in asset distribution, sticks to a definition that is less inclusive but that is available for more countries.

Comparability is also affected by other methodological differences besides the definitional issues described above. First, some differences relate to the way assets and liabilities are recorded (*i.e.* as point values, by brackets, or both) and to their accounting period (Table 10.A1.1 in the Annex). Second, the criteria used to value assets and liabilities may differ across surveys (Atkinson and Harrison, 1978). Lastly, surveys differ in terms of patterns of non-response and imputation procedures.[6] Table 10.A1.4 in the annex provides a synthetic assessment of the information contained in the LWS database by comparison with their aggregate counterparts in the national balance sheets of the household sector. This evidence suggests that, despite the considerable effort put into standardising wealth variables, there remain important differences in definitions, valuation criteria and survey quality that cannot be adjusted for. Moreover, the degree to which LWS-based estimates match aggregate figures varies across surveys. These observations have to be borne in mind in reading the results discussed in the next section.[7]

Basic patterns in the distribution of household wealth[8]

This section presents some descriptive evidence on asset-holding and participation for all OECD countries included in the LWS. It describes asset and debt participation, portfolio composition, and the distribution of net worth for the whole LWS dataset, in particular with respect to age of the household head, and presents some inter-country comparisons of wealth concentration. The definition of assets used here ("net worth 1", in the LWS nomenclature) excludes business equity; this allows covering eight OECD countries based on nine datasets. Additional information on survey features is provided in Annex 10.A1.

Asset and debt participation and portfolio composition

Table 10.1 shows that, in almost all LWS countries, over 80% of households own some type of financial assets. In most countries this is a deposit account. Stocks are particularly widespread in Finland and Sweden, while Sweden and Norway have the highest diffusion of mutual funds. In the United States, according to the SCF, holders of stocks, bonds and

Table 10.1. **Household asset participation**

In percentage

Wealth variable	Canada	Finland	Germany[1]	Italy	Norway	Sweden	United Kingdom	United States	United States
	SFS 1999	HWS 1998	SOEP 2002	SHIW 2002	IDS 2002	HINK 2002	BHPS 2000	PSID 2001	SCF 2001
All assets as recorded									
Non-financial assets	64	68	43	72	72	57	70	65	70
Principal residence	60	64	40	69	64	53	69	64	68
Investment real estate	16	27	12	22	30	14	8	–	17
Financial assets	90	92	49	81	99	79	80	83	91
Deposit accounts	88	91	–	81	99	59	76	82	91
Bonds	14	3	–	14	–	16	–	–	19
Stocks	11	33	–	10	22	36	–	30	21
Mutual funds	14	3	–	13	38	58	–	–	18
Debt									
of which:	68	52	32	22	80	70	59	68	75
Home-secured debt	41	28	–	10	–	–	39	–	46
Assets and liabilities recorded only when exceeding 2 500 euros									
Non-financial assets	64	68	43	72	72	–	70	65	70
Financial assets	48	53	49	70	70	–	58	56	60
Total debt	58	45	32	17	74	–	49	59	65

StatLink ﹅ﾟﾞﾚ *http://dx.doi.org/10.1787/423818502548*

Note: Tabulations based on a definition of household wealth that excludes business equity. Data based on household weights.
1. Most financial assets and non-housing debt are recorded only for values exceeding EUR 2 500.
Source: LWS database.

mutual funds each account for about a fifth of the population. Over 60% of households own their principal residence in all countries except Germany and Sweden, and the proportion is just below 70% in Italy, the United Kingdom and the United States (SCF). Owning a second home is most popular in Finland and Norway. There is substantial variation in the percentage owing debt: from 22% of households in Italy to 80% in Norway; and from 10% in Italy to 46% in the United States if only home-secured debt is considered.

As mentioned above, most financial assets and non-housing debt are recorded in Germany only if they exceed EUR 2 500. The data in the bottom panel of Table 10.1 are obtained by applying the same bottom coding used in Germany to the data for other countries, in order to put them on a comparable basis. On this basis, the share of households owning financial assets is similar in Canada, Finland and Germany; it is 20 percentage points higher in Italy and Norway, with the two Anglo-Saxon countries in an intermediate position. A comparison between the top and bottom panel of the table indicates that a large proportion of Canadian and Finnish households holds very few financial assets.

Table 10.2 shows a considerable variance in portfolio composition.[9] The United States exhibits the highest preference for financial assets: around 35% of total assets, over two-thirds of which are held in risky instruments like stocks and mutual funds. Sweden and Canada follow, with proportions of 28% and 22%, respectively. Financial instruments account for only 15-16% of total assets in Finland and Italy. The principal residence represents 60% or more of the value of total assets in all countries except the United States, where it accounts for close to 50%. The ratio of debt to total assets ranges from a very low 4% in Italy to 35% in Sweden. Comparing the household portfolio composition as measured in the LWS database with the composition emerging from aggregate data is an important topic for future research.

Table 10.2. **Household portfolio composition**
Percentage share of total assets

Wealth variable	Canada	Finland	Germany[1]	Italy	Norway[2]	Sweden	United Kingdom	United States	United States
	SFS 1999	HWS 1998	SOEP 2002	SHIW 2002	IDS 2002	HINK 2002	BHPS 2000	PSID 2001	SCF 2001
Non-financial assets	78	84	87	85	–	72	83	67	62
Principal residence	64	64	64	68	–	61	74	52	45
Real estates	13	20	22	17	–	11	9	14	17
Financial assets	22	16	13	15	–	28	17	33	38
Deposit accounts	9	10	–	8	–	11	9	10	10
Bonds	1	0	–	3	–	2	–	–	4
Stocks	7	6	–	1	–	6	–	23	15
Mutual funds	5	1	–	3	–	9	–	–	9
Total assets	100	100	100	100	–	100	100	100	100
Debt	26	16	23	4	–	35	21	22	21
of which:									
Home-secured debt	22	11	–	2	–	–	18	–	18
Net worth	74	84	77	96	–	65	79	78	79

StatLink ⟡ http://dx.doi.org/10.1787/423848344772

Note: Tabulations based on a definition of household wealth that excludes business equity. Data based on household weights. Shares are computed as ratios of means. Data may not add up because of rounding.
1. Most of financial assets and non-housing debt are recorded only for values exceeding EUR 2 500.
2. Figures not reported because valuing real estate on a taxable basis and debt at market prices causes a major inconsistency (indeed, most households have non-positive net worth).
Source: LWS database.

Figure 10.1. **Median wealth-holdings by age of the household head**

Values in 2002 USD

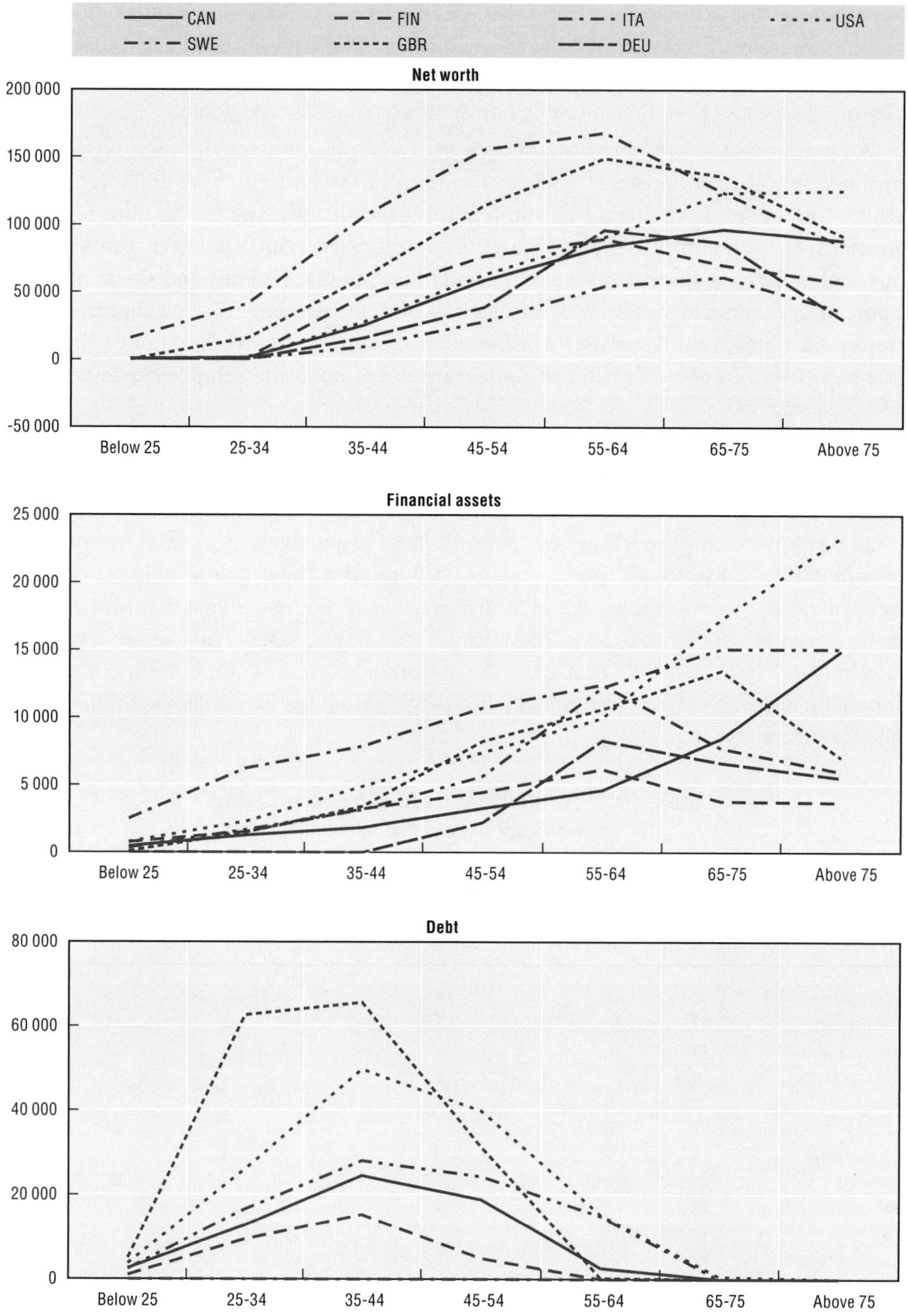

StatLink http://dx.doi.org/10.1787/423777577518

Note: Tabulations based on a definition of household wealth that excludes business equity. Data based on household weights. In the case of Germany, most of financial assets and non-housing debt are recorded only for values exceeding EUR 2 500.

Source: LWS database.

 GROWING UNEQUAL? – ISBN 978-92-64-04418-0 – © OECD 2008

Asset distribution by age of the household head

The profiles for median wealth holdings of financial assets, principal residence, debt and positive net worth by age of the household head are shown in Figure 10.1.[10] These profiles exhibit a hump-shaped pattern, although at different levels of net worth, in most countries. The young have less, the middle-aged have the most, and the older have less than the middle-aged but more than the young. The richest young are found in Italy, but their share in the population is small, suggesting that only those with enough wealth leave their parents' house. In the United States, Canada, the United Kingdom and Italy, households with older heads are also quite well-off. The patterns for financial assets are quite varied for those aged 50 and over. In all countries, the young have little debt, while those aged 35-44 are the most indebted. Unsurprisingly, indebtedness is low among the older age classes: indeed, in all countries over half of the elderly have no debt. In Germany and Italy, over half of the households have no debt at all ages.[11]

Country ranking by levels of net worth and wealth inequality

Figure 10.2 is based on the most comprehensive version of LWS wealth, with values expressed in international 2002 US dollars based on purchasing power parities and consumer price indices estimated by the OECD. Estimates indicate that the country ranking differs between net worth and household disposable income, and also that it matters which central value of the wealth distribution (i.e. mean or median) is chosen. Based on both with mean and median household disposable income, the United States is the richest country, followed by Canada and the United Kingdom, then Germany and Sweden, and lastly Finland and Italy. The country-ranking is very different based on household net worth. The United States and Italy are the richest nations in terms of mean net worth, and Sweden and Finland are the poorest ones. When switching to median net worth, the United States falls towards the middle and is surpassed by Finland and the United Kingdom. Italy and the United Kingdom show by far the highest median net worth, almost twice the corresponding values for the other countries.

The LWS database also sheds new light on international differences in wealth concentration. There are very few international comparisons of wealth distribution based on micro-data reclassified to account for differences in definitions. While Kessler and Wolff (1991), Klevmarken et al. (2003), and Faiella and Neri (2004) are among the few examples of bilateral comparisons, the LWS project is the first attempt to extend such comparisons to more than two countries. Table 10.3 shows statistics on the distribution of net worth in seven countries. The caveats mentioned above must be borne in mind: in particular, the bottom-coding implemented in the German survey is likely to overstate measured inequality. Several patterns stand out:

- Sweden records the highest Gini index for household net worth. The United States, Germany and Canada follow in that order. Finland, the United Kingdom and Italy exhibit a more equal distribution of net worth.

- In accounting terms, part of the explanation of the very high asset inequality in Sweden rests on the very high proportion of Swedish households with nil or negative net worth (32% against 23%, at most, in other countries excluding Germany, whose figure is overstated by bottom-coding).

- When the share of net worth held by top population percentiles is considered, the United States regains the lead: the richest 1% of US households control 33% of total wealth,

Figure 10.2. **LWS country rankings by mean and median of net worth and income**

Values in 2002 USD

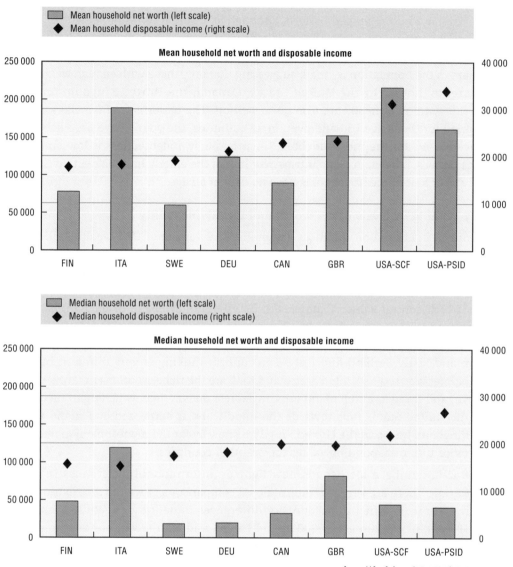

StatLink ▄▀▄ http://dx.doi.org/10.1787/423813102862

Note: Countries are ranked, from left to right, in increasing order of mean household disposable income. Tabulations based on a definition of household wealth that excludes business equity. Data based on household weights. Values are expressed in 2002 USD based on purchasing power parities and consumer price indexes.

Source: LWS database.

according to the SCF, or 25%, according to the PSID, and the next 4% cent control another 25%.[12] These proportions are far higher than in all other countries, Sweden included.

Understanding the extent to which these results are affected by the different measurement methods or the different comprehensiveness of the wealth definition is an important question for future LWS research. For instance, counting pension rights as an asset might matter more for Sweden, which should result in much greater equality than found in Table 10.3.[13]

Table 10.3. **Distribution of household net worth**[1]

Percentage

Statistics	Canada	Finland	Germany[2]	Italy	Norway[3]	Sweden	United Kingdom	United States	United States
	SFS 1999	HWS 1998	SOEP 2002	SHIW 2002	IDS 2002	HINK 2002	BHPS 2000	PSID 2001	SCF 2001
Shares of individuals (%)									
Positive net worth	77	83	63	89	–	68	82	77	77
Nil net worth	3	2	29	7	–	5	6	8	4
Negative net worth	20	15	9	3	–	27	11	16	19
Shares of total wealth (%)									
Top 10%	53	45	55	42	–	58	45	64	71
Top 5%	37	31	38	29	–	41	30	49	58
Top 1%	15	13	16	11	–	18	10	25	33
Wealth inequality									
Gini index	0.75	0.68	0.8	0.61	–	0.89	0.66	0.81	0.84

StatLink ⟲⟲ http://dx.doi.org/10.1787/423884073432

Note: Tabulations based on a definition of household wealth that excludes business equity. Data based on household weights.

1. Figures not reported because over 60% of values for net worth are missing.
2. Most financial assets and non-housing debt are recorded only for values exceeding EUR 2 500.
3. Figures not reported because valuing real estate on a taxable basis and debt at market prices causes a major inconsistency (indeed, the majority of households have negative net worth).

Source: LWS database.

Joint patterns of income and wealth inequality[14]

The joint distribution of income and wealth is of interest for a number of reasons. First, both income and wealth allow persons and households to finance their consumption. Second, in many policy circumstances, for instance support for the elderly, some people might have low incomes but also hold wealth that could be drawn upon to finance consumption. Third, assessing the effects of means-testing on benefit eligibility and take-up will often require looking at both income and asset holdings of potential beneficiaries. More generally, the higher the correlation between income and wealth, the higher is the degree of "permanent" inequality in potential consumption due to either income or wealth.

Exploring the joint distribution of income and wealth with some accuracy calls for special selections of datasets and editing procedures. This section concentrates on five nations and six datasets (two for the United States because of the SCF oversample). The definitions of income and wealth for the five countries analysed here are as follows.

● Income refers to household disposable income adjusted by the square root of household size (e = 0.5) equivalence scale. The income definition in the LWS is very similar to that used in LIS, but of a more aggregated variety. People are considered as income-poor when their income is less than half of the median, using the same equivalence scale.

● The wealth definition includes business equity within other non-financial assets ("net worth 2", in the LWS nomenclature). The same equivalence scale (e = 0.5) is used for both income and wealth. In practice, the choice of the equivalence scale makes little difference to the outcome (Sierminska *et al.*, 2006b).

This definition of net worth means that the number of countries used here is smaller than if excluding business assets (*i.e.* five countries and six datasets, Table 10.A1.2 in the Annex).[15] National data are converted into US dollars using the PPPs for personal consumption in 2002 published by the OECD; national price deflators for personal consumption have been used to express national currencies in 2002 prices.

Wealth holding of all persons and of the income-poor

Table 10.4 shows the share of people reporting positive wealth of various types (left panel) and the values for various asset aggregates (net worth, financial assets, non-financial assets and debts, right panel) for all persons and for the income poor.[16] This shows that the majority of families, including poor families, have some positive net worth. The average net worth of the income poor is positive but obviously well below as that of the entire population. The income poor have low financial assets, averaging under USD 8 812 except for the US SCF where the value is USD 26 678 (owing to a small number of outliers, see below). Between 30 and 60% of the income poor hold non-financial assets (homes or businesses) but the values are on average USD 25-50 000. The average debt of the poor exceeds their financial assets in three countries (Canada, Germany and Sweden) and is under USD 2 000 in Italy. Debt is also substantial for the poor in both of the United States datasets.

Table 10.5 indicates the dispersion of net worth, assets and debt within both the entire population and within those classified as income poor; a measure of this dispersion is provided by comparing the values of various wealth aggregates for those at the top end of the distribution (90th percentile) and at the median person is each of the two groups. Skewness

Table 10.4. Proportion with positive net worth and mean wealth and debt holdings, all people and income poor

In 2002 US PPP adjusted dollars

	Net worth	Financial assets	Non-financial assets	Debt		Net worth	Financial assets	Non-financial assets	Debt
	A. Proportion with positive amounts					*B. Average amount*			
Canada					Canada				
All persons	80.1	89.9	75.1	75.1	All persons	59 557	13 574	63 716	17 733
Income poor	58.8	76.2	40.1	61.1	Income poor	23 737	4 610	26 585	7 458
Germany					Germany				
All persons	67.2	49.7	52.7	41.1	All persons	83 063	10 870	92 206	20 013
Income poor	38.5	19.3	29.5	19.4	Income poor	31 174	2 229	35 203	6 257
Italy					Italy				
All persons	90.7	82.4	77.0	23.0	All persons	112 506	14 666	100 719	2 879
Income poor	70.3	45.0	62.0	17.6	Income poor	51 947	1 972	51 634	1 659
Sweden					Sweden				
All persons	70.5	83.1	66.6	79.4	All persons	43 000	15 808	48 761	21 569
Income poor	48.6	62.4	33.1	66.9	Income poor	20 863	8 801	25 383	13 321
United States (PSID)					US (PSID)				
All persons	78.0	83.1	71.5	73.0	All persons	104 075	36 249	94 027	26 200
Income poor	52.4	52.2	41.8	48.8	Income poor	21 784	8 238	20 956	7 410
United States (SCF)					US (SCF)				
All persons	77.0	91.3	73.3	81.5	All persons	120 553	42 058	109 180	30 685
Income poor	54.9	70.0	43.2	63.4	Income poor	75 452	26 678	59 359	10 585

StatLink 🔗 http://dx.doi.org/10.1787/424003453262

Note: Tabulations based on a definition of household wealth that includes business equity.
Source: Luxembourg Wealth Study.

Table 10.5. **Values of assets and debt for people at different points of the distribution, all persons and income poor**

In 2002 US PPP adjusted dollars

	Net worth	Financial assets	Non-financial assets	Debt		Net worth	Financial assets	Non-financial assets	Debt
	A. People in the 90th percentile					B. Median person			
Canada					Canada				
All persons	139 613	24 620	130 209	48 711	All persons	20 866	1 214	40 230	6 940
Income poor	75 521	6 132	78 850	22 662	Income poor	121	93	–	546
Germany					Germany				
All persons	196 282	26 285	209 067	58 943	All persons	20 610	–	24 136	–
Income poor	93 722	6 076	109 011	17 984	Income poor	–	–	–	–
Italy					Italy				
All persons	252 736	29 631	227 927	7 203	All persons	64 934	3 924	61 031	–
Income poor	125 360	4 562	127 776	2 113	Income poor	19 718	–	19 701	–
Sweden					Sweden				
All persons	121 202	37 979	118 261	51 411	All persons	15 325	3 493	27 384	11 374
Income poor	79 928	27 093	78 570	31 625	Income poor	–	463	–	2 451
United States (PSID)					US (PSID)				
All persons	218 016	60 940	187 899	71 097	All persons	20 657	1 877	43 790	10 871
Income poor	47 800	3 886	59 030	22 310	Income poor	65	7	–	–
United States (SCF)					US (SCF)				
All persons	249 347	72 730	211 260	73 698	All persons	21 735	2 609	44 086	13 602
Income poor	76 175	8 440	81 529	26 455	Income poor	110	91	–	453

StatLink ⌾📇 http://dx.doi.org/10.1787/424063118134

Note: Tabulations based on a definition of household wealth that includes business equity.
Source: Luxembourg Wealth Study.

is apparent in all cases. According to the left panel, 89% of the income poor (those below the 90th percentile) have financial assets below USD 8 440 in all countries except Sweden (where the 90th percentile is at USD 27 000). Median financial wealth amongst the income poor is less than USD 500 in all nations. While the net worth of the 90th percentile of the income poor is rather high in most nations (USD 47 000-USD 125 000), this is largely in the form of non-financial assets (owned homes and businesses). In contrast, the net worth of the median poor is low, under USD 121 except in Italy (where the value is all in housing). For the median poor, the reported values of debt are zero in Germany, Italy and in the US-PSID sample; in all other countries, the value of debt exceeds that of financial assets and net worth (Panel B).

Table 10.6 shows some basic measures of wealth inequality for the entire population and for the income poor. Several patterns stand out. First, the Gini coefficients for household net worth are very high (well above those reported for household income). Second, inequality in wealth is significantly higher amongst the poor than amongst the entire population, and in all nations by an order of magnitude. Last, the Gini coefficients for net worth and financial assets in the United States are higher than in any other nation, both for the poor and for the entire population. The estimates for non-financial assets and debt are more similar across nations.

Descriptive evidence on the joint distribution of net worth and disposable income

When moving beyond income poverty and considering the entire distribution of income and wealth, the issue of comparability at the top end of the distribution becomes

Table 10.6. **Gini coefficient of household net worth, all persons and income poor**

Gini coefficient	Net worth	Fin. assets	Non-fin. assets	Debt
Canada				
All people	0.67	0.87	0.63	0.66
Income Poor	0.78	0.92	0.82	0.81
Germany				
All people	0.73	0.82	0.75	0.84
Income Poor	0.84	0.92	0.84	0.92
Italy				
All people	0.60	0.77	0.61	0.91
Income Poor	0.70	0.84	0.72	0.95
Sweden				
All people	0.62	0.78	0.66	0.65
Income Poor	0.69	0.82	0.86	0.78
United States (PSID)				
All people	0.77	0.89	0.70	0.67
Income Poor	0.86	0.97	0.82	0.83
United States (SCF)				
All people	0.77	0.89	0.73	0.66
Income Poor	0.92	0.98	0.90	0.86

StatLink ⌁⫘ http://dx.doi.org/10.1787/424105231277

Note: Tabulations based on a definition of household wealth that includes business equity.
Source: Luxembourg Wealth Study.

crucial. As already noted, the US-SCF is the dataset that captures more assets in the United States, and is reputed to be the best wealth survey in the world. In order to adjust for "too good" a survey, this section relies on trimming data for the top 1% of the US SCF records but not from other datasets.[17]

The basic patterns of income and wealth (net worth) holdings are shown in Figure 10.3. Data refer to quartile groupings (QG) of both income and wealth, matched into a four-by-four picture. The dots show the relevant fraction of people in a given income- and wealth-quartile cell. Take for instance the lowest quartile group of both income and wealth (the top left-hand corner of Figure 10.3) and contrast this with the top quartile group in both distributions (the bottom right-hand corner). The United States stands out, compared to other countries, for the highest fraction of low income people that also belong to the lowest wealth quartile and, similarly, for the highest fraction of high-income people in the top wealth quartile.

A number of other patterns stand out from Figure 10.3:

- First, the concentration of people with the highest-income people in the top wealth cells is highest in the United States (nearly 15% in both datasets) and lowest in Canada (about 11%).

- Second, the distribution of people belonging to the third and the second wealth quartiles across income groups is remarkably similar in all nations (with the exception of Germany for Wealth QG2).

- Third, among people belonging to the top two wealth quartiles, their share increases uniformly as we move up the income scale (from Income QG1 to Income QG3, for people belonging to WealthQG3; and from Income QG1 to Income QG4, for those belonging to Wealth QG4).This suggests that income and wealth positions are positively correlated.

Figure 10.3. **Income-wealth quartile groups**

Share of people in each income quartile belonging to various quartiles of the wealth distribution

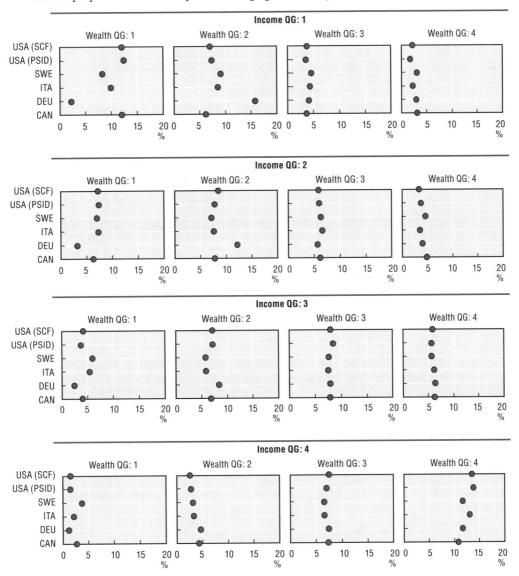

StatLink ⟨⟩ http://dx.doi.org/10.1787/423815213564

Note: Tabulations based on a definition of household wealth that includes business equity. For each income quartile, the sum of values across wealth quartiles equals 25%.

Source: Luxembourg Wealth Study.

- Fourth, few low-income people have high wealth; the share of people in the bottom income quartile (Income QG1) who also belong to the top wealth quartile (Wealth QG4) is highest in Sweden but, even here, it is well below 5%.

- Last, at the other end of the spectrum, high-income people rarely have low wealth; Sweden, again, stands out for the highest share of people in Income QG4 who are also in Wealth QG1.

The simple conclusion is that, in most nations, income and wealth are correlated, but not perfectly. The highest correlations appear to be at the top of the income and wealth scale (Income QG4 and Wealth QG4, bottom-right corner), but even here the extent of overlap is less than full.

Determinants of household disposable income and net worth

While an examination of the joint distribution of income and wealth using the proportions of persons in different parts of the (marginal) distributions is informative, the observed association between income and wealth is in part accounted for by the fact that the characteristics associated with having high income – having a high education, for instance – are also associated with having high wealth. Differences in the degree of association between countries are likely driven by both differences in the characteristics of those who hold wealth and by differences in how these characteristics are associated with wealth and income.

To examine this in more depth, this section considers patterns of disposable income and net worth while controlling for different characteristics. This is done by estimating simple bivariate regressions of household disposable income and net worth, using as covariates the *age* of the household head (four groups; age less than 30 omitted), the *education level* of the head (three levels; lowest level omitted) and the *household type* (five types; childless couples omitted). This permits a look both at how average wealth is related to household characteristics, and at how the joint distribution (as conditioned by age, education and household type) compares across countries. Figure 10.4 show regression results for income and wealth patterns: models are estimated in levels, measured in PPP US dollars, so the coefficients can be interpreted in absolute terms. The results are *not* an attempt to provide a causal model for disposable income and net worth – indeed, a causal model for these would at the very least require longitudinal data. But they do show certain patterns in the extent of the variance of disposable income and net worth that is captured by the different characteristics (for more evidence of these regression analysis, see Jantti *et al.*, 2008).

Some of the key patterns emerging from this analysis include the following:

- The calculations for household disposable income show that single parents do less well, and education positively adds to incomes, especially for the United States in the SCF sample. Incomes peak for household heads in the 50-70 age range, being lower in ages 30-50 and 70 and over. The results also suggest that a given characteristic is associated with a larger difference in income in the United States than elsewhere. For instance, having a high education is associated with a USD 30 433 disposable income advantage in the United States, but at most about USD 13 000 in the other countries.

- The net worth regressions tend to show few demographic effects but strong effects for age (older people have higher wealth) and education (higher education and net worth are positively correlated), with the strongest effects again in the United States.

- The share of variance accounted for by the age, education and family characteristics is not very large for either income or wealth. Close to 40% of the variance of disposable income is captured in Sweden, which has the most equal distribution of these nations (Atkinson, Rainwater and Smeeding, 1995; Brandolini and Smeeding, 2005), while in other countries the variance in incomes explained by these three determinants is between 20 and 25%.

- In the wealth regressions, education, age and family structure explain between 10 and 20% of the variance. The fact that the share of variance explained by the various

Figure 10.4. **Results from regressions describing the average amounts of household disposable income and net worth**

Coefficient estimates and confidence intervals

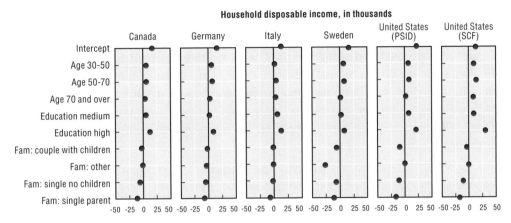

StatLink ⫘⫘⫘ http://dx.doi.org/10.1787/423816145285

Note: Tabulations based on a definition of household wealth that includes business equity.

Source: Luxembourg Wealth Study.

characteristics is less for wealth than for income reflects that we know less about what is involved in the generation of wealth, although there are reasons to believe that intergenerational transfers are a significant factor (see Chapter 8).

● Even after controlling for these factors, a sizeable correlation between wealth and income at the individual level remains. This correlation is particularly high in the United States in the SCF sample, where it exceeds 0.50, while it varies between 0.27-0.36 in the other datasets, including the PSID sample for the United States.

Conclusion

The Luxembourg Wealth Study allows for comparisons of net worth and its components across countries. Although comparability is not as great as might be hoped for, two main patterns stand out:

● First, there are both similarities and differences in patterns of wealth-holding across countries. Housing accounts for a large part of net worth in all countries. The share of financial assets is also important, although there is considerable variation across countries. Italy stands out for having very low levels of debt and few households with negative net worth. There are some differences in US results depending on whether analysis is based on the SCF or the PSID. This suggests that survey design matters a lot. It is not possible, at this point, to say whether observed country differences are due to such technical differences.

- Second, net worth and disposable income are highly, but not perfectly, correlated. Many of those who are classified as income poor do have some assets, although the prevalence of holding and the amounts held are clearly well below those of the general population, while the "median" poor has negligible financial assets in all countries covered. Part of the positive association of disposable income and net worth is related to characteristics of the household such as age and education, but a positive correlation persists even after controlling for these factors.

These results indicate that while income continues to be a crucial factor shaping living conditions and social policies, it is not the only factor that matters in determining the resources available to households. Correlation between wealth and income is high but far from perfect. In particular, the fact that assets are more concentrated than income, including among the income poor, has implications for welfare systems that rely on means-testing. All this underscores yet again the need for a common framework for the collection of data on household wealth: increased comparability can only be achieved through greater *ex ante* standardisation of measurement tools.

Notes

1. Indeed, in introducing a collection of essays on household portfolios in five countries, Guiso *et al.* (2002) mention "definitions" as the "initial problem" and warn the reader that "the special features and problems of each survey … should be kept in mind when trying to compare data across countries". Likewise, Davies and Shorrocks (2000) conclude their extensive survey on the distribution of wealth by remarking that: "Adoption of a common framework in different countries, along the lines that have been developed for income distributions, would improve the scope for comparative studies". Both considerations should be kept in mind here.

2. A recent compilation of data on wealth inequality for nine nations around the beginning of this decade shows that Sweden, not the United States, leads the ranking (Brandolini, 2006). This evidence not only runs counter to that based on income, but also to earlier evidence. According to the figures assembled by Davies and Shorrocks (2000) for 11 nations, in the mid-1980s wealth inequality was among the lowest in Sweden and greatest in the United States. Does this different ranking reflect true changes during the 1990s, or some statistical artefact? The results of Klevmarken *et al.* (2003), which show a much higher level of wealth inequality in the United States than in Sweden in the 1980s and 1990s, point towards the latter explanation. Klevmarken (2006) also reports that, in 2003, the inequality of net worth in Sweden was somewhat below the average, and lower than in France, Germany and Italy, according to the evidence of the *Survey of Health, Ageing and Retirement in Europe* (SHARE) – an international project for the collection of data standardised from the outset on the living conditions and health status of households with at least one member aged 50 or more. These findings are a clear warning that, before making cross-country comparisons and investigating the causes of different patterns, we must carefully understand the extent to which data are comparable.

3. The first LWS working papers described the main features of the LWS and some preliminary results (*e.g.* Sieminska *et al.*, 2006a and 2006b, *www.lisproject.org/publications/lwswpapers.htm*). Other recent papers on the same website look at the characteristics of individuals (median net worth) by age, gender and education. Some of these papers provide a special focus on the economic conditions of the elderly in terms of both income and assets, looking at how the combination of resources in retirement varies with the characteristics of the social protection system (Gornick *et al.*, 2006).

4. The US-SCF is by far the most detailed survey of those included in the LWS database: checking accounts, for instance, are first separated into primary and secondary accounts, and then distinguished according to the type of bank where they are held.

5. Full documentation of each survey's features is an important constituent of the LWS archive. The LWS documentation also reports which of these differences in the original surveys were corrected for in the harmonisation process, and which were not. See *www.lisproject.org/lwstechdoc.htm* for more on these idiosyncrasies.

6. For more on these differences and the efforts being made to resolve them, see Jantti *et al.* (2008).

7. Conversely, the LWS income data are almost identical to the income measures available on the LIS income surveys (Niskanen, 2007). This should come as no surprise as – for Germany, Italy and Sweden – the data are from the same surveys. While LWS income data are more aggregated than the LIS data, the former still makes it possible to separate market and disposable income uniformly across all LWS surveys.

8. The data used in this section (as well as in Annex 10.A1) are drawn from the preliminary (β) version of the LWS database.

9. Figures are not reported for Norway because of the inconsistency stemming from valuing real estate on a taxable basis and debt at market prices; also, the German data are biased by the fact that small holdings of some financial assets and debt are not recorded.

10. As wealth accumulation patterns vary over the life-cycle, it is also useful to portray the demographic structure in each country (Table 10.A1.5). The average household size ranges from 1.96 persons in Sweden to 2.65 in Italy. Italy also stands out as the country with the most pronounced ageing process, followed by the United Kingdom, Germany and Sweden, while Canada has the youngest average household head.

11. Profiles of the share of people in different age groups holding different types of assets and liabilities (not shown here) also differ across countries. Italy, again, stands out as an outlier. On the one hand, intergenerational differences appear to be dissimilar, since the hump-shape of debt-holding and home-ownership is much flatter than in the other countries. On the other hand, the low propensity to borrow and the parallel high proportion of positive net worth holders, already noted for the average, are common across all age classes. Norway and Finland show a remarkable diffusion of financial wealth in all cohorts, including the young. In Germany and Sweden the share of home-owners tends to be lower than in other countries, and it is markedly so among the elderly.

12. The over-sampling of the wealthy in the US-SCF but not in the US-PSID is a plausible reason for the difference in the estimated shares of the richest households.

13. On measuring pension wealth see Brugiavini *et al.* (2005).

14. This section relies on the α-version (*i.e.*, publicly available) of the LWS database.

15. In examining the joint distribution of income and wealth, the focus is on net worth and household disposable income. The analysis refers to both the full datasets and "shaved" datasets, where the top 1% and bottom 1% of each dataset for income and wealth are "trimmed down" to enhance comparability. For more on the methodological issues involved, such as shaved datasets, sample size, special sampling, imputations for item non-response and the handling of differences in collection methods, see Jantii *et al.* (2008).

16. Because of the omission of values for the units with financial assets below EUR 2 500, the German figures are biased downwards.

17. For more on the effect of trimming data on the comparability of the data, in particular with regard to Germany (with the omission of financial assets under EUR 2 500), Sweden (where high net debt seems to be due to tax laws that encourage debt holding) and Italy (where low net debt seems to reflect the high concentration on housing assets), see Jantii *et al.* (2008).

References

Aizcorbe, A., A. Kennickell and K. Moore (2003), "Recent Changes in the US Family Finances: Evidence from the 1998 and 2001 Survey of Consumer Finances", Federal Reserve Bulletin, January.

Antoniewicz, R., R. Bonci, A. Generale, G. Marchese, A. Neri, K. Maser and P. O'Hagan (2005), "Household Wealth: Comparing Micro and Macro Data in Cyprus, Canada, Italy and United States", Paper prepared for LWS Workshop "Construction and Usage of Comparable Microdata on Wealth: the LWS", Banca d'Italia, Perugia, Italy, 27-29 January.

Atkinson, A.B. and A.J. Harrison (1978), *Distribution of Personal Wealth in Britain*, Cambridge University Press, Cambridge.

Atkinson, A.B., L. Rainwater and T.M. Smeeding (1995), *Income Distribution in OECD Countries*, OECD, Paris.

Banks, J., Z. Smith and M. Wakefield (2002), "The Distribution of Financial Wealth in the UK: Evidence from 2000 BHPS Data", Institute for Fiscal Studies, Working Paper No. 02/21, November.

Bičáková, A. and E. Sierminska (2007), "Homeownership Inequality and the Access to Credit Markets. Can Credit Availability Explain Cross-country Differences in the Inequality of Homeownership across Income of Young Households?", Luxembourg Wealth Study Working Paper No. 5, December.

Board of Governors of the Federal Reserve System (2006), *Flow of Funds Accounts of the United States. Flows and Outstandings. First Quarter 2006*. Washington, DC, available at *www.federalreserve.gov/releases/z1/current/default.htm*.

Brandolini, A. (2006), "The Distribution of Wealth in Germany and Sweden: Discussion of the Papers by Stein and Klevmarken", in G. Chaloupek and T. Zotter (eds.), *Steigende wirtschaftliche Ungleichheit bei steigendem Reichtum?*, Tagung der Kammer für Arbeiter und Angestellte für Wien, LexisNexis Verlag ARD Orac., Vienna.

Brandolini, A. and T.M. Smeeding (2005), "Inequality Patterns in Western Democracies: Cross-Country Differences and Time Changes", Paper presented at the conference "Democracy, Inequality and Representation: Europe in Comparative Perspective", Maxwell School, Syracuse University, Syracuse, 6-7 May.

Brandolini, A., L. Cannari, G. D'Alessio and I. Faiella (2006), "Household Wealth Distribution in Italy in the 1990s", forthcoming in E.N. Wolff (ed.), *International Perspectives on Household Wealth*. Cheltenham: Edward Elgar, also available in Banca d'Italia, Temi di discussione, No. 530, December 2004.

Brugiavini, A., K. Maser and A. Sundén (2005), "Measuring Pension Wealth", Paper prepared for LWS Workshop "Construction and Usage of Comparable Microdata on Wealth: the LWS", Banca d'Italia, Perugia, Italy, 27-29 January.

Campbell, J.Y (2006), "Household Finance", National Bureau of Economic Research, Working Paper, No. 12149, March.

Davies, J.B. and A.F. Shorrocks (2000), "The Distribution of Wealth", in A.B. Atkinson and F. Bourguignon (eds.), *Handbook of Income Distribution*, Vol. 1, Amsterdam: North-Holland.

Expert Group on Household Income Statistics – The Canberra Group (2001), *Final Report and Recommendations*, The Canberra Group, Ottawa.

Eurostat (2006), *Financial Accounts*, available at *http://epp.eurostat.ec.europa.eu/portal/page?_pageid=0,1136173,0_45570701&_dad=portal&_schema=PORTAL&screen=ExpandTree&open=/economy/fina/fina_st&product=EU_economy_finance&nodeid=36598&vindex=5&level=3&portletid=39994106_QUEENPORTLET_92281242&scrollto=0*.

Faiella, I. and A. Neri (2004), "La ricchezza delle famiglie italiane e americane", Banca d'Italia, Temi di discussione, No. 501, June.

Gornick, J.C., T. Munzi, E. Sierminska and T.M. Smeeding (2006), "Older Women's Income and Wealth Packages: The Five-Legged Stool in Cross-National Perspective", Luxembourg Wealth Study Working Paper No. 3, November.

Guiso, L., M. Haliassos and T. Jappelli (2002), "Introduction", in L. Guiso, M. Haliassos and T. Jappelli (eds.), *Household Portfolios*, MIT Press, Cambridge, Mass.

Harding, T., H.O. Aa. Solheim and A. Benedictow (2004), "House Ownership and Taxes", Statistics Norway, Research Department, Discussion Papers No. 395, November.

Jantti, M., E. Sierminska and T. Smeeding (2008), "The Joint Distribution of Household Income and Wealth: Evidence from the Luxembourg Wealth Study", OECD Social, Employment and Migration Working Paper, No. 65, OECD, Paris.

Kennickell, A.B. (2000), "Wealth Measurement in the Survey of Consumer Finances: Methodology and Directions for Future Research", Board of Governors of the Federal Reserve Board, SCF Working Paper, May.

Kessler, D. and E.N. Wolff (1991), "A Comparative Analysis of Household Wealth Patterns in France and the Unites States", *Review of Income and Wealth*, Vol. 37.

Klevmarken, A. (2006), "The Distribution of Wealth in Sweden: Trends and Driving Factors", in G. Chaloupek and T. Zotter (eds.), *Steigende wirtschaftliche Ungleichheit bei steigendem Reichtum?*, Tagung der Kammer für Arbeiter und Angestellte für Wien, LexisNexis Verlag ARD Orac., Vienna.

Klevmarken, A., J. Lupton and F. Stafford (2003), "Wealth Dynamics in the 1980s and 1990s. Sweden and the United States", *Journal of Human Resources*, Vol. 38.

Niskanen E. (2007), "The Luxembourg Wealth Study: Technical Report on LWS Income Variables", mimeo, *www.lisproject.org/lws/incomevariablereport.pdf*.

Office for National Statistics (2006), *United Kingdom National Accounts. The Blue Book 2006*, edited by J. Dye and J. Sosimi, Palgrave Macmillan, Basingstoke.

Sierminska, E. (2005), "The Luxembourg Wealth Study: A Progress Report", Paper prepared for LWS Workshop "Construction and Usage of Comparable Microdata on Wealth: the LWS", Banca d'Italia, Perugia, Italy, 27-29 January.

Sierminska, E., A. Brandolini and T.M. Smeeding (2006a), "Cross National Comparison of Income and Wealth Status in Retirement: First Results from the Luxembourg Wealth Study (LWS)", Luxembourg Wealth Study Working Paper No. 2, August.

Sierminska, E., A. Brandolini and T.M. Smeeding (2006b), "Comparing Wealth Distribution across Rich Countries: First Results from the Luxembourg Wealth Study", Luxembourg Wealth Study Working Paper No. 1, August.

Sierminska, E. and Y. Takhtamanova (2006), "Wealth Effects Out of Financial and Housing Wealth: Cross Country and Age Group Comparisons", Luxembourg Wealth Study Working Paper No. 4, November.

Smeeding, T.M. (2004), "Twenty Years of Research on Income Inequality, Poverty, and Redistribution in the Developed World: Introduction and Overview", *Socio-Economic Review*, No. 2.

Statistics Canada (2006a), *Assets and Debts by Family Units, Including Employer-sponsored Registered Pension Plans, by Province*, available at *www40.statcan.ca/l01/cst01/famil99k.htm?sdi=assets%20debts*.

Statistics Canada (2006b), *National Balance Sheet Accounts, Market Value, by Sectors, at Quarter End, Quarterly (dollars x 1,000,000)*, available at *http://cansim2.statcan.ca/cgi-win/cnsmcgi. exe?Lang=E&Accessible=1&ArrayId=V1074&ResultTemplate=CII\SNA___&RootDir=CII/ &Interactive=1&OutFmt=HTML2D&Array_Retr=1&Dim=-#HERE*.

Statistics Sweden (2004). *Förmögenhetsstatistik 2002*.

ANNEX 10.A1

Features of the Luxembourg Wealth Study

This annex presents background information on some of the main features of the statistical sources used by LWS, as well as details on the definitions used. It also presents summary statistics on the distribution of household wealth in all OECD countries participating in the LWS.

A synthetic assessment of the information contained in the LWS database is provided by the comparison of LWS-based estimates with their aggregate counterparts in the national balance sheets of the household sector (which include non-profit institutions serving households and small unincorporated enterprises). This comparison is presented in Table 10.A1.4, where all variables are transformed into euros at current prices by using the average market exchange rate in the relevant year, and are expressed in per capita terms to adjust for differences in household size. Note that Table 10.A1.3 discussed above asks how well LWS covers the national accounts concept of net worth. Here, we focus on another question, namely how well the concept of net worth used in the LWS corresponds to the similarly defined concept of net worth based on national accounts. Aggregate accounts provide a natural benchmark for assessing the quality of the LWS database, but a proper comparison would require painstaking work to reconcile the two sources, as discussed at length by Antoniewicz et al. (2005). The aim of Table 10.A1.4 is more modestly to offer a summary view of how the picture drawn on the basis of the LWS data relates to the one that could be derived from the national balance sheets or the financial accounts. LWS estimates seem to represent non-financial assets and, to a lesser extent, liabilities better than financial assets. In all countries where the aggregate information is available, the LWS wealth data account for between 40 and 60% of the aggregate wealth. Note that not all of these discrepancies should be attributed to the deficiency of the LWS data, since they reflect not only under-reporting in the original micro sources, but also the dropping of some items in the LWS definitions to enhance cross-country comparability as well as the different definitions used in micro and macro sources.

Table 10.A1.1. **LWS household wealth surveys**

	Name	Agency	Wealth year[1]	Income year	Type of source	Over-sampling of the wealthy	Sample size	No. of non-missing net worth	No. of wealth items
Austria	Survey of Household Financial Wealth (SHFW)	Österreichische Nationalbank	2004	2004	Sample survey	No			10
Canada	Survey of Financial Security (SFS)	Statistics Canada	1999	1998	Sample survey	Yes	15 933	15 933	17
Finland	Household Wealth Survey (HWS)	Statistics Finland	End of 1998	1998	Sample survey	No	3 893	3 893	23
Germany	Socio-Economic Panel (SOEP)	Deutsches Institut Für Wirtschaftsforschung (DIW) Berlin	2002	2001	Sample panel survey	Yes	12 692	12 129	9
Italy	Survey of Household Income and Wealth (SHIW)	Bank of Italy	End of 2002	2002	Sample survey (panel section)	No	8 011	8 010	34
Norway	Income Distribution Survey (IDS)	Statistics Norway	End of 2002	2002	Sample survey plus administrative records	No	22 870	22 870	35
Sweden	Wealth Survey (HINK)	Statistics Sweden	End of 2002	2002	Sample survey plus administrative records	No	17 954	17 954	26
United Kingdom	British Household Panel Survey (BHPS)	ESRC	2000	2000	Sample panel survey	No	4,867[2]	4 185	7
United States	Panel Study of Income Dynamics (PSID)	Survey Research Center of the University of Michigan	2001	2000	Sample panel survey	No	7 406	7 071	14
	Survey of Consumer Finances (SCF)	Federal Reserve Board and US Department of Treasury	2001	2000	Sample survey	Yes	4 442[3]	4 442[3]	30

1. Values refer to the time of the interview unless otherwise indicated.
2. Original survey sample. Sample size can rise to 8 761 when weights are not used.
3. Data are stored as five successive replicates of each record that should not be used separately; thus, actual sample size for users is 22 210. The special sample of the wealthy includes 1 532 households.

Source: LWS database.

Table 10.A1.2. **Wealth classification matrix in the LWS**

	LWS acronym	Canada SFS 1999	Finland HWS 1998	Germany SOEP 2002	Italy SHIW 2002	Norway IDS 2002	Sweden HINK 2002	United Kingdom BHPS 2000	United States PSID 2001	United States SCF 2001
Financial assets										
Total	TFA	Σ	Σ	Σ	Σ	Σ	Σ	Σ	Σ	Σ
Deposit accounts: transaction, savings and CDs	DA	Y	Y		Y	Y	Y	Y^2	Y	Y
Total bonds: savings and other bonds	TB	Y	Y		Y	Y	Y	Y		Y
Stocks	ST	Y	Y	Y^1	Y		Y		Y	Y
Mutual funds and other investment funds	TM	Y	Y		Y	Y	Y			Y
Life insurance	LI	–	Y		–	Y	–	Y^2	Y^4	Y
Other financial assets (exc. pension)	OFA	Y	Y	Y^3	Y	Y	Y^5	–		Y
Pension assets	PA	Y	Y		–	Y	–	–	Y	Y
Non-financial assets										
Total	TNF	Σ	Σ	Σ	Σ	Σ	Σ	Σ	Σ	Σ
Principal residence	PR	Y	Y	Y	Y	Y	Y	Y	Y	Y
Investment real estate	IR	Y	Y	Y	Y	Y	Y	Y^6	Y^7	Y
Business equity	BE	Y	–	Y^6	Y	Y^6	Y^6	Y^9	Y	Y
Vehicles	VH	Y	Y	Y^8	Y	Y	–	Y^9	Y^9	Y
Durables and collectibles	DRCL	Y	Y	Y	Y	Y	–	–	–	Y
Other non-financial assets	ONF		–	–	–	–	Y^5	–	–	Y
Liabilities										
Total	TD	Σ	Σ	Σ	Σ	Y	Y	Σ	Σ	Σ
Home-secured debt	HSD	Σ	Y	Σ	Y	–	Y^{10}	Y	Σ	Σ
Principal residence mortgage	MG	Y		Y		Y^{11}	–		Y	Y
Other property mortgage	OMG	Y		Y			–		Y^7	Y
Other home-secured debt (incl. line of credit)	OHSD	Y		–		Y	–			Y
Vehicle loans	VL	Y	Y	Y	Y	Y^{11}	Y^{10}	Y^9	Y^9	Y
Installment debt (incl. credit card balance)	IL	Y	Y	Y	Y	Y	Y	Y^{12}	Y	Y
Educational loans	EL	Y	Y	Y	–	Y	Y			Y
Other loans from financial institutions	OL	Y	Y	Y	–	Y	Y			Y

Note: "Y" denotes a recorded item; "Σ" indicates that the variable is obtained by aggregation of its components. "−" denotes a not recorded item;

1. Excludes checking deposits. 2. DA and LI recorded together. 3. Includes only some pension assets. 4. Includes collectibles and some mutual funds not included in TM. 5. OFA and ONF recorded together. 6. Business assets only. 7. IR recorded net of OMG. 8. As recorded in the 2003 wave. 9. VH recorded net of VL. 10. HSD, VL and IL recorded together. 11. MG, OMG, VL and IL recorded together. 12. Includes also VL, which implies a double-counting.
Source: LWS database.

Table 10.A1.3. **Reconciling the LWS and national net worth concept**

Averages in thousands (national currencies)

	Canada	Finland	Italy	Sweden[1]	United States
	SFS 1999	HWS 1998	SHIW 2002	HINK 2002	SCF 2001
LWS net worth	103	69	154	538	213
+ pension assets	83	1	–	–	74
+ other financial assets	3	2	0	25	3
+ business equity	27	–	24	80	75
+ other non-financial assets	29	7	24	18	21
LWS adjusted net worth	244	80	201	660	396
National source net worth	249	80	204	660	396

StatLink ⟶ http://dx.doi.org/10.1787/424146383431

Note: Based on household weights.
1. LWS adjusted net worth does not include other debts.
Source: LWS database, and country sources (Statistics Canada, 2006a; Finnish data provided by Markku Säylä; Brandolini et al., 2004; Statistics Sweden, 2004; Aizcorbe, Kennickell and Moore, 2003).

Table 10.A1.4. **Per capita household wealth in the LWS database and national balance sheets**

Values in euros and percentages

	Canada	Finland	Germany	Italy	Norway	Sweden	United Kingdom	United States	United States
	SFS 1999	HWS 1998	SOEP 2002	SHIW 2002	IDS 2002	HINK 2002	BHPS 2000	PSID 2001	SCF 2001
LWS database									
Non-financial assets	28 237	31 920	53 507	50 965	14 605	33 132	61 436	63 170	77 686
Financial assets	8 018	6 181	7 971	8 913	22 066	12 943	11 036	31 332	47 059
Debt	9 577	6 032	11 202	2 590	29 561	16 159	13 572	20 857	26 707
Net worth	26 678	32 069	50 276	57 288	7 110	29 916	58 901	73 646	98 037
National balance sheet (NBS)									
Non-financial assets	32 492	–	69 234	78 417	–	–	67 728	66 679	
Financial assets	51 157	20 317	44 731	48 780	42 268	40 927	87 199	123 768	
Debt	13 813	7 147	18 750	7 089	33 629	16 577	20 471	31 003	
Net worth	69 836	–	95 215	120 108	–	–	134 457	159 444	
Ratio of LWS to NBS									
Non-financial assets	87	–	77	65	–	–	91	95	117
Financial assets	16	30	18	18	52	32	13	25	38
Debt	69	84	60	37	88	97	66	67	86
Net worth	38	–	53	48	–	–	44	46	61

StatLink ⟶ http://dx.doi.org/10.1787/424161176817

Note: LWS figures are given by the ratios between wealth totals and number of persons in each survey; household weights are used. National balance sheets (NBS) figures are obtained by dividing total values for the sector "Households and non-profit institutions serving households" by total population. All values are expressed in euros at current prices by using the average market exchange rate in the relevant year.
Source: LWS database and country sources (Eurostat, 2006 for financial assets and debt of European countries; personal communication by Ulf von Kalckreuth, Brandolini et al. 2004, and Office for National Statistics, 2006 for non-financial wealth in Germany, Italy and the United Kingdom, respectively; Statistics Canada,2006b; Board of Governors of the Federal Reserve System, 2006).

Table 10.A1.5. **Demographic structure based on LWS data**

Household characteristic	Canada	Finland	Germany	Italy	Norway	Sweden	United Kingdom	United States	United States
	SFS 1999	HWS 1998	SOEP 2002	SHIW 2002	IDS 2002	HINK 2002	BHPS 2000	PSID 2001	SCF 2001
Mean household size	2.4	2.2	2.1	2.7	2.1	2.0	2.4	2.4	2.4
Mean age of the household's head	47	49	52	55	49	51	53	48	49
Age composition of household's head (%)									
24 or less	5.9	7.3	3.7	0.7	7.2	6.6	3.8	5.3	5.6
25-34	19.6	16.7	15.2	9.4	19.3	16.9	14.3	18.6	17.1
35-44	24.7	20	20.6	21.5	19.4	17.7	19.3	22.2	22.3
45-54	19.6	21	17.5	18.8	18	17.5	17.4	22.4	20.6
55-64	11.9	13.8	16.5	16.9	14.1	16.6	14.9	12.5	13.3
65-74	10.4	11.7	14.9	18.2	9.8	10.9	14	10.9	10.7
75 and over	7.9	9.5	11.6	14.5	12.2	13.8	16.3	8.1	10.4
Total	100	100	100	100	100	100	100	100	100

StatLink ᘈᓲᓲᗖ http://dx.doi.org/10.1787/424260847544

Note: Based on household weights.
Source: LWS database.

GROWING UNEQUAL? – ISBN 978-92-64-04418-0 – © OECD 2008

PART V

Conclusions

ISBN 978-92-64-04418-0
Growing Unequal?
© OECD 2008

PART V

Chapter 11

Inequality in the Distribution of Economic Resources: How it has Changed and what Governments Can Do about it*

Better information on how cash income and other types of resources are distributed within society is critical to address rising concerns about poverty and inequality. This information has implications for policies, as it highlights the importance of national circumstances for the success of different programmes and strategies. By providing information on more homogeneous groups within society, these data are also essential to bridge the gap between official statistics based on macro aggregates for economy-wide income and individuals' perceptions of their own conditions.

*   This chapter has been prepared by Michael Förster and Marco Mira d'Ercole, OECD Social Policy Division.

Introduction

Discussions about the distribution of household income are often perceived as value-loaded and ideological, grounded more in the *a priori* prejudices of different people than on hard data and analysis. The evidence in this report is intended to help dispel this perception. While value judgments on the desirability of varying levels of income distribution will always differ across people and national cultures, all societies *do* care about the issue. How these inequalities evolve over time is one of the criteria against which all public policies are assessed.

This chapter takes stock of what can be learned from findings in previous chapters in this report. After having spelled out some of the reasons why people pay attention to income inequalities in their country (Box 11.1), the chapter draws on the evidence presented in previous chapters to summarise the main patterns characterising the distribution of household income in OECD countries, and to review the role of demographic factors, labour markets and government redistribution in shaping them. The following section discusses whether looking at current income alone is adequate if what we are really interested in is the distribution of economic resources in each country. It outlines some of the key patterns that emerge when considering items other than cash income, such as governments' provision of in-kind services and their collection of consumption taxes; household wealth and consumption patterns; and dynamic measures of how the income of the same person changes over time and compares to that of their parents. The last section highlights some of the implications of the evidence presented in this report for designing more effective policies to deal with these equity concerns by providing evidence on the potential effect of different strategies aimed at lowering poverty in different OECD countries.

What are the main features of the distribution of household income in OECD countries?

This section summarises some of the main features characterising the distribution of (equivalised) household disposable income in OECD countries. The focus is both on the overall shape of this distribution and on developments at the bottom end of the distribution, where people are at greater risk of poverty.

Levels of income inequality and poverty among the entire population

Differences in the overall shape of the distribution of household income across OECD counties are both large and persistent. The Gini coefficient of income inequality is twice as high in Mexico as in Denmark, and differences remain large when excluding from the analysis countries at both ends of the league table of OECD countries (Figure 11.1). Significant cross-country differences in inequality are found regardless of the measure used, with the ranking of countries little affected by which one is used. There are of course uncertainties about the *precise* level of inequality in any country, because of small sample sizes, under-reporting of certain types of income, and over-representation of some

Box 11.1. **Why do people care about income inequalities?**

Complete equality in the distribution of economic resources is neither attainable nor desirable. Some income disparities simply reflect differences in life-styles and preferences and are the counterpart of better incentives to work and save which, in turn, are basic requirements for strong economic growth. Because of these links, several empirical studies have investigated in recent years the effect of wider income inequalities on economic growth. Unfortunately, the results from the empirical research on this trade-off are inconclusive. For example, an OECD analysis of this issue concluded that, while evidence leaned towards suggesting that a wider income distribution is good for economic growth, the estimates as a whole explained so little of the differences in GDP growth rates across OECD countries and over time that very little, in fact, could be safely concluded (Arjona *et al.*, 2001).

There are, however, other reasons why income inequalities matter:

- First, *no society is indifferent to the distributive outcomes of a market economy*, and differences in household income are the most visible manifestation of these outcomes. Of course, voters and policy makers will have different views on the importance that should be paid to the conditions of people at different points in the distribution: for example, whether special attention should be given to the "median" person, or whether the income gains realised by the very rich and the very poor in society should be given equal weight. But, whatever these views, data on the income of individuals and families across the entire distribution are needed for spelling out the implications of different policies and structural factors. An additional reason for looking at income across the entire distribution is that both psychological and economic analyses have documented that income differences have real significance: people assess their own conditions through comparisons with others (Boarini *et al.*, 2006). This implies that information on *relative* income matters for the assessment of the living conditions of people, independently of judgements on what is "fair" in society.

- Second, *most people in OECD countries do care about income inequalities* and are capable of articulating judgements on the shape of the income distribution. When asked about whether income inequalities in their country are "too high" or "too low", a majority of respondents in all OECD countries indicated the first option, even if with large differences across countries in the size of this group.[1] Similarly, when asked to choose among different shapes of income distributions, most people expressed a preference for more equal distributions relative to more unequal ones and, among the former, for those that are more equal both at the bottom and at the top of the distribution (Kenworthy, 2007). Household surveys also highlight that one of the key determinants of different attitudes towards income inequality and poverty are people' views about the determinants of economic success, *i.e.* whether such success is thought to mainly reflect factors that are outside the control of individuals as compared to individual attitudes to work and risk-taking (see Box 5.1). While perceptions on inequality can sometimes be ill founded, people seem to care about income inequalities especially when these raise the risk of falling into poverty. In European countries, around 60% of individuals interviewed in late 2006 shared the view that everyone was at risk of falling into poverty at some point in their life, and more than 20% felt they faced such a risk personally (see figure below). Even in the United States, where (until recently) a significantly lower proportion of respondents perceived income inequality as "too large" relative to other countries, nearly three-quarters agree with the statement "today it's really true that the rich get richer while the poor get poorer", with a rise in the share of those agreeing of eight points since 2002, to the highest level since the early 1990s.[2]

- Last, even when communities downplay inequalities compared to other societal goals, *reducing income disparities may be instrumental for achieving other goals*. The effects of higher income inequality are many, including greater political influence of the wealthy, wider differences in health and educational outcomes, less capacity to undertake collective action to respond to

Box 11.1. **Why do people care about income inequalities?** *(cont.)*

Perceptions about poverty in EU countries, mid-2000s

Share of respondents agreeing with each statement

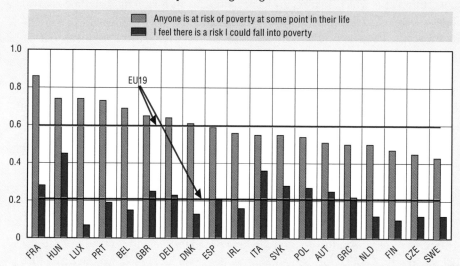

StatLink ᵒᵉᶜᵈ http://dx.doi.org/10.1787/424370547515

Note: Countries are ranked, from left to right, in decreasing order of the share agreeing that "anyone is at risk of poverty at some point in their life".

Source: Eurobarometer (2007), *European Social Reality*, Special Report No. 273, Brussels.

common threats. But one that has attracted much attention recently is the risk that these inequalities may lead to the adoption of policies that are inimical to economic performance. This risk is especially important given the strong focus in current discussions on the role of "globalisation" as a driver of greater inequalities. While it has proved difficult to quantify precisely the impact of trade, outsourcing and foreign investment in low-wage countries on earnings and income inequality in OECD countries, changes in income distribution *are* occurring in a context where the benefits of globalisation are widely shared while its costs (in terms of job displacement, earnings losses, income insecurity) are not. This asymmetry, if not addressed in an effective way, risks leading to policies (such as barriers to trade, investment and immigration) that will hurt economic growth much more than well-conceived measures to mitigate these economic inequalities.

An important limit of focusing on inequalities in the distribution of annual income is that these snapshots refer to a particular year, and do not capture differences in life-time conditions. This is an important limit, but also one that is not easily overcome – given the lack of data covering complete lifetimes of individuals and the *ad hoc* assumptions used in dynamic microsimulation models to generate hypothetical lifetime income profiles (Stånberg, 2007). Moreover, when the focus is on the immediate plight of citizens, the focus of policy discussions will be on income distribution "here and now" and on how this is changing over time. These reasons underscore the importance of closely monitoring how income inequalities change over time, and of taking corrective action when these trends are perceived as exceeding shared norms of what is "fair" in society.

1. Surveys undertaken in 1999 under the aegis of the International Social Science Programme show that the share of respondents who agreed or strongly agreed with the view that "differences in income are too large" ranged between around 65% in the United States, Canada and Japan, to between 70 and 75% in Australia, New Zealand, West Germany and Norway, to between 80 and 90% in the United Kingdom, Austria, the Czech Republic, France, Poland and Spain, and above 90% in east Germany, Hungary, the Slovak Republic and Portugal (Förster and Mira d'Ercole, 2005).

2. "Trends in Political Values and Core Attitudes: 1987-2007", Pew Research Center for People and the Press, Washington DC., 2007.

Figure 11.1. **Levels of income inequality and poverty in OECD countries, mid-2000s**

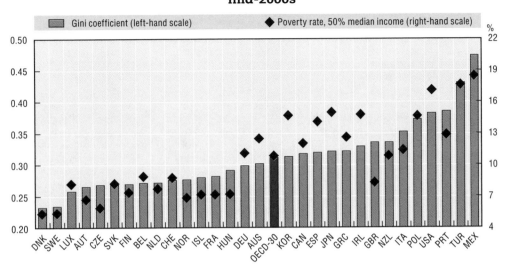

Note: Countries are ranked in increasing order of the Gini coefficient of income inequality. Data refer to the distribution of household disposable income in cash across people, with each person being attributed the income of the household where they live adjusted for household size.

Source: Computations based on OECD income distribution questionnaire.

StatLink 🔗 http://dx.doi.org/10.1787/424316682284

demographic groups, and because different statistical sources may sometime provide a different picture of how household income is distributed. But these uncertainties are not so large as to give serious grounds for doubting the broad sweep of the findings in terms of cross-country differences in inequality.

Large cross-country differences are also evident when looking at income poverty. While Figure 11.1 shows only one measure of relative income poverty (the poverty headcount, based on a threshold set at 50% of median income, shown as a diamond), cross-country patterns are fairly robust with respect to the choice of different thresholds. Relative poverty rates are always among the lowest, whatever the threshold used, in Sweden, Denmark and the Czech Republic, and always among the highest in the United States, Turkey and Mexico; they are below-average in all Nordic and several Continental European countries, and above-average in Southern European countries as well as Ireland, Poland, Japan and Korea. A composite measure of poverty – constructed by combining information on both the number of poor people in each country and how much their income falls below the poverty line – ranged in the mid-2000s from around 1% of household income in Sweden to around 7% in Mexico.

Changes in income inequality and poverty among the entire population

The past 20 years have experienced a widening of the income distribution in most OECD countries. On average, the Gini coefficient of income inequality increased by around 0.02 point, *i.e.* 7%. Other summary measures such as the standard coefficient of variation point to larger increases – by almost 30% since the mid-1980s – but these are more affected by developments at the extremes of the distribution. In all cases, these increases – while significant[1] – fall short of the sharp rises sometimes advanced in public discussion on the subject. Further, this increase has not affected all countries – as witnessed by small declines in France, as well as Ireland and Spain (where consistent time-series are limited up to the year 2000) and broad stability in another 14 countries (Table 11.1, Panel A). The

Table 11.1. **Summary of changes in income inequality and poverty**

	Mid-1980s to mid-1990s	Mid-1990s to mid-2000s	Mid-1980s to mid-2000s
A. Trends in income inequality (Gini coefficients)			
Significant increase	Czech Republic, Italy, Mexico, New Zealand, Portugal, Turkey, United Kingdom	Canada, Finland, Germany	Finland, New Zealand
Small increase	Belgium, Finland, Germany, Hungary, Japan, Luxembourg, Netherlands, Norway, Sweden, United States	Austria, Denmark, Japan, Norway, Sweden, United States	Canada, Germany, Italy, Japan, Norway, Portugal, Sweden, United States
No change	Austria, Canada, Denmark, Greece, Ireland	Australia, Belgium, Czech Republic, France, Hungary, Italy, Luxembourg, New Zealand, Portugal, Spain, Switzerland	Austria, Belgium, Czech Republic, Denmark, France, Greece, Hungary, Ireland, Luxembourg, Mexico, Netherlands, Spain, Turkey, United Kingdom
Small decrease		Greece, Ireland, Netherlands, United Kingdom	France, Ireland, Spain
Significant decrease	France, Spain	Mexico, Turkey	
B. Trends in income poverty (head-count rates at the 50% median-income threshold)			
Significant increase	Germany, Italy, Japan, Netherlands, New Zealand, United Kingdom	Austria, Canada, Finland, Germany, Ireland, Japan, Luxembourg, New Zealand, Spain, Sweden	Austria, Germany, Ireland, Japan, Netherlands, New Zealand
Small increase	Austria, Czech Republic, Hungary, Mexico, Norway, Portugal	Australia, Denmark, Netherlands, Switzerland, Turkey	Canada, Czech Republic, Finland, Italy, Luxembourg, Sweden, Turkey, United Kingdom
No change	Finland, Greece, Ireland, Luxembourg, Sweden, Turkey	Belgium, Czech Republic, France, Hungary, Norway, United States	Denmark, France, Greece, Hungary, Norway, Portugal, Spain, United States
Small decrease	Canada, Denmark, France, United States	Greece, Portugal	Mexico
Significant decrease	Belgium, Spain	Italy, Mexico, United Kingdom	Belgium

Note: For sub-periods significant increase/decrease denotes changes greater than 2.5 points (Gini coefficient) and 1.5 points (headcount); small increase/decrease denotes changes between 1 and 2.5 points (Gini coefficient) and between 0.5 and 1.5 points (headcounts); and no change denotes changes of less than 1 point (Gini coefficient) and 0.5 point (headcount). For the total period, values are double. Data in the first column refer to changes from around 1990 to mid-1990s for Czech Republic, Hungary and Portugal. Data in the second column refer to changes from the mid-1990s to around 2000 for Austria, Belgium, Czech Republic, Ireland, Portugal and Spain (where 2005 data, based on EU-SILC, are not comparable with those for earlier years); and to changes from 2000 to 2005 for Switzerland.
Source: Computations based on OECD income distribution questionnaire.

increase in income inequality was also larger in the decade from the mid-1980s to the mid-1990s than in the most recent decade, with some countries (*e.g.* Mexico, Turkey) recording large swings in performance. Since 2000, income inequality has increased significantly in Canada, Germany, Norway and the United States while declining in the United Kingdom, Mexico, Greece and Australia (see Chapter 1).

The poverty headcount, based on a threshold set at half of median income, has also risen in most countries, edging up by 0.6 percentage point in each of the two decades. While the increase in income poverty had been more moderate than for income inequality in the decade from the mid-1980s to the mid-1990s, the reverse applies to the most recent decade. Overall, over the past two decades taken together, the poverty headcount increased strongly in six OECD countries and by smaller amounts in another eight countries, while declining only in Belgium and (slightly) in Mexico (Table 11.1, Panel B).[2] Countries generally display consistent changes in terms of both inequality and poverty over the entire period, although there are exceptions – *e.g.* Ireland combines a significant increase in poverty (up to the year 2000) and a small decline in inequality.

These changes in income inequality and poverty have however occurred in a context of stronger income growth over the past decade. This increase in the absolute pace of income growth has generally benefitted people across the entire distribution, although with important differences across countries. Over the decade from the mid-1990s to the mid-2000s, the real income of people in the bottom 20% of the distribution fell in Austria, Germany, Japan, Turkey and – to a lesser extent – in Mexico and the United States. Real income growth in the middle of the distribution lagged behind the average in Canada, Finland, Italy, Norway and the United States.

Cross-country comparisons of income levels for people at similar points in the distribution

Data on the income of people and families at different points of the distribution are also important for cross-country comparisons of economic welfare. While these comparisons generally rest on estimates for "representative" agents – built by summing income flows across unattached individuals, i.e. all people resident in a country, irrespectively of the household where they live – the assumptions underlying these estimates are difficult to justify. Data on the distribution of household income allow moving beyond these comparisons of "representative agents", to look at the experiences of people at similar points in the distribution and at the pooling and sharing of resources that occur within each household. Across countries, measures of mean equivalised household disposable income are highly correlated with conventional SNA aggregates (such as Net National Income). There are, however, wide differences across countries in terms of:

- The income gap (in USD at PPP rates) between people at the top and bottom of the distribution (this gap ranges from USD 20 000 in the Slovak Republic to more than USD 85 000 in the United States, Figure 1.6).

- How people at similar points in a country's income distribution compare across countries – with the United States, for example, topping the league by a wide margin in terms of the average income of the top decile, while coming fourth (after Luxembourg, the Netherlands and Switzerland) when looking at median income, and 12th in terms of average income of the bottom decile (Figure 1.7).

Shifts in income distribution and poverty among various groups

Aggregate trends in income distribution have affected people at various points of the distribution in different ways. In Ireland, Mexico and Turkey, the decline of income inequality experienced over the past decade has mainly reflected falls in the income share accruing to people in the top quintile of the distribution and gains for people in the middle three. Conversely, in most of the countries where income inequality increased over the decade, this mainly reflected gains at the top of the distribution.

One consequence of these large gains at the top of the distribution has been that middle-class families have often lost ground relative to the economy-wide average – the so-called phenomenon of the "hollowing out of the middle-class". This is especially evident in New Zealand and the United Kingdom (in the decade from the mid-1980s to the mid-1990s), as well as Canada, Finland and the United States (where the median to mean ratio fell by around 10% over the entire period, Figure 1.3). Conversely, the relative income of middle-class families has been stable in Denmark, France and Sweden, and improved in the Netherlands and Greece throughout the period and in more countries since the mid-1990s.

These changes in economic conditions have also shifted poverty risks among various demographic groups. The most significant of these shifts has been away from the elderly and towards young adults and children (Figure 5.5). While the very old (people aged 75 and over) continue to be exposed to a greater risk of (relative-income) poverty than other age groups in the mid-2000s, this risk has fallen from a level almost twice as high as that of the population average in the mid-1980s to 50% higher by the mid-2000s. For people aged 66 to 75, this risk is now lower than for children and young adults. Conversely, children and young adults experienced poverty rates that are today around 25% higher than the population average, while they were close to and below that average, respectively, 20 years ago. Changes have been smaller when looking at poverty risks across household types, with lone parents as the group exposed to the highest risk – three times higher than average – a disadvantage that increased further over the past decade.

What factors have been driving changes in the distribution of household income?

Cross-country differences in income inequality and poverty reflect the interplay of many factors. Three, in particular, have figured prominently in discussions on the subject. These are changes in demography and living arrangements; labour-market trends; and government tax and transfer policies. While it is not always easy to distinguish among these factors, this report highlights several patterns.

Demographic factors

Demographic factors have played an important role in shaping households' living conditions. The most direct way in which this has occurred is by reducing average household size, implying that economies of scale in consumption are lost and that a higher money income is needed to assure the same level of household well-being.[3] There are, however, additional channels through which demographic factors and changes in living arrangements affect income inequalities in each country. The most important is by increasing the share in the total population of groups with below-average income (e.g. the elderly or lone parents) or with higher within-group inequality. One way of assessing the role of these demographic factors in accounting for the observed trend in income inequality is to compare the actual change in income distribution to what would have occurred had the population structure (by both age of individuals and household type) remained "frozen" at the level prevailing in some initial year. The results of such an exercise, described in Chapter 2 and summarised in Table 11.2, suggest that these structural factors have increased income inequality in a majority of countries, and significantly so (i.e. exceeding 20% of the total change in the Gini coefficient of income inequality) in Australia, Canada, France, Germany, the Netherlands and the United Kingdom. However, more important than population ageing *per se* have been the changes in living arrangements, which have implied that more people are living alone and in lone-parent households.

These shifts in the composition of OECD populations have occurred alongside changes in the relative income of different groups – with youths and, to a lesser extent, lone parents losing ground relative to others in most countries, and people closer to the end of their working life, as well as elderly people living alone, gaining the most. To some extent, these shifts in the relative income of various groups may reflect changes in their size – as in the case, for example, of lower wages following the entry of a large cohort into the labour

Table 11.2. **Impact of changes in population structure for income inequality**

Demographic change	Impact on income inequality of:		
	Change in pop. structure by both age and household type	Change in pop. structure by age of people only	Change in pop. structure by household type only
Significantly increases inequality	Australia*, Canada, France*, Germany, Netherlands*, United Kingdom	Australia*, Netherlands*	Australia*, Canada, France*, Germany, Netherlands*, United Kingdom
Slightly increases inequality	Belgium, Finland, Luxembourg, Norway, Spain, United States	Belgium, Finland, Sweden	Belgium, Finland, Luxembourg, Norway, Spain
No effect	. .	Austria, Canada, Denmark*, France*, Germany, Luxembourg, Mexico, United Kingdom, United States	Denmark*, Sweden, United States
Slightly reduces inequality	Austria, Denmark*, Italy, Sweden	Italy, Norway, Spain	Austria, Italy
Significantly reduces inequality	Mexico	. .	Mexico

Note: Results are limited to those countries where the Secretariat had access to micro-data. "Significant" contributions are those above 20% of the total change in the Gini coefficient of income inequality; "slight" contributions are those between 20% and 5% "no effects" are changes below 5%. Countries denoted with a "*" experience lower inequality over the period, implying that – had the population structure remained unchanged – the decline in the Gini coefficient would have been stronger for countries in the first two rows of the table, and smaller for those in the bottom two rows. Data for Germany refer to western *länder* only. Details on the methodology and time period considered are provided in Chapter 2.
Source: Computations of OECD income distribution questionnaire and LIS data.

market, or of adjustments in benefit income following reforms implemented to respond to the consequences of population ageing – but effects can also run in the opposite direction, as when larger population groups gain greater weight in the political process. In practice, there is little evidence of strong links between changes in the relative income of various groups and changes in their size – suggesting that shifts in the relative income of various groups have been driven more by changes in access to jobs and support from the welfare system than by demographic factors *per se*.

Labour-market trends

Labour markets are crucially important for income distribution. While much research has focused on trends in earning differentials among full-time workers – and on the role of globalisation, technology and labour-market institutions in driving them – earnings inequalities are only one of the factors at work, and perhaps not the most important. Earnings disparities among full-time workers have indeed increased rapidly since 1990, with most of the widening reflecting developments in the upper part of the distribution (Table 11.3). There are, however, exceptions to such an increase (*e.g.* France, Finland, Ireland and, to a lesser extent, Canada). This widening is also sharper for men and women, considered separately, than for all workers, irrespective of their gender – as the decline of the wage gap between men and women working full time has narrowed the "distance" between the earnings distributions of men and women.

Moving beyond full-time workers, to include people in atypical jobs such as part-time and temporary workers, significantly increases earnings inequality (by around one-half in the Netherlands and Nordic countries) and has contributed to widening the distribution of personal earnings among all workers in those countries where the incidence of atypical workers has increased in recent years (*e.g.* Germany, Ireland, Italy, Korea and Spain). Workers at the bottom of the distribution of annual earnings typically work few hours per

Table 11.3. **Summary of changes in earnings inequality among men working full time**

1990 to 2005

	Over the entire distribution (P90/P10)	Over the bottom half of the distribution (P50/P10)	Over top half of the distribution (P90/P50)
Significant Increase	Australia, Czech Rep., Germany, Hungary, Ireland, Korea, Poland, Switzerland	Hungary, Korea, Poland	Australia, Poland, Switzerland
Moderate increase	Netherlands, New Zealand, Sweden, United Kingdom, United States	Australia, Czech Rep., Denmark, Germany, Ireland, Netherlands, New Zealand, Sweden, United Kingdom, United States	Canada, Czech Rep., Denmark, Germany, Hungary, Ireland, Korea, Netherlands, New Zealand, Sweden, United Kingdom, United States
No change	Japan	Japan, Switzerland	Finland, Japan
Decline	Canada, Finland, France	Canada, Finland, France	France

Note: "Strong increase" corresponds to a rise by 20% or more in the different inter-decile ratios; "moderate increase" to a rise between 2.5% and 20%; "no change" to a change of plus or minus 2.5%; and "decline" to a fall of 2.5% or more in the different inter-decile ratios.

Source: Data from the OECD Earnings database as presented in Figure 3.1.

year, as they work either part time or full time for only part of the year. While this may reflect the voluntary choices of workers, this is only part of the story, as highlighted by the significant rise in the share of workers declaring that they would work longer hours if suitable jobs were available, as has been observed in several OECD countries.

Disparities in personal earnings among workers, however, do not necessarily translate into a wider distribution of household earnings among all people, whether working or not. This is because higher employment (especially of second earners) spread earnings among a larger number of households. However, the employment gains experienced throughout the OECD area since the second half of the 1990s have not led to significant declines in the share of people living in jobless households, with this share rising further in Turkey, Germany, the Czech Republic and Hungary and falling significantly in France, Greece and New Zealand and, to a less extent, in Australia, Italy, the Netherlands and the United Kingdom. The persistence of high household joblessness despite higher employment has partly reflected the concentration of employment gains among people with intermediate education, and the decline of employment rates among less educated people. As a result of these contrasting employment developments, changes in the concentration of household earnings have been small in most OECD countries in the period from the mid-1990s to mid-2000s, with significant rises only in Canada, the Czech Republic, Germany and Japan, and significant falls in Greece, Hungary, Ireland, Mexico and Spain (Table 11.4). Conversely, capital income and, to a lesser extent, self-employment income have become significantly more concentrated in a much larger number of OECD countries. This suggests that *non-wage income* sources – whose measurement is subject to larger uncertainties than in the case of earnings – account for a significant part of the observed widening in the distribution of household disposable income.

If changes in the concentration of household earnings account for only a part of the widening in income inequality, access to paid work remains the main factor shaping the risk of poverty. As shown in Chapter 5, among single adult households, 46% of people in jobless households have income below the 50% threshold, a proportion which falls to 28% when the household head works part time and to 8% when he or she works full time. Among people living in couple families, 33% have income below the 50% poverty line when no one in the household has a paid job, but only 19% do when one person works part time

Table 11.4. **Summary of changes in the concentration of different income components**

Entire population, period from the mid-1990s to mid-2000s

	Household earnings	Capital income	Self-employment income
Increased inequality	Canada, Czech Rep., Germany, Japan	Australia, Denmark, Finland, France, Hungary, Italy, Netherlands, New Zealand, Norway, Spain, Sweden	Belgium, Denmark, France, Germany, Greece, Hungary, Ireland, Italy, Luxembourg, Mexico, Spain, Sweden, United Kingdom, United States
Stability	Australia, Belgium, Denmark, Finland, France, Italy, Luxembourg, Netherlands, New Zealand, Norway, Portugal, Sweden, Turkey, United Kingdom, United States	Belgium, Canada, Germany, Ireland, Japan, Portugal	Canada, Finland, Japan
Reduced inequality	Greece, Hungary, Ireland, Mexico, Spain	Czech. Rep., Greece, Luxembourg, Mexico, Turkey, United Kingdom, United States	Australia, Czech Rep., Netherlands, New Zealand, Norway, Portugal, Turkey

Note: Concentration is measured by the concentration coefficient of each income component, with individuals ranked in increasing order of their equivalised household disposable income, and is computed based on data on the average value of each component for each income decile. "Stability" denotes changes in the concentration coefficient of each component between +/–0.02 point. Changes over the period from the mid-1990s to around 2000 for Austria, Belgium, the Czech Republic, Ireland, Portugal and Spain (where EU-SILC data for the mid-2000s are not comparable with those for earlier years). Income components are measured on a pre-tax basis in all countries except Belgium, Greece, Hungary, Luxembourg, Mexico, Spain and Turkey.
Source: Computations based on OECD income distribution questionnaire.

and only 4% when at least one works full time. Across countries, those with higher employment rates also record lower poverty headcounts – with countries with higher employment rates for all people as well as for mothers also recording lower poverty rates among persons of working age and among children, respectively.

Work is, however, not the only factor that matters for avoiding poverty. In the mid-2000s, for the OECD area as a whole, people living in households with workers accounted for around 60% of all the income poor (based on a threshold set at half of median income, Figure 5.10). The poverty rate among one-worker households was around 14%, and it was 3.5% for those with two workers. Even a full-time job does not always protect from the risk of poverty.

Government redistribution

Cross-country differences in the shape of the income distribution partly reflect differences in how *governments redistribute income* across individuals through the cash benefits they provide and the household taxes they collect. The effect of government redistribution in lowering income inequality is largest in the Nordic countries and lowest in Korea and the United States. The country-ranking is similar when looking at the effects of taxes and transfers in reducing poverty. Countries that redistribute more towards people with lower income also achieve a more narrow distribution of household income and lower poverty rates (Figure 4.6). Also, most of this redistribution towards people at the bottom of the income scale is generally achieved through public cash benefits – with the main exception of the Unites States, where a large part of the support provided to low-income families is administered through the income tax system.

These cross-country differences in the scale of redistribution among people with different incomes partly reflect differences in the size and structure of social spending – with spending towards people of working age achieving a larger reduction in poverty than social spending towards the elderly. Differences in spending levels and structure are, however, only part of the story. OECD countries redistribute in a variety of ways – some through universal benefits, others with more targeted programmes, some mainly relying on transfers, others mainly granting tax rebates to low-income families. Also, redistribution across individuals with different income levels always coexists with redistribution across the life-course of the same person, with some evidence that countries that redistribute more across the lifecycle spend more, in the aggregate, than those that focus more on redistribution between rich and poor.

When looking at changes over the past decade in the size of the redistribution from rich to poor, such changes differ significantly across countries and are small on average. The reduction of income inequality achieved by the combined effect of household taxes and public cash transfers declined over the past decade in around half of the countries, although it increased in the Czech Republic, France, Germany and Italy (Table 11.5). These developments were mainly driven by changes in the redistribution achieved by public cash transfers (which declined in most countries), which was partly offset by stronger redistribution through household taxes (in particular in Denmark, Germany, Italy, the Netherlands and the United Kingdom). Changes are more significant when looking at redistribution towards people at the lower tail of the income distribution, with net public transfers having weaker effects in reducing poverty than in the past in most Nordic countries (excluding Norway) as well as Canada and New Zealand, but larger poverty-reducing effect in the Czech Republic (up to 2000), Germany, Italy and Japan. These changes in redistribution may however reflect changes in market-income inequality, which tends to increase the redistributive effects for a given structure of tax and benefit systems.

Table 11.5. **Summary of changes in government redistribution in reducing inequality and poverty**

Entire population, period from the mid-1990s to mid-2000s

	Reduction of inequality			Reduction of poverty
	Due to both taxes and public cash transfers	Due to public cash transfers alone	Due to household taxes alone	
Increase	Czech Republic, France, Germany, Italy	Czech Republic, France, Germany, Italy, Japan	Denmark, Germany, Italy, Netherlands, United Kingdom	Czech Rep., Germany, Italy, Japan, Portugal
Stability	Australia, Canada, Japan, United Kingdom	Australia, Norway	Australia, Canada, Czech Republic, Finland, France, Ireland, New Zealand	Australia, Belgium, France, Netherlands, Norway, United Kingdom, United States
Decline	Denmark, Finland, Ireland, Netherlands, New Zealand, Norway, Sweden, United States	Canada, Denmark, Finland, Ireland, Netherlands, New Zealand, Sweden, United Kingdom, United States	Japan, Norway, Sweden, United States	Canada, Denmark, Finland, New Zealand, Sweden

Note: The inequality reducing effect of household taxes and public cash transfers is measured as the point difference between the concentration measures of market and disposable income, with people ranked by disposable income. The poverty reducing effect of household taxes and public cash transfers is measured as the point difference between the poverty headcount based on market income and that based on disposable income. In the case of inequality, "increase/decrease" denotes changes greater than 0.3 point in the effect of net transfers in reducing the concentration measure. In the case of poverty, "increase/decrease" denotes changes greater than 2 points in the effect of net transfers in lowering the poverty headcount rate at 50% median income. Changes refer to the period from the mid-1990s to around 2000 for Belgium, the Czech Republic, Denmark and Ireland (where EU-SILC data for the mid-2000s are not deemed to be comparable with those for earlier years).
Source: Computations based on OECD income distribution questionnaire.

Summing-up

The importance of each of these drivers of income inequality – changes in demography and living arrangements, labour-market trends, and government redistribution – has varied across OECD countries, and no single "story" holds for all. The factors involved are many and, because of their interdependencies, disentangling their importance is difficult. One measure of their role is provided in Table 11.6, which shows results of a simple shift-share decomposition applied to changes in the poverty headcount for households with a head of working age (left-hand panel) or of retirement age (right-hand panel) over the past decade. Available data allowed applying this decomposition to 14 countries.

Table 11.6. **Summary of various factors for changes in poverty rates for households with a head of working age or of retirement age**

Entire population, period from the mid-1990s to mid-2000s

	Persons living in households with working-age head				Persons living in households with retirement-age head			
	Total change in poverty rate	Due to changes in:			Total change in poverty rate	Due to changes in:		
		Market-income poverty	Taxes and public cash transfers	Household structure		Market-income poverty	Taxes and public cash transfers	Household structure
Australia	=	+	+	–	+++	–	+++	=
Canada	+++	+	+++	–	+++	=	+++	=
Denmark	+	=	+	=	⸺	=	–	–
Finland	+++	–	+++	+	+++	–	+++	–
France	=	+	=	=	..	..	..	..
Germany	+++	=	+	+++	–	=	–	–
Italy	–	+++	–	–	–	=	–	+
Japan	+	=	=	+	–	+	–	+++
Netherlands	+	=	+	=	+	=	+	=
New Zealand	+++	+++	+++	–	+++	=	+++	=
Norway	+	–	+	+	⸺	=	⸺	=
Sweden	+	–	+++	=	+++	=	+++	=
United Kingdom	–	–	=	–	–	=	–	=
United States	=	=	=	=	+++	=	+++	=
Average	+	=	+	=	+	=	+	=

Note: The table is based on a decomposition analysis described in Chapter 5. Household structure refers to ten groups distinguishing work attachment (households with no workers, with one adult working, and with two or more adults working) and household types (singles and couple families, with and without children). The analysis is limited to countries for which the data allow distinguishing between market- and disposable-income poverty. "+++"/"–" denotes changes greater than +/–1.5 points, "+"/"–" denotes changes between +/–0.5 and +/–1.5 points and "=" denotes changes of less than 0.5 point. See Chapter 5 for a more detailed description of methodology.
Source: Computations based on OECD income distribution questionnaire.

For both household types, the rise in the poverty headcount over the past decade mainly reflected a small fall in the redistributive effects of taxes and transfers, with negligible effects for changes in market-income poverty and population structure. Country experiences, however, differ significantly, especially for working-age households. Demographic factors have been important in Germany, where they contributed to increasing the poverty headcount of working-age households, as well as in Italy and New Zealand, where they had the opposite effect. Conversely, a greater concentration of market income has increased poverty in Italy and New Zealand and, to a lesser extent, in Australia, Canada and France. Finally, the reduction in the size of interpersonal redistribution achieved by the tax and benefit system has been significant in Canada, Finland, New Zealand and Sweden, and – to a lesser extent – in Australia, Denmark, Germany, the Netherlands and Norway. In the case of households headed by a person of retirement age, all countries where the poverty headcount increased significantly over the past decade (Australia, Canada, Finland, New Zealand, Sweden and the United States) also experienced a fall in the effect of the tax and transfer system in reducing poverty. Better identifying the role of the various factors at work – a task that is best undertaken through country-specific analysis – is important for designing appropriate policy responses.

Can we assess economic inequalities just by looking at cash income?

The short answer to this question is "no". There are three reasons why cash income is a limited measure of the economic resources of households. First, people can have quite high living standards even if they have low incomes – because they have built up their savings, because government services such as health and education may be provided free of charge, or because they can produce much of what they need through home production. Second, income is only an indirect measure of people's consumption opportunities, and better proxies – such as household wealth and actual consumption – are sometimes available. Third, the calendar year underlying the concept of annual income is an accounting concept with no intrinsic economic significance, and the situation that prevails at a point in time may be a poor guide to people's conditions over their life-course. Cash income is easily measured, and this helps cross-country comparisons, but any serious attempt to assess developments in economic inequality has to consider whether these other factors validate or invalidate conclusions based on static income measures alone.

Non-cash income sources

Household cash disposable income excludes a range of flows that affect a household's consumption possibilities. These include services provided by firms (which are important in some countries) as well as other resources (such as time and home production) that contribute to households' living standards and to their ability to attend to their needs. Among the factors omitted from the "standard" accounting framework are government activities that impact on household well-being through the in-kind services they provide and the consumption taxes they collect.

The case for including *in-kind public services* in a broader measure of the economic well-being of households is straightforward. Households pay taxes to finance these public services. However, while these taxes are deducted from their disposable income when making studies of the distribution of income, the services provided in return are *not* included.

While, in theory, all public services confer benefits to households (from education to defence), the case for their inclusion in a broader measure of household economic resources is most compelling for those that confer a personal benefit to users. The value of these public services (for education, health and other social services) varies significantly across countries (from less than 10% of household disposable income in Turkey to more than 40% in Denmark and Sweden), as well as over time (mainly reflecting the expansion of publicly provided education and health services). This suggests that including them in a more comprehensive measure of households' economic resources will significantly affect any assessment of cross-country comparisons of levels of inequality and of changes in individual countries.

There is no unique way to include household services in income distribution analysis, and sometimes conclusions differ according to the different techniques that can be used. Nevertheless, some patterns (described in Chapter 9) are consistent across studies:

● Public in-kind services tend to be distributed rather uniformly across people belonging to various income groupings, implying that they account for a larger share of household income at the bottom of the distribution than at the top. As a result, inclusion of these in-kind services narrows the Gini coefficient of income inequality at a point in time, by around 0.07 point on average, and by larger amounts in Sweden, Norway, Australia, Denmark, New Zealand, Portugal, France, Italy and the United States (Figure 11.2).

● This equalising effect, however, differs among programmes – with large reductions due to compulsory education, non-specialist health care and public housing, and negligible ones for non-compulsory education. Indeed, non-compulsory education is more unequally distributed than income in one in three countries.

● The effect of government services in narrowing the Gini coefficient of income inequality is quite large. It is equivalent to about half the equalising impact of household taxes and cash benefits. In the United States, public services have the same impact in reducing inequality as do taxes and transfers.

Figure 11.2. **Influence of in-kind public services and consumption taxes on income inequalities**

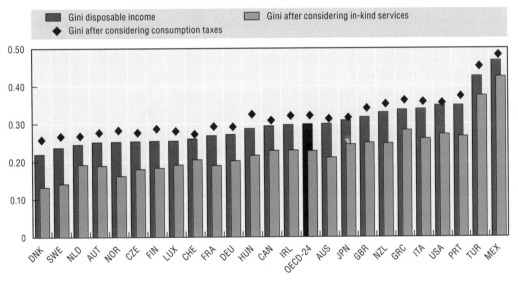

StatLink 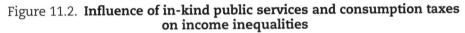 http://dx.doi.org/10.1787/424330428204

Note: Countries are ranked from left to right in increasing order of the Gini coefficient of income inequality. Estimates of the effect of public in-kind services in narrowing income inequality are those based on grouped data described in Chapter 9. Estimates of the effect of consumption taxes in increasing income inequality are illustrative only: they are based on applying the distributive profile of general consumption taxes and of excises in one country (Australia) to income values by deciles in other countries (as described in Warren, 2008).

Source: Computation based on OECD income distribution questionnaire and other data.

Consumption taxes also fall outside the standard accounting framework generally used to assess income inequality. Considering how consumption taxes affect the distribution of household resources is however much more difficult than for in-kind services for both conceptual and empirical reasons. Despite these difficulties, a long tradition of research has considered the distributive impact of consumption taxes in individual countries. This research highlights two consistent patterns.

● First, consumption taxes are heavily concentrated on people with lower income.

● Second, this is more the case for taxes levied on specific goods and services (alcohol and gasoline) than for those on general consumption.

There are few comparative studies of the distributional impact of consumption taxes, but those that have been done highlight large differences in the burden of consumption taxes as a share of income for people in different deciles (with more regressive impacts in Nordic countries than in Belgium, the Netherlands and Ireland). Unfortunately, these studies do not yet allow assessing whether these cross-country differences reflect the specific features of the tax systems of various countries or other factors.[4] Even so, the fact that consumption taxes are now often relatively high (VAT rates often exceed 20%, and excise taxes are often a considerably higher proportion of final prices) imply that they do have a significant effect on the distribution of resources. One way to illustrate the scale of this effect is though a simple "what if" scenario, which applies the distributive profile of taxes on general consumption and specific goods prevailing in one country (Australia) – based on the "preferred" methodology described by Warren (2008) – to the income distribution of others. This simple scenario adjusts for differences in the overall level of consumption taxes and in their composition (between general consumption and excises) across countries, but not for differences across countries in the detailed characteristics of national tax systems and in consumption-to-income ratios across income groupings. Results (shown as diamonds in Figure 11.3) suggest that consumption taxes could raise the Gini coefficient of income inequality by around 0.02 point, i.e. around 5%, with larger effects in Denmark, Hungary, Finland, Norway and Sweden. This effect of consumption taxes in raising income inequality offsets a large part of the combined effect of income taxes and workers social security contributions in lowering it – even if it is considerably lower than that (in the opposite direction) of in-kind public services.[5]

Does the exclusion of these non-cash income sources matter for policies? It obviously does for countries that have undergone significant changes in the mix of support they provide to households (for example, by switching from in-kind services to cash transfers as

Figure 11.3. **Static and dynamic measures of poverty and inequality**

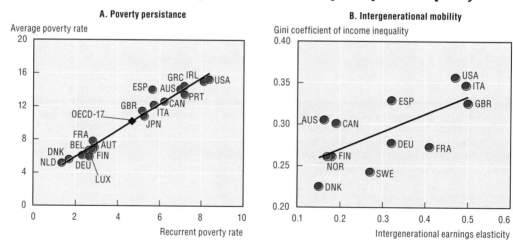

StatLink http://dx.doi.org/10.1787/424352834355

Note: Panel A: Dynamic measures of income-poverty rates based on a threshold set at half of median equivalised household disposable income. OECD-17 is the simple average of the countries shown except Japan, for which estimates are based on an income definition (household income before taxes and after public transfers) that differ from the disposable income definition used for other countries. The "always poor" poverty rate is the share of people with income below the poverty threshold in each of three consecutive years; data refer to the early 2000s. Panel B: The intergenerational earnings elasticity is a measure of the extent to which the earnings of sons are correlated to those of their fathers at a similar point in their life-cycle, meaning that high elasticity levels reflect low mobility. For further details on both sets of data, see Chapters 6 and 8.

Source: Detailed sources are provided in Chapters 6 and 8.

in the reforms implemented in several transition countries, or by moving from provision of public housing at subsidised rates to rent allowances targeted to low-income households) or that have implemented reforms that change the tax mix in the direction of greater reliance on taxes on general consumption. In these cases, governments need to assess the consequences of these reforms for the well-being of beneficiaries, and may want to mitigate some of the adverse distributive effects of these reforms through specific measures. But the consideration of these non-cash income sources also raises a more general question that matters for policy design, namely, how best to mix cash transfers and in-kind services to meet any particular redistributive goal: while people may value cash transfers more than services tied to a specific use, such services can often be better targeted to those in need and may contribute more to improving their living conditions in the longer term.[6]

Non-income measures

The rationale for relying on income as the yardstick for assessing the living standards of individuals and households is that income effectively constrains their consumption possibilities. Income is, however, only a partial measure of these possibilities and other measures are important in their own right.

One of these measures is *household wealth*. Surveys measuring household assets and liabilities exist in several OECD countries, but differences in survey design in this field are much larger than in the case of income. This makes their use for cross-country comparisons much more problematic. Comparative information on household wealth is, however, becoming more easily available with the "public use" version of the *Luxembourg Wealth Study* – a collaborative project that aims to do for household wealth what the LIS has achieved for income.

Despite the difficulties in making international comparisons, the first results that are emerging from the LWS (as described in Chapter 10 of this report) shed new light on the assessment of living conditions and how these vary among the population.

● One result, which is now well established in country-specific research, is that the distribution of wealth is much more unequal than that of income: this reflects differences in saving patterns across the income distribution (with small savings among those at the bottom of the income scale, and much larger ones for people at the top), and the importance of bequests for the transmission of market wealth *across* generations.

● Less well established is how wealth inequality compares across countries. In the early 2000s, the Gini index for the distribution of household net worth (based on a definition that included business equity) was highest in Sweden (one of the countries with a more narrow distribution of household income), closely followed by the United States and, further behind, by Germany and Canada, with Finland, the United Kingdom and Italy having the most equal distributions of wealth. However, other measures of wealth inequality (such as the share of total wealth held by people in the top decile) and other definitions of household wealth (i.e. excluding business equity) lead to a country ranking that is more similar to that based on household income. More generally, comparisons of wealth inequality across countries partly reflect the exclusion from the LWS of some wealth components (such as pension assets) for which information is currently limited to only some countries.

Country rankings also differ significantly when comparing the absolute level of household assets and income, with Italy having the highest median net worth (followed by the United Kingdom) despite having the lowest equivalised household income among the OECD countries included in the LWS. Sweden has the lowest median net worth, despite an income value that is above that of many other OECD countries. This suggests that differences in average income across countries might exaggerate comparative differences in household access to resources – although it may also reflect the partial coverage of the wealth data currently available.

Other patterns emerge when looking at the wealth holdings of people with different characteristics. Median net wealth varies with the age of the household head, generally rising until the end of working life and then declining during retirement. This inverted-U profile is, however, *less* steep than for income, with only small declines taking place in Canada and a continued increase by age of the household head in the United States.

The data used in Chapter 10 also allow looking at the joint distribution of income and wealth for a subset of the countries covered by the LWS. Across individuals, income and net worth are highly correlated, but this is not perfect. In general, income-poor people have fewer assets than the rest of the population, with a net worth generally about under half of that of the population as a whole.

The second non-income measure of households' "command over resources" is provided by *direct measures of household consumption*. Household consumption is, in theory, less affected by temporary disturbances in income, and so is better suited to making assessments of inequalities across different people. Students, for example, may be income-poor but not consumption-poor, as they are able to borrow against expected future earnings and are often supported by their family. Similarly, people who suffer a *temporary* setback in income might not feel the need to reduce their consumption immediately, relying on savings from previous years or hoping that things will get better in the future.

In recent years, several studies have looked at trends in consumption expenditure inequalities. The results show that consumption inequality has risen more slowly than household income inequality in the United States, the United Kingdom and Australia (see Table 11.A.1 available at *http://dx.doi.org/10.1787/424402577838*), which suggests that annual incomes have become more volatile, but the volatility of lifetime income has not changed by as much. This is a case of data confirming what has long been the popular perception of change in these countries. However, this is not a general pattern across all countries – consumption inequality has increased by as much as income inequality in Japan and has risen *more* rapidly than income inequality in Poland and Turkey.

One area where consumption data hold special promise is for developing direct measures of poverty. "Material deprivation" refers to the extent to which people in each country can afford those items and activities that are typical in their society. This approach has a long tradition in individual countries but can also be implemented in a comparative setting in two different ways, both of which are used in Chapter 7 of this report.

- The first looks at the average prevalence of different deprivation items (for example, the inability to pay for a holiday or to socialise with friends) in each country, and then derives a summary measure by averaging across these items. This approach, when applied across a broad range of items, highlights large differences in the extent of material deprivation across OECD countries. This measure of material deprivation is higher in countries with high income poverty – suggesting that, at least at the aggregate level, relative income poverty is indeed identifying difficult living conditions. However, the prevalence of material deprivation is also higher in countries characterised by lower national income – suggesting that relative income poverty rates may be a poor proxy for hardship in countries with a relatively low, but equally distributed, standard of living.

● The second approach reverses the order of aggregation: a composite measure of material deprivation is derived by looking first at the extent to which each person lacks various items, and then by looking at how many people are in these conditions. Results based on this second approach show that, across individuals, the experience of deprivation declines monotonically as income rises. It also declines with age, in contrast to the U-shaped relation between relative-income poverty and age found in most countries, suggesting that income-poor older people are not necessarily experiencing material hardship. Results also suggest that, while there is some overlap between low income and deprivation, a large share of income-poor people are not materially deprived and that, conversely, a large share of those materially deprived are not income-poor.

Information on these non-income measures of economic well-being is important for social policies. This is most evident when considering ways of improving the targeting of social programmes to reach those with greater needs. Income may be a poor proxy of economic needs, and equity concerns may relate to a range of inequalities (*e.g.* in education and health) that have not been addressed in this report.[7] Indirectly, the non-income measures considered in this report also point to the importance of looking at factors that go beyond the income and earnings capacity of people, to other constituents of an acceptable standard of living. More comprehensive information on asset holdings would also allow assessing the effects of the assets tests embodied in the social programmes of several countries on the behaviour of social-assistance clients, and the effect of the various asset-based welfare programmes recently introduced in several OECD countries.

Dynamic measures

Measures of economic resources that look at income – or even wealth, or material deprivation – at a single point in time are to a lesser or greater degree "static". Something could happen shortly after the sample period that could change the standard of living of households. This is important, as what matters most for policies are not the blips of fortune that can lead anyone to experience a period of low income at some point in their life, but the *persistence* over time of these unfavourable conditions. The importance of dynamic measures of economic inequality is illustrated by longitudinal data that track the income of the same person over time and by studies that compare the income of an individual with that of their parents.

The value-added of longitudinal data that track the income of the same person over time is best illustrated by focusing on income poverty. Longitudinal data enable a distinction to be made between three groups of people: i) those who are temporarily poor; ii) those who are continuously poor; and iii) those who cycle in and out of income poverty over a given number of years. While such data are generally available for only a minority of countries, the evidence discussed in Chapter 6 for 17 OECD countries, based on information on income over three consecutive years, shows that:

● Around 45% of people counted as poor based on static income will move above the (50%) poverty threshold over the next three years; however, less than 10% of them have income above the median in the final year.

● On average, about 5% of the population were poor in all three years, and a further 4% in two of the three years considered.

- A higher proportion of the population (17%) experiences a drop in their income below the poverty threshold at some point in any three-year period.

Across countries, however, those characterised by a higher poverty headcount based on static income also record higher persistent poverty (Figure 11.3, left-hand panel), and indeed higher proportions of the population who experience low income at some point in the three-year period. There is a strong correlation between measures of income poverty calculated on an annual basis and both the narrower and wider measures of poverty that can be calculated using longitudinal data. Further, when looking at the importance of various events, entries into poverty are mainly associated with family- and job-related events, although their importance varies between various types of income-poor (i.e. temporary and recurrent).

The second way to move beyond static income data is to look at *income mobility across generations*. Surveys in all OECD countries show that a majority of people declare that income inequalities are acceptable when they are matched by greater equality of opportunities. Indeed, striving to achieve equality of opportunity better corresponds to most people's notions of equity and fairness than looking at final income inequalities. Unfortunately, equality of opportunity is hard to define, even harder to measure, and exceptionally difficult to achieve – not least because the endowments of each individual partly reflect factors and decisions taken by their parents.

One way, however, to give practical content to the notion of equal opportunity is through measures of the extent to which children of low-income households move up the income ladder when they reach adulthood. While information suitable for this type of study exists only for a few countries and domains, the measures presented in Chapter 8 suggest that parental background remains a very strong determinant of success, be it assessed in terms of students' achievement in secondary education or in terms of the position on the earnings ladder of sons relative to fathers. Cross-country differences in the degree of this inter-generational elasticity are large. There is evidence that the intergenerational transmission of advantage and disadvantage is particularly high in the United Kingdom, the United States and Italy, and is much lower in most Nordic countries. This suggests that countries with lower income inequality based on static income (in the lower corner of the right-hand panel of Figure 11.3) also have greater social mobility, although there are exceptions – *e.g.* Australia and Canada, which combine high mobility with moderately high inequality, and France which has lower mobility than would be expected from its level of inequality.

As Chapter 8 makes clear, one of the conclusions to be drawn from this way of looking at inequality is that those people who claim that they are indifferent to the distribution of resources at any one point in time, as long as everyone has an equal opportunity to achieve success, are effectively deluding themselves. Equality of opportunity often requires an equal starting point. While this suggests that a more equal distribution of resources is a necessary precondition for providing fair opportunities, these resources and parental endowments go well beyond current income. This calls for attention on ensuring that no children are left behind in the education system, and that opportunities are provided for access to further education by all.

Summing-up

Because conventional measures of inequality based on the annual cash incomes of households are so limited, information on additional dimensions of household well-being has much to offer. There are drawbacks to all the measures considered in this section, so it seems unlikely that we can put aside annual income-based estimates of inequality or poverty yet. But we can *tentatively* conclude that:

- Measures of inequality based on annual cash incomes overstate the overall inequality of resources available to households relative to measures that consider publicly-provided services. This conclusion needs to be modified to the extent that consumption taxes widen the distribution of resources, but the evidence is that this effect is smaller than the equalising effect of these other factors. Other factors that are not considered in this report (such as employer provided benefits, and imputed capital income flows) may, however, have the effect of widening inequalities relative to measures based on cash income alone.

- Poverty measures based on annual income are moderately good indicators of the extent of hardship across countries. They are strongly correlated with measures that look at longer periods of time, as well as with measures of material deprivation. But they are much poorer indicators of the extent of poverty the more that average living standards differ across countries. And while they are good indicators of poverty in different countries, income-based measures are poor measures at the individual level. Changing the time period taken into account has an enormous effect on who is and who is not considered poor. The overlap between income poverty and material deprivation is far from perfect. Such conclusions point to the importance for policies of considering a range of factors beyond current income when assessing the need for social support.

- There is substantial evidence that the living standards of older people are higher than is indicated by annual cash-income measures. The older people are, the less likely they are to be deprived materially and the more likely they are to hold greater assets. Income distribution results show that families with children are now on average more likely to be poor than people aged 65-75; the true gap in living standards is probably even larger than this statistic suggests.

What are the implications of these findings for policies aimed at narrowing poverty and inequalities?

This report has mainly focused on the "facts" characterising inequalities and poverty in OECD countries. But many of these facts have implications for designing more effective policies to deal with these problems. This section provides an illustration of these implications based on conventional measures of cash income. In discussing such implications, it is useful to distinguish policies along two dimensions:

- The first relates to the precise nature of the equity goal pursued by governments. While much of this report has discussed income inequalities over the entire distribution, for many OECD countries the most immediate concern is poverty rather than inequalities *per se*. Because of this consideration, this section looks at the effect of different strategies in reducing relative income-poverty among people of working age. The exact nature of the equity goal pursued by governments is important as the effects of different policies will depend on the characteristics of the people who are supposed to benefit from them.

- The second distinction is between two different strategies to narrow poverty. The first aims at remedying inequalities *after* they have occurred in the market place, and the primary tools used to achieve this goal are public cash transfers and household taxes (the "redistribution strategy"). The second approach aims at making the distribution of market income less unequal, and the main instrument through which this goal is pursued is that of increasing the level of employment and spreading work opportunities across a larger number of households (the "work strategy").

This section first describes some of the features of these two strategies to lower poverty, and then presents evidence on their potential effect in lowering poverty in different OECD countries.

The redistribution strategy

While redistribution from rich to poor is only one of the objectives of government policies, the size and channels of its effects will come under increased scrutiny as communities become more concerned about a widening divide in economic conditions and opportunities. Two set of considerations are relevant to the design of redistributive policies.

- A first relates to the relative role of cash transfers and household taxes. Several factors bear on establishing the most appropriate balance between these two elements. On one side, cash transfers may be regarded as effectively equivalent to negative taxes, suggesting that only the "net" should matter for the individual. However, a large amount on "churning" of benefits and taxes (where the same person pays and receives a large amount of both) may be expected to lower the well-being of people – either because of differences in the timing of various measures, or because taxes lower the discretionary control of people on how to allocate their resources. In practice, people at the bottom of the income distribution are likely to pay few taxes, so that supporting them will typically depend on cash transfers. These benefits may be administered in different ways (*i.e.* either through a specific benefit administration or through the tax system) and tied to different conditions, with implications for the well-being of people receiving them.

- A second consideration relates to the balance between the overall size of public transfers and the amount of redistribution achieved per dollar spent. As argued in Chapter 4, a given redistributive goal can be pursued through different combinations of level and targeting of social spending. The evidence there presented suggested that countries that redistribute more per dollar spent have lower outlays on social expenditures than others. This trade-off implies that more redistribution could be achieved, for a given amount of taxes, by targeting social programmes more tightly to people in greater need or, conversely, that the same redistribution could be achieved with a lower tax pressure. While different considerations will bear on the "optimal" amount of targeting, one simple option for shifting public efforts towards those in greater needs is to re-direct spending away from earnings-related programmes (such as old-age pensions) and towards programmes that are subject to some conditions on resources. However, for programmes directed at people of working age, greater targeting may come at the costs of larger disincentives for participation and work effort in the income range where benefits are withdrawn. Targeting may also alienate support from higher income groups, pushing them to "opt out" of public programmes towards private alternatives and to vote against political parties supporting higher spending.

While various features of the tax and benefit system will influence the efficiency loss that is associated with fiscal redistribution, all forms of redistribution distort the behaviour of agents, hence they imply *some* losses in economic efficiency. Such losses explain the bad press that often surrounds redistributive policies. Indeed, poorly-designed transfer policies have sometimes undermined the incentive to work and weakened the link between effort and reward. But these negative effects are not, by themselves, an argument against fiscal redistribution. Most communities will generally care about *both* efficiency *and* equity goals, suggesting that the relevant question is how to ease the trade-off between these two objectives. Whatever the views on this trade-off, fiscal redistribution remains a better response to the anxieties linked to wider inequalities than the protectionist threats that loom on the horizon in some countries as a response to globalisation. As governments have long realised, the question is not whether or not to redistribute, but how to do so without damaging market signals too much.

The work strategy

Redistributive policies are, by definition, "remedial" – mitigating poverty and inequality after these have materialised in the market place. But redistribution is only one possible response to concerns about poverty. Another approach to concerns about inequality is to introduce preventive policies that lessen the likelihood that poverty develops in the first place; and the best way of achieving this is by facilitating access to paid work. Helping people to move from benefits to work is a central element of "active social policies" (OECD, 2005). These policies rest on the idea that governments cannot simply mitigate the consequences of a wider distribution of market income through more redistribution (especially when other pressures on public spending are also rising) but should, more ambitiously, aim to change the conditions in which people develop.

"Welfare-to-work" has featured prominently in reforms pursued by several OECD countries in recent years. These policies, which have first been introduced with respect to people receiving unemployment benefits, have since been extended to other categories of beneficiaries, such as lone parents and people with disabilities. Welfare-to-work policies typically combine more active interventions of the public agencies administering these programmes; automatic referral of beneficiaries to available vacancies; services aimed to facilitate the transition from benefits to work; changes in tax and benefit rules to reduce possible "unemployment traps"; tighter obligations on beneficiaries to accept suitable job offers; time limits on the periods when benefits can be drawn; and benefit sanctions in the case of non-compliance. In many respects, the effects of these policies in reducing welfare rolls and increasing employment have exceeded expectations, although increased employment has not always translated into large improvements in people's living conditions. While moving people from benefits to work will lower poverty when the earnings paid are above the poverty thresholds, these policies often face a trade-off of a different type, *i.e.* worsening the conditions of those who remain on benefits or leave the welfare rolls without moving to work. While "welfare to work" policies are not always aimed only (or even mainly) at lowering poverty, their significance for anti-poverty strategies is that they help to achieve *both* equity and efficiency. By helping people to move into jobs and to become autonomous members of societies, these policies help prevent a widening in the distribution of market income from occurring in the first place.

What works best in reducing poverty?

The practical question about these two strategies is the size of their effects on poverty. As the effects of most policies on poverty are debatable, it is difficult to say what works best in the abstract. One way of illustrating their potential pay-off is to compare their effects in a simple "what if" scenario. The approach used here is similar to the one described by Whiteford and Adema (2007) with respect to families with children. This starts by setting a benchmark in terms of either the effect of taxes and benefits in reducing poverty, or of employment levels, and assuming that countries can somehow be moved to this benchmark. The "redistribution strategy" assumes that all OECD countries could achieve the poverty reduction (i.e. the proportional difference in poverty rates before and after taxes and transfers) currently achieved by the third best-performing country; while the "work strategy" simulates the impact on poverty of achieving the level of household joblessness in the country where this is currently the third lowest, and the share of two-earner families that prevails in the country where it is currently the third highest.

Figure 11.4 compares the effect of the two strategies on the poverty headcount (based on a threshold set at 50% of median income) for people living in households with a head of working age. The results partly reflect the (arbitrary) nature of the benchmark set. For example, the larger effects of the "redistribution strategy" compared to one based on raising the prevalence of two earners-households simply reflects the wider distance relative to the third best-performing countries in terms of redistribution than in terms of prevalence of two earner households.[8] Similarly, the size of these effects partly depends on the specific income threshold used (i.e. the higher the threshold, the greater the share of households with workers among the poor and the larger the effects of the "redistribution strategy"). Despite these caveats, Figure 11.4 point to two main conclusions.

- The first is that the effect of various strategies depends on national circumstances, i.e. no set of policies will work under all conditions. In the scenario presented above, the reduction in the poverty headcount achieved through the "redistribution strategy" is less than 1 point in Belgium, the Czech Republic, Denmark, France and Sweden, while it exceeds 6 points in Canada, Japan, Korea, Poland and the United States: of course, most of these countries have low social spending, so the size of spending increase is considerable. Conversely, in the lower joblessness scenario, the fall in the poverty headcount is 1 point or less in half of the countries, while it exceeds 4 points in Australia and Germany, and it is significant (between 2 and 4 points) in Belgium, the Czech Republic, Ireland, Norway and the United Kingdom. Similarly, in the scenario with a higher prevalence of two earner families, the change in the poverty headcount is of 2 points or less in half of the countries, but above 4 points in Poland and Italy.

- The second conclusion is that the two strategies work best when combined. Countries that do best in respect of poverty headcounts typically combine both high benefits granted to jobless household and an emphasis on facilitating access to work for those that are without it. For example, of the eight countries with the lowest poverty headcount, six also belong to the third of countries that redistribute more to people at the bottom of the income scale, two to the third of countries with the lowest incidence of household joblessness, and two to the third of countries with the highest prevalence of two-earner households. Similarly, among the eight countries with the highest poverty headcount, six belong to the third of countries that redistribute the least, three to the

Figure 11.4. **Poverty reductions achieved through "redistribution" and "work" strategies, mid-2000s**

Poverty rates among people living in households with a head of working age, based on a threshold set at half of median equivalised disposable income

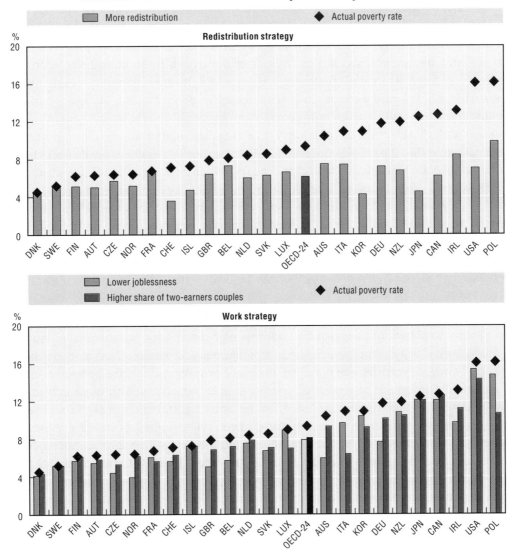

StatLink ᗰᔕᒪᗠ http://dx.doi.org/10.1787/424354624210

Note: Countries are ranked, from left to right, in increasing order of the actual poverty rate. The "redistribution strategy" assumes that countries achieve the same percentage reduction in market-income poverty that is currently achieved by the country with the third highest reduction. The "work strategy" embodies two different variants: in the first, countries achieve the same prevalence of household joblessness (as measured by the share of people living in households where no one works) that is currently realised in the country with the third lowest level; in the second, countries achieve the same prevalence of two-earners families as in the country with the third highest level. Countries that perform better than the benchmark are assumed to be unchanged. Benchmarks for the "redistribution strategy" refer to the aggregate poverty reduction. Benchmarks for the "work strategy" are specific to four household types (single and two-or-more-adult households, with and without children). The scenario is limited to those countries where information is available on market-income poverty.

Source: Calculations based on the OECD income distribution questionnaire.

third of countries with the highest prevalence of joblessness and three to the third of countries with the lowest prevalence of two-earner households. This suggests that *both* access to work and redistribution are important to reduce poverty.

A final consideration is that the two strategies described here are not two poles opposing each other but part of a continuum of options. Disincentive effects of the "redistribution strategy" are especially large when it takes the form of paying subsidies to people who are not working. But as the risk of poverty shifts to households with some earnings, successful inroads into poverty can increasingly rely on programmes that top-up the earnings of low paid workers. Such schemes are important as it is not enough to move people from the welfare rolls into poorly-paid jobs that do not provide them or their families with a viable route out of poverty. To achieve lasting reductions in poverty, policies need to insure that the people concerned keep these jobs (many currently do not), that the earnings paid are high enough to escape poverty (which does not always happen) and that these workers progress towards better jobs (which typically requires training and human capital accumulation). To this end, measures to promote "welfare-in-work" could include employment-conditional benefits granted to low-paid workers according to their family characteristics, wage subsidies to employers for hiring or retaining low-paid workers, portable retraining and health care, measures to enable and promote up-skilling, as well as services that allow parents to reconcile work and care – though flexible working patterns, access to quality and affordable child care, and changes in the organisation of schools to fit the needs of working families.

These considerations suggest that addressing concerns about economic inequalities requires both a *shift* in emphasis in social programmes and a *balanced* set of interventions. Making "work" the centrepiece of efforts to reduce poverty and inequality recognises that a narrower distribution of economic resources is better achieved through subsidies to low-paid workers than through payments for not working, and that transfers to those with no jobs are more effective when supported by services aimed at moving them from benefits to work. The need for balance stems from the recognition that some people face more deep-seated obstacles to participating in the labour markets than others, that many jobs do not pay wages adequate to escape poverty, and that, anyway, children cannot be held responsible for the sins of their parents (Ringen, 2007).

Conclusion

Whatever the mix of intervention chosen, society's goal of reducing economic inequalities – at least when these are perceived as conflicting with shared norms of what is fair in society – should be clearly formulated and given the place they deserve within the range of goals that governments pursue. While the specific formulation of these objectives will differ across countries – ranging from poverty goals for children (as in the United Kingdom) or for the population at large (as in Ireland), to goals referring to the growth in a suitable measure of household income (*e.g.* the median)[9] – what matters is that these are set clearly, that policies in all fields (*e.g.* fiscal, health and education) are assessed for their contribution to their attainment, and that governments are accountable for their success or failures in achieving them. Monitoring the achievement of these goals requires an adequate statistical infrastructure and suitable indicators in each country, as well as comparative data to assess the influence of common and country-specific factors on their evolution. For all these reasons, the information presented in this report is critical for designing better policies to promote growth that is more equitable.

Notes

1. The average change of the Gini coefficient over the past two decades is equivalent to around 15% of the gap in income inequality that separates Denmark from the United States; in the case of the inter-decile ratio (P90/P10), the average change over this period is equivalent to less than 10% of the gap between the same two countries.

2. Data for Belgium for 1983 and 1995 are based on fiscal data and are not strictly comparable with those for later years (see note 7, page 148). In particular, estimates of changes in poverty are likely to be downward biased compared to other national surveys.

3. Childbearing decisions are an important determinant of household size and – when fertility rates evolve differently across the income distribution – they will also affect income inequalities. On average, fertility rates have declined slightly more at the bottom and middle of the income distribution than at the top, especially in the United States and most European countries, with the opposite pattern occurring in Mexico, Poland and Sweden. A stronger decline in fertility rates at the bottom of the income distribution allows these household to spread the available resources over a smaller number of people; this will dampen the increase in income inequality relative to what it would otherwise have been.

4. Among the features that most immediately impact on these distributive impacts are the zero VAT-rate on food in Australia and the United Kingdom. Other mechanisms – which may be captured through income surveys – are VAT-credits targeted to low-income households (as in Canada) or cash transfers used to compensate low-income groups following the introduction of VAT (as in New Zealand).

5. Ideally, a comprehensive assessment of all government activities on the distribution of household incomes would consider all these flows simultaneously. In practice, this is difficult, as the data requirements are daunting. Based on a variant of the "what if" scenario presented above, the combined effect of public in-kind services and consumption taxes may narrow the income distribution by 0.05 point on average, but by much more in Australia, Sweden, the United States, Italy, New Zealand and Portugal and by much less in the Netherlands, Luxembourg, Turkey, Finland and Greece (Warren, 2008).

6. Public in-kind services may also be especially important to reduce income poverty. In Japan, for example, including the value of childcare services in household income would lower child poverty by more than 2 points (from around 14% to 12%).

7. The most obvious dimensions of equity in education are ensuring a basic minimum standard of educational competencies to all students; and ensuring that personal and family circumstances do not become an obstacle to achieving their educational potential. Cross-country differences in these respects are large (OECD, 2007a). Differences are also important when looking at health inequalities, whether these are measured by the dispersion in the age of death or in terms of mortality differentials between groups of people with different education or social class within countries (OECD, 2007b).

8. For example, the median country achieves less redistribution than the third best performing one by around 13 points, while its level of household joblessness is around 4 points higher than the third best performing country, and the prevalence of two-earners households is around eight points lower.

9. Atkinson (2007) recommends that "when reporting the change in *living standards* the OECD and national governments should measure the change in *median* income … This simple change should not … be controversial; its implications are however far-reaching. It means that the macroeconomic discourse would have to consider the distributional implications of policy. It would require the acquisition of distributional information alongside the national accounts".

References

Arjona, R., M. Ladaique and M. Pearson (2001), "Growth, Inequality and Social Protection", OECD Labour Market and Social Policy Occasional Paper, No. 51, OECD, Paris.

Atkinson, T. (2007), "EU Social Policy, the Lisbon Agenda and Re-Imagining Social Policy", Henderson Oration, Centre for Public Policy Conference, 21-22 February, Melbourne.

Boarini, R., A. Johansson and M. Mira d'Ercole (2006), "Alternative Measures of Well-being", OECD Economics Department Working Paper, No. 476 and OECD Social, Employment and Migration Working Paper, No. 33, OECD, Paris.

Förster, M. and M. Mira d'Ercole (2005), "Income Distribution and Poverty in OECD Countries in the Second Half of the 1990s", OECD Social, Employment and Migration Working Paper No. 22, OECD, Paris.

Kenworthy, L. (2007), "Jobs with Equality", mimeo.

OECD (2005), Extending Opportunities for All – How Active Social Policy Can Benefit Us All, OECD, Paris.

OECD (2007a), No More Failures: Ten Steps to Equity in Education, OECD, Paris.

OECD (2007b), Society at a Glance – OECD Social Indicators 2006, OECD, Paris.

Whiteford P. and W. Adema (2007),What Works Best in Reducing Child Poverty: A Benefit or Work Strategy?, OECD Social, Employment and Migration Working Paper, No. 52, OECD, Paris.

Ringen, S. (2007), "What Do Families Do?", Chapter 5 in What Democracy Is For?, Princeton University Press.

Ståhlberg A.-C. (2007), "Redistribution across the Life Course in Social Protection Systems: An Overview", Modernising Social Policy for the New Life Course, OECD, Paris.

Warren, N. (2008), "A Review of Studies on the Distributional Impact of Consumption Taxes in OECD Countries", OECD Social, Employment and Migration Working Paper, No. 64, OECD, Paris.

OECD PUBLICATIONS, 2, rue André-Pascal, 75775 PARIS CEDEX 16
PRINTED IN FRANCE
(81 2008 05 1 P) ISBN 978-92-64-04418-0 – No. 56247 2008